THE CROSSES OF AUSCHWITZ

THE CROSSES OF AUSCHWITZ

Nationalism and Religion in Post-Communist Poland

GENEVIÈVE ZUBRZYCKI

THE UNIVERSITY OF CHICAGO PRESS
CHICAGO AND LONDON

GENEVIÈVE ZUBRZYCKI is assistant professor of sociology at the University of Michigan.

The University of Chicago Press, Chicago 60637
The University of Chicago Press, Ltd., London

Printed in the United States of America

15 14 13 12 11 10 09 08 07 06 5 4 3 2 1

ISBN-13 (cloth): 978-0-226-99303-4
ISBN-10 (cloth): 0-226-99303-5
ISBN-13 (paper): 978-0-226-99304-1
ISBN-10 (paper): 0-226-99304-3

Library of Congress Cataloging-in-Publication Data

Zubrzycki, Geneviève.
The crosses of Auschwitz : nationalism and religion in post-communist Poland / Geneviève Zubrzycki.
p. cm.
Includes bibliographical references and index.
ISBN 0-226-99303-5 (alk. paper) – ISBN 0-226-99304-3 (pbk. : alk. paper)
1. Nationalism—Religious aspects—Poland. 2. National characteristics, Polish. 3. Auschwitz (Concentration camp). 4. Post-communism—Poland I. Title.
DK4121.Z83 2006
320.5409438′09049—dc22

2005030833

This book is printed on acid-free paper.

À PAUL, POUR TOUT.

CONTENTS

ILLUSTRATIONS

PLATES (AFTER PAGE 140)

FIGURES

TABLES

PREFACE

This project has deeper roots than the doctoral dissertation from which the book ultimately bloomed. Its seeds were sown in the summer of 1989, when I first set foot in Poland. I arrived two days before the first semidemocratic elections of June 4, the historic date marking the end of Communism in Poland. On election day, my host took me to St. Stanisław Kostka's Church, where Father Jerzy Popiełuszko, murdered by the secret police for his political activism, lies at rest in a large, cross-shaped tomb. I did not yet speak a word of Polish, but the sea of Polish flags in the overcrowded church, many bearing the famous Solidarity logo, was so striking that the image remained etched in my memory. To be sure, as a francophone Québécoise raised during the 1970s in a family where politics was always on the menu, nationalist iconography and the collective effervescence generated around key events like elections and commemorations were not unfamiliar. What was new was the massively popular confluence of religious and national sentiments. So profound were the impressions of that summer that they shaped my future interests and goals, eventually leading me toward sociology. I became deeply intrigued by the relationship between national identity and religion, puzzled by their near-total fission in Québec after the 1960s' "Quiet Revolution" in sharp contrast with what appeared to be their nearly absolute fusion in Poland.

This is, broadly speaking, what this book is about. It is about the relationship between Polish national identity and Catholicism, the post-Communist transition's redefinition of that relationship, and how national identity is given form, transmitted and transformed by specific symbols, rituals, and events. The focal lens through which I analyze these sociological processes is that of the War of the Crosses, an event in which self-defined "Poles-Catholics" erected hundreds of crosses in the immediate proximity of Auschwitz. Because this event was deeply controversial and emotional, pricking nerves not only in Poland but also internationally, my deciding to proceed with research on such a freighted and consequential case was a difficult choice. Nevertheless, it became clear that the War of the Crosses afforded an unusually clear window through which to study questions I was already researching.

Those questions were formed during a long period of "participant observation" that predated the more formal fieldwork conducted specifically for the book. Beginning in 1989, I spent more than thirty-six months in Poland, witnessing the progressive transformations of that decade. Interactions with Poles "on the ground" in myriad social venues and circles, and in different institutional settings—at families' dinner tables, in university classrooms, in student clubs, at soccer games, during informal gatherings with friends and colleagues at cafés, as well as at formal events like weddings, graduations, popular festivals, and street rituals—all subtly informed my analyses of texts, specific allocutions, events, and symbolic representations. Moreover, my own "national" position as betwixt and between gave me a unique vantage point and often provided an opportunity for my interlocutors in these informal venues to discuss what constitutes "Polishness." As I am culturally Québécoise, Canadian by citizenship, American by residency, and a native speaker of French who bears a Polish surname and is fluent in Polish, Poles' reactions to my own identity(ies) were most telling. I learned volumes from the various criteria and classifications employed by Poles to "figure me out."

The following analysis is therefore inseparable from my lived experience in Poland both before and during this project—in the moments, to enumerate a few representative examples, when Lech Wałęsa declared to a huge crowd packed into Cracow's market square that people should vote for him because he is "a pure Pole" (1990); when infuriated listeners on call-in talk shows denounced the attempts to relocate a Carmelite convent away from Auschwitz (1992); when criticism of the church was so pervasive that special public discussion forums were initiated by the Dominicans in Cracow (1993); when the broadcasts of Radio Maryja, a right-wing Catholic radio station, turned so radical that mainstream Catholics perceived it as a dangerous new sect, prompting questions on the fragmentation and potential breakdown of the church (1997); and when Poles underwent a serious "narrative shock" following the "revelation" and investigation of the 1941 pogrom in Jedwabne (2001).[1]

1. Pronounced Yed-WAB-neh.

That shock, triggered by the publication of *Neighbors* (2000), forced Poles for the first time into a head-on confrontation with their own role in the Holocaust. A short book by Polish-born Princeton University professor Jan Tomasz Gross, *Neighbors* describes how ethnic Poles murdered their Jewish neighbors in the small town of Jedwabne during the summer of 1941. It provoked a discussion and soul-searching about Polishness and Polish-Jewish relations across society.[2] "Jedwabne" was on everyone's lips—in stores, buses, radio talk shows, café discussions, public seminars in cultural centers, churches, and so forth. In fact, my fieldwork at Auschwitz in the winter and spring of 2001 was all performed in the context of the watershed public debate on what had become not just the name of a town but a full-blown cultural phenomenon, "Jedwabne." Although rarely the direct subject of lectures at the Auschwitz-Birkenau State Museum or of my interviews, it came up again and again. For a scholar of nationalism, it was a most fruitful time to analyze representations of Polishness through those of Jewishness, and of Polish-Jewish relations. *Jedwabne* became a cipher of repressed Polish memory suddenly uncovered; a hissing serpent that had been asleep before the rock was turned over.

"Jedwabne" was, after all, the *second* blow inflicted on Poles' self-representations as victims cheated by history, abandoned by friends, and invaded by foes, within the last decade. The first was the post-Communist narrative reconfiguration of Auschwitz in Poland from being the symbol of Polish martyrdom to becoming that of the Shoah and of universal evil. "Jedwabne" forcibly revealed to many that not only were Poles *not* World War II's main victims, but that they were even the perpetrators of some of its horrors.

Trained as a cultural and historical sociologist, I have tried to identify and interrogate the multiplicity of actors, ideas, and social forces behind the social drama that unfolded as the War of the Crosses. Still, no account is ever truly complete, and this one is no exception. Readers expecting an exhaustive analysis of contemporary Polish-Jewish relations or Polish

2. *Neighbors* was first published in Polish in 2000. Its English translation appeared a year later, allegedly to allow enough time for the Polish government to make appropriate apologies and officially recognize the role of ethnic Poles in the pogrom before the book became available to the American public. Following its Polish release, the Institute of National Memory (Instytut Pamięci Narodowej) opened an official investigation of the murders and published its findings in two volumes (Machcewicz and Persak 2002a, 2002b). *Neighbors* also produced an important debate among historians in the form of lengthy editorials in the Polish press (see *Jedwabne* 2002). Gross's own responses to the debates appeared in a collection of essays published in 2003. Other interventions by prominent public intellectuals in Poland and abroad, as well as by Polish Catholic personalities and official statements, can be found in English in Brand (2001) and Polonsky and Michlic (2004).

anti-Semitism will be disappointed. While these topics are important and directly relevant to my analysis, they do not lie at the center of this book. Given how I define my research object, I address them within the broader context of Polish nationalism and religion in the post-Communist period.

This book is also bounded temporally, focusing as it does on the "long decade" following the post-Communist transition, from 1989 to Poland's official entry into the European Union on May 1, 2004. "Historical sociologists of the present" such as myself face the irresolvable problem of circumscribing a "moment" for analysis, even while knowing full well that the cultural processes described continue to evolve, bursting the temporal frames assigned to them. We do not enjoy the same luxury as those who analyze more distant histories, namely those of the relative fixity of "the past" and the dead. Moreover, the cases of post-Communist societies present additional challenges, since their intense transformation continues. I aim, then, at a still rapidly moving target. Polish-Jewish relations, along with Polish nationalism and Catholicism, continue to assume new forms, whether with the sixtieth anniversary of the liberation of Auschwitz or the recent death of John Paul II. While the swirl of events may at times seem to overtake us, peering beneath the surface turbulence can offer useful insights of a more enduring kind into the relationship between religion and nation, as I hope this book demonstrates.

ACKNOWLEDGMENTS

Many friends and colleagues have played a role in seeing this book come to life and to light. I am grateful first of all to Martin Riesebrodt, who was my mentor from my first days as a graduate student at the University of Chicago. His critical readings and advice were crucial to the book's definition, especially when I resisted entering a territory that seemed filled with hidden landmines. His and Brigitte's friendship, humor, art, and joie de vivre were important as I navigated the tempests of graduate life; together they richly and indelibly marked my years in Chicago. Andy Abbott, Bill Sewell, Ron Suny, and Roger Gould also were great supports and brilliant conversation partners in the initial stages of the project. Tragically, Roger passed away before I completed the book, but he remained a critical reader in many imagined dialogues we had, and continue to have. My numerous conversations with Moishe Postone and Andreas Glaeser were always illuminating, and an endless source of new perspectives and challenges.

I also benefited enormously from the critical comments and insights of my colleagues at the University of Michigan. Michael D. Kennedy, Howard Kimeldorf, and Brian Porter forced me to clarify arguments and offered invaluable advice on the art of scholarly writing, as did Julia Adams even after she left Michigan for Yale. Thanks also to Jonathan Huener, who meticulously read and commented on chapter 3; to Krisztina Fehervary, for her detailed comments on the introduction; and to the two anonymous reviewers, who made important suggestions. I count myself fortunate for having worked with the legendary Doug Mitchell; his assistant, Tim McGovern; and Senior Manuscript Editor Sandy Hazel at the University of Chicago Press—all were generous and untiring shepherds of the book.

Research for this study was funded in part by the Social Sciences and Humanities Research Council of Canada and the MacArthur Foundation's Council for the Advanced Study of Peace and Cooperation (CASPIC); its writing phase was supported by the Charlotte Newcombe Foundation (Woodrow Wilson National Fellowship Foundation) and a postdoctoral fellowship from the Center on Religion and Democracy at the University of Virginia. An additional research trip to Poland in the summer of 2004 also was generously funded by UVA's Center on Religion and Democracy, and supplemented by the University of Michigan's Department of Sociology. Finally, I was fortunate to be awarded a publication subvention from the Office of the Vice President for Research at the University of Michigan, which allowed me to obtain rights to many photographs I was unable to take myself.

My field research in Poland would not have been as fruitful, rewarding, and enjoyable without the help of several colleagues, institutions, and friends. I am grateful to Zdzisław Mach for granting me institutional affiliation with the Center for European Studies at Jagiellonian University in the winter and spring of 2001. I am especially indebted to the personnel of the Auschwitz-Birkenau State Museum in Oświęcim, who assisted my research in countless ways and directed my attention to issues, sources, materials, and people I would not have otherwise found. I also thank all informants and interviewees for taking the time to offer thoughts, perspectives, and opinions, and, in some cases, generously giving me access to their personal photographic archives.

I benefited enormously from meetings with Polish scholars in Cracow and Warsaw over the last decade. Aleksandra Jasińska-Kania, Joanna Kurczewska, and Annamaria Orla-Bukowska were especially helpful, pointing the way through the maze of Polish academia and research facilities and proffering interesting leads. I was also fortunate to have gained the research assistance of Małgorzata Hulboj-Kuleta in the summer of 2004 when I returned to Poland to collect additional data for the book. Professor Irena Borowik at Jagiellonian University regularly supplied me with fresh literature, and her insights, contacts, and solid research instincts provided a constant support through the years. More than this, her friendship was invaluable; she made Cracow seem warm even during the harsh winters. Jan Rogoyski's house became a home away from home until his death in 2003, and Paweł Walczak's support was important from the time I learned my first Polish words in the summer of 1989.

My thanks to *Studies in Contemporary Jewry* and *Theory and Society* for their permission to reproduce portions of text that first appeared in their pages. Passages from the introduction, chapter 5, and the conclusion were published as "'Poles-Catholics' and 'Symbolic Jews': Jewishness as Social Closure in Poland" in *Studies in Contemporary Jewry*, vol. 21, "Jews, Catholics, and the Burden of History," edited by Eli Lederhendler. Copyright © 2005 by Oxford University Press, Inc. Portions of chapter 2 were published as "'We the Polish Nation': Ethnic and Civic Visions of Nationhood in Post-Communist Constitutional Debates" in *Theory and Society* 30, no. 5 (2001): 629–69.

Finally, I want to thank my family. I am especially grateful to my two sets of parents, Andrée Gendreau and Denys Delâge, and Pierre and Lynne Zubrzycki. They laid the foundations of the world I occupy—a world in which serious inquiry and the academic vocation have intrinsic value and are never doubted—and from them I learned that history always matters. But my deepest gratitude is reserved for my husband, Paul Christopher Johnson. His support sustained me through the research and writing stages, and his confidence in me gave me courage when I lacked it. The help most needed often comes in the little things. Paul walked me to the bus on every early morning when I could not bear the prospect of yet another day at the Auschwitz Museum; he often occupied the chair next to me in the long hours at the library of Jagiellonian University; and read, edited, and reread several drafts of the manuscript over the last several years. But even more than this, he created with me a life outside and beyond this book, without which this project would not have seemed worth sustaining. I dedicate the book to him.

ABBREVIATIONS

AWS	Akcja Wyborcza "Solidarność"—Electoral Action "Solidarity"
KOR	Komitet Obrony Robotników—Workers' Defense Committee
KPN	Konfederacja Polski Niepodległej—Confederation for an Independent Poland
LPR	Liga Polskich Rodzin—League of Polish Families
PD	Partia Demokratyczna—Democratic Party
PSL	Polskie Stronnictwo Ludowe—Polish Peasants' Party
ROP	Ruch Odbudowy Polski—Movement for the Reconstruction of Poland
SLD	Sojusz Lewicy Demokratycznej—Alliance of the Democratic Left
UD	Unia Demokratyczna—Democratic Union
UW	Unia Wolności—Freedom Union
ZchN	Zjednoczenie Chrześcijańsko-Narodowe—Christian-National Union

PRONUNCIATION KEY

The following provides a guide to the pronunciation of Polish words and names.

a is pronounced as in *nap*
c, as /ts/ in *cats*
ch, as in *loch*
cz, as hard /ch/ in *church*
ć, as soft /ch/
g, always hard, as in *girl*
i, as /ee/
j, as /y/ in *yes*
u and ó, as /oo/ in *boot*
w, as /v/
sz, as hard /sh/ in *ship*
ś, as soft /sh/
rz and ż, as /zh/ in *Zhivago*
ź, as softer /zh/
ę, as French /ain/ in *bain*
ń, as Spanish ñ in *año*
ą, as French /on/ in *avion*
ł, as /w/

INTRODUCTION

Introduction and Theoretical Orientations

Figure 1 Pope John Paul II and Chief Rabbi Pinchas Menachem Joskowicz, June 11, 1999. Photo: PAP/Jacek Turczyk.

The Pope, the Rabbi, and the Crosses of Auschwitz

"I have a request for Mr. Pope. . . . I ask Mr. Pope to order his people to also remove this last cross from the camp" (*Gazeta Wyborcza*, June 12–13, 1999).[1] As he spoke, Poland's chief rabbi, Pinchas Menachem Joskowicz, waved a finger under the nose of a frail, stooped John Paul II (fig. 1). Poles held

1. All translations, unless otherwise noted, are mine.

their breath in disbelief, witnessing this televised incident live immediately following the pope's historic visit to the Polish parliament, where he had addressed the nation on June 11, 1999. The rabbi was referring to the so-called "papal cross" standing just outside Auschwitz. During the summer and fall of 1998, some three hundred crosses had been erected on the grounds adjacent to the former concentration camp by self-defined "Poles-Catholics" in response to the rumored imminent removal of the eight-meter-high "papal cross." The War of the Crosses, as I call the event, created turmoil at the national and international levels, and in the spring of 1999 all but the "papal cross" had been removed by the Polish army.

The rabbi's informal address of the pontiff and his accusatory wagging finger spoke volumes, quite apart from the request itself.[2] The following morning, newspapers exploded with indignant editorial reactions. The Union of Jewish Communities in Poland immediately issued a statement distancing itself from Rabbi Joskowicz's "scandalous" and unjustifiable behavior:

> Rabbi Joskowicz does not represent Jewish communities in Poland. Today's declaration, addressed to John Paul II, had a scandalous form that can in no way be justified. In accordance with earlier agreements, on June 13 [Rabbi Joskowicz] will officially stop fulfilling the function of chief rabbi. It is imperative to speak about the large cross at the gravel pit at Auschwitz, whose presence is difficult to accept for many Jews, in a fashion that does not offend anyone. We appreciate the last actions of the Polish government in the gravel pit affair. Our common goal is to create a situation in which all victims of the camp can be honored. We are grateful to John Paul II for his previous declarations that permitted the overcoming of earlier controversies linked with the terrain of Auschwitz, which is the symbol of the most tragic event of our century. (Katolicka Agencja Informacyjna, *Biuletyn*, no. 46, June 15, 1999)[3]

2. Although born in Poland, Rabbi Joskowicz's native tongue is Yiddish, and he lived most of his life in Israel. His limited linguistic skills account for his awkwardly addressing John Paul II in Polish as "Mr. Pope."

3. The gravel pit is the fenced area just outside the walls of Auschwitz where the "papal cross" is, and where the hundreds of other crosses were erected in 1998–99. The area takes its name from its function during World War II. Despite several suggestions in the Polish press that Rabbi Joskowicz had been dismissed as a result of the specific incident with the pope, the above statement indicates that his retirement had already been planned, and therefore was not prompted by this faux pas. It was, nevertheless, related to his handling of the War of the Crosses at Auschwitz during the past year. The rabbi's dismissal-retirement was ultimately linked to

Even though the Jewish community in Poland agreed with the nature of Rabbi Joskowicz's request—to remove the "papal cross" from the grounds just outside Auschwitz—it disagreed with the place, timing, and tenor of the rabbi's intervention: "I completely agree that the cross should not be there," declared Jewish public intellectual and editor Konstanty Gebert, "but the image of an insolent Jew treating the nation's most respected leader in that way confirms the worst stereotypes and that really hurts us" (*New York Times*, June 12, 1999). The editor of another Jewish publication wrote that "the mistake of Joskowicz was to do what he did at the wrong place, at the wrong moment and in the wrong way. The resolution of complicated and difficult problems demands patient, often long-lasting diplomacy, conducted away from television cameras in an atmosphere of dialogue. In the case of Joskowicz, it was rather a monologue that the pope listened to without a word, because there was no other way" (Adam Rok, *Słowo Żydowskie*, July 2–16, 1999).[4]

These reactions must be placed in the context of long and difficult negotiations concerning the crosses, which had recently been removed from the immediate vicinity of Auschwitz. The restored order still appeared fragile and the situation potentially volatile. Given the history of controversies surrounding the former concentration camp and the symbolic import of the rabbi directly and personally confronting the pope, immediate reactions from various members of the Jewish community in Poland were meant to appease spirits and maintain calm.

The most significant of the "earlier controversies" linked with the terrain of Auschwitz, alluded to in the declaration of the Union of Jewish Communities in Poland and in editorial reactions to the pope-rabbi interaction, involved the presence of a Carmelite convent just outside Auschwitz

his "poor understanding of the Polish situation" (interviews with Stanisław Krajewski, cochair of the Committee on Christian-Jewish Dialogue, member of the International Council of the Auschwitz-Birkenau State Museum, and consultant for the American Jewish Committee, May 2001; and with Piotr Kadlčik, president of the Jewish Community in Warsaw, May 12, 2004).

4. The quick and unequivocal condemnation of the rabbi's action was so complete that after a few days several felt the need to come to his defense. Konstanty Gebert, for example, reiterated that the rabbi's form of address resulted not from bad will but from bad Polish, and his overall request not from insolence but from emotional distress (*Gazeta Wyborcza*, June 14, 1999). Jacek Kuroń, cofounder of KOR, former deputy and minister of labor, and chair of the parliamentary commission on national minorities at the time, qualified the reactions as an "attack" on the person of Rabbi Joskowicz (*Gazeta Wyborcza*, June 16, 1999), and Father Stanisław Musiał indicated that since the cross was commonly called the "papal cross," even by church authorities, it was natural for the rabbi to request its alleged owner to take action.

from 1984 to 1993.[5] The War of the Crosses, which is the main case of this book, is closely related to that conflict. The pope-rabbi confrontation actually marks the unsatisfying conclusion of a social drama in three acts spanning fifteen years. It gained in currency, however, in the decade following the fall of Communism and the "recovery of national independence," as Poles commonly refer to the period.[6]

Acts One and Two: The Carmelite Convent and the "Papal Cross"

The first act opened in 1984, when Carmelite nuns established a convent in Oświęcim,[7] a small town of approximately fifty thousand people in southwestern Poland, about seventy-five kilometers from Cracow. Oświęcim could not be distinguished from myriad other small Polish towns, were it not for the fact that this is where Nazis built the world's most notorious

5. The Carmelites are a cloistered religious order that cultivates contemplative life. They live in silence, devote themselves to prayer, and do not engage in evangelization. They have little, if any, contact with the world outside the walls of the convent. For detailed accounts of the Carmelite convent dispute, see Bartoszewski (1991); Głownia and Wilkanowicz (1998); Rittner and Roth (1991); and T. Klein (1991). Klein's account is especially valuable, since he acted as the main Jewish negotiator with church authorities regarding the convent's relocation. For a pro-Polish, conservative view that includes several documents, see Raina (1991).

Another controversy, occurring after the relocation of the Carmelite convent and before the War of the Crosses, raised the problematic issue of religious symbols' presence at Auschwitz. In 1995, a group of scouts that had completed community work at Birkenau, Auschwitz's sister camp three kilometers away, planted small crosses and Stars of David in the former camp's ash field. These religious artifacts went unnoticed by the museum authorities until Elie Wiesel forcefully demanded their removal during his participation in the fiftieth anniversary of the Kielce pogrom in 1996, arguing that the place should remain silent, and therefore devoid of religious symbols (Christian or other). Wiesel's position was widely reported in Polish news media, and provided the opportunity for renewed anti-Semitic discourse. The crosses and Stars of David were removed by the museum staff by order of the government quickly thereafter. I return to the theological underpinnings of the need for silence at Auschwitz in chapter 4.

6. The term *social drama* is more than an apt metaphor to describe the War of the Crosses and its place in relation to other crises at Auschwitz. As developed by Victor Turner (1974), it is a useful conceptual tool to help us make sense of the event in all its complex layers and as it is related to the broader context of the Polish post-Communist transition. Social dramas are conflicts expressed in periodic public contestation of "root paradigms," social narratives and cultural scripts that orient social action and give meaning to that action. In the case at hand, the root paradigm at the source of the conflict between Poles and Jews is that of martyrdom: who suffered most at Auschwitz and therefore who "owns" the memory of the camp and the right to commemorate their dead? The root paradigm contested among Poles, as we shall see, is that of an eternally and intrinsically Roman Catholic Poland, which the cross is said to symbolize. Social dramas are therefore conflicts that tend to bring fundamental aspects of society into the foreground, thereby bringing out divisions between social groups, with people taking sides in terms of firmly anchored moral imperatives.

7. Pronounced Osh-VYEN-chim.

Figure 2 Gravel pit, separated from the former concentration camp Auschwitz I and the current Auschwitz-Birkenau State Museum by a cement wall and a double row of barbed-wire fences. The large building in the background is where the former Carmelite convent was housed in the years 1984–93. The "papal cross" stands in the center of the green area, on the top left corner of the photograph. Photo: PAP/CAF Jacek Bednarczyk.

concentration and extermination camp, Auschwitz. The convent was established in a building that, while being outside Auschwitz per se, overlooks the site (fig. 2). During the war, that building (Theatergebaübe, or Old Theater) was a storehouse for Zyklon B, a chemical used in Germany before and during World War II as a disinfecting and pest-control agent—and, beginning in 1941, to asphyxiate camp prisoners. After protests from Jewish groups (mostly outside Poland) objecting to the presence of the nuns at the site, in 1987 an agreement was reached and ratified in Geneva between representatives of the Roman Catholic Church and European Jewish leaders. The accord stipulated that the convent would be moved from the vicinity of Auschwitz by 1989. For various reasons, the nuns failed to move by that date, and tensions escalated as a group of Jews from New York, under the leadership of Rabbi Avraham Weiss,[8] occupied the convent grounds in

8. Rabbi Avraham Weiss is most famous in Poland for occupying the Carmelite convent in the summer of 1989; protesting the presence of a church in Brzezinka in a building across the road from Birkenau, which had been occupied by Nazis during the war; and mobilizing some American congressional representatives to demand from the Polish government the removal of crosses at the gravel pit.

July of that year and were forcibly ousted from its premises.[9] Protests and resistance followed in Poland, including many declarations by the head of its Catholic Church, Józef Cardinal Glemp, that were often unabashedly anti-Semitic in content and tone.

Rabbi Weiss's protest at the Carmelite convent took place in July 1989, roughly coinciding with the fall of Communism in Poland. Many Poles perceived the pressures from outside Poland to relocate the convent as an insult and a threat to, or even an assault on, their state's newly regained and still fragile sovereignty. Moreover, the "Weiss incident" explosively mixed gender, religion, and nationality: Jewish males jumping over fences and demanding to meet with cloistered nuns had been understood not as a "peaceful protest" but as an attack on saintly women and the profanation of a sacred site. The imagery and symbolism of Rabbi Weiss's protests had made a strong impact on the Polish social imagination. Certainly, the language in which the incident was reported and discussed in the Polish media as well as by the Roman Catholic Church clearly influenced how it was interpreted in the population at large. The same was true outside Poland, where the event was often portrayed as a "minipogrom" confirming Polish hatred of Jews and the persistence of traditional Polish anti-Semitism.

Act 2 actually began quietly almost a year before these incidents, when in the fall of 1988 a tall cross appeared on the grounds of the convent, the so-called gravel pit.[10] Brought there by a local priest and a group of former

9. The deadline by which the nuns were supposed to relocate was, by all accounts, unrealizable. Two years to find a new site that would be acceptable to all parties, obtain city permits and government clearance, secure materials, and ensure the proper construction was unrealistic in Communist Poland. There was also clear resistance and some ill will on the part of the sisters, whose vows were made to that specific convent at that specific site, and who stubbornly refused to leave. Finally, the affair was further complicated by the fact that as a monastic order, the Carmelites are not under the jurisdiction of the diocesan bishop but under the head of the Carmelite order in Rome. Although Polish, the nuns therefore refused to submit to an agreement ratified by representatives of the Polish Roman Catholic Church.

10. The exact date of the appearance of the "papal cross" at the gravel pit is unclear. Some sources point to the summer of 1988 (T. Klein 1991, 202), some to the fall of 1988 (Głownia and Wilkanowicz 1998, 226; Kucia 2005, 243). Other authors date its installation at the gravel pit in the winter of 1989, on February 22, to protest the second anniversary of the Geneva accord (E. Klein 2001, 12); in March 1989 (Bartoszewski 1991, 73); or in the early summer of 1989 to commemorate the tenth anniversary of John Paul II's Mass at Birkenau in 1979. Yet another commentator, Stanisław Krajewski (1997), dates its appearance at the gravel pit more vaguely in the summer and fall of 1989, in the context of the escalating Carmelite convent conflict following Rabbi Weiss's protest in July of that year. My own research suggests that the cross was erected at the gravel pit in the fall of 1988, but removed in June 1989, at the occasion of a Mass celebrated by Cardinal Macharski at Birkenau to commemorate the 1979 papal Mass. It was returned to the gravel pit shortly thereafter. The movement of the cross may explain some of the confusion

(Polish Catholic) Auschwitz prisoners, the cross had been part of an altar on the grounds of Birkenau, Auschwitz's sister camp three kilometers away, where John Paul II celebrated Mass in 1979 during his historic first visit to Poland as pontiff—hence its popular naming as the papal cross.[11] The cross had been dismantled and stored in the basement of a local church during the decade that separated the pope's Mass at Birkenau from the night it appeared in the convent's yard. It was erected at that site without witnesses and without any public or known ritual or ceremony. Though we cannot say with certainty that social actors did not act out of religious motivations, we can certainly say that the practice was also, if not primarily, politically motivated. Indeed, the planting of crosses to sacralize a site, to give it sacred immunity, had been a common practice under Communism. Most frequently, this tactic was used to defend church property, but the symbol was also used as a "protective weapon" against the Communist state during protests and rallies.[12] In this case, the erection of the papal cross in the yard of the Carmelite convent was clearly such a tactic as well as a form of protest against the planned relocation of the Carmelite nuns.

The nuns finally relocated in 1993, when John Paul II personally intervened in the conflict by asking them to leave. The papal cross, however, remained on the site, since it had not yet been erected there when the Geneva accord was negotiated and ratified.

---

regarding the moment of its planting at the gravel pit. That confusion also points to the fact that the installation of the cross was neither a public nor a publicized event, so it did not attract the attention of the parties involved in resolving the Carmelite convent conflict until well after the fact.

11. Father Stanisław Musiał argued that the designation "papal cross" is misleading and manipulative, a "terminological dissimulation" (*Gazeta Wyborcza*, June 25, 1999). The cross, according to him, could be rightfully called or qualified as the "papal" cross had it been specifically blessed by the pope, and had the pope identified the gravel pit as the rightful site for its emplacement. Neither was the case (*Gazeta Wyborcza*, April 22, 1998). In the news media and public discourse of the Far Right, one could also often hear or read that the pope had celebrated Mass by that cross at that site, which was not the case. It is possible to interpret that "rumor" as an attempt to further sacralize the site by attributing the pope's presence there. I use the term, even though that designation is contested, since it is referred to as such in public discourse. Henceforth, I will for simplicity's sake not use quotation marks. Nevertheless, they remain implied in all instances.

12. For an interesting radio documentary comparing the defense of a cross in Nowa Huta in 1960 with the War of the Crosses in Oświęcim during the summer of 1998, see transcripts in *Tygodnik Powszechny* (August 11, 1998). The editors' stated intent in juxtaposing the two events was to highlight how seemingly similar gestures have very different underpinnings, tenor, and outcomes. *Tygodnik Powszechny*, a liberal Catholic weekly, was very critical of the War of the Crosses, which it interpreted as an act of anti-Semitic aggression and the hurtful manipulation of religious discourse and symbols contrary to Christian teachings.

Figure 3 Prayer vigil by the papal cross early in the spring of 1998. Photo: from the personal archives of Kazimierz Świtoń.

Act Three: The War of the Crosses

The third act of the drama, the War of the Crosses, started five years after the nuns' relocation. In February 1998, Krzysztof Śliwiński, plenipotentiary to the foreign affairs minister and responsible for contacts with the Jewish Diaspora, mentioned in an interview conducted by the French newspaper *La Croix* that the papal cross, which had been the object of contention in various Jewish circles, would also be removed from the grounds of the former Carmelite convent.[13] A series of commentaries by political figures immediately followed and were thrust into the public arena. Antoni Macierewicz, a well-known member of the Right, qualified the intended removal as "religious profanation and national humiliation." One hundred and thirty deputies and a group of senators from right-wing parties signed a

13. Such negotiations were indeed under way (interview with Stefan Wilkanowicz, editor-in-chief of Znak publishing house and cochair of the International Council of the Auschwitz-Birkenau State Museum, April 23, 2001).

Figure 4 View of the gravel pit fence from the street in April 1998. On the left, the former Carmelite convent; in the background, behind the papal cross, Auschwitz buildings. On the fence, banners proclaiming "Here in the years 1940–45 Germans murdered Poles"; "Keep Jesus at Auschwitz"; and "Polish Holocaust by Jews 1945–56," referring to the commonly held belief that the Secret Police during Stalinism was primarily constituted by Jews. Photo: from the personal archives of Kazimierz Świtoń.

petition to the government advocating the continued presence of the cross at the gravel pit, and Lech Wałęsa spoke out against the removal of the cross in a letter to Bishop Tadeusz Rakoczy, under whose jurisdiction Oświęcim falls. By mid-March, popular mobilization was under way: some parishes celebrated special Masses for "the respect and protection of the papal cross" alongside vigils for the defense of crosses in Poland (fig. 3). At the annual, Jewish-sponsored "March of the Living" in April that year, banners and posters with slogans such as "Defend the Cross," "Keep Jesus at Auschwitz" (in *English*), and "Polish Holocaust by Jews, 1945–56" were displayed on the gravel pit fence (fig. 4). By spring, the issue had become an affair involving, at the domestic level, government officials, the opposition, the Roman Catholic Church, and various civic organizations.

In June, Kazimierz Świtoń, ex-Solidarity activist and former deputy from the right-wing Confederation for an Independent Poland, initiated a hunger strike at the gravel pit that lasted forty-two days, demanding from the

Roman Catholic Church a firm commitment that the cross would remain.[14] After failing to secure such a commitment, Świtoń appealed to his fellow Poles to plant 152 crosses on the grounds of the gravel pit, both to commemorate the (documented) deaths of 152 ethnic Poles executed at that specific site by Nazis in 1941 and to "protect and defend the papal cross." This appeal proved successful: during the summer and fall of 1998, the gravel pit in Oświęcim was transformed into the epicenter of the War of the Crosses as individuals, civic organizations, and religious groups from every corner of Poland (and from as far away as Canada, the United States, and Australia) answered Świtoń's call to create a "valley of crosses," encouraged by the popular and controversial radio station Radio Maryja (plates 1–3).[15] By August 21, 135 crosses stood on the site; a month later, on September 26, 236 were in place, 96 of them measuring four meters or more in height. Later that fall, on the initiative of some Cracovians, stations of the cross were installed. By the time the Polish army finally removed them in May 1999, 322 crosses stood at the gravel pit (fig. 5).

During that summer, the site became the stage for prayer vigils, Masses, demonstrations, and general nationalist agitation. It was the destination of choice for pilgrims, journalists, and tourists in search of a sacred cause, a good story, or a free show, respectively (fig. 6). Religious images of the national Madonna (Our Lady of Częstochowa), as well as secular symbols such as red-and-white Polish flags and national coats of arms featuring a crowned white eagle,[16] commonly adorned the crosses and added to their symbolic weight and complexity. The papal cross itself was transformed into an improvised altar, with flowers, candles, and small flags spread at its foot (plate 4). The fence surrounding the area, where crowds of the curious gathered to observe the spectacle, was similarly covered with political banners and flowers.

14. Kazimierz Świtoń (1931–) organized in 1978 the first Committee of Free Professional Unions in the People's Republic of Poland (Komitet Wolnych Związków Zawodowych); was a member of Solidarity, 1980–89; and was a deputy in the Sejm 1991–93. As he participated in several hunger strikes in the late 1970s and throughout the '80s, his hunger strike in defense of the papal cross should be understood as the continuation of a popular strategy of resistance to the authorities under Communism.

15. Radio Maryja was established in 1991 as a local radio station in Toruń, and has since expanded into a nationwide network with an estimated six million listeners. In addition to its radio network and television station, Radio Maryja has developed into a genuine social movement, with various religious and social organizations, political groups, and publications more or less loosely affiliated with it (Jasiewicz 1999).

16. The crown is not the symbol of royalty, but of sovereignty. See Zdzisław Mach's interesting article on the Polish coat of arms (1992).

Figure 5 The papal cross surrounded by smaller crosses planted in the summer of 1998 at the invitation of Mr. Świtoń. Photo: from the personal archives of Kazimierz Świtoń.

Figure 6 Pilgrimage of followers of the schismatic Society of Saint Pius X to the gravel pit on the Feast of the Assumption. On that day (August 15, 1998), the society celebrated a Tridentine Mass and erected a cross, second-highest after the papal cross. Photo: from the personal archives of Kazimierz Świtoń.

At the national level, the fourteen-month-long "war" was marked by a series of debates and legal battles, numerous declarations from public officials, and accusations and counteraccusations that embroiled the government in conflicts with the opposition, Polish public intellectuals, Polish-Jewish activists, groups from the Far Right, the Roman Catholic Church, and a schismatic brotherhood claiming to represent "true Catholicism in defense of the Nation." The affair took on international and transnational dimensions as well, as a group of U.S. congressional representatives and the Israeli government demanded the removal of all crosses while members of the Jewish and Polish diasporas added their own salt to the boil. Ultimately, then, the conflict mobilized constituencies at the national, international, and transnational levels.[17] The Polish government thus found itself in a peculiar position: that of mediator between the demands of states, transnational civil society, and supranational organizations on the one hand, and ultimatums from a part of its own civil society on the other. Its partly conflicting objectives were to regain control over rebellious citizens and maintain its sovereignty in the international sphere in the face of proposals for the extraterritoriality of Auschwitz and Birkenau from some Jewish organizations, while appeasing supranational organizations to which it aspired to belong.[18]

It took the involved authorities several months to find a solution to the crisis. In the meantime, the cross(es) became a hot potato thrown back and forth between the government and the Catholic Church. At first, the government stood on the sidelines, invoking the principle of separation of

17. I distinguish between the international and the transnational levels in the following way: the international sphere represents relations between states (*interstatal* would be a better term), while *transnational* refers to relations between groups and institutions whose actions cross over sovereign polities (here again, *trans-statal* would be an analytically more precise term). (See Verdery [1994] for a useful discussion and differentiation between trans-ethnonational and trans-statal). The case is a good example of the mobilization of transnational civil society, with the involvement of the Polish and Jewish diasporas. For an analysis of religion, states, and transnational civil society, see the edited volume by Rudolph and Piscatori (1997), and especially the editors' useful introduction.

18. It was suggested that Auschwitz-Birkenau be removed from the Polish nation-state to become extraterritorial. This proposal was articulated, among others, by Rabbi Avraham Weiss, one of the main protagonists of the Carmelite convent controversy, but also by Kalman Sultanik, then vice-president of the World Jewish Congress, and by Menachem Pinchas Joskowicz, then chief rabbi in Poland. Sultanik proposed that the former camp be under the joint jurisdiction of UNESCO, Jewish organizations, and the Polish government (*Polska Agencja Prasowa*, June 4, 1998), while Rabbi Weiss and Rabbi Joskowicz independently suggested that it be under Israeli control. The Association of Jewish Communities in Poland quickly declared in a statement that this was Rabbi Joskowicz's private opinion and that it in no way represented the communities' views. This incident was one of the rabbi's faux pas that eventually led to his retirement-dismissal.

church and state as defined in the concordat of 1997 in arguing that the papal cross was the property of the Roman Catholic Church, which was responsible for the use of its religious symbols.[19] The church countered that the crosses stood on government property and that the Roman Catholic Church had no monopoly on the symbol of the cross, which belonged to the entire Christian community of believers. Over time, however, as a growing number of crosses appeared at the gravel pit, the crisis became more acute for both the government and the church. For the government, the situation was exacerbated by demands from Israel and pressure from representatives from the U.S. Congress at precisely the time when Poland was negotiating the terms of its NATO membership. For the church, it was rendered more acute by the disobedience by Catholics of the episcopate's request in late August to stop planting crosses, and in the persistent involvement of the Society of Saint Pius X, a schismatic group (plates 5–7).

In the end, the Polish government and the Catholic Church made concerted attempts to find a solution and regain control of the gravel pit. Following many legal battles and the passage of a law regarding "the protection of the grounds of former Nazi camps" on May 7, 1999, a 100-meter zone was established around Auschwitz, thereby giving the government the legal means to evict Kazimierz Świtoń from the gravel pit, where he had been encamped in a trailer for nearly a year, while the church arranged for the crosses to be relocated to a nearby sanctuary.[20]

19. A concordat is an agreement negotiated by the Vatican with a given state that regulates the relations between the secular power and the Roman Catholic Church in that state. This one with Poland was reached in July 1993, but was only ratified four years later. Some saw in the official reestablishment of diplomatic relations with the Vatican, broken unilaterally by the Communist regime in September 1945, a return to normalcy that Communism had interrupted. Others saw it as an outdated project that threatened the separation of church and state. The concordat has been at the center of Polish public debates throughout the 1990s. In addition to hot issues such as the question of religious instruction in public schools and the recognition by the state of church weddings, its validity itself was questioned, since the agreement was made before one of the two parties involved, the Republic of Poland, had new legal foundations. How could a diplomatic treaty between two states be made before one of them had a (new) constitution? The conflict was structured along two familiar poles: prochurch, conservative Center-Right Catholics versus liberal Center-Left secularists.

20. Świtoń was eventually arrested for threatening to blow up the gravel pit and served a brief jail sentence. Although some report that the War of the Crosses was an illegal action because Świtoń and the Defenders of the Cross were trespassing on state property (e.g. Holc 2005), this is not quite accurate. In its negotiations to relocate the Carmelite convent away from Auschwitz, the Polish state acquired, in 1993, the building and its grounds. Just before the sale, however, the Carmelite nuns rented the property to the Association for the Victims of the War (Stowarzeszenie Ofiar Wojny) in a thirty-year lease. While the Polish state was the formal owner of the former Carmelite convent, its lawful occupant was therefore the Association for the Victims of the War, whose leader, Mieczysław Janosz, was allowing Kazimierz Świtoń and pilgrims on the grounds.

The papal cross, however, remained. There was thus no resolution of the *initial* conflict concerning the presence of that specific cross. For this reason, the social action of cross-planting could therefore be qualified as "successful," and is regarded as such by Świtoń himself: by escalating the conflict and radicalizing the demands—from the retention of one cross to the retention of hundreds—the Defenders of the Cross, Świtoń's ad hoc advocacy group, successfully altered the terms for what a compromise would entail. In fact, by the end of the affair, removal of the papal cross was not even considered an option and was not open to negotiations; the removal of Świtoń and the 300-odd crosses was the principal objective of most of those involved. If at the outset the papal cross's presence at the gravel pit was not inevitable and different authorities considered the possibility of its removal and relocation, by the drama's conclusion its presence at that site had been naturalized and made a permanent monument in the landscape of Auschwitz's perimeter (plate 8).

As the encounter between Rabbi Joskowicz and John Paul II suggests, the papal cross now stands as a multivalent and overdetermined symbol: a reminder of the conflict, a scar on the ground, a polluting emblem in a taboo zone—the protection zone around the former camp, a legal and symbolic buffer between the sacred and the profane, between Auschwitz and the town of Oświęcim. Although the drama is over, there is no closure to the conflict; rather, the papal cross now monumentalizes the dispute.

The War of the Crosses as Nationalist Event

As we shall see in greater detail in later chapters, in terms of Poland as a whole, the primary actors were fringe characters associated with marginal parties and groups from the Far Right. The event itself, however, did not remain on the periphery of Polish public life but occupied its very center (fig. 7). The performance captivated the media and both national and international audiences: in Poland, political figures, government officials, public intellectuals, church authorities, and clergy members as well as ordinary citizens were rapt in the debates it generated about anti-Semitism, history and memory, Polish national identity, and the place of religion and religious symbols in their newly independent country.[21] The War of the

---

In the summer of 2004, the Old Theater and the gravel pit were officially placed under the jurisdiction of the Auschwitz-Birkenau State Museum, which plans to house an international center for teaching about Auschwitz and the Holocaust in the building.

21. Ninety-six percent of Poles had heard of the event by mid-August, according to a poll conducted by CBOS (1998, $N = 1{,}085$), and 59 percent said they were interested in and following

Figure 7 Kazimierz Świtoń at a press conference, enjoying his fifteen minutes of fame as the War of the Crosses becomes a media event and the focus of debates in the public sphere. Photo: from the personal archive of Kazimierz Świtoń.

Crosses became yet another occasion to discuss these familiar key issues in post-Communist Poland. But in many ways it became *the* occasion. In the process, it highlighted and sharpened conflicts between ethno-religious and civic-secular nationalists, between members of the church hierarchy and clergy who supported the action and those who did not, and between the institutional church, self-defined Poles-Catholics planting crosses, and a schismatic group celebrating religious services at the site. The War of the Crosses at Auschwitz galvanized existing divisions and conflicts within the church and highlighted with alarming clarity the institution's crisis in post-Communist Poland.

The War of the Crosses (and the controversy around it) was both like and unlike other, earlier key symbolic sites and events where the meaning of the nation was (re)defined and (re)interpreted (such as the constitutional

the event (OBOP 1998, $N = 1{,}011$). As I define it, an event is constituted not only by specific social actions, but also by the reactions these generate in the public sphere. The War of the Crosses, as an event, was therefore constituted by the actions taking place at the gravel pit and the societywide debate these engendered. I return to a discussion of Events as an analytical category and of an eventful sociology of nationalism as a theoretical framework later in this chapter.

preamble I also discuss in this work) in that its terms were familiar and important to all strata, not merely to politicians and intellectuals, and it attracted international attention. At the outset, then, we should recognize both the familiarity and the distinctiveness of the War of the Crosses. The event was built out of symbols and narratives of the nation that had been spun and woven over decades (and even centuries), but this familiar repertoire did not have the same meaning or resonance in the post-1989 context. With Poland now open to the West, "Oświęcim," the symbol of Polish martyrdom, was overshadowed by "Auschwitz," the international epicenter of Holocaust memory-making.[22]

The "Pope-Rabbi" incident described above was revealing, but its headline-grabbing appeal obscures important aspects of the controversy. By showing the two elderly religious leaders at odds, the photograph muscles the viewer into a specific interpretive corner. In that corner, the event's meaning is primarily related to religious conflict and, more specifically, Christian-Judaic and Polish-Jewish antagonism. The War of the Crosses was indeed widely represented in the international news media as yet another gesture of Christian anti-Judaism and Polish anti-Semitism. While anti-Semitism undoubtedly was an important element of the controversial action, it was not the only significant one. The event was not solely an interfaith and interethnic conflict. I argue that key axes of the conflict were actually *intra*religious and *intra*national.

Consequently, the story I will tell is much more complex and multilayered than the "religious war" theme suggests, however compelling and memorable it may be. My "caption" to the pope-rabbi photo will be longer and more circuitous. Once read, it will grant the photo deeper texture, richer colors, and clearer resolution than it has in its present black-and-white patina. In this long caption, the photo's theme is Polish nationalism. It is, to be sure, about a battle between Poles and Jews over the meaning of Auschwitz and its memory; a competition between two groups whose identities crystallize around messianic myths of chosenness in which suffering plays a central role; and about the presence of the Christian symbol at the former camp.[23] But the theme is also, if not primarily, the ongoing debate

22. The symbolic representations of the site should not be conflated with the site itself. I therefore use quotation marks to emphasize the construction and porousness of "Oświęcim" and "Auschwitz" as meaningful symbols. The names appearing in the text without quotation marks refer to physical sites, as I explain in more detail in chapter 3.

23. A few terminological clarifications are in order at this point. The reader should note that although I speak of "Poles" and "Jews," it is far from my intention to imply that these are

among Poles about the meaning of the nation in post-Communist Poland, and the nation's relationship with Roman Catholicism. The event and the controversy around it cannot be understood without looking at the historical construction of Polish national identity through Poland's three-time territorial partition and disappearance from the European map (1795–1918), the context of twentieth-century Communism, and the meaning of the current post-Communist transition.

As we leave behind the thin caption accompanying the photo of the pope and the rabbi, the one describing their argument as merely religious, it will not prove useful to replace *religious* with *national* in any straightforward sense, since this would merely expose and trim the photo in a different way. The conundrum is to understand the ways in which the evident religious sentiments are national, and the ways in which the national ones are religious. This study, therefore, ultimately aims to use the War of the Crosses as a catalyst for theoretically clarifying the relationship between nationalism and religion.[24] Let's begin by briefly looking at how that relationship has been conceptualized in the literature on nations and nationalism.

---

homogeneous or distinct groups. As I show throughout the book, reactions to the War of the Crosses from members of both "groups" were highly diversified. Groupness, here, is constituted dialectically in relation to the "Other." Poles and Jews are therefore categories that make sense here insofar as they are distinct vis-à-vis each other, even though great variation exists within each. I am also aware that classifying actors in two camps, Poles and Jews, creates a certain ambiguity for people who are embedded, in some way or another, within both groups, such as Jews living in Poland. Are these Jewish Poles or Polish Jews? Jews with Polish citizenship? All these identities are possible, but I refer to that group as they refer to themselves in Poland, as Polish Jews (*polscy Żydzi*). As I use the term, *Polish Jews* describes not the entire Polish Jewry (those living in Poland and those living outside its borders, the Polish Jewish Diaspora), but more narrowly those Jews currently living in Poland as well as those who may have emigrated from Poland anytime after World War II but who still participate in Polish public life. This level of generalization, while not ideal, is essential to capture the main lines that characterize each group vis-à-vis the other.

24. Although I use the War of the Crosses as a window into the broader sociological problem of nationalism and religion, this book constitutes the only exhaustive study of the event. E. Klein (2001) wrote a journalistic account of the event; Ryzner (2000) has a short article analyzing the reaction to the event in the international press; Kuleta (2001) has conducted a content analysis of the coverage of the event in Polish newspapers in an unpublished master's thesis; and Holc (2005) has a short article on the topic. The War of the Crosses is also addressed in some of the articles published in a volume edited by Berger, Cargas, and Nowak (2004), but most of those consist of translations of primary documents and key Polish interventions, such as those from Father Stanisław Musiał, Józef Cardinal Glemp, Stanisław Krajewski, and Konstanty Gebert. To the best of my knowledge, my book provides the only exhaustive analysis of the event.

Theories of Nationalism and Religion

Surveying the Field

Mainstream scholarship on nations and nationalism often points out that the emergence and rise of nationalism as an ideology is linked to the general trend of the secularization of society (Kedourie 1960; Anderson 1983; Gellner 1983; Hobsbawm 1983a, 1983b; see A. Smith 2003, 9–18).[25] Historically, politics has replaced religion as the ultimate reference, a process referred to as the "disenchantment of the world" (M. Weber 1978; Gauchet 1985). In view of this historical fact, some scholars have concluded that religion's demise is responsible for the extent of nationalism's success.[26] The argument most paradigmatically goes as follows: starting with the Reformation, the authority of the church was seriously diminished in temporal matters. The Enlightenment and later the French Revolution further diminished religion's power as a principle of social organization, as a basis for political legitimacy and sovereignty, and as the source of knowledge. Once the way was cleared, rationalism, politics, and eventually nationalism would become the new sacred principles of the modern era.

Historical arguments of the *longue durée* identify these secularizing processes as turning points in the creation of a world system of nation-states, with nationalism as the new secular orthodoxy. There is no doubt that these ideological revolutions and the structural changes that accompanied them had a tremendous impact both on the decline of religion as "sacred canopy" (Berger 1969) and on the slow emergence of the nation form. There is also no doubt that nationalism was often draped in religious robes, as Revolutionary France (and other cases) teaches us. What is problematic in this scholarly narrative is the conclusion that nationalism's emergence and success was (and is) related to religion's demise; that the emergence of nationalism was

25. Secularization theory is highly differentiated. José Casanova, in his remarkable historical-comparative study of public religions in the modern world, argues that secularization, commonly thought to be a single phenomenon (and consequently often developed into a single theory), is actually composed of "three very different, uneven and unintegrated propositions: secularization as differentiation of the secular spheres from religious institutions and norms, secularization as decline of religious beliefs and practices, and secularization as marginalization of religion to a privatized sphere" (1994, 211; see especially chapters 1 and 8). Philip Gorski (2000a) differentiates between four main types of secularization theories. Whereas some posit the disappearance and the decline of religion, others emphasize its privatization and transformation.

26. Although Benedict Anderson links the dusk of the religious mode of thought and the dawn of nationalism, he does not claim that the latter was produced by the erosion of the former, but more productively, that nationalism is both born out of and against religious systems ([1983] 1991, 12). A similar argument is more consistently developed by David E. Bell in his book *The Cult of the Nation in France: Inventing Nationalism, 1680–1800* (2003).

caused by secularization.[27] As Liah Greenfeld points out, "The fact that nationalism replaced religion as the order-creating system . . . implies nothing at all about the historical connection between them and lends no justification to the kind of sociological teleology that is the essence of such reasoning" (1996, 176). In fact, historical sociologists have recently argued that nationalism has roots *not* in religious decline, as is commonly maintained, but rather in moments of religious fervor and renewal (Greenfeld 1992, 1996; Gorski 2000b, 2003; Calhoun 1993; Gillis 1994; Marx 2003).[28] One moment of such religious élan was the Reformation, which "replaced the universalistic notion of Christendom with local and regional variants of the common faiths, mobilized popular participation, promulgated vernacular discourse and printed texts, and invoked the theological sovereignty of the people against the Church and monarchs" (Calhoun 1993, 219). Culturally, it allowed the development of a different kind of memory, one that was neither purely local nor cosmopolitan, as well as a new type of identity among elites, who came to share a bounded self-conception as "God's Englishmen," a protonational (or national, according to early modernists) identity (Gillis 1994, 7). The Reformation's subsequent launching of national churches throughout Europe is seen as the basis for the development of nation-states, since it emancipated regions from Rome, fractured the political establishment, and furnished new political alliances along confessional lines. The point here is that there is convincing evidence that nationalism's success is not necessarily attributable to religious decline, and that we should not take the relationship between nationalism and religion as a zero-sum game in which one can win only at the expense of the other.

27. The inverse causal relation is also commonly assumed: the contemporary rise of religious movements and the "re-enchantment of the world" are often attributed to the decline of the nation-state in the face of globalization.

28. The Reformation is seen either as containing the seeds of secularization or as a source of religious revival. According to either interpretation, however, it is a significant event in the formation of nations and nationalism. "Modernists" argue that nationalism is in essence a modern phenomenon, originating in the late eighteenth century, its birth often corresponding to the French Revolution. They look at the Reformation from a greater historical distance, seeing in it its long-term impact on the place of religion in public life. The Reformation, for them, therefore contains the seed of secularization that ultimately allowed the emergence of the nation form. "Early modernists," such as Greenfeld and Gorski, question the modernist position and identify the rise of nationalism in the early modern period. As a result, instead of seeing the Reformation as the beginning of the end of religion that then caused the emergence of nationalism, they understand it as a wave of religious élan whose *immediate* effect was to instigate nationalist movements and create national identities. While both positions link the Reformation with the eventual emergence of nationalism, each conceptualizes the relationship between religion and nationalism differently: modernists see nationalism resulting from religious decline, and early modernists see its roots in religious enthusiasm.

The evolutionist view of the rise of nationalism is taken one step further by scholars who suggest, after Émile Durkheim, that nationalism is a substitute for religion in modernity, with immense integrative power in an age of anomie or atomization (Durkheim [1912] 1995; Kohn 1944, 1946; Hayes 1960; Tamir 1995; Llobera 1996; Marvin and Ingle 1999). Nationalism is portrayed as being pervasive in modernity because it fills the void left by religion's retreat. According to this evolutionist-functionalist view, nationalism has not only superseded religion, it has actually replaced it by *itself* becoming a modern religion, fulfilling functions of integration that traditional religions once performed. At the individual or psychological level, nationalism is seen as a functional substitute for religion in modernity because it fulfills deep human needs (Hayes 1960; Llobera 1996; Hobsbawm [1992] 1995, 172–73), whereas at the social level, it fulfills the essential function of consolidating the group and its identity above and beyond individual needs (Tamir 1995).

These arguments are problematic at several levels. First, equating nationalism and religion erases the distinct characteristics of each phenomenon. Second, presupposing psychosocial needs as natural—or eliding the process by which these needs are created and then fulfilled—mystifies as much as it explains. The reification and primordialization of needs imply that national identity is a "natural" phenomenon instead of the product of human agency, and suggests the inevitability of nationalism rather than its historical contingency. Finally, the functional equivalence of nationalism and religion is dubiously premised upon a historical narrative of the secularization of the West, the vacuum of which was filled by nationalism. The varied and complex history of the relationship between nationalism and religion cannot be restricted to a simple linear sequence in which one form of social organization is replaced by another (from Gemeinschaft to Gesellschaft), and one type of integrative cement is replaced by another (from religion to nationalism).

In addition to being theoretically and logically flawed, the evolutionist-functionalist perspective is empirically wrong. Religion is obviously not part of some prior stage, but very much present in the modern world and highly significant in defining the nation and its discourse, as well as in shaping nationalist practices. Moreover, that perspective prevents us from understanding and explaining cases in which religious beliefs, symbols, and practices play a salient role in national identity and nationalism, leading us to treat these as a residue or "survival" from a premodern period, thereby endowing them with primordial, atavistic powers. To escape these problematic generalizations, we need to rethink the relationship in a way that does not preclude the coexistence of religion and nationalism, but instead attends to the historical contingency, the institutional and cultural embeddedness, and the social dynamics of the religion-nation relation. The question is not to determine the relative primacy of one or the other as carrier of collective identity, but rather to identify the conditions under which religion and nationalism are fused, split, or juxtaposed, and to pinpoint how exactly these categories are imbricated in social identities.

Unlike the evolutionist-functionalist view, which posits the disappearance of religion as a sine qua non for the emergence of nationalism and sees the "age of religion" and the "age of nationalism" as two radically different historical periods, the "perennialist" position is one that stresses continuity between religion and nationalism: according to its proponents (A. Smith 1986, 2003; Armstrong 1996; Hastings 1997), ancient religious communities provided the materials from which modern nations could later be built. This view is troubling insofar as it assumes a historical continuity between premodern communities, what Anthony D. Smith calls *ethnies*, and modern nations. The problem is that there is no necessary continuity here, although—and this is key—such continuity is retrospectively constructed and reinforced in nationalist discourse and narratives. As we will see in the case of Poland (chapter 1), the identity of the nation as primordially and eternally Catholic was created and reinforced in a particular period by interested actors, and is intimately related to structural changes, ideological developments, and political interests. This is not to say that Roman Catholicism before the age of nationalism did not play an important role in premodern Poland and in the lives of many of its inhabitants. It surely did. But Catholicism has not always been, as nationalists claim, the hallmark of the Polish nation. The construction of national identity involves the creation of collective memories, rituals, and symbols, their institutional maintenance and renewal, and the selective appropriation and annihilation of divisive memories and alternative identities (Renan [1882] 1996; E. Weber 1976; Gellner 1983; Hobsbawm and Ranger 1983; Anderson [1983] 1991; Hobsbawm [1992] 1995; Duara 1995). Claiming a direct continuity with ancient forms of community is therefore far-fetched, although the modern process of nation creation involves the borrowing from these older communal forms of myths, heroes, and symbols to create the illusion of the modern nation's ancient origins and therefore legitimize its modern existence.

To understand the relationship between religion and nation in all its complexity, we must shed modernization theory's a priori but without reifying the link between premodern and modern communal bonds, as perennialists do. The way forward is to highlight how religion can frame identities, shape actions, and be used to mobilize masses, as well as to show how nationalism impacts the definition of religious identities and religious movements. Several important works in the last decade have undertaken this task under the rubric of Religious Nationalism (Juergensmeyer 1993; Van der Veer 1994; Sells 1996; Tambiah 1996). Although this literature is certainly important, it tends to focus on violent interreligious and interethnic conflicts and the logic of that specific kind of group antagonism. It does not take as its specific object of study how religion and ethnicity have become entangled in a given group in the first place—what the fusion or fission between ethnicity (or national identity) and religion is dependent on, nor when and how that relationship can be renegotiated and reconfigured. These are the questions I attend to in this work. Using the War of the Crosses as my window into the relationship between religion and nationalism in Poland allows me to examine both dimensions of that relationship: between religious and ethnic groups, and also within them—how the nation is constituted vis-à-vis others, but also achieved through contests among social and political actors within the nation.[29]

Moving Ahead

Despite the academic buzz around religious nationalism in the last few years, a midrange theory that shows how macrostructural transformations such as state formation and regime transformation impact the relationship between religion and nationalism within one national group remains to be developed. This is one of the contributions of this book to the literature on nationalism: instead of looking at grand historical trajectories, I examine critical historical junctures and political crossroads in Polish history—most specifically the post-Communist period—where the relationship between religion and nationalism is being renegotiated. This strategy allows me to identify the causes of that renegotiation and the mechanisms behind that process.

I argue that there exists in Poland a triangular relationship between the form of the state, the definition of national identity, and the place and role of religion and the Catholic Church in society. Put very schematically, in the absence of a national state (or of a state perceived as *genuinely* representing *Polish* interests, as was the case under Communism), religion and

29. By focusing on inter- and intragroup dynamics via the study of Jerusalem as a contested symbol and place, Friedland and Hecht's book, *To Rule Jerusalem* (2000), has a similar sociological agenda.

national identity become fused; Roman Catholicism is used as an ethnonational marker. The mobilizing discourse of the nation is primarily defined in ethno-religious terms, and the Roman Catholic Church is represented as the legitimate guardian and carrier of national values, providing institutional, ideological, and symbolic support to civil society. With the creation of a legitimate national state, however, the fusion between nation and religion—and the tight bond between civil society and church—is called into question: religion becomes less significant in defining Polishness, and the church loses its centrality in society. Post-Communist Poland, I argue, is characterized by the redefinition of the triadic relationship between state, nation, and religion. But if this suggests *why* the relationship between religion and national identity is currently being redefined in Poland, the challenge remains to actually show *how* this is occurring. The next section assembles the tools for a cultural approach to meet that challenge. This approach uses *events, symbols*, and *narratives* as its key terms.

A Cultural Approach to the Study of Nationalism and Religion

The primary goals of this study are to show why religion and nationalism become fused or dissociated in the Polish case, and how this is achieved on the ground. To achieve both these goals, I firmly anchor my analysis of the current period in relation to perduring narratives of the nation that have become historically sedimented. I also focus my investigation on specific events through which the relationship between national identity and religion is crystallized and debated by competing social groups, so that it can be observed empirically. Such an approach allows me to grasp the processual dynamics of nationalism and to tease out how identity formation on the ground is related to broad institutional and structural changes such as state (re)formation and regime transformation.

History, Narrativity, and Events

The post-Communist transition cannot be understood without considering how Poles interpret, understand, narrate, and configure the decade following the fall of Communism. It is by first historicizing the transition—that is, by placing it within the context of Polish history and Poles' *interpretations* of that history—that the meaning of the transition emerges: Poles inject Communism into a long narrative vein of conquest, occupation and oppression by powerful neighbors, and their historical struggle for independence. The current period is therefore plotted as the latest phase in a narrative about Poland's fight for independence; it is commonly evoked as the "recovery of national independence." Historical linkages are constantly forged between the interwar period, when Poland reappeared on the European map, and the remapping of post-Soviet Europe. In this narrative, Poland's fateful destiny (independent nation-statehood) was interrupted by forty-four years of Communism, a dark stain requiring permanent removal from collective memory.[30]

The post-Communist transition is therefore first and foremost understood by Poles as a *national* one; it is a period characterized not merely by democratization and marketization, but primarily by the construction of a national state, a state *of* and *for* Poles, to borrow Rogers Brubaker's formulation (1996).[31] Given this project, the issue of what exactly constitutes "Polishness" has been a recurring theme in public discourse and debates; in the process, Polish national identity's "traditional" association with Catholicism has been seriously questioned. It is in this broader context that the War of the Crosses takes on its full meaning and can shed light on the relationship between religion and nationalism.

The study of events such as the War of the Crosses, then, is important for two reasons: first, such events make readily observable ongoing processes which may not be otherwise apparent; and second, it is through them that the nation is (re)constructed. And here I answer Brubaker's summons for an "eventful" sociology of nationalism. Following the theoretical leads of Sewell (1996a, 1996b), Abbott (1990), and Sahlins (1985), an eventful perspective is one that pays theoretical attention to contingent events and to their transformative consequences. Events as I define them, however, are not necessarily those that change structures and create new cultural forms (Sewell 1996a). They are meaningful and consequential in that they sporadically create, recreate, define, refine, and redefine the nation through social contestation. Nationalism, then, is best described as a series of intermittent bursts of creativity, contestation, and redefinition of the nation that are embedded in and caused by *longue durée* social, historical, and cultural environments. As a coveted symbol constructed out of subsymbols, events,

30. The post-1989 naming of the state as the *Third* Republic of Poland is indicative of this symbolic attempt to mnemonically erase Communism from Polish history. Continuity is claimed with the Second Republic (1918–39), and just as the People's Republic of Poland (1945–89) marked a rupture with the Second Republic, the Third Republic (1989–) breaks off with the previous era by bypassing and eliding it altogether.

31. The transition to post-Communism is therefore a "triple transition," marked by marketization, democratization, and the less studied nationalization of political space (Brubaker 1996).

and narratives, the nation is a crossroads where diverse discourses and practices intersect, with political and cultural actors fighting over the direction of advance. Instead of treating the nation as a "thing" or a historical and sociological "fact," the nation is a work in progress constituted through nationalist events such as the War of the Crosses.

Symbols and Nationalism

Three symbols intersect in the War of the Crosses: the cross, as it bears the nation; the nation, as it provides the grain of the cross's wood; and "Oświęcim"/"Auschwitz," whose soil nourishes this forest of symbols. Symbols, Victor Turner (1967) taught us, are polysemic or multivocal; they condense multiple meanings and remain semantically open. Their meaning is not absolutely fixed, and new significations can be added to traditional ones by collective fiat. Precisely because meanings are not fixed, social contests center on the question of a symbol's definition. A symbol's meaning depends on the power, authority, or prestige of the social groups that compete for its control, as well as each group's rhetorical effectiveness at locating the symbol within mobilizing narratives and contexts of action.

The nation itself, for example, is a dominant symbol with multiple possible meanings "offered as alternatives and competed over by different social groups maneuvering to secure the monopoly on its definition" (Verdery 1993, 39). In this contest, agents fight for the control of official (that is, explicit and public) representations of the social world, to impose their own visions as the legitimate one to be reproduced in common sense (Bourdieu 1980, 1991b, 2000). This means that studies of nationalism must identify the particular fields—social, historical, cultural, and even global—in which different groups compete to control the nation and its meanings, and to what ends. The conflict *within* the nation over the nation's meaning, project, and destiny provides a fruitful site for the investigation of the internal dynamics of nationalism.

I therefore pay attention to the actors' multiple, often contradictory interpretations of key symbols, what Turner has termed a symbol's "exegetic meaning," and to the "operational," or practical, meaning: how given symbols are actually used by social actors, toward what ends, and with what techniques.[32] As we shall see in subsequent chapters, the cross in Poland

32. Note here that the operational or practical meaning of a symbol may be attributed consciously or unconsciously in that social actors may be manipulating the symbol with definite ends in mind, but their actions may lead to outcomes different from those they intended. "Operational"

might be described by certain Poles who use it as the symbol of the nation, of national unity in the face of adversity. But in practice, the cross is used by these same actors as a tool of exclusion and division in the specific context of post-Communism. It is also said to represent the "essence" of Polishness and its fusion with Roman Catholicism when, in fact, analysis of debates surrounding the symbol during the War of the Crosses reveals that it stands for the profound contestation—even fission—of that fusion. Quite counterintuitively, the disputed symbol ultimately represents the *dissociation* of religious and ethno-national identity in post-Communist Poland.

I also study each symbol in relation to the others, what Turner called a symbol's "positional" or "relational" meaning. Since symbols are intrinsically involved in social processes, they must be studied in relation to other symbols, within the contexts in which they are evoked and used by social actors. And vice versa: to comprehend the semantics of key Polish symbols—such as the nation as defined in its constitution's preamble, "Oświęcim" as a locus of Polish collective memory, or the cross in the public sphere—as they are used in specific events, we must examine the debates between social groups about their key signifiers before and during these discrete events (Turner 1974, 141–42). But even more broadly than this, we must examine the specific social, institutional, and political contexts in which these symbols, as well as the debates about them, become meaningful (Bourdieu 1991b, 2000).

Consequently, theories that view culture as a coherent, uniform, and static system of symbols and meanings (for example Geertz 1973) are of questionable utility for this study. Culture, after the "cultural turn," is more fruitfully addressed in performative terms: humans are not the passive recipients of cultural systems that constrain their action. They are, rather, the active users of cultural tools in practice. Following Sewell (1999, 48–49), I view culture as a network of semiotic relations that has a certain coherence. This coherence, however, is "thin" at best: users of culture form a semiotic community in that they recognize the meaning of signs and symbols and are able to engage in meaningful action, but without necessarily agreeing in their emotional or moral evaluations of these recognized symbols. Such a perspective avoids the uniformizing view of culture as consensual, shared, clearly bounded, and static, and is especially useful for the study of nationalism. For example, all Poles, regardless of religious affiliation and level of

---

meaning is a concept that captures the ultimate outcome of symbolic ritual action, not its stated objectives ("exegetical" meaning).

commitment, recognize the cross as a key Polish symbol; not all, however, agree on its meaning and place in Polish society.

Broadly, then, this work focuses on key symbols that generate, condense, and mobilize—but can also divide—sentiments within a society. The meaning of symbols is radically indeterminate and contested, and this social contestation is deeply ideological, in the sense of being consciously "worked" by different groups toward different political objectives. But symbols are not only relationally constructed; they are also historically constituted by key narratives and events. The historical process was mostly overlooked by Turner, but will take center stage in my investigation. I give attention, for example, to how the cross comes to signify Poland's status as the dying and rising "martyr of nations" at one historical juncture, and Solidarity's resistance to Communism at another. Since symbols and meanings change over time, we must attend to their meaning as they are embedded in layers of historical narratives.

Aesthetics and Emotions

The focus on symbolic action is important for the study of nationalism because symbols typically evoke and stimulate emotional responses, what Turner (1967) has termed the "orectic" pole of symbols. The study of emotions has made a much-needed comeback in the study of collective action and nationalism (Yang 2000; Goodwin, Jasper, and Polletta 2001; Berezin 2001; Aminzade and McAdam 2001; Kaufman 2001; Petersen 2002; Suny 2004). With the move away from primordialism toward constructivist theories of nationalism, emotions—traditionally associated with the irrational and "primordial"—were discarded. Nationalism was now seen not as the result of irrational crowds, but rather as the work of calculating elites and institutions, the result of specific rationalizing processes of modernity. While this move toward the social and intellectual creation of nations and nationalism was essential, with regard to the role of emotions the baby had been thrown out with the bathwater. National identity and nationalism are potent social phenomena precisely because of the emotions they evoke, generate, and manipulate (Anderson [1983] 1991). These emotions, of course, are not "primal" or "primordial" (as some of the functionalist authors discussed above imply or maintain) and should not be viewed as solely individual phenomena. They are obviously socially constructed (Reddy 2001). Scholars of nationalism thus must now work at breaking down the association "emotional-primordial-primitive-irrational," and bring emotions into a constructivist framework of national identity and nationalism.

A further contribution of this book, then, is to show how emotions are mobilized by specific symbols and the narratives they carry. The symbols and iconography of the War of the Crosses were crucial in evoking key historical events with varying emotional resonances. As a Christian symbol, the cross summons sentiments related to suffering and martyrdom, but also of hope and renewal. In its more specifically national dimension, it arouses feelings of pride in Polish national identity and independence—conjoining connotations of both the oppression from, and resistance to, foreigners. The scarred face of the Black Madonna, Our Lady of Częstochowa, also reminds Poles of their historical suffering and their "miraculous" survival as a nation. I show that the specific iconographic collage used by the Defenders of the Cross (crosses, flags, flowers, posters, pictures of John Paul II, paintings of the Black Madonna) and the specific ritualizations at the gravel pit (prayer vigils, Masses, patriotic chants, hunger strikes) were borrowed from a cultural repertoire of nationalist mobilization that carried high emotional resonances. The summoning of emotions created through the specific aesthetics of the event is undoubtedly behind the mobilization of different groups for, but also *against*, the cross-planting action.

The role of nationalist aesthetics—its symbols, stories, and rituals—must be brought to the fore of analyses of nationalism, since it is through these aesthetics that people become emotionally invested in the nation. I show that the aesthetics of the War of the Crosses and the emotions they generated were central to the relatively successful mobilization of nationalist groups that led to the symbolic appropriation of Auschwitz. Through their flamboyant, graphic aesthetics, marginal groups took on a high profile in the ongoing war of positions over what Polishness "truly" is.

Relevance of the Polish Case for a Cultural Approach

The book fills a large gap in the literature on nationalism by providing the only extensive sociological analysis of Polish nationalism that focuses on the post-Communist period. Polish nationalism, despite its richness and complexity, has received relatively little attention in the field. Few studies are devoted to the Polish case, and even fewer focus on the post-Communist period, despite the massive geopolitical import of this transition. Brubaker published an excellent sociological analysis of the dynamics of interwar Polish nationalism in a short chapter of his influential *Nationalism Reframed* (1996), but the great majority of works on Polish nationalism, such as the seminal studies of Andrzej Walicki (1982, 1989, 1990, 1999), focus on political philosophy and Polish nationalism's ideological roots. Brian

Porter's study (2000) is attentive to the sociological aspects of Polish nationalism, but remains primarily focused on the nineteenth century. The single serious work specifically devoted to nationalism in post-Communist Poland is from Joanna Kurczewska (2002), who studied the various forms of national identifications and patriotism expressed by political elites.[33] To date, there exists no book-length study of nationalism and religion in Poland, or of nationalism in post-Communist Poland. How do we account for this lacuna?

Just like their Western counterparts, most Polish sociologists and other social scientists have preferred to study "more important" topics related to the post-Communist transition, such as democratic reform, the development of a market economy and the processes of privatization, European integration, and the like.[34] Another reason Poland has received relatively little attention in the area is because it has not suffered from "significant" nationalist problems: there has been no war (Yugoslavia), no separatist movements (Yugoslavia, Czechoslovakia), and no officially mandated discrimination against minority groups (Baltic states). Poland, it would seem, is boringly quiet on the national(ist) front. One obvious reason for this relative calm is the demographic structure of postwar Poland: for reasons I will discuss in the next chapter, Poland has one of the most ethnically and religiously homogeneous populations in the world, as approximately 97 percent of Polish citizens are ethnically Polish, and 95 percent are Roman Catholic (at least nominally).[35]

Yet this apparently tedious lack of intrigue can be turned from liability to luster. For despite such overwhelming homogeneity, nationalism has in fact been one of the defining issues of the post-Communist years. This suggests that nationalism is not always and necessarily the result of some "objective" structural problems. In this study, I show that nationalism stems

33. Other Polish scholars touch upon nationalism through the analysis of other problems, such as Ewa Nowicka's work on stereotyping (1991; Nowicka and Łodziński 2001) or Jerzy Szacki's essays on liberalism after Communism (1994).

34. This absence is even more conspicuous given the attention Polish social scientists have given to the national question in the late nineteenth and twentieth centuries. Because of the national situation, Polish sociology was actually born out of concerns about the nation, and Polish social thought was shaped by important works on the nature of the national community and the strength of national bonds (Thomas and Znaniecki 1927; Znaniecki 1952); the relationship between nation and state (Limanowski 1906) and culture and nation (Chałasiński 1968); the relationship between folk and national cultures (Czarnowski 1956, [1934] 1988) and the difference between regional and national feelings of belonging (Ossowski 1984); the challenges facing small nations and borderland populations (Chlebowczyk 1980); and the construction of national identity in borderlands and in borderline situations (Kłoskowska 2001).

35. Data from the 2002 Polish census, available at http://www.poland.gov.pl.

from perceptions of history, their aesthetic representation, and the understandings of political change that succeed in taking hold as a thinly coherent culture.

Data, Methods, and Organization of the Book

Several chapters pay careful attention to intellectuals' articulation of the nation and of the state, since this social group plays a central role in the ongoing project of national (re)definition in Poland.[36] But the book is equally attentive in its method to the analysis of discourses and practices of "everyday people." This offers a more complete picture of national identity and nationalism than has been offered by most scholarly works, one that is at once top-down and bottom-up.

Data and Methods

The evidence for the book was collected via archival research, fieldwork interviews, and participant observation pertaining to selected issues, events, and symbols. I reviewed and analyzed editorials and letters to the editor in Polish newspapers (dailies, weeklies, and monthlies) from diverse political and ideological orientations, covering a wide spectrum from Left to Right.[37] The press in Poland provides a forum where different ideological positions are articulated and diverse political opinions are expressed and defended. Newspapers are used here not as a source of objective information, but rather as primary documents for the analysis of ideological debates.[38]

36. See Suny and Kennedy (2000) for an analysis of intellectuals' crucial role in the shaping and dissemination of national identity, and Kurczewska (2002) on the role of Polish political elites more specifically, as they act as "final instances" in processes defining the parameters of contemporary social reality (ibid., 12).

37. A list of publications reviewed along with circulation figures are provided in appendix A. It is important to note that the Left-Right cleavage is defined in ideological terms, not in socioeconomic ones (although they may sometimes overlap). The Left-Right opposition should thus be understood not as one between support for state intervention in the economy versus neoliberal free-market economy, but one between a secular and a confessional conception of the social order and between a civic and an ethnic vision of the nation (Jasiewicz 2000). Moreover, in Poland values and beliefs have been shown to have a greater impact on voting behavior than socioeconomic status (Markowski 1997).

38. The Polish word for this literary genre is *publicystyka* (German *publizistik*). It is translated in English as "journalism," but its meaning is actually quite different. *Publicystyka* is "a type of writing that presents important current problems of social, political, economical, cultural life etc., from a definite point of view, aiming at the shaping of public opinion" (*Mała Encyklopedia Powszechna* 1997). It is thus not mere description of an event, but partisan analysis. It is comparable to the op-ed pages in American newspapers.

Other primary documents include official church publications, pastoral letters, sermons, homilies, and texts of "spontaneous" public prayers; political speeches and pamphlets; inscriptions left on the crosses and placards brought to the site of the War of the Crosses; and other nontextual artifacts such as posters, postcards, icons, and altars. I also gathered archival data such as meeting minutes, exhibit plans, and internal memos from the Auschwitz-Birkenau State Museum's records, as well as unpublished documents relating to the guides' training, educational programs, and statistical data on visitors at the museum's Pedagogical Section.

I conducted formal and informal interviews with priests, Roman Catholic intellectuals, social activists, and actors directly involved with or especially vocal in the cross-planting action, as well as with key Auschwitz-Birkenau State Museum personnel. Participant observation also yielded significant data for the study and assumed many forms. As a visitor of the Auschwitz-Birkenau State Museum, I took multiple guided tours for Polish-speaking groups as well as for English and French ones in order to establish the "typical" narrative of the visit (and compare the discourse addressed to Polish audiences with that addressed to foreign ones). I spent hours in the "Polish Block," which is not included in the tour circuit but instead visited by individual visitors, during which I observed their reactions to the exhibit and its narrative.

On the production side of museum activity, I frequented special training sessions for the tour guides, who must pursue their education after certification, and attended lectures, workshops, and meetings with camp survivors offered to humanities teachers in a special course organized by the museum's Pedagogical Section and the Akademia Pedagogiczna in Cracow. My informal interactions with fellow students, all certified high school teachers, during lunch hour, coffee breaks, and carpooling were most fruitful. Moreover, I met several times with nuns who pray by Saint Maksymilian Kolbe's cell in the "Block of Death," and I attended numerous gatherings of the Covenant in Defense of the Papal Cross in Oświęcim, a small group of men and women who have been meeting by the fenced area surrounding the papal cross every day since the relocation of the Carmelite convent in 1993. The group meets to pray for the nation, and more specifically for the defense of the papal cross and the prompt return of the Carmelite nuns to the site.

Lastly, I participated in special events such as the March of the Living, when Jewish youth march from Auschwitz to Birkenau, where special commemorations take place; and the March of Memory, during which participants and activists walked from the former Cracow ghetto to the Płaszów camp to commemorate the fifty-eighth anniversary of the ghetto's liquidation.[39]

Organization

The book's largest window onto the relationship between nationalism and religion, the War of the Crosses, will not be clear enough until we draw open the curtains and polish the glass. The next chapter therefore takes a closer look at the myths and symbols that make up the dominant Polish national narrative, the very narrative and symbols at the heart of the War of the Crosses. More than a historical survey that provides the background for understanding the current period, this chapter aims to analytically deconstruct "the nation" and rethink some of its myths by examining the various stories and symbols comprising the dominant national narrative(s), and to identify in which particular contexts they surface and become mobilizing.

Following this historical excursus, chapter 2 addresses the question of what the process of building a legitimate national state after the fall of Communism implies for the definition of national identity, and for the role of religion and the church in shaping nationalist discourses and practices. It pays particular attention to debates surrounding the production and ratification of the preamble to the Constitution of 1997. More specifically, it analyzes disputes over the definition of the constituent entity ("the nation" or "citizens") and over whether an *invocatio Dei* (a reference to God) should be included in the constitution's solemn opening. The preamble as symbolic product and the process by which it came into being as an "event" offer a point of entrée to consider the post-Communist political field in Poland as it has (re)defined the relationship between religion and national identity, and between church and state.

We then turn to the study's main case, the War of the Crosses at Auschwitz in 1998 and 1999, a privileged site where questions of identity are condensed, crystallized, and fiercely contested by different social groups. First,

39. Most formal interviews were audiotaped and lasted between one and four hours. Subjects who were talking to me in their official capacity are named in the text. The identity is not revealed for those subjects who expressed personal opinions that they preferred not to be tied with their professional status. Valuable interview data were also collected from more than 150 subjects in informal ethnographic interviews during participant observation. These conversations were not taped, and their duration varied greatly depending on the nature of my interaction with the subjects. These subjects are not identified in the text. A list of formal interviews is included in the references.

chapter 3 analyzes the making of Auschwitz as a contested, multilayered symbol, and the role of the Auschwitz-Birkenau State Museum in that process. Whereas Auschwitz is, for Jews and the world, the place and symbol of the Holocaust (and now of universal evil), for Poles it signifies Polish martyrdom. This chapter shows that the War of the Crosses, at the level of the Polish-Jewish conflict, is a fight over memory and the appropriate ways to commemorate the unspeakable. It also shows the perverse effects of Socialism's civic nationalism and its enduring effects on the Polish memory of Auschwitz as a Polish site of martyrdom.

Chapter 4 consists of a close investigation of another potent symbol throughout Polish history, the cross, through an analysis of the discourses of the Defenders of the Cross and of those who brought crosses to the gravel pit. It offers an analysis of not only the inscriptions left on the crosses, but also the general aesthetics of the War of the Crosses. Key to the relative success of the action, I argue, was the deployment of religious and nationalist iconography that had strong emotional associations with potent historical events.

The last empirical chapter based on the War of the Crosses, chapter 5, investigates the discourses about the controversial event in the Polish public sphere and points to changing and plural conceptions of the cross, and more broadly of the nation and its relation to Roman Catholicism in post-Communist Poland. I show that the War of the Crosses was not only a conflict with Jews over the meaning of Auschwitz, but also a debate about the place and role of religion in the new polity.

The conclusion returns to theoretical implications of the case for thinking about the relationship between nationalism and religion.

CHAPTER ONE

Genealogy of Polish Nationalism

L'incompréhension du présent naît fatalement de l'ignorance du passé.[1]
—Marc Bloch, *Apologie pour l'histoire*

In the Polish tradition, the historical image has proved far more convincing than the historical fact.
—Norman Davies, *God's Playground: A History of Poland*

Introduction

Every nation has its myth of foundation: its linked plots of growth and development, crisis and resistance, doom, victory, and rebirth. These myths change over time, with the times, but always remain, their origins occluded; it is in that sense, and only that sense, that they are timeless. The most common and pervasive Polish myth is that of Poland's intrinsic Catholicity: *Polonia semper fidelis* (Poland always faithful), the bulwark of Christendom defending Europe against the infidel (however defined); the Christ of nations, martyred for the sins of the world, resurrected for the world's salvation; a nation whose identity is conserved and guarded by its defender, the Roman Catholic Church, and shielded by its Queen, the miraculous Black Madonna, Our Lady of Częstochowa; a nation that has given the world a pope and rid the Western world of Communism . . . If this representation is a caricature of the myth, it is, like all caricatures, distorted only by the picture's being drawn with rather oversharp angles.

In this chapter, I analyze the formation and transformation of Polish national identity and nationalism, and investigate the construction of the

1. "The incomprehension of the present is fatally born of the ignorance of the past."

association between Polishness and Roman Catholicism, too often taken for granted. Before undertaking an anatomy of the War of the Crosses and its multiple layers, we must know something of its constituent parts: the making of the cross as a dominant symbol and martyrdom as a core narrative, the representation of Jews as "Other," and Catholicism as a key element of Polish identity.

To go forward, we must first go back. It is for that reason that I now invite the reader on a fairly whirlwind historical tour of the formation and transformation of Polish national identity and nationalism. The tour will not be an exhaustive (or exhausting) survey of Polish history, but rather a discussion of the historical constitution of the nation focused on the questions defined in the book's introduction.[2] The objective is not only to provide the reader with the historical background necessary for understanding the current period and the War of the Crosses, but also to identify key events, narratives, symbols, and rituals out of which the nation was and is created, and which specifically were brought to bear in the recent crisis at Auschwitz. The current strategies of discourses and practices are delineated by the parameters of historical narratives. It is through these key narratives and symbols that religion and national identity were intertwined during the War of the Crosses. It is therefore crucial for us to uncover their origins.

The pervasive myth of Poland's intrinsic Roman Catholic identity is based on a specific telling of national history, argues Brian Porter: "The Catholic narrative of Polish history is far more than a recognition that Roman Catholicism was and is important in Poland: it is an ideologically loaded conceptual framework that gives specific meaning to the past and helps determine what is remembered and what is forgotten" (2001, 291). Echoing Prasenjit Duara's call, our goal should thus be to rescue Polish history from the ethno-Catholic narrative of the nation[3] by deconstructing

2. For detailed surveys of Polish history in English, see Łukowski and Zawadzki's concise political history of Poland (2001); Wandycz's classic history of partitioned Poland (1974); and Davies' two-volume history (1982). In Polish, see Tazbir (1980); Kieniewicz (1987); Łepkowski (1989); Kamiński (2000); Chwałba (2000); Szczur (2002); and Markiewicz (2004). On the history of Christianity in Poland, see the classic work of Kłoczowski, recently translated into English (2000). On nationalism more specifically, see Walicki (1982, 1989, 1990, 1999); Brock (1994); Blanke (1981); Stauter-Halsted (2001); and especially Porter (2000). For a history of Poland and its eastern neighbors, consult T. Snyder (2003).

3. Duara's agenda is more ambitious: it is to rescue History from the nation, that is, to move outside and beyond the narrative framework of national history, which depicts the nation as a collective subject steadily evolving through time instead of seeing the nation as a "complex project of repressions and recreations, the sublation of the other in the self" (1995, 33). Duara redefines history as a configuration of narratives created at the national, local, and transnational levels and attempts to recover the voices muted by the totalizing narrative of nationalism.

and analyzing the different threads of the Polish national narrative(s), and by identifying in which particular contexts the stories and symbols comprising the various visions or versions of Polishness were woven into more or less durable fabrics. The chapter shows how the political history of Poland and the making of a dominant national narrative are imbricated, and highlights the processes by which a specific amalgam of "stories," rituals, and symbols came to form that dominant narrative.

The tour we now undertake includes two aspects: a study of the national narrative's components, and the analysis of the processes of their legitimation and canonization as "national." This is important because in contrast with Poland's national mythology, religion has not always played a role in Polish nationalism. Systematically looking for traces of it would further reify that association instead of deconstructing it. It is precisely the process by which religion came to be entangled with a specific form of nationalism that is the question at hand. Until the Polish nation was constructed along ethnic lines at the end of the nineteenth century, I show, religion played but a secondary role in conceptions of nationhood.

In the first part of the chapter I analyze the Polish protonation, defined in civic terms and centered on the Polish-Lithuanian Republic (1569–1795). I then discuss the implications of the Polish state's disappearance (1795–1918), which led to the reorientation of the emerging nation in ethnoreligious terms. In part 3 I analyze the stereotype of the "Polak-katolik" as it was codified in the "Reborn Poland" of the interwar period; and finally, in the last section of this chapter, I analyze the relationship between nation and religion, as well as between church, state, and civil society, during the Communist period.

The Civic Protonation

In today's Poland, the nation is primarily understood in ethnic terms. It is conceived as a community of history and culture, whereas the state (and "society"—*społeczeństwo*) proceeds from an associational-political relation. *Nationality* and *citizenship* are thus distinct: the first term has a clear ethnic and cultural connotation, referring to one's tie with a historical and cultural community, a community of descent, "Poland," whereas the second strictly reflects the legal-political relationship between the individual and the state.[4] Although the ethnic conception has been the dominant

4. The predominance of the ethnic understanding of the nation, the dichotomy between "nation" and "state," and the distinction between nationality and citizenship are not unique to

one since the late nineteenth century, and "nation" and "state" have been understood as distinct if not antagonistic since then, in the seventeenth and eighteenth centuries the term *naród* (nation) had a political connotation detached from linguistic or ethnic considerations. The nation (or protonation) was, rather, conceived as a political relation between citizens-noblemen: it was a political body composed of and limited to the nobility, the *szlachta*, whose members were equal in rights regardless of fortune, bound by their loyalty to the state. To a modern reader, this status-based definition of the nation may be too restrictive to be significant, closer to the Athenian *demos* than to modern democracy, and infinitely removed from what the civic nation ideally embodies since the French Revolution. But note that the Polish nobility was one of the largest in Europe, constituting 10 to 13 percent of the republic's total population. Civic participation in the Republic of Nobles was far greater than in nineteenth-century France or England. In the bourgeois France of Louis-Philippe (r. 1830–48), for example, only 1.5 percent of the population had the right to vote (Walicki 1991, 24).

Polishness was in principle blind to ethnic or religious background: one could be "*natione Polonus, gente Ruthenus, origine Judaeus*" without arousing the suspicions such an identity could evoke today.[5] Polish protonationalism was instead defined by territorial patriotism and loyalty to the state that guaranteed the *szlachta*'s "golden freedom."[6] This liberty stood in sharp contrast with the rest of Europe at the age of absolutism. The Democracy of Nobles, as the Polish-Lithuanian Republic is often

---

Poland but are, rather, characteristic of central and eastern Europe. On the distinction between ethnic and civic nationalism, see the classic work by Meinecke (1970); the no less classic by Brubaker (1992); and the articles by Yack (1996) and Nielsen (1999). For a discussion of the distinction's problematic uses, see Zubrzycki (2002).

5. "A member of the Polish nation, of the Ruthenian people, of Jewish origin" was how a seventeenth-century cleric allegedly described himself (in Tazbir 1978, 91). In an unpublished dissertation, David M. Althoen (2000, 115–51) discusses the disputed origins of the descriptive line.

6. The Golden Freedom is the general designation given to the nobility's privileges and freedoms in the republic from the sixteenth to the eighteenth century. At the election of Henri de Valois to the Polish throne in 1573, articles that formed a fixed constitutional contract between the *szlachta* and the elected king were drawn up, the so-called Henrician articles. They stipulated, among other things, the *szlachta*'s right to approve all declarations of war, all impositions of taxes, and all summons of *levée-en-masse*. One article concerned the *szlachta*'s right to freely elect kings in the future, legally abolishing the possibility of a dynastic monarchy. At the next election only three years later, the *Pacta Conventa* added several articles concerning the specific concessions made by Stefan Bathory, the newly elected king. "Henrician articles" are therefore the constitutional promises that every monarch had to accept upon taking the throne, whereas the "Pacta Conventa" was a list of specific pledges drawn up for each individual king.

called,[7] was characterized by the active and direct participation of the nobility in the political affairs of the country. The republic was based on an elective monarchy, and had, since 1493, a parliamentary system in which the Sejm (assembly of nobles, now Parliament) retained legislative power. The principle *Nic o nas bez nas* (nothing concerning us without us) and the (in)famous *liberum veto*, which allowed for a single nobleman to refuse the sanctioning of a king's election, the ratification of a law, or the levee of a new tax simply by uttering "Nie pozwalam" (I do not allow), are representative of a protodemocratic political culture that valued consensus and unanimity (Kamiński 2000). The potential for anarchy was kept in check by strong social norms that prevented the abuse of the principle; the *liberum veto* actually existed for a very long period without being used. It was only when the social norms of political behavior that kept it under control were loosened that the *liberum veto* was unleashed and became a problem. Hence its portrayal, often caricatured, as the cause of a political anarchy that paralyzed the development of essential reforms and inhibited the economic modernization of the country, consequently facilitating foreign intervention in domestic affairs, a pattern that allegedly resulted in the dissolution of the state and the partitioning of its territory.

The First Partition, when Russia, Prussia, and Austria divided up among themselves much of the territory of the Polish-Lithuanian Republic in 1772, shook up the *szlachta* enough to prompt an era of reforms that resulted in the proclamation of the Constitution of May Third in 1791. This constitution remains a potent symbol in Poland, even though it was abolished in 1792, a year after its proclamation and a year before the Second Partition.[8]

7. This appellation comes from the fact that the king's power resided in the sovereignty of the people, the noble nation (*naród szlachecki*). The *szlachta* was extremely differentiated socioeconomically: from the powerful *magnateria*, a class of rich landowners, to the petty nobility, who lacked either land or serfs—or both—and whose noble title and rights were the only elements distinguishing them from poor peasants. Despite this stratification within the nobility, all members enjoyed formal political and legal equality (in this case the right to elect a new king), hence the popular saying "The nobleman in his small plot of land is the equal of the Palatine" (Szlachcic na zagrodzie równy wojewodzie).

8. The Constitution of May Third was the culmination of an era of reform, a final attempt at sovereignty after the First Partition in 1772 and before the two subsequent ones that would soon follow (1793, 1795), eventually erasing Poland from the European map. In contemporary Poland, the Constitution of May Third symbolizes democracy, sovereignty, Poland's entrance into modernity, and its "Westernness": Poland was definitely modern and Western, since it was the first to institute a constitution in Europe—as the story goes, in an attempt to assuage a common inferiority complex, but also, especially under Communism, to align Poland culturally and politically with the West. The constitution symbolically places Poland with the United States

While it did not extend full equality for all citizens, it called for a broadening of the "nation": political membership was now dependent on landownership, not on noble birth. The landless nobility was therefore excluded from the nation, while the burghers were its new members. The peasantry was overlooked altogether.

Some thus see in the Democracy of Nobles an embryonic form of civic nationalism, though still far from modern nationalism (if by modern we mean mass-based)[9]—a form of nationalism that could not develop further at that time, but nevertheless left its traces in the contemporary Polish social imagination.[10]

Ethnicity, Religion, and Status

While ethnicity was not a criterion for membership in the nation, its ideologists were not completely satisfied with a purely political basis for national unity. A myth of common origins thus integrated the multiethnic nation of

---

and France. That symbol is widely shared throughout the ideologically divided political spectrum, although liberals and conservatives attribute different meanings to it. In post-Communist Poland, intellectuals of the Left use it to emphasize the civic heritage of the nation, while those of the Right emphasize the constitution's association with sovereignty. May 3 has been a legal holiday since the fall of Communism.

9. For a useful overview of the main tenets of modernist theories of nationalism, see Gorski (2000b, 1430–34).

10. Some historians argue that remnants of Poland's civic traditions aided the resistance to foreign domination under the Partitions as well as under state-Socialism (Walicki 1990, 27–28). In the words of historian of ideas Wojciech Karpiński, "Solidarity was the product of the best features of the democratic tradition of the gentry" (in Gomułka and Polonsky 1990, 3). Norman Davies believes that without the civic sense inherited from the Democracy of Nobles, it would have been difficult if not impossible to organize resistance to Communism. He even sees in the organizational structure of Solidarity the continuation of Polish parliamentarism (1982, 2:723–24). This seems a bit romantic to me. To be convincing, one would have to explain the process by which these traditions were not only transmitted to future generations, but spread from one narrow stratum to the entire population, and show how institutional structures were maintained (despite their actual disappearance) and handed down to the end of the twentieth century. That dissidents referred to these traditions in their discourses and even in their enactments, however, is another story, and one of significance for my purpose here. Whether the structures of Solidarity or the rhetorical style of its activists were actually, "factually" historically transmitted is less important than the fact of the activists' appropriation, interpretation, and reworking of that history, actively writing a new chapter in a familiar narrative. In acting like democratic heroes, the shipyard workers were emulating models in Polish history: the Democracy of Nobles and the Romantic insurgents that they had learned about from their history textbooks, family accounts, literature, and films. What they were reproducing, then, were the *representations* of Polish history and not the actual structures or practices.

nobles within one large family. All nobles of the Polish-Lithuanian Republic were said to descend from the ancient Sarmatians, themselves descendants of the Scythians, ultimately related to the biblical Adam. This mythic tribal identity superseded regional and ethnic differences, explained the association of ethnically diverse (noble) groups, and legitimized the noble nation's privileges.[11] Nevertheless, Polonization was often a requirement for ascension and integration into the *szlachta.* It frequently meant adopting Polish as the common language in the public sphere and converting to Roman Catholicism.[12] It would thus be a misrepresentation to claim that ethnicity as a category was simply absent from the conceptual universe of the *szlachta*'s ideologues. It was present; but as a defining element of the nation and the principle for inclusion in or exclusion from the nation, ethnicity was not, as it would later become, the focal point of the Republic of Nobles' protonationalist ideology.

Similarly with regards to religious affiliation. In addition to being ethnically diverse, the population of the Polish-Lithuanian Republic was a complex religious mosaic: it included not only Catholics (of both Latin and Greek rites), but also Orthodox, Jews, and a small number of Muslims.[13] The nation of nobles, because it was status based, was ethnically and religiously somewhat porous: some nobles never converted to Roman Catholicism, while others converted to Protestantism during the Reformation. Indeed, Calvinism spread rapidly among the nobility in the sixteenth century, and by midcentury, Protestants were a majority in the senate. Protestants and Catholics were equally "Polish," equal compatriots, which earned Poland the reputation in Europe of being the land of religious tolerance. In 1572, the Sejm issued a declaration assuring "that we who are divided by faith will keep peace among ourselves, and not shed blood on account of differences in

11. On the Sarmatian myth of common descent, see Walicki (1999, 263–64). As an ideology and cultural movement, see "Le sarmatisme et le baroque européen" in Tazbir (1986, 7–27).

12. The term *Polonization* is used here to denote the process by which Roman Catholicism came to represent the ideology of the nation of nobles, not to refer to the ethnicization of Roman Catholicism. According to Janusz Tazbir, Catholicism was Polonized in the seventeenth century through its sarmatization, that is, through the "adaptation of religious beliefs and ritual forms to the political ideas of the gentry" (1990, 118). On this question, see Tazbir's "La polonisation du catholicisme" (1986) or its abridged English version, "The Polonization of Christianity" (1990), which also discusses at length the place of Protestants in the political and religious life of the First Republic.

13. Approximately half the population of the entire state was Roman Catholic. Religious divisions often went hand in hand with ethnic and class ones. In the Eastern Kingdom, for example, Ruthenians were often Orthodox peasants, while Poles were Catholic nobles—a common situation that would eventually lead to nation formation and modern conflicts.

faith or church" (in Porter 2001, 291). Religious divisions would not shatter the collective "we" alluded to in the declaration. Just as being ethnically Lithuanian would not prevent a noble from being Polish, a noble's religious affiliation would not threaten his membership in the Polish nation. With the Counter-Reformation, however, Roman Catholicism was naturalized and "indigenized" as the religion of Poland. It was contrasted with Protestantism, a "new" and "foreign" religion: "Your religion is a newcomer which recently came to us from foreign countries, while the Catholic faith was and is mistress in her own house," declared a chancellor at the Sejm in 1648 (in Tazbir 1990, 120). Protestants responded by "indigenizing" Protestantism: just like Catholicism, Protestantism had come to Poland via the Czech lands.

Already in the mid-fifteenth century, Poland had started to be known in Europe as *Antemurale christianitatis*—the bulwark of Christendom—a reputation that was confirmed and reaffirmed after King Jan III Sobieski liberated Vienna from the Turks in 1683, a victory important enough to be commemorated in a mural in the Vatican.[14] And a few decades earlier, in 1653, in what belongs to legend as much as to history, Pauline monks in Częstochowa resisted and defeated Swedish invaders, a miracle attributed to the presence of the icon of the Black Madonna in the monastery (fig. 8). As a sign of his gratitude, King Jan Kazimierz dedicated Poland to the Virgin Mary and consecrated the icon as "Queen of Poland." It is probably from the king's vows of faithfulness to the Virgin that Poland's traditional motto, *Polonia semper fidelis*, originates.[15] Her cult began to spread during the Catholic

14. See the interesting essay by Janusz Tazbir, "Le rempart—Place de la Pologne en Europe" (in 1986, 83–102). Until its fall in 1453, the title had been held by Constantinople. From the fifteenth to the seventeenth century, it was transferred to several countries that were directly (like the Balkans and the Iberian Peninsula) and indirectly (like Poland) threatened by Muslim expansion. Machiavelli, in his *Discourses*, wrote about Poland as a bulwark defending Europe against invasions from Asia. Erasmus of Rotterdam picked up that thought, and Pope Urban VIII, in 1627, conferred the title Bulwark of Christianity on Poland. Half a century later, in 1678, Pope Innocent XI stated publicly that Poland was "*praevalidum ac illustre christianitatis Republicae propugnaculum*" (mighty and noble Republic, bulwark of Christendom) (Brzozowski 1990, 143). The notion, in Poland, initially concerned the defense of Europe against the Muslim threat, but was soon broadened to include the defense of Western Christianity from Eastern Orthodoxy, coupled with Romantic messianism's idea of the propagation of freedom and peace among the nations of Europe. In the twentieth century, Poland's mission was to protect itself and Europe from Soviet atheism. Nowadays, certain Roman Catholic groups reaffirm the mission of Poland as the fortress of Catholicism and redefine the rampart: Poland is no longer defending Europe from the infidel, but defending *itself* from Europe. The wall is now erected on Poland's western, not eastern, edge.

15. Cardinal Wyszyński reiterated these vows of faithfulness to Roman Catholicism and to the Virgin in 1956 by rededicating the nation to the Queen of Poland on the three hundredth

Figure 8 Icon of the Black Madonna, Our Lady of Częstochowa.

Counter-Reformation, under the shadow of conflicts with Ottomans and the threat from the infidel (Tazbir 1990, 119). A major symbol and a central trope of the Catholic narrative of the nation and of modern Polish nationalism thus were born.

There is therefore no doubt that religion occupied an important place in the Polish-Lithuanian Republic and its politics, and punctuated the everyday life of its inhabitants. The conversion of Mieszko I to Christianity in 966 had had important historical consequences: it marked the inclusion of Polish lands into the Latin world and "Western culture," and propelled the Polish crown into a network of alliances, influences, and conflicts tightly related to that event (a historical "fact" constantly evoked by Poles whenever their nation gets lumped together with "eastern Europe"). The Catholic Church

anniversary of Jan Kazimierz's vows (*śluby jasnogórskie* [Jasna Góra's vows]), and welcomed John Paul II with those words on the occasion of his first visit to Poland as pontiff in June 1979. The pope also used this phrase to qualify Poland's "profoundly Christian legacy."

was also an important player in the life of the kingdom: from the sixteenth century onward, for example, the archbishop of Gniezno, Primate of Poland, even assumed the role of the Interrex, holding power between the death of a king and the election of his successor.

What must be emphasized here, however, is that the religious (that is, Roman Catholic) element, although definitely present by the mid-seventeenth century, did not play a defining role in the noble nation's identity. We do not find the clear association between Polishness and Roman Catholicism in the protonational ideology of the nation of nobles as would later be claimed by the church and nationalists alike, in part because Polishness was not defined in ethnic terms. Ethnicity and religious affiliation were not yet firmly tied into the definition of the nation. Catholicism would become central to Polish national identity and ideology, as well as instituted by a national political program, only toward the end of the nineteenth and during the twentieth century.

The existence of this civic protonation is significant given the persistent tendency in the literature on nationalism to map a caricatured dichotomy between civic and ethnic nationalisms onto the geographical divide between (modern) western Europe and (backward) eastern Europe (Zubrzycki 2002). The Polish case shows that ethnic nationalism is not intrinsic to eastern Europe; rather, it was, as we shall soon see, a set of specific political conditions that reoriented Polish nationalism away from a civic understanding of the nation toward an ethnic one.

Statelessness and the Ethnicization of the Nation

The Partitions of Poland were a transforming trauma in Polish historical and social imagination, and continue to shape understandings of the nation's past, present, and future. The Partitions period (1795–1918) is important for several reasons: it interrupted efforts at state formation and reoriented an emerging national identity along new lines; it redefined the relationship between nation and state (and between the notions of nationality and citizenship); and it provided the narrative structure of modern Polish nationalism. It is during that period that modern Polish nationalism was forged and became mass-based: the state's dissolution was the catalyst for the form this nationalism would eventually take. In what Rogers Brubaker has called the "social deepening" and the "ethnic narrowing" of the nation (1996, 84–86), Polishness was in the late nineteenth century reimagined along ethnolinguistic lines. Moreover, Roman Catholicism, already a salient feature of Polish society, became a definitive marker of the nation at the critical period of the democratization of the national sentiment (Blanke 1981; Brock 1994; Walicki 1990, 1999; Porter 2000).[16]

If the Polish-Lithuanian Republic provided the "original matrix" of Polish protonationalism (Brock 1994, 310), its dissolution, following the Third and last Partition of Poland in 1795, was bound to alter the course of what followed. As Peter Brock points out, "The fact of political annihilation became the cornerstone of the Polish national idea" (ibid., 309). With the last Partition's coup de grâce, the political definition of nationhood and the conception of Polishness focused on the multiethnic republic became increasingly difficult to sustain. Some patriots even equated the death of the republic with the end of the Polish nation. To contravene this apocalyptic vision, a distinction was made between a mere state and a "genuine" nation: the state is the nation's outer envelope, the soul's body, a mere artifact, whereas the nation is a community held together voluntarily by a shared history and the common will to regain independent statehood. The nation would from then on reside not in institutions but in ideas: it was conceived as a moral entity, an ideal that resides in the hearts and souls of Poles. Poland was not yet lost as long as Poles lived, to paraphrase the opening line of the national anthem. This reflected a very different posture than the exclamation "We shall *again* be Poles" (that is, once the republic would be restored), uttered in despair immediately after the shock of the last Partition.[17]

Romantic Messianism and Roman Catholicism

Romantic poets played a critical role in the creation and diffusion of this novel notion of the Polish nation. They were proclaimed the nation's "apostles," the "missionaries of the Polish soul," moral authorities describing in their work the suffering of the enslaved nation and supporting personal sacrifice in the name of the fatherland, supreme ideal, and sacred value. For Romantics, the nation was a community of history and tradition guided by

16. I distinguish *society* from *nation* here. *Nation* is an ideological category, whereas *society* refers to the population of the lands of partitioned Poland.

17. The national anthem originates from the mazurka of General Dąbrowski's legions, raised in 1798 for the Army of Italy: "Poland has not yet died / So long as we live / That which alien force has seized / We at sword point shall retrieve / March, march, Dąbrowski! / From Italy to Poland / Under thy command / We shall rejoin the nation." The anthem's first line, "Poland has not yet *died*," was replaced, after Marshal Józef Piłsudski's coup in 1926, with "Poland has not yet *perished*." The original, composed in 1797, seemed to imply that Poland had disappeared from the European map owing to natural causes rather than illegitimate assault—a representation of history that later seemed unacceptable (Davies 1982, 2:16).

a unique mission: to free nations from oppression, thereby placing them on the road to universal salvation. Poland was represented as the Christ of nations: crucified for the sins of the world, it would be brought back to life to save humanity from dangerous political idols and satanic rulers. This historical interpretation of the Partitions was coupled with the prophetic revelation of Poland's victory qua resurrection in poems, plays, and other writings, such as Adam Mickiewicz's *The Books of the Polish Nation and the Polish Pilgrim*, a national-biblical parable (first published anonymously in 1832):

> And finally Poland said: "Whosoever will come to me shall be free and equal, for I am FREEDOM." But the kings when they heard of this were terrified in their hearts and said: "We drove out freedom from the earth, and behold it returneth in the person of a just nation that doth not bow down to our idols! Come, let us slay this nation." And they plotted treachery among themselves. . . . And they martyred the Polish Nation and laid it in the grave, and the kings cried out: "We have slain and we have buried Freedom." But they cried out foolishly. . . . For the Polish Nation did not die: its body lieth in the grave, but its soul hath descended from the earth, that is from public life, to the abyss, that is to the private life of people who suffer slavery in their country, that it may see their sufferings. But on the third day the soul shall return to the body, and the Nation shall rise and free all the peoples of Europe from Slavery. . . . And as after the resurrection of Christ blood sacrifices ceased in all the world, so after the resurrection of the Polish Nation wars shall cease in all Christendom. (1944, 379–80)

As this archetypal messianic text illustrates, religious vocabularies and metaphors were used as a powerful medium for the expression of nationalist opinions, feelings, and actions. The Partitions were widely described in religious metaphors and allegories: it was the period of "Babylonian captivity," the "Descent into the Tomb," and "the Time on the Cross" (Davies 1982, 2:18). The depiction of the Partitions as a *via Dolorosa*, with Poland cast in the role of Christ, made Roman Catholic practices the "natural" vehicle for the popularization of this narrative and this definition of the nation. Sunday Mass in churches of all the lands of partitioned Poland ended with the singing of "Boże coś Polskę" (God Who Saved Poland), a hymn composed in 1816: "O God, who through the ages / Has girded Poland with power and fame / Whose shield hath kept Her in Thy care / From evils that would cause Her harm / Before Thy altars, we bring our entreaty / Restore,

O Lord, our free country."[18] Easter week became the occasion to commemorate Poland's "crucifixion" and pray for its resurrection.[19] The Virgin Mary was represented as the crucified nation's protectress and comforter; her cult was unparalleled in the territories of the former republic. The icon of Our Lady of Częstochowa, by far the most popular Virgin of the lands of partitioned Poland, resonated with special intensity (fig. 9). Her scarred face and the miracles associated with her both represented Poland's mutilation and gave hope for its independence. She had saved Poland from the Swedish invasion during the Deluge; she could certainly defend the nation from the Muscovite and German tyrants. The Black Madonna of Częstochowa was the object of intense popular devotion: in addition to numerous pilgrimages in all seasons of the year, numerous prayers, songs, and patriotic hymns were addressed to her.[20]

With Poland transformed into the Christ of nations, the cross was metamorphosed into a core Polish symbol. In the nineteenth century, it was common to iconographically represent Poland in the figure of Christ on the cross (fig. 10). The cross, the crown of thorns, and a laurel branch became typical symbols to represent the plight of the nation and its noble fight for freedom.

Even before the January Uprising (1863–64), during which Poles rebelled against Russia, but mostly after its crushing in 1864, Poland underwent what Maria Janion and Maria Żmigrodzka have called a "national ritual of martyrdom and death" (1978, 549), with political manifestations taking place at various memorial sites and in cemeteries during funerals. Noblewomen

18. The last line of the hymn was adapted to the political situation: in the reconstituted state during the interwar period, people sang "*Bless*, O Lord, our free country" instead of the version used during the Partitions: "Restore . . . our free country." Under Communism, the Partitions version returned. Masses typically ended with that hymn, which was sung as the recessional.

19. As a tradition from the baroque period, Easter Sepulchers during Holy Week were elaborately decorated, complete with special effects (adornments, trompe-l'oeil, lights, etc.), often reflecting patriotic themes. On Good Friday, as Jesus-Poland lay in the tomb with guards keeping watch nearby, people prayed for his Resurrection and attended the mandatory confession. On Saturday night, during an evening service, Christ would symbolically resurrect, and his tomb would be found empty the following morning. The tradition was revived during the Second World War and remains to this day. Every church has its own sepulcher with its own scenographic style, and participates in an unofficial competition. People go from church to church to compare and evaluate the representations of the entombment. The Easter Sepulchers of Father Jankowski (Solidarity's chaplain in the 1980s) in Saint Brygida's parish in Gdańsk are infamous for their controversial nationalist depictions, which are often anti-Semitic in content.

20. For a comprehensive anthology of patriotic prayers from the sixteenth century to the present, see Gach (1995).

Figure 9 Postcard, circa 1905. "Greetings from Poland," with a naïve reproduction of Our Lady of Częstochowa, flags commemorating the November (1830) and January (1863) Uprisings, and the coats of arms of Poland, Lithuania, and Rus (the territory of the First Republic). Reproduced from Kłoczowski (1991), with permission of Editions Spotkania.

mourned the nation by wearing gowns only in black, adorned by patriotic jewelry: crosses engraved with "Poland," bracelets and necklaces reminiscent of rosaries, pins with the supplication "God save Poland," and brooches in the form of a crown of thorns (ibid. 1978, 548–50; Kłoczowski 1991, 36–37 for photographs).

Yet the relationship of this specific form of nationalism to Catholicism and the Roman Catholic Church is more complex than the borrowing of Catholic symbols, rituals, and liturgical forms suggests, and is certainly less idyllic than what the Catholic narrative of the nation maintains. That narrative has been very successful in retrospectively building the identity of Poles as intrinsically related to their Catholicism, and their national aspirations as supported and defended by the Catholic Church. This is historically inaccurate, however. Romantic messianism, "Poles' singular secular gospel" (Janion and Żmigrodzka 1978, 10), was quite heterodox and even, for some,

Figure 10 Popular postcard published circa 1891, commemorating major events in the life of the nation. In the background, Cracow's Wawel castle (the panorama was sometimes changed to a view of Warsaw). A cloth draped around the cross bears the inscription "The Time of Redemption has not yet Come." Poland is represented both as Jesus and as the Virgin Mary, whom he consoles. The dates on Jesus's staff are of the Partitions (1772, 1793, 1795); on the cross's beam, of the Centennial of the Constitution of May Third (1791–1891). Hence Jesus represents the union of the nation and the state, crucified (repeatedly partitioned) but certain to rise again. The pages ripped from Jesus's book, appearing against the background of Mary's cloak, mark key national uprisings. The Virgin appears to represent the nation mourning the loss of statehood; though presently in chains, she will one day be "free" (regain independence). Reproduced from Kłoczowski (1991), with permission of Editions Spotkania.

heretical, since it promised an earthly incarnation of the divine (Porter 2000, 28).[21] If members of the lower clergy were often actively involved in insurrectional movements, the episcopate, following the Vatican's line, preferred

21. For a recent discussion of the "Romantic religion" and heresy, see the texts of Przybylski (1995, 99–108) and Rutkowski (1995, 111–21) as well as the forum following them in Siwicka and Bieńczyk (1995, 123–41).

to limit its interventions. Polish Catholics were instructed by the church hierarchy to focus their thoughts on things eternal and to leave worldly affairs to the anointed authorities, the partitioning rulers. Rome had recognized the Partitions of Poland and consequently disapproved of insurrectional movements. The Holy See dreaded more generally the growing national agitation in eastern Europe at the beginning of the nineteenth century, and advocated the maintenance of the Congress of Vienna's map (1812). Polish bishops saw in revolutionary politics a greater threat than the Orthodox tsar, and denounced the national struggle even before Pope Gregory XVI did (ibid., 31).[22]

Yet the dedication of the lower clergy to the national cause offset the position of the hierarchy and the Vatican (Casanova 1994, 93). Indeed, political and institutional circumstances were instrumental in making the Catholic Church a major "national" institution at the center of a civil society in which education, publishing, and freedom of organization were seriously limited, and Polish was banned from public usage. In this context, religious worship and practices—in Polish—provided a significant space for Poles to affirm their sense of community. Although it had neither created nor openly endorsed this fusion of religious symbols and practices with nationalism, the Roman Catholic Church therefore became the "carrier" of Romantic civil religion (Morawska 1984).

The symbiosis between Catholicism and Polishness, and between church and civil society, was achieved through a long process in which national identity was Catholicized and Catholicism was nationalized. Nineteenth-century messianism was key in defining the form of this not-so-Catholic "Catholicization" of national identity. Messianism, moreover, gave not only a narrative structure to the situation of Poles under the Partitions, but a framework for the entire Polish history. Poles are the chosen nation, "the spiritual leaders of mankind and the sacred instrument of universal salvation" (Walicki 1990, 30–31), innocent sufferers at the hands of evil oppressors. The messianic vision of Poland as martyr and savior became a

22. The Vatican's support of the Partitions has a long history. In 1792, Pope Pius VI blessed the efforts of the Confederation of Targowica, which brought about the Second Partition, for "bringing calm and happiness to the Republic." After the Third and last Partition, in 1795, he ordered the ecclesiastical hierarchy to fully cooperate with the partitioners. Pope Gregory XVI, in his 1832 encyclical *Cum Primum*, condemned Poles for their attempt to overturn "the authorities established by God." At the end of the nineteenth century, Pope Leo XIII praised the loyalty of the Polish bishops to the partitioning powers. On the Vatican's position toward "the Polish Question," see Pomian (1982, 120–21); Cywiński (1993, 1:57–58); Davies (1982, 2:212–16); and especially Żywczyński ([1935] 1995).

core narrative, or what Victor Turner called a "root paradigm," referring "not only to the current state of social relationships existing or developing between actors, but also to the cultural goals, means, ideas, outlooks, currents of thought, patterns of belief which enter into those relationships, interpret them, and incline them to alliance or divisiveness" (1974, 64). Romantic messianism gave meaning to events and social relationships by offering a framework through which to interpret them. It also provided a script for collective representations and action, and a semiotic center for clustering religious and national symbols, as we will see in subsequent chapters.

For most of the nineteenth century, the government authorities banned the dense and cryptic Romantic philosophical treatises and literary works. This action did not lead to their loss, but rather to their assuming more easily transmissible forms. In their more or less covert diffusion to the masses, Romantic literature and wisdom were condensed and simplified: the Polish public was introduced to the Romantic ideas in popularized imitations of poetry, legends of heroes and martyrs, quotations, slogans, images, and rituals that captured the imagination (Janion and Żmigrodzka 1978; Jedlicki 1990). "The constant repetitions of the symbols on innumerable ritual occasions," Morawska notes, "made the national romantic faith personally and intensely familiar to generations of Poles" (1984, 31). The representation of Polishness in the Romantic creed and its wide popularization led to a "stereotyped canon of simplified romanticism" that became the basis of the "Polish sanctuary" (Jedlicki 1990). The canon was fashioned from a tight narrative fabric woven from historical legends and accounts of heroes and martyrs such as Tadeusz Kościuszko and the peasant insurrection he led (1794), the Republic of Nobles and the Constitution of May Third, as well as from political and religious symbols including "The Song of the Legions," which later became the Polish national anthem; the hymn "Boże coś Polskę"; the crowned white eagle; and above all the Black Madonna of Częstochowa, Queen of Poland (ibid., 55). This "simplified Romanticism" acquired its canonical value when Poland regained independence after the First World War; some of its elements became part of state rituals, while others made it into school textbooks and thereby socialized generations of children.[23]

23. Maria Janion and other prominent literary theorists and writers have argued that the hegemony of the Romantic vision and discourse in Polish national imagination has seriously dwindled if not disappeared after 1989 (Siwicka and Bieńczyk 1995). I return to this issue in the next chapter.

Toward the Modern Ethnic Polish Nation

Toward the end of the nineteenth century, Polish nationalism shifted from a political to a linguistic-cultural emphasis.[24] Until then, the nation still had been "open," regardless of ethnicity or religious identity. Some Jews, for example, were referred to as "Poles of the Faith of Moses," which suggests that the nation had undergone a social deepening to include non-nobles, but had not yet undergone a process of ethnic narrowing.[25] Thus, Polish nationalism between 1830 and 1863 was more inclusive than it had ever been and perhaps would ever be again (Porter 2000, 37). Membership in the nation was determined by one's active participation in the struggle for independence. As Jews participated in the January Uprising against Russia, they became, with Christians, brothers-in-arms in the fight for a free and independent Poland:

> Another visible grace of Providence for Poland, which is only now being redeemed from the sins of captivity, is the union, sealed by the joint martyrdom of Poland's Christian and Israelite sons: these arks of a funeral covenant were borne on the shoulders of both Levites and Christians to the fraternal cemetery and thus to a joint resurrection. Since this day there have no longer been two population groups on the common soil of oppression, but one nation. (From The Manifesto of the Revolutionary Underground, in ibid., 40)

Jewish and Christian Poles were regarded as "the two Israels," two chosen nations fused into one Romantic messianic narrative. Polish bards were compared to biblical prophets, and insurgents to the Maccabees; Poland itself was referred to as Zion, and Warsaw as the new Jerusalem (Walicki 1999, 275; Opalski and Bartal 1992, 51–54). This union, however, was short lived: Jews quickly regained their status of "internal Other," and as we will see in subsequent chapters, the very notion of the chosen people that

24. This section is primarily based on the work of Brian Porter (2000). See especially chap. 2, "The Social Nation."

25. Two qualifications must be made: first, the "Poles of the faith of Moses" referred to here were assimilated Jews. This inclusiveness was thus limited to a small group of Jews. Second, this inclusiveness in the ideological sphere does not mean, of course, that anti-Semitism did not exist. It surely did. But as Porter points out, "hatred was exiled, at least temporarily, from the rhetoric of nationalism and was relegated to other, less potent spaces" (ibid., 37). For a succinct history of Polish-Jewish relations, see Blobaum (2005).

had united Christian and Jewish Poles in a single narrative about Poland's struggle for independence is now what divides them. No longer brothers-in-arms, Poles and Jews fight over chosenness and martyrdom in their battle over Auschwitz and its memory.

The defeat of the Uprising in 1864 marked a turning point in the definition of the national cause and, ultimately, the nation. In addition to the countless killed and executed, thousands were afterwards deported to Siberia, and thousands of others left Poland for western Europe in more or less self-imposed exiles. In the critical decades following the tragedy, the Romantic creed was denounced as naïve: it was time, a new generation of intellectuals claimed, to forget futile dreams and focus the nation's energy on constructive work. The novelist Bolesław Prus (1847–1912) summarized Positivists' bitterness toward and revulsion from the Romantic insurrectionist tradition:

> If all the blood spilled by Poles in the cause of freedom were poured together, it would fill the biggest lake in the country; and if all the bones of those who have died in battles, on the gallows, in the camps, or in exile were collected into one heap, they would make another Wawel. But what benefit has there been? None, and there never can be any, since Polish patriotism is made up of violent explosions of emotion which are not illumined by understanding and are not transformed into acts of creative will. (In Davies 1982, 2:49)

The messianic myth was therefore rejected: sacrifice did not lead to resurrection, but to immoveable death. Positivists consequently advocated working within the existing political structures to make the best of what the situation had to offer. Positivism provided a new language for talking about and representing the nation, as well as imagining its future: "organic work" was the peaceful economic and cultural activity that would promote the health and increase the strength of the social organism (Millard 1995, 110).[26] Its proponents took the nation out of the political framework, which was centered on the active struggle for independence, and reconfigured it within a *social* mode of thought. It is this precise move, according to Porter, which is at the root of the reorientation of the nation along ethnic lines. "Poland" was from then on based on the actual, existing society subjected to the laws of nature, and not a grand abstract cause defined by poets and national prophets. The

26. Polish positivism is primarily Spencerian in its orientation, not Comtean. See ibid., 46–48.

language of science replaced that of poetry in the discursive elaboration of the nation. The nation was now a sociological formation—an actual, visible community of Poles linked by sharing "objective," concrete characteristics such as language, faith, and history, and by their daily enactment of cultural and folk practices.

These changes in the intellectual construction of the nation went hand in hand with the emerging democratization of national consciousness among the masses in the last third of the century. It became obvious, especially after the 1846 *jacquerie* in Galicia (during which some eleven hundred noblemen were killed) and the defeat of the January Uprising (1863–64), that regaining national independence would be impossible without the support and participation of peasants, the bulk of Polish society. Since building a Polish national consciousness among this class was crucial, the nationalist program started to include the education of the peasantry and a project for the abolition of serfdom. This aimed at suppressing class lines in order to create a common national identity, enabling all strata to work side by side for Poland instead of as class antagonists (Stauter-Halsted 2001). In the words of Roman Dmowski, the father of modern Polish nationalism, "Men are first and foremost members of a nation; only secondly are they divided into social classes within the nation.... The first commandment of the citizen's catechism is solidarity, a sense of union with the entire nation" (in Millard 1995, 111). This is consistent with Benedict Anderson's observation that "regardless of the actual inequality and exploitation that may prevail... the nation is always conceived as a deep, horizontal comradeship" ([1983] 1991, 7).

Far from being a natural process, this national "awakening" required the hard labor of nation-builders (Chlebowczyk 1980; Hroch 1996; Stauter-Halsted 2001). Journalists, teachers, writers, and ethnographers were the main artisans of this process of creating a national ideology and diffusing it. Noblewomen also played an important role in the transmission of patriotic values from one generation to the next, and in their dissemination to other classes: they socialized their children and grandchildren in a familiar narrative of ancestor-heroes, and often held clandestine classes, teaching peasant children how to read and introducing them to the glory and tragic faith of Polish history (Staszyński 1968). The Endecja was especially active in the building of national consciousness among peasants.[27] They edited

27. The Endecja is the name given to the political formation associated with the right-wing National Democracy. The term comes from the party's acronym, ND. Members were referred to as Endecy or, in its Anglicized version, Endeks.

Polak-Katolik, a newspaper specifically addressed to peasants that provided them with information on current events, offered political guidance, and disseminated a popularized Polish history. At the turn of the century, this project of nationalizing the masses was institutionalized in the Society for Popular Education, an organization comprising more than six thousand teachers and educational workers that had a lasting influence on rural and small-town activists (Walicki 2000, 22).

The nationalization of the masses was concurrent with, and to a certain extent facilitated by, the increased repression of Poles in the Russian and Prussian lands.[28] In Russian Poland, the use of Polish was severely curtailed, whereas attacks on the Roman Catholic Church (*Kulturkampf*) and policies of denationalization (*Polenpolitik*) characterized Prussian Poland. The pernicious anti-Polish policies of the Prussian government created a strong sense of collective grievances that would be exploited by Polish nation-builders. By targeting language and religion simultaneously, the Prussian government's discriminatory policies had the adverse effect of arousing the very national consciousness it sought to repress, and connecting it to confession (Brock 1994; Blanke 1981; Kulczycki 1981; Osa 1992; Bjork 2004).[29]

Modern Polish national identity by the end of the century was being constituted and reconstituted through the opposition to "Others": Protestant Germans in the west and Orthodox Russians in the east.[30] The initial impetus for this oppositional identity was thus rooted in cultural and political geography, though it was reinforced through colonial domination by

28. In Austrian Poland, the situation was quite different, and perhaps best characterized by accommodation rather than repression and resistance. Consult the excellent study of Keely Stauter-Halsted (2001) on Galicia.

29. One such policy was the elimination of Polish-language classes and of religious instruction in Polish. Through their passive resistance, pupils from the lower and middle schools protested against this policy by, for example, refusing to answer the questions posed to them in German during religion classes. As a result, children were often beaten, and their parents were fined. These educational policies were especially significant in linking linguistic and religious issues in Prussian Poland, as were the school strikes of 1901–6 in mobilizing the population for the Polish cause. On the Polish school strikes, see the interesting study of John Kulczycki (1981).

30. The vivid depiction of these "Others" in popular novels such as Henryk Sienkiewicz's (1846–1916) *Trilogy* deeply influenced the social imagination of the reading public. The historical saga and love story was published over five years in the 1880s initially as newspaper *feuilletons*. Set in the time of the Deluge, when Cossacks, Russians, and Swedes assailed Poland, it captivated the reading public. The text is a brilliant case of "invented tradition" (Hobsbawm and Ranger 1983) in that it was written in an invented "Old Polish" that contemporary Poles could understand as it transported them to a different era. Another popular novel by Sienkiewicz told the story of Polish resistance against the Teutonic Knights, a tale that resonated especially with readers in Prussian Poland.

these "external Others" and exploited as such by Polish nation-builders.[31] Foreign domination and religious repression contributed to the linking of national consciousness and religious identity in the dominant national narrative (Casanova 1994; Hobsbawm [1992] 1995, 67–68), as well as to the strengthening of the ties between civil society and the church (Michel 1988; Morawska 1984; Casanova 1994).

By the time Poland regained its independence at the end of the First World War, the nation was conceptualized as a community of language, culture, and faith. In reaction to the experience of statelessness, which prevented the maintenance, development, and solidification of a civic understanding of nationhood in the century following the last Partition of Poland, the nation had come to be seen by its ideologues as a body embracing all strata of the Polish-speaking population (although certain strata, such as peasants, had yet to identify with this body). "Fighting for the nation" no longer meant fighting for abstract universalist ideals, but combating "visible" enemies. The relationship between Polishness and Roman Catholicism would be codified in the writings of modern Polish nationalism's main ideologue, National Democracy (Endecja) founder Roman Dmowski (1864–1939), and ossified during Communism.

"Polak-Katolik"

The long-awaited return of Poland to the European map did not arise out of the struggle for independence but more contingently, as a result of the First World War and the collapse of the three empires that had kept the territories of the Polish-Lithuanian Commonwealth apart. The Second Republic (1918–39) was conceived as a state *of* and *for* the ethno-linguistic Polish nation, to borrow Brubaker's formulation (1996), yet its territory included large parts of Lithuania and Ukraine. In 1931, ethnic Poles constituted approximately 64 percent of the republic's population, Ukrainians 16 percent, Jews 10 percent, Belarusians 6 percent, Germans 2 percent, and Lithuanians 1 percent—demographic "facts" that, given the mission of the state, would not be without repercussions.[32]

31. Identity is obviously constructed not only in opposition to "external Others." "Internal Others" play a crucial role in that process as well. In Poland they are also defined along ethnoreligious lines, and Jews have been the "internal Other" par excellence as a result.

32. The demographic data on interwar Poland is problematic for several reasons and should therefore be treated as approximate: first, the data assume clear and unambiguous divisions between ethnic groups; second, the criteria used to classify individuals into neat categories were not always consistent in that language, religious affiliation, or self-identifications were sometimes

It is in this context that the intricate process of nationalizing the masses was accomplished. As for its minorities, the Polish state was to assimilate the population in the east through their cultural Polonization, and nationalize the territory and economic life in the west by replacing Germans and Jews with Poles in key political and economic positions (Brubaker 1996, 79–106). The nationalization of ethnic Poles was also intensively under way. Being a Pole was a multifaceted affair, a matter of the mind, body, and soul. Above all, Poles were increasingly encouraged, in political discourses and church sermons, to imagine their national identity in association with their Roman Catholicism. Roman Dmowski was especially significant in disseminating this version of Polishness; he is perhaps best known and remembered for his intellectual codification and politicization of Polishness and Catholicism into a single category, that of "Polak-katolik."[33] Indeed, on the sixtieth anniversary of his death on January 8, 1999, the Polish Sejm adopted a resolution to pay tribute to "this outstanding Pole." Dmowski is remembered and celebrated for "his struggle and work . . . for the reconstruction of the independent Polish state," for creating "a school of political realism and responsibility," and for contributing to "the establishment of our frontiers, and especially the western border." But his greatest contribution, according to the representatives of the Sejm, lies in "[his] role in underlining the tight association of Catholicism with Polishness for the survival of the Nation and the rebuilding of the State."[34]

---

used. Lastly, there were some cases of data tampering for political reasons. The figures used here are based on Jerzy Tomaszewski's correction of the 1931 census data (1993), which slightly downplayed the numbers of national minorities. According to the linguistic criteria of that census, Poles formed 68.9 percent of the total population, Ukrainians 13.9 percent, Yiddish-speaking Jews 8.7 percent, Belarusians 3.1 percent, and Germans 2.3 percent (Davies 1982, 2:404). Waldemar Michowicz's corrected figures (1988) approach those of Tomaszewski: Ukrainians, according to him, constituted 16.2 percent of the total population, Jews 10 percent, Belarusians 5.6 percent, and Germans 2.6 percent.

33. My comments on Dmowski in this subsection are primarily based on the excellent analysis and synthesis of Andrzej Walicki, "The Troubling Legacy of Roman Dmowski" (2000). Consult Grott (1993) for a collection of original texts focused on the place of Roman Catholicism and of the Roman Catholic Church in the thought of the Right from the end of the nineteenth century up to World War II, and Grott (1999) for an analysis of Catholic nationalism in the Second Republic. On the relationship of the Endecja to the "Jewish problem" from 1918 to 1929, see Bergmann (1998); on its relationship to national minorities more generally, see Radomski (2000).

34. See "Uchwała Sejmu Rzeczypospolitej Polskiej z dnia 8 stycznia 1999 o uczczeniu pamięci Romana Dmowskiego," *Monitor Polski*, January 15, 1999, no. 3, position 12 (http://www.abc.com.pl/serwis/mp/1999/0012.htm). The resolution was adopted by a right-wing government, but won the support of a significant portion of moderates and members of the Left (Walicki 2000, esp. 43–46). Two things are worth noting: first, the association between Polishness and Roman Catholicism is taken for granted. It is represented here as a fact that Dmowski merely—yet

The following passage from Dmowski's brochure *Church, Nation, and State*, originally published in 1927, is characteristic of his thought:

> Catholicism is not an appendage to Polishness, coloring it in some way; it is, rather, inherent to its being, in large measure it constitutes its very essence. To attempt to dissociate Catholicism from Polishness, and to separate the nation from its religion and the Church, is to destroy the very essence of the nation. ([1927] 1964, 15)

As a result, he insisted that

> The Polish state is a Catholic state.
>
> It is not Catholic only because the great majority of its population is Catholic, and it is not Catholic in some or other percentile. From our perspective, it is Catholic in the full sense of that term because our state is a national state, and our nation is a Catholic nation. (Ibid., 27)

In Dmowski's ideological and political universe, the nation's identity and moral power was rooted in its Catholic religious and cultural heritage, and the Roman Catholic Church was at once at the source and the guardian of nationhood. The Endecja created and actively promoted in their publications and through their activities the view that Poles are intrinsically Catholic, and that Catholicism is the only true and natural expression of Polishness. As the 1999 tribute to Dmowski indicates, this "Polak-katolik" vision of modern Polish national identity endured; indeed, it even grew more strident and insistent under Communist rule.

In interwar Poland, the fusion of Roman Catholicism and national identity led to a hierarchization of national groups, with (Catholic) Poles at the top and Jews at the bottom. For the Endecja, the state was to be the exclusive property of Catholic Poles, and Poland was to be the Catholic state of the Polish nation. This juxtaposition of religious and national terms into a single category served to conceptually order and give meaning to anti-Semitism (Walicki 2000). Jews were not only ethnically or racially alien, to use the terms of the period; they were also cultural (that is, religious) "Others."

Jews were second-class citizens, acting as the prime "internal Other," portrayed as dangerous chameleons and parasites on the Polish Catholic body. Now that the nation was a social organism based on ethnic and

significantly—underlined. Second, a causality is posited between the association of religion and nationality and the survival of the nation and the state's restoration.

religious criteria, Jews suffered from ethnic, religious, and economic anti-Semitism. In the context of the Endecja's ideology of the struggle of the fittest, Jews had to be eliminated from the economic sphere for the Polish nation to grow in strength. Several boycotts of Jewish-owned business were organized,[35] and a law prohibiting the conducting of business on Sunday was ratified, leaving religious Jews who observed the Sabbath at a disadvantage compared with their Christian counterparts.[36] The state also instituted, in 1923, a quota on the number of Jewish students that could be admitted to universities, infringing on the National Minorities Treaty and some articles of the 1921 Constitution. The *numerus clausus* stipulated that the number of students from any given national group ("or of the Mosaic faith") could not exceed the percentage that this given group represented in the republic. Consequently, the enrollment of Jews was severely limited. Right-wing student groups also implemented "ghetto-benches" in some Polish universities: Jewish students were segregated in the classroom by being forced to sit in assigned benches in the back. The enforcement of this practice was often violent, and tolerated by the academic administration as a way to "maintain peace" in teaching facilities.

The church played its own role in the promotion of anti-Semitism.[37] Newspapers like *Rycerz Niepokalanej* and *Mały Dziennik*, edited by future Auschwitz martyr Father Maksymilian Kolbe, warned Poles against the alleged Jewish practice of ritual murder, and reminded Catholics that Jews were Christ-killers. The Roman Catholic Church saw Jews as especially dangerous because of their social radicalism, for they represented both

35. The Endecja organized an important economic boycott in 1912 that lasted well into the interwar years. Dmowski saw in this a nonviolent, civilized strategy of interethnic struggle (ibid., 28–29). Boycotts were far from always being peaceful, however, and were often physically implemented. Polish youth from the Fascist group Falanga would, for example, verbally abuse and physically assault Jewish business owners, as well as post themselves in front of Jewish businesses to intimidate and physically prevent ethnic Poles from entering them. Customers were sometimes beaten for buying "at the Jew." It is interesting to note that even before the Endecja-inspired boycotts, opposition to Jewish businesses served nationalist interests: the founding of Christian-owned stores in the countryside in the last quarter of the nineteenth century had been a way to forge cross-class alliances between (Polish) peasants and the gentry, and to foster Polish national identity in the peasantry (Stauter-Halsted 2001, 133–41). On the 1912–14 boycott as an effort to dislodge Jews from the urban economy, see Blobaum (2001).

36. It is difficult to assess the extent to which the Sunday Rest law was enacted in order to curtail Jewish-owned businesses. For example, the Left saw it as progressive legislation, since it benefited the working class (Mendelsohn 1986, 133). In any case, there is no doubt that it affected Jewish small-business owners. On anti-Jewish legislation in interwar Poland, see Rudnicki (2005).

37. On the process through which Catholic rhetoric and modern anti-Semitism became compatible at the turn of the twentieth century in Poland, see Porter (2005).

liberalism and Communism, equally godless and antinational.[38] Secularism and liberalism were more specifically associated with assimilated Jews, whereas Communism was seen as a dangerous weapon wielded by Russian Jewish intellectuals, the *Żydokomuna*. Many of these themes are still present in current discourse more than half a century later.

But a key caveat here: my attempt to unravel the ideological bundle of the Polak-katolik and its politicization has created an overly unified narrative of the period. The Polak-katolik was but *one* representation of Polish national identity, and one that was far from unchallenged. The interwar period was characterized by tensions between visions of the nation and of the state, but also, and related to the former, by quarrels between the officially nonconfessional Polish state and the Roman Catholic Church. These tensions, argues Paul Zawadzki (1996, 173), are precisely what structured the political game in interwar Poland. Though the church was careful not to openly support the Endecja's political program, its loyalty leaned toward the nationalist Right, and as a result alienated other political parties and antagonized religious and national minorities. The period is marked by the unmistakable emergence of anticlericalism, strong among large sectors of the intelligentsia, within the Socialist Left, and to a certain extent within the peasants' movement (Michnik 1993; Casanova 1994, 93–94). The Endecja's Polak-katolik, then, was a strategic discursive move to construct and mobilize a political constituency, an attempt vigorously contested by the secular Left. At the same time, it cannot be said that the ideological representation of Poles as Catholics was merely a rhetorical ploy.

Although the association between ethnicity and faith powerfully propagated by Dmowski was more a slogan and a political program than the faithful representation of all ethnic Poles, it was not invented in a vacuum. As we saw above, approximately two-thirds of the Second Republic's population was ethnically Polish, and the same proportion was also Roman Catholic (Tomaszewski 1993). The portrayal of Poles as Catholics therefore had some empirical ethnographic basis. The key question, whether or not people actually linked these identities, is more difficult to answer.[39]

38. For an analysis of modern anti-Semitism and its "double character" from a Marxian perspective, see Postone (1986, 302–14).

39. Some peasants, according to Durkheimian ethnographer Stefan Czarnowski, conflated "church" and "Poland" and "religion" and "nation" in what he called "confessional nationalism," concluding that the emergent national bond in that social group was religious, primarily focused on the exercise of the cult ([1934] 1988). But the process of nationalization of peasants is very uneven and multifaceted, with great variation from one region to the next. Joseph Obrebski (1976) conducted fieldwork in the eastern borderlands (now part of Ukraine and Belarus) during the same period (1930s), and found that peasants maintained local, hybrid, or in-between identities

Dmowski did not invent the *ideological* association between Polishness and Roman Catholicism either: before he even started using it, the Polak-katolik formulation was commonly found in a periodical of the same name (founded in 1906), and the formulation was frequently used in other Catholic publications, such as the Poznań-based weekly *Przewodnik Katolicki*.[40] What is significant for our purpose, however, is that Dmowski forged a unified identity out of these two categories, and then politicized that identity and articulated a program around it. By doing so, he gave new meaning to difference. The Second World War and important structural changes in its aftermath would generalize and ossify the Polak-katolik stereotype.

The Polish Nation versus the Communist State

Poles' experience of the Communist period was plotted onto a familiar and potent narrative of national and religious oppression by a powerful neighbor. They commonly understood Poland's postwar condition as the continuation of its historical subjection to foreign domination, and Yalta was often referred to in popular discourse as yet another Partition. Michael D. Kennedy notes that already by 1948, the "principal recurrent theme of protest for subsequent decades had been established: the identification of communism with foreign occupation and repression" (1991, 21). In that common script, the Roman Catholic Church took on its "traditional" role of guardian and defender of the nation against a "foreign" state. Imposed from above and from abroad, the political regime and its elite were regarded as illegitimate by the bulk of Polish society.[41] The state was perceived as fulfilling neither of its nationalist *sine qua non*: it was neither of nor for the Poles. In contrast, the church enjoyed an immense popularity and authority, built

---

that were contextual, not the clear-cut association between national identity and religion reported by Czarnowski—a finding consistent with those of Janina Kłoskowska at the end of the twentieth century (2001). On the complex process of the nationalization of peasants in Galicia at the end of the nineteenth and beginning of the twentieth century, see Stauter-Halsted (2001). On the various aspects of Polish religious culture during the same period, see Olszewski (1996).

40. It should be noted that the meaning of the Polak-katolik formulation itself was not unequivocal in the early twentieth century: tensions actually existed among its users as to what it meant. For some, it was a way to stress the essential religiosity of the Poles; for others it was a way to critique the church's accommodating stance toward the partitioning powers and to push for the institution to be more patriotic; for yet others is was a coded speech for anti-Semitism. I'm grateful to Brian Porter for pointing this out to me in a personal communication, January 2005.

41. Legitimacy is not an immutable state of affairs: it rises and declines, is defined and redefined according to different principles (M. Weber 1978). One should therefore be cautious in asserting a complete lack of legitimacy of the Polish Communist state and its ruling elite, as we shall see in the following pages.

most recently through its oppression by and resistance to the Nazis. There thus existed in Communist Poland two rival institutions claiming to represent the nation. In this competition for legitimacy, a complex relationship between the state, the church, and civil society took shape. It is this relationship and its implication for Polish national identity that I analyze next.[42]

Competing for Legitimacy

In its search for at least a semblance of legitimacy, the Communist Party falsified elections to "prove" to its citizens and to the world that it legitimately represented the people it claimed to represent, and invested massive effort in portraying the Polish People's Republic as the "inevitable culmination of a historical process leading toward the realization of 'freedom and progress' " (Kubik 1994, 115). The elites represented the Socialist state as the only legitimate state Poles could have, since it was the heir and defender of the "truly historic Polish land" covering the western territories acquired in the peace settlement.[43] In that nationalist narrative, these territories were referred to as the "Recovered Lands" (*ziemie odzyskane*), lands Poland had long ago unjustly lost but had now regained, secured by the Communist regime.[44] The party prided itself on constituting the People's Republic as a state based in the Piast dynasty's ancestral land, thereby recreating the only "true Poland," that is, an *ethnic* Poland. The Recovered Lands became the cornerstone of the state's nationalistic propaganda in the years immediately following the

42. For a collection of documents related to church-state relations, consult *Tajne dokumenty: Państwo-Kościół 1980–1989* (1993) and *Tajne dokumenty: Państwo-Kościół 1960–1980* (1996). For analyses of the Roman Catholic Church in Communist Poland and the relationship between the ecclesial institution, the state, and civil society, see Michel (1990); Osa (1996); Dudek and Gryz (2003); Anusz (2004); and Pawlicka (2004). On civil society and oppositional politics more specifically, see Lipski (1986); Ost (1990); Kennedy (1991); and Bernhard (1993).

43. As a result of the Second World War and the peace agreements, Poland ceded to the USSR 170,000 square kilometers of its eastern territory, divided up between the Ukrainian and Belarusian Socialist Republics, and received in exchange 100,000 square kilometers in the west, amputating from Germany Silesia, eastern Pomerania, and a part of Brandenburg.

44. The so-called Recovered Lands constitute a third of the current Polish state. Most of that territory had once been under the rule of the Piasts, the first Polish dynasty; but some portions of it had been part of the state only very briefly, and scarcely any of it had been part of the state since the twelfth century (Kulczycki 2001a, 216). The concept of a Piast Poland referred to the alleged ethnic purity of the primitive state of the early Piast dynasty (tenth and eleventh centuries), "the Poland of the early Polish tribes as yet undiluted by German colonists, Jewish refugees, or Ruthenian conquests" (Davies 1992, 325). Consult the articles by John Kulczycki on this topic: on the Communist appropriation of the Piast concept as a strategy of internal legitimation and external justification for the annexation of the western and northern territories from Germany (2001a); and on the state's nationalist discourse of "autochthonization" of the Recovered Lands and the treatment of the populations of these territories (2001b).

end of the war. Despite its official civic nationalism, in an attempt to build its legitimacy the state made recourse to ethnic arguments and practices. Through its policies of ethnic cleansing,[45] it actually built an ethnic Poland and naturalized that idea to such a degree that the postwar Polish state's borders and population became the sole imaginable political entity. Moreover, the notion of a "return to normalcy" discursively eclipsed the historical reality of the ethnically and religiously diverse First and Second Republics, the memory of which now became a mercurial anomaly.

Poland's post–World War II population became strikingly different from what it had ever been: Jews had been exterminated and survivors had massively emigrated after liberation; eastern minorities were incorporated into the Soviet Union; and German populations were expelled. As a result, ethnic Poles now constituted about 95 percent of the Polish People's Republic. The population's religious makeup was also dramatically altered: while in 1931 Roman Catholics comprised 65 percent of Poland's population, by 1946 the proportion of Catholics had increased to 96.6 percent of the population within the new borders (Casanova 1994, 260).[46] The new Poland was free of its national minority "problem." Ironically, Dmowski's dream of a Piast Poland made up of Catholic ethnic Poles was largely created by historical accident and by the Communist regime he so vehemently opposed before the war. This was to have a significant impact not only on Poles' identity, but on their collective memory of the war as well: with very few Jews left in Poland to remember the Holocaust, Poles remained with their own, uncontested memory and narrative of the events (Young 1993, 116).

Polak-Katolik bis

It is in this specific context that the "Catholicization" of the national tie and the corollary equation between ethnicity and faith—exemplified by the Polak-katolik stereotype—was accentuated and generalized after the Second

45. I mean by "ethnic cleansing" the expulsion of the German population of the Recovered Lands, the deportation or forced relocation of Ukrainians (1945–47), the party-inspired pogrom in Kielce (1946), and the wave of anti-Semitism in 1968 that led to the massive emigration of Jews who had remained after the war.

46. In addition to the "physical-geographical" construction of the postwar nation-state's homogeneity, "Polishness" is, of course, constructed and maintained through a myriad of cultural forms (myths, commemorations, traditions, literature, and music) and institutional settings (museums, schools, the military, etc.) (Hobsbawm [1992] 1995; Anderson [1983] 1991; Gillis 1994; E. Weber 1976) as well as through the annihilation of other potential identities (E. Weber 1976; Duara 1995).

World War. In addition to the ethnic and confessional reconfiguration of the nation-state, key in that process were the state's failure to stimulate loyalty to its principles and its inability to create a mobilizing Socialist Polish identity (Babiński 1993; Nowicka 1991; Kubik 1994; Morawska 1995; Osa 1996), as well as the Roman Catholic Church's effective opposition to the Communist party-state (Casanova 1994; Zawadzki 1996). The church provided an infrastructure for the resistance to the regime and drew support from the West, mainly through Catholic organizations. Religion and the church eventually became the site of moral and political resistance to the totalitarian regime, and served as an alternative legitimate system assuming symbolic and organizational functions (Walaszek 1986).

Given the state's lack of popular support and doubtful mandate, political legitimacy was symbolically transferred to the church. During Stalinism, Stefan Cardinal Wyszyński (1901–81) was significantly called Interrex, in reference to the tradition, during the period of the elective monarchy, in which the Primate assumed the interregnum. He developed a conception of the nation that successfully integrated various strands of Polish nationalism: a theology of the nation characterized by both a religious and a historical perspective, influenced by the biblical notion of the chosen people and by nineteenth-century Polish messianism while incorporating Dmowski's ethnic definition of the national community (Bartnik 1982; Lewandowski 1989). For Cardinal Wyszyński, the nation was an "organic community which has a determined model of life, conscience and spirit, and whose concrete tradition, common fate and the traces of the historical existence give a unifying force" (Lewandowski 1989, 153). The nation, in this view, is biological and historical, a living organism constituted of families and common land, with a common fate and tradition, a common language, culture, and spirit (Bartnik 1982, 9–10). "The nation," stated Wyszyński, "is a lasting phenomenon just like the family from which the nation originates" (in Houle, Łukasiewicz, and Siciński 1990, 153).

The tension between "us," the Polish Catholic nation, and "them," the alien atheistic party-state, was symbolically represented in myths and allegories, and sometimes enacted in rituals. The most powerful example is that of the Great Novena, which lasted a little over nine years, from August 1956 to May 1966. During his internment, Cardinal Wyszyński dedicated his life and office to the Virgin Mary, and promised to renew the nation's vows of faithfulness to her on the occasion of the millennial anniversary, in 1966, of Poland's conversion to Christianity (Wyszyński 1995). After his release, he organized a series of celebrations centered on Our Lady of Częstochowa to promote religious renewal and mass mobilization.[47] Each year was assigned its own dedication (fidelity to God, the cross, the gospel, and the church; the Roman Catholic family; love and social justice; the Holy Mother, and so on), and was initiated on August 26, 1956, by an opening Mass in Częstochowa attended by *one million* pilgrims. A replica of the holy icon of Black Madonna was made and taken on its own pilgrimage across the country, visiting several dioceses and being hosted in manifold private households for twenty-four hours per stop. The popularity of the Novena overshadowed the state's own secular and political celebrations of the Polish state's one-thousandth birthday that same year.[48] It organized counterdemonstrations in the hope of diverting attention from the popular celebrations of the church, provoking a veritable war of slogans: banners on churches proclaimed *Sacrum Poloniae Millennium*, whereas civic buildings were adorned with posters proudly announcing "A Thousand Years of the Polish State"; *Deo et Patriae* was matched by Socialism and Fatherland; "The Nation with the Church," by "The Party with the People"; and *Polonia Semper Fidelis*, by "Socialism as the Guarantee of Peace and Frontiers" (Davies 1982, 1:21; Dudek and Gryz 2003, 234–50).

Finally, the authorities, facing the increasing popularity of the church's celebrations and the competition posed by them, confiscated the wandering replica of Our Lady of Częstochowa. This action only heightened the determination of the faithful: devotional processions continued to march, this time bearing an empty frame, symbolizing through the absence of the Black Madonna the oppression of the religious and national identity of Poles (Kubik 1994, 116). From the perspective of the faithful, not surprisingly, the confiscation and confinement of the Virgin confirmed both her essential kinship with Poles—also arrested and confined—and her power: otherwise, why would Communist authorities regard her as a special threat? Like a martyr who becomes powerful in and through her fiery apocalypse, Our Lady of Częstochowa accrued more potency than ever in her disappearance. The empty frame summoned and catalyzed Polish sentiment as much as the Madonna's presence had; with the Catholic icon removed, the index

47. Maryjane Osa argues that the Great Novena, as pastoral mobilization, linked intellectuals and the working masses under the leadership of the Roman Catholic Church, the outcome of which was a reorganization of religious culture around unifying national themes (1992, 118–59). For a collection of sermons by Cardinal Wyszyński during that busy year of 1966, see Wyszyński (1996a, 1996b).

48. The Polish state was founded in 966 by Mieszko I through his conversion to Christianity. The year 966 thus marks the simultaneous birth of Polish statehood and the baptism of Poland. Both the state and the church competed over the meaning of 966 in 1966. For an analysis of that competition in greater detail, see Kubik (1994, 110–17).

remained, the empty frame a sign and cipher of the empty state, a shell without content that might be, and should be, cast down and filled with something new.

The millennium of Polish Christianity was celebrated as planned on May 3, 1966, which was also the anniversary of the 1791 Constitution and the Feast of Our Lady. The fusion of three significant events into a single date and commemoration created a powerful symbolic picture: that of a profoundly Roman Catholic nation whose sovereignty and independence resided in its belief in God and the Virgin Mary. As French sociologist Patrick Michel notes, the very reference to Mary, Queen of Poland, was a way to symbolically draw the borders of the imaginary territory of an independent Poland. According to Michel, when John Paul II declared in Częstochowa that "here we have always been free," he meant that the religious space is also the site of national independence, which the party-state could in no fashion pretend or even aspire to appropriate (1986, 84).

The symbolism of Karol Wojtyła's first visit to Poland as pope in June 1979 provided another key enactment of the tension between church and state. The pontiff's visit was dedicated to the commemoration of martyr Saint Stanisław, the "Polish Thomas Becket," patron saint of Poland and bishop of Cracow, who had been killed and dismembered by King Bolesław the Brave in 1079 for competing with the secular power. The papal visit on this nine hundredth anniversary of the churchman's slaying and the celebrations organized around it pointed to the clear and dramatic victory of civil society and the church over the party-state. In the legend, Saint Stanisław's mutilated and scattered body was miraculously reconstituted, symbolizing the reunification of the kingdom, whose land had been divided during preceding reigns. In the context of the Partitions, the legend implied the impending reunification of the Polish lands under one (Polish) state; under Communism, it highlighted both the rivalry between the church and the state, the oppression of the former by the latter, and finally the unifying power of the church.

Beyond its symbolism, the papal visit highlighted the authority and popularity enjoyed by the church and the Polish pope in contrast with that of the state and its party. As much as 20 percent to 25 percent of Poland's population gathered along the pope's motorcade route, and about three million Poles were present in the Błonia krakowskie, a park in the center of Cracow, to participate in the papal Mass.[49] That event was likened to a

49. The pope also celebrated Mass at Birkenau, Auschwitz's sister camp, during that first official visit. I return to that event in chapter 3.

"psychological earthquake" and a "massive political catharsis" (Szajkowski 1983, 72), an authentic moment of Durkheimian collective effervescence. The impact of the visit was indeed so great, in the words of a Polish activist, that Poland before and after June 1979 were two completely different countries (Lipski 1986, 331). According to Jan Kubik, John Paul II's first visit was the single most important factor leading to the final collapse of the official discourse in the 1970s (1994, 150).

The pope's religious message on human rights and human dignity provided a powerful emancipatory vocabulary; unlike terms derived from Marxism, it could not be co-opted and corrupted by the party-state. The appropriation, by a regime not recognized as legitimate, of words such as *exploitation, justice,* and *equality*, deprived the opposition of a vocabulary for social protest and reform, what sociologist Jadwiga Staniszkis has aptly called the "semantic problem of workers' protest" (in Kennedy 1991, 45). The pope's discursive framework therefore became the "verbal arsenal with which intellectual and worker could in common criticize the regime without shame" (ibid., 45).

As Kennedy points out (1991, 43–45), the pope's religious message resonated with the population for three main reasons: first, the pervasiveness of lies in a Soviet-type society made claims to an absolute truth more plausible to the system's subjects; second, these claims to "truth" were enhanced because they were associated with forms of community considered everlasting (the nation and the church) as opposed to structures considered ephemeral (the state and its party); and lastly, these communal identities took on life because the population could transpose them onto a charismatic individual, who in return sent back the image of a nation unified behind its moral guardian, the church.

Beyond discourse and the "political economy of truth," the election of the "Polish pope" and the first papal visit are regarded as the midwife of the Solidarity movement because they provided "a new cultural foundation for national self-identification, and the organizational experience for mobilizing it" (Kennedy 1991, 43). With the papal visit organized outside state structures and without its assistance, and with the peaceful and orderly participation of millions of Poles in events surrounding the pilgrimage, a formerly atomized population[50] recognized that its members constituted a community, a civil society whose social bonds were solid enough to organize

50. I am referring here to the studies conducted by Stefan Nowak (1981), in which he measured the strength of social bonds. Nowak found that Poles identified first and foremost with the concrete family and the abstract nation, with a large void in between these two forms of communities: the structure of Polish society, he concluded, appeared to be "a 'federation' of primary

significant opposition to the party-state. In this sense, the 1979 papal visit was a "dress rehearsal" for Solidarity, the self-organized and self-governed trade union to be born a year later, in August 1980 (ibid., 45). The aesthetic impact of the pope's visit was also notable. Michael Bernhard points to the contrast in the symbols employed in workers' protests before and after that visit: conspicuously absent during the 1976 protests, religious symbols became a "ubiquitous sign of workers' identity as Poles both at the strike at the Gdańsk shipyard and throughout the Solidarity period" (1993, 139).

By the beginning of the 1980s, three collective actors were therefore at the center of Polish politics: the party-state, the church, and Solidarity, what David Ost (1990) has called "tripartism." Solidarity recognized the moral authority of Roman Catholicism and the church, and constructed its discourses on those foundations.[51] The church and its social teachings provided Polish society with the unified worldview that would be significant in the years of opposition under the leadership of Lech Wałęsa and the trade union.

This is not to say, of course, that Solidarity's religious foundations explain the movement's emergence, and that there were no tensions between the opposition and the church (or within the opposition and within the church itself, for that matter). Although Cardinals Wyszyński and Wojtyła were supportive of KOR (Komitet Obrony Robotników—Workers' Defense Committee) in the late 1970s (Kennedy and Simon 1983, 135; Bernhard 1993, 119), some in the church (especially in the period before John Paul II's first visit to Poland) interpreted the struggle between KOR and the party-state as one between "pinks and reds," and many political dissidents saw the church as a bastion of right-wing politics.[52] It is far from my intention

groups unified in a national community" (p. 51). Associations of all kinds—civil society—were found to be absent from Poles' conception of their social universe.

51. Interesting regional patterns exist with regards to Solidarity's understanding and portrayal of the Roman Catholic Church. French sociologist Alain Touraine and his collaborators (1982, 44–49) found that the church was characterized as either identical with the nation, an ally in the defense of civil society, or an institutional body with its own conservative interests in different research sites.

52. On KOR and the genesis of Solidarity, see Bernhard (1993); Ost (1990); and Kennedy (1991). On the complex relationship between the church and the secular Left, see Michnik's influential essay, initially published in 1977, with its excellent introduction by David Ost in its English translation (1993). Elsewhere, Ost characterizes the complicated relationship between Solidarity and the church's hierarchy as one of unreciprocated affection: not only was the church generally suspicious of Solidarity's radicalism, but "Solidarity always felt far closer to the Church than the Church felt to Solidarity" (1990, 157). Both Ost and Michael Bernhard (1993, 137–38), however, point to the church hierarchy's and activist clergy's different attitudes toward

Figure 11 Gate 2 at the Lenin shipyard in Gdańsk during the historic August 1980 strike that marked the birth of Solidarity. Flowers, flags, and a picture of Pope John Paul II adorn the fence as workers kneel during the celebration of Mass. Photo: Nieznalski/KARTA Center.

to portray a perfect harmony between the institutional church and the organized opposition. My focus here is less on the organizational and institutional aspects of the union of church and opposition, and more on the discourse and symbolism of the anti-state protest, which after the pope's historic first visit was undeniably and powerfully garbed in religious robes, puzzling many Western observers (figs. 11, 12).[53]

In the 1980s, Catholicism and the Roman Catholic Church were portrayed by the opposition as the basis for a moral community fighting an "evil" totalitarian regime imposed from outside and from above. This depiction succeeded in providing a very powerful narrative of the nation, one

and differing levels of support and involvement in Solidarity, and the tension these differences sometimes created within the ecclesial institution. Finally, Solidarity itself was riddled with internal conflicts, especially after the declaration of martial law (1981–83). Tensions between its left and right wings, as well as between workers and intellectuals (Ost 1990, 162–63), grew in significance after the fall of Communism, as we will see in chapter 2.

53. Solidarity is often characterized as the first genuine Leninist workers' revolution; the sight of revolutionary workers kneeling in outdoor Masses celebrated during strikes is therefore an image that is difficult to reconcile with that of revolutionary leftist politics.

Figure 12 Mass celebrated by Father Henryk Jankowski of St. Brygida parish at the Lenin shipyard in Gdańsk during the August 1980 strike. Photo: KARTA Center.

able to mobilize support against the party-state. The narrative evoked a glorious past and carried emotionally loaded analogies between present misery and the painful experience of the Partitions. It was built around Poland's historical suffering, the alleged role of the church in the nation's survival, the notion of Poland as chosen people (*lud polski ludem Bożym*—"the Polish people is God's people"), and that of Poland as *Antemurale Christianitatis*, defending Europe against the infidel (Islam in the seventeenth century, atheist Soviets in the twentieth). The iconography of national identity and resistance to the oppressive foreign regime was largely borrowed from Romantic messianism. It emphasized symbols traditionally associated with the nation, such as the miraculous Black Madonna of Częstochowa, as well as motifs taken from the Passion, such as the cross and the crown of thorns (figs. 13–15).

The cross especially became a significant element of collective consciousness, which together with other symbols, signs, and gestures created a language to express rebellion against the authorities (Rogozińska 2002, 28).[54] Crosses were carried during political manifestations, and it is with

54. The marrying of paschal symbols to national ones was most evident in the arrangement of Easter Sepulchers, which in the 1980s were one of the most important places of patriotic manifestations. For a discussion of this phenomenon and descriptions of Easter Sepulchers in

Figure 13 Postcard circulated in 1980. The tall cross is the sign of individual and collective liberation. A worker broke his chains and spread his arms into the V shape of victory, which became the emblematic gesture of Solidarity, following its use by Wałęsa during the August strikes and throughout the 1980s. The cross is the "cross of gratitude, symbol of the workers' strikes in July 1980 in Lublin." It is dedicated by the Lublin Car Repair Workshop. At the top of the postcard, a quote from John Paul II: "You are not a slave, you must not be a slave. You are a son." Photo: KARTA Center.

three giant crosses that the victims of the 1970 strikes were memorialized a decade later, a demand explicitly formulated by the Gdańsk shipyard strikers on August 14, 1980 (figs. 16, 17).[55]

Solidarity's historic twenty-one-point agreement, the Gdańsk Accord, was signed two weeks later by Lech Wałęsa, who wore a rosary around his neck and used a giant souvenir pen of the pope's 1979 visit. Masses and political meetings typically ended with the nineteenth-century patriotic hymn "Boże coś Polskę," with the congregants linking arms as they exited, in preparation for possibly facing antidemonstration police units (fig. 18).

Warsaw in 1982 and 1983, see Renata Rogozińska's fascinating study on paschal themes in Polish art in the period 1970–99 (2002, 29–31).

55. Other political events were observed with the installation of crosses in the 1980s. For example, the 1956 Poznań uprising, during which several dozen people were killed, was commemorated with a monument consisting of two giant crosses. The first was engraved with the date 1956 and the other with 1968, 1970, 1976, and 1980, years of the other major uprisings in Communist Poland. The monument was unveiled in 1981, and the accompanying celebrations lasted three days.

Figure 14 The use of religious symbols became commonplace during strikes in the 1980s. Here Lech Wałęsa and Tadeusz Mazowiecki leave the Gdańsk shipyard on May 6, 1988. Photo: PAP/CAF Stefan Kraszewski/AW.

The solidarity, enthusiasm, and spontaneity deployed in these mass demonstrations contrasted sharply with the carefully coordinated actions of the state, one increasingly weakened by the opposition and the church.

Church, State, and National Identity

Because of the widely shared perception of the state as illegitimate, the party-state could not afford, politically speaking, to crush the Roman Catholic Church; the latter's authority was too imposing and the potential risk too costly. In fact, the state in a sense *needed* the church's support to gain legitimacy in the eyes of the people. Although the ecclesial institution did not legitimize the regime per se—as it did elsewhere in the Communist Bloc—it did help to "stabilize" society in exchange for some rights, which in the long run further fomented resistance to the state. Through a tacit agreement, the party-state refrained from attacking the church, and the church refrained from openly undermining the party-state, resulting in a period of relatively peaceful coexistence that gave the church a field through which it could accomplish its mission.

Figure 15 Lech Wałęsa represented as Poland's martyr-savior, with a barbed-wire crown on his head. On the original poster, the lower portion is red and the upper is white, alluding to the Polish flag. Photo: KARTA Center.

Within this system, the church secured for itself a realm of autonomy—that of spirituality and national identity—and became the *mediator* between the opposition and the state, from the beginnings of Solidarity (Kennedy and Simon 1983, 141–42; Jerschina 1990, 89–90; Ost 1990, 156–60) to the Round Table negotiations and historic Agreement in 1989 (Kennedy 2002, 82). From victim to mediator to uncorrupted partner, over the years the church gradually became the institution with which Poles most readily identified. Aided by the election of Karol Wojtyła to the papacy, it became the unrivaled central locus of authority in Polish society. The appearance of a structured opposition, first with KOR in the 1970s and then with Solidarity in the 1980s, did not weaken the church's power for two reasons: they were on the same side in the fight against Communism and the party-state, and both operated in distinct spheres. The church therefore occupied a distinctively privileged position: it served as the legitimizer of Solidarity while serving as the mediator between the opposition and the state. Ironically, because of its lack of initial legitimacy, the very Communist regime that aspired to create a purely secular system ended up creating one in which the

Figure 16 Wooden cross consecrated by "Solidarity's chaplain," Father Henryk Jankowski, on the first Sunday of the August 1980 strike. It was erected at the spot where workers were killed almost a decade earlier, in December 1970, and was replaced by the official monument in December 1980. Photo: KARTA Center.

Roman Catholic Church became the legitimate—and to a large extent the legitimizing—institution.

Poles could not construct their identities through a state and institutions they felt not only did not represent them, but actually oppressed them and embodied the opposite of what they claimed to stand for: freedom, justice, and social equality. In this context, the church and the opposition were able to provide a mobilizing discourse of the nation, using primarily the familiar, Romantic messianic narrative with its religious symbols. This narrative and its aesthetics resonated with Poles' framing of the Communist experience as the imposition of a foreign system by the usual suspect. There is little doubt that the official civic-secular discourse of the state actually helped consolidate an ethno-Catholic vision of nationhood. And that vision was now more plausible than ever, given the ethnic and confessional makeup of the People's Republic of Poland.

Yet if the state's official civic discourse and secular symbols failed to mobilize people, this does not mean that it failed to shape its citizens overall: the state still controlled the efficient means of socializing the population through powerful institutions—the school, the workplace, the military,

Figure 17 Nearly complete Gdańsk monument commemorating the death of workers killed during the December 1970 manifestations. The commemoration of the victims, the nation's martyrs, was one of Solidarity's demands during the August 1980 strike. The three crosses were erected where the workers were shot; the monument was officially unveiled in December 1980. Photo: Nieznalski/KARTA Center.

the media, and myriad other cultural and social institutions. The Recovered Lands and the new geographical outline of Poland were soon taken for granted, and recognition was given to the state for making the defense of the western border a *raison d'état*. The state might have spoken in a language that did not resonate, but the creation of an ethnically homogeneous nation did have a serious impact on Poles' conception of their country and of themselves as a nation, as well as on their collective memory.

Figure 18 Religious services were often the occasion for political expression in the 1980s. Here congregants exit St. John's Cathedral in Warsaw's Old Town after Mass on May 1, 1983. The Mass marked the beginning of an independent May Day manifestation. Photo: Wilkońska/KARTA Center.

There thus existed, under Communism, a double tension between ethnic and civic nationalism: that of the state's official civic discourse in contrast with its significant ethnic practices and/or effects, and that of the church's ethno-religious discourse in contrast with its civic practices, since it served as the umbrella institution of the opposition. I discuss the implications this semantic confusion now has in post-Communist Poland in subsequent chapters.

Conclusion

As this exploration of key events, processes, core narratives, and mythic tropes of Polish history shows, Polish nationalism is multilayered, constituted through time in relation to its political and cultural environments. Polish protonationalism was founded on civic principles—albeit severely stratified ones—and grounded in republican institutions. The Partitions interrupted and inhibited the further development of this vision of nationhood. More than a century of statelessness progressively reoriented conceptions of the nation around language, ethnicity, and eventually religion as cultural responses to that loss of statehood. Religious symbols and messianic metaphors were significant in giving a language and a narrative structure for the national struggles. They not only provided a grammar for sentiments already extant, a hook on which to hang the nation's coat, but proved *constituent* of the form and density of that coat's weave. Religious symbols and narratives, we have now seen, became the stitching of the nation itself.

The association between Polish national identity and Roman Catholicism is therefore historically determined and contingent. It was first articulated in the last third of the nineteenth century, when the stateless nation was rearticulated on ethnic bases and when policies targeting both language and faith linked ethnicity and religion in the emerging national consciousness of the masses. It was ideologically codified into the Polak-katolik ideal in the first half of the twentieth century and further politicized during the Socialist period. The conjoining of Polishness and Roman Catholicism into a single—albeit hyphenated—category occurred at the key moment of the nationalization of the masses. It is an inescapable feature of modern Polish nationalism that is constantly grappled with by social and political groups who aspire to define Polishness and Poland in other terms. This narrative of Polish history, with its potent symbols, myths, and customs, shaped protest in Communist Poland. The narrative also shapes interpretations of the present, and structures the political field: now that it has once again "recovered national independence," should Poland be a nation with the cross, or without it? This question, often repeated at key junctures, is more than mere metaphor. The cross is a debated symbol that carries dramatic social consequences, as the War of the Crosses revealed.

CHAPTER TWO

"We, the Polish Nation": Redefining the Nation in Post-Communist Poland

> After several tremors, two great political camps were constituted: the anti-Communist Right (AWS) and the post-Communist Left (SLD). It was the year 1997. The rivals wheeled out two cannons against each other: The Lord God and History. In economic programs they differed insignificantly; the battle for the souls of Poles was to be fought in the sphere of values and memory. It was a question of identity, and not opinions about taxes, education, the reform of the health system, and social security. . . . The first chased the "Bolsheviks," the second the "occupants in cassocks."
>
> —Artur Domosławski in *Gazeta Wyborcza,* February 5, 2001

Introduction

Before turning to the site of Auschwitz and Oświęcim, where the War of the Crosses was fought, we must consider the broader sociopolitical landscape in which the event took place. It is in the specific context of post-Communism that the War of the Crosses takes on its full meaning.

In light of the previous excursus into Polish history and, more important, the understanding and framing of that history by Poles, the fall of Communism in Poland has not only meant the transition from a totalitarian to a democratic system of government, and from a state-controlled to a free-market economy. Poles have also understood it in terms of the recovery of a sovereign state and of national independence. As such, the post-Communist period is seen as a critical historical juncture, that of the (re)constitution of a *national* state, a state *of* and *for* Poles. This nationalist project requires the specification of what Polishness "is" and should be. If under Communism the Roman Catholic Church held a quasi monopoly on the production and reproduction of national identity and could articulate an integrative, operative, and mobilizing discourse of the nation—because of the party-state's perceived illegitimacy—the fall of Communism and the building of a legitimate Polish state have reopened the discursive field on the "nation." What is the Polish nation? Is it defined by Catholicism, as its traditional motto *Polonia semper fidelis* calls for, and therefore should the state be confessional; or should Polishness be understood in secular terms, with a state transcending religious membership through official religious neutrality?

The post-Communist period has thus been shaped by a societywide debate in which some preach the maintenance of a Catholic Poland, united under the cross, while others demand the confessional neutrality of the state and advocate a more inclusive definition of national identity, based not on religious affiliation but on political-legal principles. Debates concerning the place of religion and religious symbols, and the role of the Catholic Church in the new polity have punctuated and structured public life in the first decade following the fall of Communism: What should the church's status be in the Third Republic, and should Christian values be legally enforced? Should religious instruction in public schools be mandatory? Should there be an *invocatio Dei* in the new constitution? Should there be crosses in the classroom, in state buildings, and, more controversially, at Auschwitz?

De-Churching Civil Society, Secularizing National Identity

The issues outlined above are being considered and debated within a new context: that of an order characterized by a plurality of institutions, political groups and associations, within the framework of a legitimate, democratic, and national state. With the advent of a legitimate state, the Catholic Church has lost the ability to credibly portray itself as the nation's keeper. As a result, almost three-quarters of Polish society in the 1990s thought that the political influence of the church was too great; and this regardless of which parties' bottoms warmed the seats of Parliament (Gowin 2000, 35). The approval of the church's activities, moreover, dropped from 90 percent in 1989 to an all-time low of 38 percent in 1993 (Centrum Badania Opinii Społecznej [CBOS] 1999, 2004a). This approval rating stabilized at the upper fifties toward the end of the decade, and has gained a few percentage points since the beginning of the new century (CBOS 2004a).[1]

1. These findings are consistent with those of the Statistical Institute of the Catholic Church (Instytut Statystyki Kościoła Katolickiego SAC). In surveys conducted at the end of 1997, as many as three-quarters of Poles disapproved of the church's giving its opinion on government affairs,

This seismic shift in attitudes cannot be explained by the secularization thesis, since the process is not accompanied by an increase of religious indifference: in 2000, 96 percent of Poles declared themselves to be "believers," and 58 percent said they participated in religious services *at least* once a week (CBOS 2001).[2] Nor can the decrease in church credibility be explained by a generalized crisis of authority in social institutions during the transition from Communism, since other institutions, like the police and the army, maintained theirs (Gowin 1995, 8). The drop in approval could, rather, be explained by the fact that many Poles have changed their expectations of the church since the fall of Communism. The opinion polls cited above suggest that the religious and the political spheres are now dissociated in the minds of the respondents, and that religion and the church no longer occupy the same place in the political field. In the new political constellation, Poles have found compelling themes other than religion for the construction of their social identities. Polish national identity can now express itself through channels other than those of the church, and there exists a plurality of institutions through which Poles make their voices heard. The new institutional pluralism has important implications, foremost among them being the end of the Roman Catholic Church's quasi monopoly on national identity.

As I have suggested elsewhere (Zubrzycki 1997a, 1997b), the advent of a legitimate, democratic state ruptured a pattern of relations between church and civil society, and introduced a new dynamic characterized by growing criticism of the church and by the church's consequent attempt to increase its institutional power by intervening in the political sphere in

---

and 60 percent considered it inappropriate for the church to voice its opinion about mass media content and style. Moreover, about 60 percent of those polled thought that in the first eight years following the fall of Communism, the church was too involved in public life (Zdaniewicz and Zembrzuski 2000, 435).

2. $N = 13{,}166$. According to the same dataset, an additional 15 percent attend Mass once or twice a month. Therefore, 73 percent of Poles go to church at the very least once or twice a month. The best and most extensive work on religious change since the fall of Communism and on church-state relations from a sociological perspective has been produced by Irena Borowik, a sociologist of religion. Her monographs on the institutionalization and privatization of religion in postwar Poland (1997) and on religious transformations in Central and Eastern Europe since the fall of Communism (2000) are especially valuable. See also her work, with Tadeusz Doktór, on religious and moral pluralism in Poland (2001). On the faith and religious practices of the intelligentsia, see Libiszowska-Żółtkowska (2000); on the religious faith of youth, see Szawiel (2003); on vocations, see Pawlina (2003). For statistical data and its analysis published by the Statistical Institute of the Catholic Church, see Zdaniewicz and Zembrzuski (2000); for a testing of the rational-choice paradigm in the sociology of religion using the cases of the post-Communist period in Poland and (East) Germany, see the article by Froese and Pfaff (2001).

order to compensate for the loss of its social influence. This model was the predominant one from roughly 1989 to 1993, after which the church became subtler in its interference. However, its political interventions in the first years following the fall of Communism were extensive. They consisted of publicly endorsing certain political candidates and parties, posting lists of the "right" candidates for whom "good Catholics" should vote, and voicing its opinion on and organizing a strong political lobby for issues close to its heart: the shape of the state, the return of mandatory religious instruction in public schools, the respect of Christian values in the media, the concordat with the Vatican, and the criminalization of abortion, to mention only the most important topics debated in the public sphere.[3]

If the church's involvement in political life was perceived as necessary under Communism, it is clearly seen as unacceptable in a fully sovereign and democratic Poland. Long before the fall of Communism, Jan T. Gross and Leszek Kołakowski captured the challenge the church would face in a democratic Poland: "When denied freedom to preach its doctrine, the Church becomes a champion of democratization by demanding that freedom be restored. But in a free Poland, where it would have the monopoly of religious worship, would the Church continue to be a pillar of democracy?" (1980, 321). Although the Polish Catholic Church fought for the establishment of democracy, it must now redefine its position within a democratic environment, a circumstance which implies the abandonment of the institution's centrality (Michel 1992b, 188). The church's claim to owning the "ultimate truth," a powerful antidote to the pervasive lies in real Socialism, is now incompatible with the pluralism characterizing the democratic marketplace of ideas. The post-1989 situation has posed severe challenges for the institution.

I argue that the declining social power of the church and the rise of integrist tendencies in its midst are therefore closely related, and linked to a twofold process: the decline of the social influence of the church can be explained on the one hand by the introduction of a legitimate state and a plurality of institutions, and on the other hand by the church's own reactions,

3. See CBOS (1999) for statistical data on social approval of the church as it corresponds to specific debates in the public sphere, and Gowin (2000) for an essayistic analysis of the evolution of the church in the 1990s. One public statement by Bishop Michalik during the 1991 electoral campaign epitomized and came to symbolize the church's problematic involvement in politics: "It would be bad if a Catholic nation found itself again in a situation where it has to be ruled by a non-Christian parliament. . . . I often say, and I will say again: a Catholic has the duty to vote for a Catholic . . . a Muslim for a Muslim, a Jew for a Jew, a Mason for a Mason, and a Communist for a Communist" (*Więź*, no. 1, 1992).

characterized by an interference in public and political life that Poles now clearly reject.

It is in this context that in the 1990s, Roman Catholic political groups who strongly advocated an ethno-religious definition of the nation were promoting the creation of a confessional state. Politician Wiesław Chrzanowski of the right-wing Catholic Zjednoczenie Chrześcijańsko-Narodowe (ZchN—Christian National Union) declared that "the nation is constituted of the people among whom certain values are formed, a certain culture which is the heritage of the past," adding that this was why he did "not believe in the denominational neutrality of the state" (*Tygodnik Powszechny*, no. 17, 1992). The pressure from the church and the Right for the institutionalization of the Polak-katolik vision, especially strong in the first few years following the fall of Communism, called for the urgent broadening of national identity, according to Adam Michnik:[4]

> The most important debate now concerns the question asked by [Ernest] Renan in the title of his famous work *Qu'est-ce qu'une nation?* If we define the nation simply as belonging to a group, one will always be able to find some criteria, such as race, blood or any other arbitrary criteria only chauvinists allow themselves to define. How to know if someone is Polish, Ukrainian, Jewish, or German? In this context, the problem of national [and] religious minorities constitutes a vital test for the nascent democracies in post-Communist Europe. (1991, 46)

There has thus been an attempt by liberal intellectuals to renegotiate the church-state and church-society relationships and to somehow reorient Polish national identity along civic terms. I am referring to the public intellectuals associated with publications such as *Polityka* and Adam Michnik's *Gazeta Wyborcza*, and to some extent the editors and contributors of the liberal Catholic weekly *Tygodnik Powszechny* and Znak, its publishing house. This attempt at fostering a civic nationalism is characterized by the presentation and promotion, in speeches, essays, and editorials, of the principles of the civic nation and the condemnation of a narrower, ethno-religious vision. However, not only does that vision of the nation run counter to the general understanding of it in Poland, but its discourse about "citizens," "social justice," and "civic rights and duties" is sometimes *heard* as an echo of

4. A historian by training, Michnik (b. 1946) is one of the most influential intellectuals and activists of postwar Poland. He cofounded KOR in 1976, was adviser to Solidarity in 1980–81, and since 1989 is the chief editor of Poland's most important daily, *Gazeta Wyborcza*.

Communist rhetoric and *langue de bois*, a semantic problem akin to that faced by workers under Communism, as we saw in the previous chapter. Public intellectuals have therefore tried to sell this vision to the population by reconstructing a distinctively *Polish* narrative that emphasizes the civic heritage of the Polish nation by, for example, referring to sixteenth-century religious tolerance; the First Republic's multiethnic and multiconfessional state; the Democracy of Nobles' elective monarchy; the Constitution of May Third; the Polish legions fighting "for your freedom and ours"; interwar liberal traditions; and to a certain extent KOR's and Solidarity's peaceful resistance and civic activism.[5]

A few things are worth noting here: first, the liberal intellectuals' attempt at "indigenizing" a seemingly foreign vision of the nation by appealing to various (glorious) historical precedents; and second, their deliberate effort to bypass the political system most clearly associated with the civic discourse in contemporary social consciousness, namely Communism. The civic vision must be made legitimate and desirable by showing it to be firmly rooted in Polish history. This strategy aims at replacing an abstract notion of civic nationhood that is often understood and rejected by national-Catholic milieus as an antinational (Communist, internationalist, cosmopolitan) and therefore anti-Polish and anti-Catholic (atheist, Jewish, Masonic) ideology, with its more concrete, historicized, and "genuinely Polish" version.

Additionally, the civic discourse often stresses that Poland could only "make it to Europe" as a modern, civic nation.[6] "Europe" signifies, in Poland

5. The relationship of liberal intellectuals to Solidarity is complex: on the one hand, many were members and central actors in the movement and its oppositional politics. As such, they feel entitled to the legacy of Solidarity. On the other hand, they do not identify with the turn to the right that Solidarity took after the fall of Communism, and have been pushed to the margins of the union's legacy by its Right-leaning members. This tension is perhaps best symbolized in the numerous public conflicts and eventual rift between Tadeusz Mazowiecki (see note 21) and Lech Wałęsa, and their running against each other in the first post-Communist presidential elections in 1990. *Gazeta Wyborcza* endorsed Mazowiecki with an outspoken editorial by Michnik, who explained why he could not vote for Wałęsa, seeing in him the dangers of populism. Wałęsa retorted that he was not interested in what the "professors" had to say about him, Solidarity, or Poland: he said *he* was Solidarity, after all, and belittled the role and contribution of the intelligentsia in the social movement. On the post-1989 divisions within Solidarity, see chapter 1 of David Ost's book *The Defeat of Solidarity: Anger and Politics in Postcommunist Europe* (2005); on the Wałęsa-Mazowiecki breakup and the events leading up to it, see chapter 2 ("Market Populism and the Turn to the Right") in the same book.

6. On the meaning of "Europe" in post-Communist Poland, see Kaldor (1996); Paszkiewicz (1996); and Zubrzycki (1998). On the meaning and usage of "Europe" in Polish right-wing circles more specifically, see Kowalski and Tulli (2003, 495–497). For Hungary and Romania respectively, see the analyses of Gal (1991) and Verdery (1996) (chap. 5, "Civil Society or Nation? 'Europe' in the

and elsewhere in the region, civilization and progress. As stated in the program of the Democratic Union, "Belonging to Europe is to belong to a world of democracy, peace and economic progress" (1993, 3).[7] Although there was and is a certain amount of skepticism over Europe and Poland's so-called return to it in certain milieus of the Catholic Right (Skotnicka-Illasiewicz and Wesołowski 1995; Zubrzycki 1998; CBOS 2004b), and consequently the emergence of a new Polish messianism which aims at bringing back to Europe the human values it has lost to "secularism, liberalism, and capitalism,"[8] there is widespread popular belief that Poland rightfully belongs in the European Union: almost two-thirds of Poles surveyed on the eve of Poland's joining the EU supported European integration (CBOS 2004b).

It is important to note, however, that discourses of the nation are not only addressed to national audiences: they also communicate and forward claims intended for international ones. In a historical context of international institutional reorganization marked by aspirations for NATO and EU memberships, and in a period in which ethnic nationalism has been widely and loudly denounced in response to bloody ethno-nationalist conflicts that have afflicted many countries of the region, the representation of one's nation and nationalism as the "good," "Western," and "civic" kind has been crucial, and notable in the constitutional symbolism of many post-Communist states.[9]

Symbolism of Romania's Postsocialist Politics," reprinted in Suny and Kennedy [1999, 301–40]). For Latvia, see Eglitis (2002, 119–26).

7. The Democratic Union (1990–94) became the Freedom Union (Unia Wolności) in 1994, and was reconfigured in May 2005 as the Democratic Party (Partia Demokratyczna). For a history of the party, its origins in the Solidarity movement, and its subsequent transformations, consult http://demokraci.pl/. For a useful guide through Polish political parties and coalitions (and their frequent reconfigurations and metamorphoses) in the 1990s, see Paszkiewicz (2000).

8. As articulated by the pope in *Veritatis Splendor* (1993, 326–27) and in *Tygodnik Powszechny* (on February 22, 1998). Cardinal Glemp also argued that Poland should enter the European community, but bring to it what defines Poles: their faith (in *Gazeta Polska*, March 15, 1998). On the Polish Catholic Church's position(s) on European integration and various laypeople's visions of Europe, see Grosfeld (1996); Leszczyńska (2002); Muszyński (2002, 2003); Fedyszak-Radziejowska (2003); and Stępniak (2004).

9. The International Institute for Democracy, for example, states that "the rights of national minorities have . . . been enshrined in the constitutions, *albeit in response to urgent requests from European organisations and notably from the Council of Europe*" (1996, 6; my emphasis)—a testament to the influence of supranational organizations in the design of the constitutions of Central and Eastern European states and the symbolism included in preambles. See The International Institute for Democracy (1996) for preambles and full constitutional texts; for a comparison with the constitutions of the states of the European Union, see Grewe and Oberdoff (1999).

The civic discourse—or "counterdiscourse," since it is trying to establish itself against the commonsensical ethnic understanding of the nation—is met with especially harsh resistance by the Roman Catholic Church.[10] The church supports the preservation of an organic nation in which Roman Catholicism would still be the principal feature of Polishness, and the family, tradition, and history would constitute the nation's hallmark. Józef Cardinal Glemp, the Primate of Poland, repeated many times that the "nation" (that is, a community of culture) prevails over "society" (that is, a political community of citizens). Pope John Paul II also saw the family and the nation as the most significant elements of human identity (Lecomte 1992, 115–24). These conceptions are in accord with the theology of the nation developed by the late Cardinal Wyszyński, as discussed earlier.

The civic vision of Polishness is also resisted by those who define themselves in ethno-Catholic terms, as will become evident in my analysis of constitutional debates below. In the political field, this position is most clearly associated with the coalition Akcja Wyborcza "Solidarność" (AWS—Electoral Action "Solidarity") and the members of Liga Polskich Rodzin (LPR—League of Polish Families). LPR explicitly defines itself in its program as a "political formation reverting to the thought of the interwar national-democratic camp and its most outstanding representative, the Polish statesman Roman Dmowski."[11]

A vocal segment in the public sphere also defends a vision of Poland intrinsically linked with its Catholicism. The daily and weekly publications *Nasz Dziennik*, *Gazeta Polska*, and *Nasza Polska*,[12] as well as the controversial Catholic radio station Radio Maryja, also advocate a vision

10. I do not mean here the community of Roman Catholics, but more narrowly the institutional church, the episcopate, and the clergy. There are of course different tendencies within the church itself, and within the active Catholic community at large. The most obvious orientations are those of a "closed" Catholicism and church, and of a more "open" church that is conscious of the need for a greater flexibility and adaptability and, most important, of the urgent need to return to the essence of its role, religion. One of the church's most daring characters, priest and philosopher Józef Tischner (1931–2000), warned against the integrist tendencies of the institution and had publicly promoted a rapprochement with intellectual elites of the Center-Left, most notably through his association and collaborative work with Adam Michnik (Michnik, Tischner, and Żakowski 1995). The goal of "open" Catholics is to reform the institution along the spirit of Vatican II, help it to adjust to the new situation, and understand the criticisms it increasingly faces. Advocates of an open church are members of the editorial board of the liberal Catholic *Tygodnik Powszechny*, and lay journalists from Michnik's *Gazeta Wyborcza*. For a more complete description of the various orientations within the institutional church, and an analysis of these internal divisions since 1989, consult Gowin (1995, 2000) and Zubrzycki (2005).

11. For the full program and statute of LPR, visit their Website, http://www.lpr.pl.

12. Although very vocal, right-wing news media are nowhere as popular as ones from the Center-Left. For a discussion of newspapers and their circulation, see appendix A.

of the nation and of the state reminiscent of Dmowski's.[13] Jan Maria Jackowski, a conservative public interlocutor frequently heard on Radio Maryja and a contributor to *Nasz Dziennik*, perhaps best articulated the vision of this "new Endecja" in a series of best-selling books titled *Battle for Poland* and *Battle for the Truth*, in which he describes liberalism as the source of totalitarianism and calls for the Polish nation to remain close to the church and to Roman Catholicism, with the (Catholic) family as the source of national vitality. Echoing Dmowski, Jackowski argues that a confessional state is necessary for the health and survival of the nation (1993, 1997).

Debates about the nature of the nation and political fights about the shape of the state have therefore punctuated the decade following the fall of Communism in Poland. Other recurrent (and related) themes in public life include those concerning the place of the Catholic Church in the Third Republic, the importance of Catholicism in defining Polishness, and issues of collective memory and rapport to the immediate (Communist) past. To reiterate the argument of this chapter so far: the fall of Communism has reopened the discursive field on the nation and national identity. While the ethnic vision of nationhood is still the predominant one in Poland, it is being seriously challenged by a legitimate civic counterdiscourse that is making its way into the Polish national consciousness.[14] In a dynamic analogous to the one described above regarding the Catholic Church, one can see in the virulent ethno-Catholic discourse of the Right an attempt to gain moral capital that it hopes to transform into political credibility in a decade that has been largely dominated by the post-Communist Left.[15] It is in the face

13. Most of the airwave minutes on Radio Maryja are filled with religious content: Masses, rosaries, individual prayers, call-in shows where listeners can ask priests questions, etc. The overtly political segment is "Unfinished Conversations" (Rozmowy niedokończone), an evening program in which a special guest discusses a specific topic with a priest-moderator, taking calls from listeners.

14. The research of Joanna Kurczewska supports my claim that the ethnic understanding is the commonsensical one in Poland. Kurczewska interviewed fifty-two political leaders about their vision(s) of the nation and national identity and found that the Polak-katolik model is largely taken for granted regardless of politicians' political orientation. Although there was wide disagreement in the normative evaluations of the model, the Polak-katolik stereotype was perceived as an accurate representation not only of "the past," but of present-day Poland as well (2002, 287). Kurczewska is the principal investigator of nationalism and national culture in post-Communist Poland; see her other works (1997, 2000).

15. The post-Communist Left in Poland (as in many other countries of the region) has had a surprisingly strong comeback in the 1990s. The parties of the Left won the parliamentary elections in 1993 and 2001, forming governments in 1993–97 and 2001–5. The office of the presidency has been held by Aleksander Kwaśniewski, former leader and current member of SLD, from 1995 to 2005.

of attempts at redefining the nation along new lines that the ethno-Catholic vision is affirming itself with such vitality.

Let's now consider the debate over the 1997 Constitution's preamble, a prime case in which these competing visions of the nation were set in confrontation.

One Nation under God?

> Having regard for the existence and future of our Homeland, which recovered, in 1989, the possibility of a sovereign and democratic determination of its fate, we, the Polish Nation—all citizens of the Republic, both those who believe in God as the source of truth, justice, good and beauty, as well as those not sharing such faith but respecting those universal values as arising from other sources . . . beholden to our ancestors for their labours, their struggle for independence achieved at great sacrifice, for our culture rooted in the Christian heritage of the Nation and in universal human values . . . recognizing our responsibility before God or our own consciences, hereby establish this Constitution of the Republic of Poland as the basic law for the State.[16]

It took nearly a decade for Poles to draft and enact a new constitution. In 1996 and 1997, the preamble of the Constitution of the Republic of Poland became the arena in which opposed visions of the nation and of the state were made especially apparent, and became the source of an even greater radicalization and polarization. The drafting of the preamble crystallized and intensified questions and debates that have been central in post-Communist Poland: questions of identity and collective memory, the meaning of recent history within broader modern Polish history, and the "historical" place of the Roman Catholic Church and its new role in post-Communist Poland.[17]

A significant portion of the debates focused on the drafting of the constitution's solemn preamble. It may seem, at first glance, a little odd that this would be so in a country facing the pressing practical needs of legally redefining the relationship between its legislative and executive powers, reorganizing the economy, and undertaking its reprivatization. But the preamble acts as the symbolic site par excellence where the nation is explicitly

16. Extracts of the preamble of the Third Republic of Poland's Constitution (in its official English translation). The full text of the preamble is presented in appendix B.

17. For a fuller discussion of constitutional debates as they were shaped by political and institutional arrangements, see my article (Zubrzycki 2001).

defined, providing the basis for the constitution of a new, post-1989 Polish state. The document itself, as symbolic product, and the process by which it came into being as an "event," offered a clear window into the main axes that have structured the post-Communist political field in Poland. Regardless of its legal value or lack thereof,[18] the preamble itself and the debates generated by its drafting arc indicative of its central symbolic role in the reconstruction of "Poland." That its status is primarily symbolic does not diminish its importance; to the contrary, from the cultural perspective the preamble's perceived importance (despite any direct legal utility) and the complex layers of meaning behind its construction as a symbol make its interpretation all the more crucial. Because it is an attempt to reify and stabilize the nation's identity in the past and to fixate it by extending it into the future in the most official way, the constitution's preamble and the debates over what it should and should not include motivate powerful sentiments of affiliation and division. By their very nature, therefore, the document and its crafting were contentious.[19]

"Citizens" or "Nation"? Debates on the Nature of the Community

One of the most heated issues in the constitutional debates of 1996 and 1997 concerned the naming of the constituent entity: the Center-Left insisted that it be defined in the most inclusive terms, and therefore proposed "We, Polish citizens," whereas the Roman Catholic Church and the Right would settle on nothing less than "We, the Polish Nation."[20] The former defined Poles as citizens, bypassing the idiom of nationhood altogether. The preamble's

18. It is unclear here if the content of the preamble would indeed have legal force—it is generally not the case, since preambles are not part of constitutions per se. Rather, the preamble is an axiological document of a symbolic nature and celebratory tone, placed *before* the actual articles of law. Some legal scholars (e.g., Brzezinski [1998]), however, argue that preambles can serve an *interpretive* function: reference to the preamble can be made to clarify an ambiguous article of law by identifying the values on which the constitution is based.

19. For a detailed analysis of visions of nationhood in Polish constitutional debates and how various positions were related to institutional arrangements, see Zubrzycki (2001). For other works specifically devoted to the analysis of preambles as political, legal, and symbolic texts, see Koubi (1996) on France, and Markadan (1984) on India. On constitutionalism and constitution-making in Poland and in Eastern and Central Europe, see Brzezinski (1998); Graczyk (1997); Grewe and Oberdoff (1999); Grudzińska-Gross (1994, 1997); International Institute for Democracy (1996); Łętowska (1995, 1997); Ludwikowski (1996); Mathernova (1993); Osiatyński (1995, 1997); Preuss (1995, 1998); Rapaczyński (1993); Schwartz (2000); Sokołewicz (1995); and Śpiewak (1997).

20. Note how the Right frequently capitalizes the word *nation* to indicate (and emphasize) its sacredness.

first version, prepared by Tadeusz Mazowiecki,[21] opened with the words "We, Polish Citizens" and was at once rejected by the Catholic Church and Solidarity, which demanded that the word *citizens* be replaced by that of *Nation*: "Recognizing the Polish Nation as the creator of the Constitution," according to Solidarity leader Marian Krzaklewski, "underlines the state's sovereignty" (*Non Possumus*, text addressed to the Sejm on February 28, 1997, printed in *Gazeta Wyborcza* on March 3, 1997). In a poll conducted earlier that month, 70 percent of Poles agreed that the constitution should open with the words "We, the Polish Nation," against the 20 percent who thought it should start with "We, Polish citizens" (Ośrodek Badania Opinii Publicznej [OBOP] 1997, 23).[22]

For supporters of the civic vision of the nation, however, the concept of "citizen" is better than that of "nation," because "it includes everyone regardless of ethnicity" (*Gazeta Wyborcza*, February 26, 1997). The Constitutional Commission consented to include the concept of "nation," but refused to exclude that of "citizens." Wiktor Osiatyński[23] clarified the commission's intention: "If the concept of nation is to be included, it can only be in its civic version, not the ethnic" (*Gazeta Wyborcza*, March 3, 1997). The final version of the preamble thus juxtaposed "citizens" with "Polish Nation," thereby giving a civic meaning to the concept of nation—a resolution positively welcomed by Michnik's *Gazeta Wyborcza*, which reported the final formulation with the front-page headline "A Nation of Citizens" (February 27, 1997).

The church initially characterized the addition of the term *Nation* as "satisfying," but described the preamble as "sterile in its conception of the national character" (B. P. Pieronek in Katolicka Agencja Informacyjna, *Biuletyn*, no. 8, February 28, 1997). The Far Right treated the project with less diplomacy. The formula "We, the Polish Nation, all citizens of the Republic" was perceived by conservative milieus of the Right as reducing a quasi-sacred community of descent and culture, the Nation, to a "meaningless"

21. Tadeusz Mazowiecki (1927–) is the principal author of the preamble, an intellectual and politician, and a deputy at the Sejm. In 1957 he cofounded the Warsaw KIK (Klub Inteligencji Katolickiej—Catholic Intelligentsia's Club); in 1958 he launched the Roman Catholic monthly *Więź*. Adviser to Lech Wałęsa during the August 1980 strikes, Mazowiecki was one of the coauthors of the Round Table Agreements (1989). In 1989–90, he was Poland's prime minister. He cofounded one of the most important parties of post-Communist Poland, Unia Demokratyczna (Democratic Union), which later became Unia Wolności (Freedom Union), and now is known as Partia Demokratyczna (Democratic Party).

22. $N = 1{,}116$ of Poland's inhabitants over 16 years of age.

23. Fervent supporter of the constitution, Osiatyński was an adviser to the Constitutional Commission from 1990 to 1996.

political association that dangerously opens the door to non-Poles. According to the opinion expressed in nationalist newspapers of the Far Right,[24] such as *Gazeta Polska* and *Nasza Polska*, the civic project is thus unfair to "real" Poles and ultimately threatens the nation's very existence:

> The NATION is obviously a community of blood, history, language, religion, traditions, territory. . . . It is impossible to become a member of a nation by being granted, by administrative decision, the citizenship of a certain state. . . . The principle that "the Nation, it is all the citizens of the Republic" will cause every citizen from the administrative point of view to have the right to decide about Polish national affairs. A foreigner who settled in Poland and received Polish citizenship not long ago will have identical rights in the affairs of our Nation as the descendants of Tadeusz Kościuszko. . . . How could none of the deputies present at the enactment of the preamble not cry TREASON? (Wojciech Cejrowski in *Gazeta Polska*, no. 16, 1997)

The preamble's civic definition of the nation is thus seen not only as antithetical to the Polish nation; it threatens the nation's very existence:

> This project hurts Polishness . . . [Citizens] are all those who possess the passport of a given state. . . . But it is the Polish nation, as the democratic majority in its country, that decides about the shape of the state—not all the citizens. All Polish citizens, regardless of nationality, religion, or skin color, of course have equal rights and benefit from Poland's traditional tolerance. But they cannot significantly influence the shape of Poland just like the sons of the nation who created this state. It is worth here repeating the words of Primate Stefan Cardinal Wyszyński from 21 years ago: "The state is not a lasting phenomenon. . . . What is a lasting phenomenon is the family and the Nation. That is why the church always builds on the family and the Nation." The Left's constitution is antinational and anti-Polish. In it is contained not only a new totalitarianism, but also a new de-nationalization. (Wiesław Magiera in *Nasza Polska*, April 30, 1997)[25]

24. For works on right-wing politics and the Far Right in Central and Eastern Europe, see Fischer-Galati (1993) and Ramet (1999). On Poland more specifically, see Korboński (1993); Terry (1993); and Ost (1999). For an analysis of the relationship between conceptions of the nation and the success of right-wing movements, see Koopmans and Statham (1999).

25. The term *denationalization* (*wynarodowienie*) has very strong connotations in Polish. It refers to attempts by Prussia and Russia in the nineteenth century to annihilate the sentiment

These views are representative of a discourse of exclusion that emphasizes the sharp dichotomy between citizenship and nationality (with nationality superseding citizenship in importance), and stresses that the newly sovereign state should be a state for ethnic Poles and not for citizens at large (the remaining 3 percent of the population). This is precisely the discourse of exclusion Adam Michnik was worried about in 1991.

As we have seen in the last chapter, Jews have been the traditional "internal Other," but "bad Catholics," "cosmopolitan secularists," and Freemasons (the last two categories, however, working as code words for "Jews") also have been categories of symbolic exclusion from the nation in ethno-Catholic milieus. The 1990s have witnessed significant anti-Semitic discourse in the public sphere despite the virtual absence of Jews in Poland.[26] This phenomenon could be explained by the fact that Jews, in Poland, serve as the prime "symbolic Other." Michnik calls this peculiar phenomenon "magical anti-Semitism": "The logic of normal, correct and healthy anti-Semitism is the following: Adam Michnik is a Jew, therefore he is a hooligan, a thief, a traitor, a bandit etc. . . . Magical anti-Semitism however

---

of belonging to the Polish nation. The standard Polish dictionary (*Mały słownik języka polskiego*) defines the verb *wynaradawiać* (denationalize) as follows: "to deprive someone of his or her national traits, of his or her national distinctiveness; to deprive someone of the consciousness of belonging to some nation."

26. It is very difficult to establish the number of Jews in Poland. Estimates vary greatly, ranging from 1,055 individuals (2002 Polish census) to 40,000 (*American Jewish Year Book* 2003). The wide variation in these data is the outcome of different measures of "Jewishness": self-declaration in the census versus ancestry or formal membership in Jewish organizations. The numbers have steadily grown in the last decade as better sources for estimating them have become available, and as the Jewish community has witnessed a cultural, religious, and institutional renaissance. In 1989 and 1990, the *American Jewish Year Book* estimated the total Jewish population of Poland to be 5,000, of which nearly 2,000 were "registered"—that is, formally affiliated with one or more religious or secular Jewish organizations. This figure was widely cited in Polish publications throughout the 1990s. During that decade, however, the total number of Polish Jews was re-estimated to be closer to 10,000 (*American Jewish Year Book* 1992, 1995). By the beginning of the new millennium, the number of Polish Jews affiliated with religious or secular Jewish organizations totaled 7,000–8,000. Moreover, between 10,000 and 15,000 people showed interest in rediscovering their Jewish ancestry, and as many as 40,000 Polish citizens were now thought to have "some" Jewish forebears (ibid., 2002, 2003). The numbers cited by Piotr Kadlčik, the president of the Jewish community in Warsaw and president of the Union of Jewish Communities in Poland, are slightly more conservative: according to him, there are now 4,000 to 6,000 "registered" Jews and approximately 20,000 to 25,000 Polish citizens of Jewish descent who do not maintain a formal connection to any Jewish institutions (personal communication, May 2004. Listen also to the radio interview in English with Kadlčik, available at http://www.fzp.jewish.org.pl/english/present.html). For Polish census data, see http://www.mswia.gov.pl/index_a.html; for other Polish estimates, see Łodziński (2003).

works this way: Adam Michnik is a thief, therefore he is most probably a Jew" (1999, 73). Any opponent of the ethnic vision of the nation, therefore, is accused, through a series of associations and double entendres, of being a "Jew."[27] The editor of *Nasza Polska*, for example, declared the civic nation an invention of Jews: "Not everyone knows that one of the inventors of this new 'meaning' of the word 'nation' is Tomasz Wołek, editor-in-chief of the daily *Życie*. Who is Tomasz Wołek, and what is *Życie*? To this question, we can answer indirectly by noting that the vice-editor-in-chief is a certain Bronisław Wildstein" (Stanisław Krajski in *Nasza Polska*, April 23, 1997).[28]

In the Name of God

Tellingly, the other contentious aspect of the constitutional debates concerned whether to include an *invocatio Dei* in the constitution's preamble. Given that the overwhelming majority of Poles are Roman Catholic (at least nominally), the preamble should include, according to the advocates of the

27. The quotation marks indicate the symbolic and discursive nature of the category. It is the *image* of Jews and *representations* of Jewishness—not real, existing Jews (even when actual Jewish persons are referred to or are verbally and symbolically abused)—that I emphasize here.

I address the question of Polish anti-Semitism more exhaustively in the chapters on the War of the Crosses at Auschwitz, and discuss magical anti-Semitism and the phenomenon of the "symbolic Jew" in the book's conclusion. The most exhaustive research on Polish anti-Semitism can be found in the volume edited by Ireneusz Krzemiński (1996), based on survey data collected in 1992. Krzemiński and his colleagues found that although more prevalent in Poland than in other European countries or in the United States, modern (or "political") anti-Semitism of the type "Jews control the world" is not specific to Poles. Traditional (or "religious") anti-Semitism, however, based on the portrayal of Jews as Christ-killers, is more specific to Poland, although that form of anti-Semitism is relatively weak and less common than its modern kind. Religious anti-Semitism is most popular among older and less educated Poles, and among those residing in villages and small towns. The higher the level of education, the less religiously founded anti-Semitic attitudes the respondents expressed. The percentage of respondents expressing anti-Semitic views, however, had increased between 1992 and 1996, when CBOS conducted a survey repeating several questions from Krzemiński's study. But so did the percentage of those opposing anti-Semitism, which led the Krzemiński team to conclude that the 1990s had witnessed a clear polarization of attitudes toward Jews and anti-Semitism. For a discussion of the 1992 and 1996 surveys in English, see Krzemiński (2002). For an annotated bibliography of works on Polish-Jewish relations and Polish anti-Semitism published since 1990, see Corrsin (2005).

28. What is interesting to note here, besides the blatant anti-Semitism and the association civic nation = cosmopolitan = anti-Polish = Jews, is that the newspaper *Życie* is itself on the conservative Right in the political ideological landscape. This shows how far to the Right *Nasza Polska* (and *Gazeta Polska*) are. Thanks to Krzysztof Jasiewicz for stressing this in a personal communication.

national-Catholic vision, an *invocatio Dei*, or reference to God. The following comment by Alicja Grześkowiak, then senator from Solidarity, is representative of this position:

> A preamble characterizes the identity of the nation, underlines that what is instituted on earth is not perfect. Referring to God confirms human dignity; it indicates that the true guarantee of human rights and dignity is God Himself. For believers, such a preamble has an additional value: it motivates them to live not only in compliance with the constitution, with the law, but also with certain values. A preamble referring to God also reflects the face of the nation. The constitution cannot negate the fact that the majority of the nation is Catholic. The formula "in the name of Almighty God" is an ecumenical formula that can be accepted by all believers. 98 percent of Poles are believers, and the constitution should be written for the believers, which does not reduce the role of nonbelievers nor discriminate against them. For nonbelievers the [*invocatio Dei*] will only be a linguistic expression deprived of content. For believers, it is an important issue that allows them to feel at home in Poland. A constitution without a preamble referring to God will be, in fact, the constitution of another nation. (*Życie Warszawy*, September 19, 1996)

Referring to God as the ultimate source of dignity and justice not only specifies the Roman Catholic identity of Poles—thereby breaking from an officially atheist People's Republic of Poland—but moreover implies the predominance of natural law over positive law.[29] It was argued on both

29. Natural law refers to "principles of law and morality, supposedly universal in scope and binding on human conduct" (*Oxford Dictionary of Sociology*, 348). Following Thomas Aquinas, it was believed to be God-given; but from the Reformation onward, natural law was also given secular foundations in human nature and reason. Natural law stipulates that there is a normative system given in nature; that norms are not subject to change in time or place. In contrast, the logic of positive law is that it defines the normative system; norms are a human creation and therefore are subject to change and interpretation. Thus, this form of law could define norms that are against natural law or humanity. (Nazi Germany is often given as an example of the dangers of a strict positive law.) This is why it is often insisted that positive law be based on natural law. The Polish case is complex in that regard. The church insisted that the constitution be *directly* based on the first version of natural law (as God-given), when the constitution actually was founded on positive law based on natural law's secular version (human nature and reason). The members of the Constitutional Commission thus argued that even without the *invocatio Dei*, the constitution was still ultimately—although indirectly—founded on natural law.

sides of the Left-Right divide that this could potentially have concrete legal consequences. The church frequently declared that the *invocatio Dei* and the primacy of natural over positive law would ensure the constitutional ban on abortion, a highly contentious issue in post-Communist Poland.

Since the constitution is instituted as the highest law of the republic, placing natural law above positive law by referring to God as the legislator would, according to the Left, the Center, and even liberal Catholics, run counter to the establishment of the *Rechtsstaat* (state under the rule of law), and would imply the granting to religious authorities of a privileged position as "subsidiary of truth," a situation incompatible with the principles of a secular state. "It is the constitution, not the Decalogue," wrote an editor in *Polityka* (no. 20, 1996). A deputy from Sojusz Lewicy Demokratycznej (SLD—Alliance of the Democratic Left) insisted that the *invocatio Dei* not be included, since "believers look for God at church, not in the constitution" (*Życie Warszawy*, September 19, 1996); and President Aleksander Kwaśniewski emphasized that "in no secular country with a neutral worldview does natural law stand above positive law" (*Gazeta Wyborcza*, February 25, 1997). According to the Left and liberal circles, a strict *invocatio Dei* would open the door for the establishment of a confessional state.[30]

The Constitutional Commission's final resolution was to include a general reference to God and to religious values, but *juxtaposed* with that of the Enlightenment's humanist tradition. This compromise, however, could not satisfy the Roman Catholic Church, which fiercely criticized the preamble's "pagan conception of God": "God is not a kind of philosophical, Masonic idea, or a vague New Age god. The point is to recognize Him as invariable, the highest Being who is the Creator of the moral and legal order" (B. P. Michalik in Katolicka Agencja Informacyjna, *Biuletyn*, no. 10, 1997). Cardinal Glemp expressed himself in similar terms in an Easter sermon: "What we have here is atheism enriched by Masonic ideology. . . . As Catholics, we will decidedly stand for the presence of a reference to God in the [preamble]. We want the real God in the constitution" (Katolicka Agencja Informacyjna, *Biuletyn*, no. 20, 1997). The God evoked in the preamble did not meet the standards of the church, and the ecclesial institution soon resorted

30. This position has not prevented the same social and political actors to push for the inclusion of an *invocatio Dei* in the European Union's constitution. This suggests that the opposition to the *invocatio Dei* was not only ideological but also contingent upon political structures and institutional arrangements.

to nationalist arguments by advocating that the "Polish Nation had the right to its Christian God":

> The formulation "we, Polish citizens, who believe in God as the source of truth, justice, beauty and goodness, as well as those who do not share this faith . . ." is not a classical *invocatio Dei*, but is at most a substitute that informs us that in Poland there are people believing in "some kind" of God. Showing off God as a source of only those values, with the omission that He is the Creator, the living God, Legislator before Whom one has to settle accounts . . . is dangerous. . . . Such a god can . . . only be the intellectual construction of philosophers. Meanwhile, in a Christian nation, we have the right to hear about our living God, our creator and savior. This is the God of our faith and only this God do we call upon in the *invocatio Dei*. . . . We must clearly say that a constitution with no perspective should not be ratified, and that a nation with a Christian tradition of over one thousand years must, on the basis of its roots, order thoughts, law, and actions, and that is why it has a right to the *invocatio Dei*. (B. P. Michalik in *Nasza Polska*, no. 5, 1997)

Discourse and Representations

The analysis of public discourses surrounding the preamble highlights significant differences between the languages used by each camp, constituting coherent "subfields" within the discursive field on the nation. The Center-Left speaks of "citizens," "civil society," and the "civic nation," and aims at creating a modern Poland open to Europe, oriented toward the future, and based on universal human values. In contrast, the conservative Center and the Right speak of "Poles" and their "ancestors" and reach to the past, to Poland's thousand years of history. It aims at preserving a national tradition, emphasizing the national-Christian heritage and values. The first is legitimized according to rational-legal principles, the other by the weight of tradition.

These two schemes of thought make dialogue difficult, and the different discursive subfields cause misunderstandings to abound. For example, in circles of the Left and Center, *citizen* is a neutral term that avoids the exclusion of those who are not ethnically Polish. For the Right, however, it echoes jargon from the Communist period. Similarly, liberal intellectuals treat *civil society* neutrally, whereas for right-wing Roman Catholics the term is understood as an ideological project aiming at depreciating "natural" forms of community such as the family and the nation (Gowin 1995). Proponents of the state's religious neutrality see the Catholic Right's efforts to include the *invocatio Dei* as an instrument serving to divide and exclude rather than unite and include, whereas the Catholic Right actually presents it as a path to unity. Other examples include *religious neutrality*, *tolerance*, and *pluralism*, understood by the Roman Catholic Right and the conservative wing of the church as "atheism," an "extreme moral relativism," a dangerous "moral nihilism" that "does not respect the nation" (Alicja Grześkowiak in *Gazeta Wyborcza*, February 25, 1997). Cardinal Glemp frequently declared that the preamble had no soul, and Bishop Józef Michalik stated that it was "a bad project because it has no ethical values" (*Polityka*, no. 20, May 18, 1997).

Similarly, the Constitutional Commission stressed the democratic spirit of the preamble and the democratic process surrounding the drafting of the document, while the church called it a "democratic totalitarianism." Whereas the constitution's authors spoke of the ratification of the document as the "great consensus," the establishment of a "social contract," the result of a "historical compromise," the editorialists of newspapers from the Right called it a "treason," a "conspiracy against the Nation":

> They shout with a great voice about the great compromise, the national agreement, the Polish *raison d'état* etc.... It is an anticonstitution, a constitution against Poland, the nation, man, the family, God, and democracy; an encore to the People's Republic of Poland, a Constitution of targowica.... On May 25, we, the Polish nation, will reject the bad, pagan, and non-Polish Constitution of the Left!!! (*Nasza Polska*, April 23, 1997)[31]

The ideals of the civic nation and universal values are understood positively by some, and as ideological, cosmopolitan, and ultimately anti-Polish by others. Of course, the Right is not the only group demonizing the opponent's position. Some circles associated with the Left characterize the Right's emphasis on the nation as a provincial chauvinism, qualify religion as superstition, call tradition ignorance, and so on.[32]

31. Targowica was a town in the Ukraine where in 1792–93 some Polish magnates conspired against Poland in order to abolish the Constitution of May Third (1791). They sought the protection of Catherine II, which gave the pretext for the Second Partition of Poland (1793). The word *Targowica* since then has been synonymous with high treason and conspiracy against the country.

32. This is especially true of Jerzy Urban's weekly, *Nie*. Urban describes his paper as "a satirico-critical newspaper, attacking nationalism, clericalism, parties from the right, parties

These discourses are not only the result of different views of the nation and of the state: they also result from the logic of the political field itself (Bourdieu 1991b). The actors compete with each other for symbolic power by formulating their position vis-à-vis the other camp. The subfields are thus relational and dialogical: actors engage, speak, react, and reply to the other group.[33] In this case, this process slowly led to an escalation in the accusatory tone of discourse, especially from the Right campaigning against the ratification of the constitution. Not surprisingly, the language used to describe opponents became more bitter, and the polarization sharper, from March to May 1997—that is, from the final works on the constitutional project and its submission to the National Assembly, until the referendum on it held May 25. Despite strategies of delegitimation used by the Right, Poles voted for the final ratification of the constitutional project (52.7 percent for, 45.9 percent against, 1.4 percent invalid votes). Voter turnout, however, was very low,[34] which seems to indicate that the debates that fascinated the elites did not resonate as strongly with the masses. It should be noted, however, that the Right's slight defeat in the referendum did not prevent it from winning the parliamentary elections a few months later in the fall of 1997. One might argue that the debates over the preamble gave the Right the opportunity to solidify its coalition and mobilize constituencies that contributed to the power of AWS in establishing a base to effectively counter SLD in the elections.

Conclusion

This chapter had two objectives: first, to outline the post-Communist lay of the land in terms of the issues that have defined the period, along with describing the main actors and their discourses; second, to discuss one key event that has, like the War of the Crosses, condensed and crystallized debates about Polish national identity and Roman Catholicism. The analysis of constitutional debates suggests that national sentiments of affinity become

---

issued from Solidarity and Wałęsa." *Nie* is on the extreme left, not so much in terms of the content of its interventions but in its form. Famous for its satire, hostility toward the church, and vulgar caricatures, the weekly is comparable to the *National Lampoon*. Urban was the spokesman of General Wojciech Jaruzelski (b. 1923), first secretary of the party and prime minister in the 1980s infamous for imposing martial law (1981–83).

33. For a fascinating analysis of hate speech in five right-wing publications (and a useful glossary of the most often used "code" terms), see Kowalski and Tulli (2003).

34. Voter turnout was 42.86 percent, which means that about 23 percent of eligible voters were for the ratification of the constitution, and about 17 percent were against (official figures reported in *Gazeta Wyborcza*, May 26, 1997).

powerfully activated when relatively abstract discursive constructs are condensed and affixed in symbols of the nation's representation—in the case at hand, in the contested preamble of Poland's 1997 Constitution.

In the next chapters, we turn our attention to another key symbolic event, in this case a site, that mobilized the sentiments and actions not only of elites, but of elites and "the masses" in equal measure. Having now laid out the major vectors of the religion-nation fusion and its partial fissures, we now turn to the ways Auschwitz was signified, battled over, and endowed with new meaning in the last decade. This will move us one frame closer to the War of the Crosses as a specific social drama and event.

CHAPTER THREE

"Oświęcim"/"Auschwitz": Archaeology of a Contested Site and Symbol

Les lieux de mémoire naissent et vivent du sentiment qu'il n'y a pas de mémoire spontanée, qu'il faut créer des archives, qu'il faut maintenir des anniversaires, organiser des célébrations, prononcer des éloges funèbres, notarier des actes, parce que ces opérations ne sont pas naturelles. C'est pourquoi la défense par les minorités d'une mémoire réfugiée sur des foyers privilégiés et jalousement gardés ne fait que porter à l'incandescence la vérité de tous les lieux de mémoire. Sans vigilance commémorative, l'histoire les balaierait vite. —Pierre Nora, *Les lieux de mémoire*[1]

Memory is never shaped in a vacuum; the motives of memory are never pure. —James E. Young, *The Texture of Memory*

Introduction

An interpretation of the War of the Crosses at Auschwitz first requires a textured reading of the symbol of "Auschwitz" itself.[2] If "humanity's largest cemetery" is known in the world by its German designation, in Poland

1. "Realms of memory are born out of, and live from, the feeling that there is no spontaneous memory; that we must create archives, observe anniversaries, organize celebrations, pronounce eulogies, and notarize documents, because these operations are not natural. This is why minority groups' defense of a memory whose only refuge is in carefully chosen sites only brings to light the truth of all realms of memory: without commemorative vigilance, History would quickly sweep them away."

2. As noted in the book's introduction (note 22), the symbolic representation(s) of Auschwitz should not be confused with the physical site itself. The names without the quotation marks refer to the place, while they refer to the symbol(s) when placed in quotation marks. Auschwitz is

it is known and referred to as "Oświęcim," the Polish name of the small town annexed to the Reich during World War II where the Nazis set up the world's most infamous concentration and extermination camp. The different names for the same site are related to its respective meanings for the different parties involved. Whereas "Auschwitz" is, for Jews and the world, the symbol of the Holocaust and now of universal evil, "Oświęcim" is for Poles the symbol of Polish martyrdom.[3] It is also the symbolic terrain where Poles articulate their relationship to various Others: Germans, who created the camp; Russians, who liberated it; and especially Jews, with whom Poles compete for the ownership of the former camp as a symbol of their own martyrdom. Finally, Auschwitz is the site of the dramatization and enactment of nationalist discourses which have shaped—and divided—Polish public life in the last decade.

"Oświęcim"/"Auschwitz" are multivocal symbols that simultaneously condense and polarize disparate significations. Auschwitz is also what Pierre Nora calls a *lieu-carrefour* (1997, 15), a privileged site where questions of identity are crystallized and fiercely contested by different social groups. Oświęcim the town and within it Auschwitz the former camp constitute the physical battleground of the War of the Crosses and, before it, of the Carmelite convent controversy. In this chapter, I analyze "Oświęcim"/

therefore the former camp and current museum, while Oświęcim is the town in which Auschwitz is located. Although Poles only very rarely use the name Auschwitz to denote the former camp and current museum, this is the term I privilege to reflect the historical record. I use "Oświęcim" to refer to the Polish symbol, Oświęcim to refer to the town; "Auschwitz" to refer to the Jewish and universal symbol, and Auschwitz to refer to the former camp and current museum. When quoting someone, I keep the term used in the original language.

3. Note that the Greek-derived word *holocaust* is rarely used in Polish (but increasingly so) and the Hebrew *Shoah* even less. In Polish, *extermination* (*zagłada*) is the term most often used to describe the mass killings during World War II. There is thus talk about the extermination of Jews, of Poles, and of Gypsies. See Novick (2000) on the process through which the extermination of Jews during World War II became "the Holocaust" in the United States; Cole (2000) for the varying and shifting meanings of the Holocaust in western Europe, Poland, the United States, and Israel; and Alexander (2002) for an analysis of how the Holocaust became a universal symbol. On the various meanings of "Oświęcim" and/or "Auschwitz," see Irwin-Zarecka (1989a, 1989b); Tanay (1991); Gitelman (1993); Goban-Klas (1995); Steinlauf (1997, 122–44); Sułek (1998); Kapralski (1998); Novick (2000); Cole (2000); and Kucia (2001, 2005). For an excellent analysis of the meaning of "Auschwitz" and its mythologization by Israeli and Diaspora Jews, Soviet Russians, and Poles, as well as for the multiple—often contradictory—philosophical preoccupations the Holocaust raises, see Webber (1992). For a study of Holocaust memorial sites in Communist and post-Communist Poland, see chapters 5, 6, and 7 in Young (1993). The most extensive analysis of the politics of commemoration at Auschwitz in Communist Poland is by Huener (2003). On another contested site and symbol and the conflicts it provokes between Israelis and Palestinians as well as within each nation, see Friedland and Hecht's outstanding study, *To Rule Jerusalem* (2000).

"Auschwitz" as core symbols, and their respective relation to Auschwitz and Oświęcim.[4] More specifically, I dissect the various layers of meaning "Oświęcim" carries for Poles and discuss the role of the Auschwitz-Birkenau State Museum in the symbol's ideological configuration and reconfiguration. After decades of socializing Poles into a specific reading of history, changes in the narrative of the museum (and other state institutions) are seen by many Poles as a sudden "Judaization" of Auschwitz, resulting in a "de-Polonization" of "Oświęcim" and its (Polish) memory. Unpacking the meanings attributed to the site itself and interpreting the changes taking place in the discursive field about the symbol are keys to understanding the War of the Crosses.

Geography and History of Auschwitz

Before undertaking our excavation of symbols, let's take a bird's-eye tour of the physical site. What is commonly referred to as Auschwitz is actually a large complex of camps and subcamps, including concentration, extermination, and forced-labor camps covering some forty square kilometers (fig. 19). Auschwitz (or Auschwitz I) was the mother camp, established in 1940 outside Oświęcim mostly for Polish political prisoners; Birkenau (or Auschwitz II) was the largest one, established three kilometers from Auschwitz I in 1942 in the small village of Brzezinka, with the main purpose of exterminating the European Jewry;[5] and Monowitz (or Auschwitz III, which is not part of the museum) was established in Monowice to provide forced labor to nearby factories such as the large I. G. Farben works.[6] The geography of these camps in relation to the small villages and towns in which they were established during the war is important, since it comes up frequently in debates between Poles and Jews. According to many Poles, controversies arise from avoidable misunderstandings, which they see as the result of a lack of knowledge of the spatial organization of what is called indiscriminately "Auschwitz."

4. For Marvin Prosono (1994), disputes over Auschwitz are less about physical territory per se than about the symbolic nature of the territory. He therefore analyzed the controversy over the Carmelite convent through the conceptual lenses of what he terms "symbolic territoriality." My own view and goal in this work is to show how the physical territory and its symbolism are distinct entities that sometimes intersect, overlap, or contradict each other depending on various groups' theologies, interpretations of history, and collective memories.

5. The hurried construction of Birkenau was prompted by the overflow of Soviet prisoners of war in late 1941, and was initially intended for several groups of prisoners, to be divided in various sections of the camp. The same year, Himmler had also designated Birkenau to become the largest site for carrying out the Final Solution (Huener 2003, 6–7).

6. For detailed descriptions of the Auschwitz system, see van Pelt and Dwork (1996).

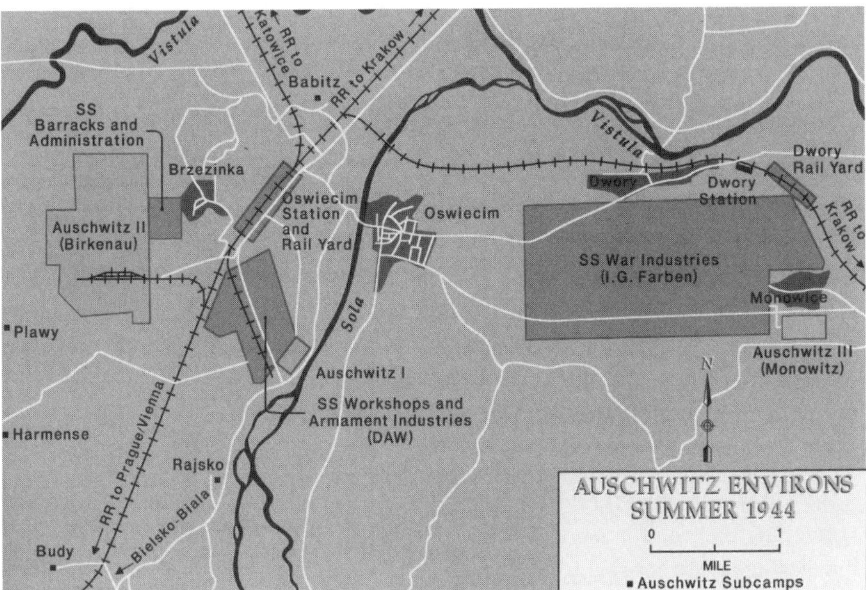

Figure 19 Map of Auschwitz I, Auschwitz II (Birkenau), and Auschwitz III (Monovitz). Used with permission of the United States Holocaust Memorial Museum, Washington, DC.

Several factors have made KL (for *Konzentrationslager*) Auschwitz the site around which collective memories of the Holocaust for Jews and of World War II for Poles have coalesced. Unlike the camps in Treblinka, Bełżec, and Sobibór, which were dismantled by the Nazis in 1943 after most Jews of Poland had been killed in the so-called Aktion Reinhard,[7] Auschwitz-Birkenau was still operating shortly before the Soviets liberated the camp on January 27, 1945. Because of the rapid advance of the Soviet Red Army in the last months of the war, Nazis abandoned the camp, leaving ample evidence of their crimes (Webber 1992, 3). Moreover, the Red Army actually liberated prisoners at Auschwitz, whereas at most other camps they stumbled over ruins with little or no traces of survivors.[8] These factors had important

7. In all, approximately 1.7 million Jews were killed as part of Aktion Reinhard; the overwhelming majority of them were from Poland. The victims of Bełżec were mainly Jews from the ghettos of southern Poland, and those deported to Sobibór came primarily from the Lublin area and other ghettos of the eastern *Generalgouvernement*. Victims of Treblinka originated mainly from central Poland, primarily from the Warsaw ghetto and Radom (United States Holocaust Memorial Museum, *Holocaust Encyclopedia*, http://www.ushmm.org/wlc/en/).

8. The Red Army liberated approximately 7,000 prisoners at Auschwitz, who remained in the camp after the Nazis had forced approximately 60,000 others to march west as the Soviets

repercussions for memory-making: first, Auschwitz's relatively large number of survivors lived to tell their stories in Poland and throughout the world (although these stories were different, depending on the identities of those doing the telling); second, the camp's surviving structures provided solid evidence of the Nazi crimes as well as an infrastructure that could house a state museum; and lastly, the number of survivors liberated by the Red Army, the evidence left behind, and the enormity of the crime provided an "ideal" prompt through which the Communist state could construct a shrine to Socialism's victory over Fascism, and a warning against the excesses of capitalism.

"Oświęcim" as a Core Polish Symbol

"Auschwitz." "Oświęcim." The former is the symbol of the Holocaust; the latter, of Polish martyrdom. "Oświęcim" condenses multiple layers of meaning that reinforce one another and serve to justify the position of those insisting on the presence of the cross at the site. Let's look at the origins of the signification of "Oświęcim" for Poles.[9]

The Polish Experience of Auschwitz during World War II

The first layer of meaning is that of the camp's history during World War II. Already during the war, the name "Oświęcim" signified Polish suffering under German occupation. KL Auschwitz was initially created for Polish political prisoners: intellectual and professional elites, members of the resistance, priests, and nuns were the main groups imprisoned there until the Final Solution was implemented in 1942, after which the camp was given the additional and henceforth main function of death camp for the European Jewry, through the creation of Auschwitz II-Birkenau.[10] While in the Polish

approached. With those who had been released from the camp and those transferred from the Auschwitz system to other camps, the total number of Auschwitz survivors is much larger, in the tens of thousands (Hilberg 2003, 3:1046–48). By contrast, it is thought that less than 10 people survived Bełżec, where approximately 500,000 perished, the great majority of whom were Jewish. Between 800,00 and 850,000 Jews were killed at Treblinka, with less than 100 surviving to see liberation.

9. While "Auschwitz" is a complex symbol in its own right, because Polish nationalism is the subject of this book my primary focus is on "Oświęcim."

10. Other prisoners in this early period of the camp's history included Soviet prisoners of war, Germans opposed to the Nazis, homosexuals, and Jehovah's Witnesses. Poles, however,

consciousness the camps in Treblinka, Bełżec, Chełmno, and Sobibór were and are synonymous with the extermination of Jews (because this is primarily where Polish Jews from the liquidated ghettos of Warsaw, Cracow, Łódź, and Lublin were killed), "Oświęcim" became and remained the symbol of Poles' martyrdom during World War II, representing the attempt by Nazis to physically and culturally annihilate the Polish nation—an interpretation that fit neatly into Polish scripts of denationalization by their western neighbor.

The Socialist Appropriation of the Symbol

After the war, the Communist state built onto this already common understanding of the camp by creating the State Museum Oświęcim-Brzezinka in 1947 on the basis of a law "on the remembrance of the martyrdom of the Polish Nation and other Nations."[11] As the name of that law suggests, Poles, although not the camp's sole victims, were its main martyrs. The museum was indeed squarely Polish from its inception, but the national narrative was told in the Socialist mode and according to Socialist parameters.[12] In it, "Victims of Fascism" from Poland and from twenty-seven other nation-states were exploited and exterminated at the camp, later liberated by the

constituted the main group during the early period of the camp's history. Since those who were targeted by deportations were primarily members of the Polish intelligentsia, assimilated Polish Jews were also imprisoned.

11. For a detailed history of postwar Auschwitz and its various narratives, see Huener (2003).

12. This can be seen, for example, in how the State Museum Oświęcim-Brzezinka inserted Auschwitz into a narrative about Poles' constant fight against the German threat: the Teutonic knights in the fifteenth century, Prussian participation in the Partitions of the eighteenth, oppressive Prussian rule in the nineteenth, and Nazi occupation in the twentieth. This narrative was especially powerful since it deemphasized the Polish-Russian enmity and cast Russians/Soviets as allies. However powerful and ideologically useful, the narrative nevertheless presented an important political problem for the historical commission in charge of designing the various exhibits: how to represent the German Democratic Republic? The members proposed that there had always been "good" and "bad" Germans, the bad part being the capitalists turned Nazis, now constituting the Federal Republic of Germany. The "good" Germans had resisted Nazism and now constituted the friendly German Democratic Republic, which had even returned land to Poland (the Recovered Lands) (archival material from the Auschwitz-Birkenau State Museum, minutes from the historical commission, 1948–49, pp. 72–76, 92–100; call number 942). The transcripts from the historical commission are revealing in terms of the ideological parameters set by the new political situation in Poland, which ultimately impacted the narrative of the museum. See also the official guidebook to the museum, which contained two full pages on the opposition led by the German Communist Party against the "monopolists and militarists" (Smoleń 1960, 7–9).

victorious and just Red Army.[13] According to a Polish publication about the camp,

> In KL Auschwitz, there were prisoners of various nationalities, creeds, and professions. They included Americans, Austrians, Belgians, Britons, Bulgarians, Chinese, Croats, Czechs, Dutchmen, Egyptians, Frenchmen, Germans, Greeks, Gypsies, Hungarians, Italians, Jews, Letts, Lithuanians, Norwegians, Persians, Poles, Romanians, Russians (and other citizens of the Soviet Union), Slovaks, Spaniards, Swiss, Turks, and Yugoslavs. (Iwaszko 1985, 63)

Stated in this fashion, Jews constitute only one among many groups enslaved and murdered at the camp. That most of the nationals listed above were Jewish was concealed. Note also that the listing is made alphabetically; in the original Polish version, Jews (Żydzi) were last on the list, implicitly distorting reality one step further. Another example of this bias can be found in the official guidebook to the museum, in which a short paragraph informs the reader-visitor of the Nazis' use of Auschwitz for the total extermination of Jews, but under the subheading "The Nations' Room" (Sala narodów). Other groups' fates, such as those of Soviet prisoners of war or Romas, were described using the same term, *extermination*, but were brought to the reader's attention with clear subheadings: "The Extermination of Soviet Prisoners of War" and "The Extermination of Gypsies" (Smoleń 1960, 15–16).[14] Jews got no subheading.

Through these subtle and not-so-subtle semantic formulations and editorial formats, the Jewish fact of Auschwitz was forced into the background, whereas the extent of Polish suffering was brought closer to the fore. Polish Jews, moreover, were included among Poland's victims. By conflating Polish

13. For a succint presentation of the Socialist-nationalist narrative of Nazi camps in which Jews were barely mentioned, see also the erratum to the 1966 *Wielka Encyklopedia Powszechna PWN*, included with volume 11 of the encyclopedia (1968).

14. The guide to the State Museum Oświęcim-Brzezinka, *Oświęcim 1940–1945*, was written by Kazimierz Smoleń, former prisoner and director of the museum from 1955 to 1990. It was revised and reedited several times until the narrative revision of the museum in the early 1990s, when it was pulled out of circulation. Although the current vice-director of the museum insisted that it was not reedited because it was now obsolete, Mr. Smoleń told me with obvious rancor that it had been discontinued because the current administration thought it was "too political" (interviews with Krystyna Oleksy, museum vice-director and director of the Pedagogical Section, March 19, 2001, and with Kazimierz Smoleń, May 9, 2001).

Jews and gentile Poles into the category of Polish Citizens or sometimes simply Poles, Poland, it was implied, had suffered the most deaths. While the use of a "neutral," civic language of *citizens* was meant to avoid the reproduction of the very categories defined by the Nuremberg Laws (Huener 2003), it is my contention that the diminution of Auschwitz's Jewish fact was also, if not primarily, a strategic ideological manipulation by the Communist state intended to create a Socialist shrine, replete with victims (the "victims of Fascism," Poles at the head) and heroes (the liberating Red Army, the resistance movement, and so on). Although it was known that most of the victims of Auschwitz were Jewish, the historical commission in charge of designing the museum's main exhibit did not want that fact to "distract" from the Socialist narrative.

The number of victims was established at four million, a figure that came to symbolize Nazi atrocities, Polish martyrdom, and the importance of Soviet liberation. That number was established, James Young points out, "by a combination of the camp commandant's self-aggrandizing exaggerations, Polish perceptions of their great losses, and the Soviet occupiers' desire to create socialist martyrs" (1993, 141). It is the contention of some that the Soviets inflated the number of the camp's victims more than threefold, partly to boost the significance and role of the Red Army in the Socialist narrative of World War II, diminish Stalin's own crimes, and create the impression that the great majority of the victims must have been non-Jews, with Poles and Soviet prisoners of war at the top of the list (ibid., 141; Krajewski 1997, 240). It is difficult to establish whether the inflation of that number was the result of straight political disingenuousness, but it certainly abetted the creation of a powerful narrative around Nazi atrocities and Soviet liberation.

The (civic-Socialist) nationalist appropriation of the site went hand in hand with the Socialist narrative of World War II in general and of "Oświęcim" in particular: people died there not because of their ethnic origins, or "race," as defined by Nazi ideology, but because they were opposed to Fascism, an evil political and economic system. Poles, as *résistants par excellence,* were thus portrayed as the camp's main martyrs and heroes. Communist propaganda made the Nazi camp *the* symbol of Fascist oppression, the culmination of bourgeois society's aberrations. It came to symbolize not only German occupation, but also the victory of Socialism over Fascism and capitalism. "Oświęcim" was widely used as such in the official propaganda, school textbooks, and at the state museum. In the 1959 commentary to the film shown to every group of visitors at the museum until 1990, the camp is described as a well-organized, rationalized capitalist enterprise. Here's a sample of what the visitor heard:

> "Oświęcim": Symbol of Hitlerism. Here Germans created a huge experimental laboratory of Fascism, a factory of death that served Fascist science and technique..... Raw matter for German factories: 700,000 kilograms of cut hair from 140,000 murdered women. Fascists were trading in death.... [T]hey sold hair to factories and state-operated upholstery workshops. In another division in this business, bandits ripped out teeth from corpses to remove gold crowns. (Personal transcripts from taped film *Oświęcim*, shown from 1959 to 1990, archives of the Auschwitz-Birkenau State Museum)

Liberated by the Red Army, Auschwitz became a Socialist shrine, visited every year by tens of thousands of Soviet Bloc citizens, and "Oświęcim" a potent Socialist symbol. It was an important symbol used in legitimating new geopolitical alliances, however jury-rigged—much more a forced marriage than a love story with a happy ending. By emphasizing Nazi Germany's crimes, moreover, Communists were minimizing the Soviet Union's own offenses, whether against its own civil population or Poland's. Indeed, the emphasis on "Oświęcim" was a way to distract from the tragedy of Katyń, where some fifteen thousand Polish officers and members of the intelligentsia were killed by the Soviet NKVD in 1940.[15]

In the 1960s, the museum administration conducted studies to measure the pedagogical effectiveness of the guided tours offered to Polish schoolchildren. These help us identify the pedagogical mission of the institution. What was most important for children to learn from their visit? Before the tour, pupils were asked three questions: who created the camp and when, how many victims, and who liberated the camp and when. After the tour, they were to be able to answer additional questions regarding the name of the camp, the date of its establishment, the name of the first commandant, the date of the first transport of Poles, the number of victims, and the names of the nation-states whence those victims came. The young visitors were also to know which groups were sentenced to be exterminated (answer: Jews, Gypsies, and Slavs/Poles), and to have learned

15. "Katyń" has come to stand for a series of executions of Poles by the Soviets. Approximately 4,500 Polish officers were killed in the Katyń forest, near Kozielsk; another 4,000 in Starobielsk; and approximately 7,000 in Ostashkow. The NKVD was the predecessor of the KGB.

about the Resistance Movement (Ruch Oporu) and its leaders. Finally, the museum was interested in knowing which exhibits made the greatest impressions on them, where they left flowers, and whether they wanted to visit again.[16]

From the questionnaires distributed to school groups before and after the three-hour tour, we learn what the main pedagogical goals were. These conform to the narrative I present above, with its emphasis on the martyrdom of Poles "and other groups," the resistance to the Nazis in the camp and to Fascism more generally in Poland, and the salvational liberation by the Soviets.

We also learn much from essays submitted to a contest organized in 1970 by the museum on the occasion of the twenty-fifth anniversary of the liberation of Auschwitz, with the theme "My reflections after the visit of the extermination camp in Oświęcim." In addition to emphasizing the struggle against Fascism and the liberation of the camp by the Soviets, several contestants' entries identify Poles as the camp's main victims. Here are representative passages from two students:

> "Why"? We Poles, a nation destined to biological extermination, to complete disappearance and in the best-case scenario to the function of slaves, know the answer to this question. We, who to this day are healing bloody wounds and remember the days of national martyrdom, days of contempt and death, know that Germans were taken by an obsession of grandeur that had tragic effects.
>
> Concentration camps, also known as "death factories" or extermination camps, were the main tool in the insane and criminal program of the Hitlerites for the "liquidation" of entire nations, in the first place the Polish nation, so that the rule of the German Reich would extend on the lands inhabited by these nations.[17]

Whether the students "truly" viewed the camp and its history in this way is perhaps impossible to say. What those essays nevertheless do tell us is what the students thought the museum, which organized the contest, and

16. From an undated and unpublished report prepared by curator Jadwiga Bezwińska, "Stan wiedzy młodzieży szkolnej o obozach koncentracyjnych na podstawie badań prowadzonych przez Państwowe Muzeum w Oświęcimiu," Referaty/Bezwińska/214, inventory no. 158004, Dział dokumentacji archiwalnej Państwowego Muzeum Auschwitz-Birkenau w Oświęcimiu.

17. Both extracts are from essays found in the Auschwitz-Birkenau State Museum's archives, call number 1013a, inventory no. 156621, Dział dokumentacji archiwalnej Państwowego Muzeum Auschwitz-Birkenau w Oświęcimiu.

their schoolteachers, who encouraged their participation, wanted to hear. These two types of documents—the questionnaire and the contest essays—therefore provide us with the narrative through which the museum was socializing visitors, in this case children. As we shall see, the museum has revised its narrative in recent years. It has dropped the Socialist rhetoric and, most important, now stresses that Jews constituted 90 percent of the camp's victims. For Poles, however, who for three generations were socialized to the implied "fact" that they had constituted the majority of prisoners and victims of the camp, this revision of history is not easily or unquestioningly accepted.

"Oświęcim" as Roman Catholic Symbol

To recapitulate so far: "Oświęcim's" first layer of meaning is related to Poles' historical experience at the camp during World War II; the second, to the Socialist narrative built on the historical one. The third layer, probably the most counterintuitive and controversial for non-Polish audiences, is that of "Oświęcim's" Roman Catholicism, to which I now turn.

Members of the Catholic Church's clergy and religious orders were among the camp's first victims, and two were later canonized. Father Maksymilian Maria Kolbe gave his life in exchange for that of a fellow (Polish Catholic) prisoner. He died in the so-called Block of Death, where his cell has been transformed into a shrine (figs. 20, 21). Edith Stein, Sister Teresia Benedicta of the Cross, was a German Jew from Breslau (now Wrocław). A student of Edmund Husserl, she converted to Catholicism, joined the Carmelite order, and died in one of Birkenau's gas chambers. Saint Maksymilian Kolbe and Saint Benedicta of the Cross are both sources of tensions between Catholics and Jews. The canonization of Father Kolbe is controversial because before the war he was editor of *Mały Dziennik*, a daily with strongly anti-Semitic content, and also because his martyrdom at Auschwitz offers a narrative of the camp's history that goes against that of the Shoah.[18] Edith Stein's sainthood was contested (by Jews) because of her Jewishness. While she died in the camp as a Jew in accordance with Nazi racial laws, Catholics understand her death as a religious sacrifice and revere her as a Catholic martyr.

The Roman Catholic identity of the camp was grafted onto the previous layers of meaning of "Oświęcim" in the 1980s, with the pope's Mass at

18. Thanks to Jonathan Huener for pointing out this last element of controversy to me in a personal communication.

Figure 20 Starvation cell in Block 11, commonly called the Block of Death, where Maksymilian Kolbe died. The cell has been transformed into a shrine commemorating the saint. The tall candle was brought there by John Paul II, and fresh flowers are commonly left in the cell through the iron grid. From a postcard sold at the Auschwitz-Birkenau State Museum's gift shops.

Birkenau in 1979 and the canonization of the martyrs Edith Stein and Maksymilian Kolbe.[19] As Jonathan Huener shows in his excellent study of commemorations at Auschwitz in Communist Poland (2003, 185–225), the Mass at Birkenau—celebrated by John Paul II during his first visit to his homeland as pontiff—was a turning point in the postwar history of Auschwitz. The papal pilgrimage "to Poland's 'Golgotha' represented the triumph of Polish vernacular notions of Auschwitz and its role in postwar Polish culture" (ibid., 186–87). While that Mass affirmed and legitimated the Polish-narrative idiom of "Oświęcim," it also extended it by proclaiming the universal lessons of "Auschwitz." This move from the national to the universal, however, was cast in a Christian framework that ultimately opened the way for a national-*Catholic* reframing of the site and symbol, which in turn set the

19. Father Kolbe was beatified as confessor by Pope Paul VI in 1970, and canonized as martyr by John Paul II in 1981. Edith Stein was beatified on May 1, 1987, in Cologne during John Paul II's pilgrimage to Germany, and canonized on October 11, 1998. On October 1, 1999, she became patron saint of Europe, a title she shares with Saints Birgitta of Sweden and Catherine of Sienna. (These three female saints were added to complement Saints Cyril, Methodius, and Benedict, Europe's male patron saints.)

Figure 21 Altar consecrated to Saint Maksymilian Kolbe at the sanctuary of Jasna Góra in Częstochowa. The altar is prominently placed in a room adjacent to where the icon of the Black Madonna is adored. In the painting, Kolbe wears his prisoner's uniform. A banner tells the story of Polish martyrdom during the Second World War, listing along a strand of barbed wire the names of the numerous camps where Poles were interned. That martyrdom is personified by the use of prisoners' personal identification numbers, with the saint's given the place of honor at the center of the banner. Note that Auschwitz is referred to as Oświęcim. The red triangle with the letter *P* stands for political prisoners, as per Auschwitz's classification system. Photo: Geneviève Zubrzycki.

stage for some of the most significant controversies surrounding the former camp in the 1980s and 1990s.

The commemoration of Edith Stein and Maksymilian Kolbe provided the initial impetus for the planning of a convent in the immediate vicinity of Auschwitz. In their first letter to Poland's Department of Religious Affairs in January 1983, the Poznań Carmelites wrote,

> Edyta Stein, a sister of our order, and Father Maksymilian Maria Kolbe, our great compatriot, were killed in the Oświęcim camp. We greatly desire to pray at that very place for peace on earth, so that the hatred and crimes of man against man shall never be repeated, as Sisters of our Order have been doing in Dachau since many years. (In Raina 1991, 8)

After the government's initial denial of the Carmelites' request, a new missive was sent by the Carmelite provincial. This time, however, the order's reasons for soliciting the state's permission to establish a new convent by the former camp were revised. Instead of casting the two martyrs as the basis for the request, the provincial more politically emphasized the significance of the convent for Poland's *raison d'état*: using the Socialist discourse of Poland's fight against Fascism, he argued that the presence of the convent at that site would highlight the martyrdom of (Socialist) Poles at the hands of (capitalist) Fascists:

> What is at stake, here, is not the least the mere foundation of another religious establishment. This cloister will have the significance of a great symbol. The crimes committed *against Poles and the representatives of many other nations* at this place are so great that they demand ceaseless expiation. I want to emphasize that a cloister with a similar idea has been in existence for a dozen years or so in the Federal Republic of Germany, where German Carmelites are praying and expiating just next to the former concentration camp in Dachau near Munich. The presence of such cloisters is a *reminder for public opinion of the pain inflicted on our nation by Fascism*. It is therefore not a question of founding a monastic house just anywhere on the territory of the town of Oświęcim, but rather at this specific site and in this specific building on Finder Street, not far from the Wall of Death. (Raina 1991, 9; my emphasis)

If the presence of the Carmelite convent in the proximity of the site was for many Poles (and even for some Polish Jews) "natural" because it reflected the Catholicity of the site, it was, for the very same reason, objectionable for most (non-Polish) Jews.[20] In the Polish imagination, however, the camp's grounds were ultimately fused into a coherent and potent whole, conjoining the highly emotional memory of the wartime "Oświęcim," the ideological-Socialist narrative given to it in the People's Republic of Poland, with the religious significance of Roman Catholic shrines.

"Oświęcim" and Polish Sovereignty in the Post-Communist Period

The fourth and last layer of meaning of "Oświęcim" concerns its status in post-Communist Poland. With the conflict over the Carmelite convent and its escalation in the early 1990s just before its relocation, "Oświęcim" has

20. For an account of Polish Jews' and non-Polish Jews' different reactions to the Carmelite convent, see Krajewski (1997, 228–31).

come to stand, in the last fifteen years or so, as a symbol of Polish autonomy and sovereignty over what Poles regard as their main site of martyrdom. The national significance of the symbol was heightened with attempts at what have been understood by many Poles as the "de-Polonizing" of the site and the memory of Polish suffering, perceived as a threat to the Polish state's sovereignty. The idea of "Oświęcim" being "de-Polonized" has been expressed or reported to me by several informants during fieldwork interviews or participant observation. The debates surrounding the relocation of the Carmelite nuns, the attempts at removing the papal cross, the revision of the camp's history, and the proposal for the extraterritoriality of the site in order to detach Auschwitz and Birkenau from the Polish nation-state have all coincided to reinforce nationalist sentiments regarding the camp, its history, and its future, and to refuse the de-Polonization of this important site and symbol of the Polish nation.

Before moving on to the current reconfiguration of "Oświęcim," it is necessary to place the Polish symbolization of Auschwitz and its commemoration of the Holocaust (or lack thereof) within a wider comparative framework. James E. Young (1993) has shown, through an incisive comparative study of Holocaust memorials in Germany, Poland, Israel, and the United States, that the memorialization of the Holocaust is embedded in each country's own national memory, meanings, and (changing) national projects. While Poland's commemoration of the Holocaust is effected within the core narrative of Polish martyrdom, Young showed that in Israel, Holocaust memorialization and commemorations are entrenched in the building of the state; in the United States, the Holocaust is framed within specifically American ideals and experiences, such as liberty, pluralism, and immigration. The Polonization of the Holocaust, while clearly problematic, should therefore not be seen as a unique phenomenon.

De-Polonizing "Oświęcim" by Judaizing Auschwitz

Since de-Polonization is a notion that frequently arises in discussions of the War of the Crosses, Polish-Jewish relations, and recent trends at the Auschwitz-Birkenau State Museum, it is important to investigate it further. De-Polonization is often polemically presented as being related to the "Judaization" of the site and its memory. Those who use these notions deny the right of Jews to control the memory of the former concentration camp, and insist that the museum, which holds the legitimate monopoly on knowledge about the site, has gone too far in its revision of history.[21] The term de-Polonization is also used to refer to Jewish protests against Christian forms of commemoration and to an entire set of restrictions applied to the former camp and its immediate (and not-so-immediate) surroundings. De-Polonization, according to those who use the term, basically stands for the attempt by Jews to manage and control the physical site, and for the exclusive (and illegitimate) control of the symbol by them.

This is, to take one example, the argument of Father Waldemar Chrostowski, former codirector of the Committee on Christian-Jewish Dialogue. According to Father Chrostowski, dialogue between Poles and Jews is impossible, since dialogue for the latter means that Poles must "sit tight, listen and comply" with whatever demands Jews make. The de-Polonization of the former camp (and consequently the downgrading of "Oświęcim" as a symbol) is the result of an unequal, unilateral imposition of views, in which Jews appropriate Auschwitz as their own exclusive site of martyrdom, dictating a series of conditions to be met by the Polish side. The priest-professor's comments were met with warm applause by a room full of teachers during a three-day workshop, "Totalitarianism, Nazism, Holocaust," held at the museum in 2001. Many students left the room talking among themselves about how refreshing it was, for a change, to have someone acknowledge the "Polish point of view" and speak "more objectively" than the program's numerous "philo-Semitic lecturers."[22]

21. This monopoly is held not only in the field of research, but also in the communication of that knowledge. While individuals may visit the former camp on their own, the Auschwitz-Birkenau State Museum has a strict policy regarding groups. Every group must be accompanied by a licensed guide in order to enter the museum's grounds, as a means of controlling the information given to the visitors and the way it is disseminated, as well as to monitor the behavior of the visitors and ensure their proper decorum (no eating, drinking, or smoking on the entire terrain of the former camp; no talking at specific sites such as the wall of death, the urn of ashes, and so forth). When groups arrive at the museum with their own guide (from a tourism agency from Cracow or Warsaw, for example), a licensed museum guide must be hired to "supervise" the discourse of the private guide. The only case in which this rule is not enforced is for groups of Jewish visitors-pilgrims, who come with their own guides and combine the visit with the reading of testimonies and prayers. I was told by a member of the museum administration, "What can we do? We can't force them to listen to us. And this is, after all, a cemetery, a memorial site. You can't monitor the way people commemorate their dead."

22. Father Chrostowski has published widely on the subject (1999, 2001), and was at the center of a controversy in 1997 about anti-Semitism in the Roman Catholic Church. In a groundbreaking op-ed article in *Tygodnik Powszechny* entitled "Black Is Black" ("Czarne jest czarne," November 16, 1997), Stanisław Musiał, a Jesuit priest, openly criticized the church hierarchy for tolerating anti-Semitism within its ranks, taking as his point of departure the episcopate's soft stance toward Father Henryk Jankowski, the renowned Solidarity chaplain who has since

The Museum's Narrative Revision

What some Poles interpret as de-Polonization has been brought about by a set of related and concurrent processes. First and foremost, although the museum's main exhibit has remained basically the same since 1955, when it was initially designed, some revisions were introduced after the fall of Communism. Most of these changes concerned the numbers and identities of Auschwitz victims. During the Communist period, the total number of victims at the camp had been inflated to four million. Moreover, it had been implied that Polish citizens constituted the largest group of prisoners and victims there. Now the total number of victims is estimated to be 1.1 million to 1.5 million, 90 percent of whom were Jews from all over Europe. As for the Polish population, it is now established that approximately 375,000 Polish Jews and 150,000 gentile Poles had been deported to Auschwitz. Of those prisoners, an estimated 80 percent of Jews and 50 percent of gentile Poles were killed. Taken together, almost 400,000 Polish citizens perished at Auschwitz. (Hungary's losses are even greater: 438,000 Hungarian Jews were killed in the Birkenau gas chambers [Piper 1992].) Overall, during World War II Poland lost about six million citizens (approximately 17 percent of its pre–World War II population): 3.2 million Jews (almost the totality of its Jewish population) and nearly three million "ethnic," or non-Jewish, Poles.[23] The number of Polish citizens who perished during World War II (six million) and the number of European Jews killed during that period (six million) appear to

---

become notorious for his stridently anti-Semitic sermons and his controversial Easter Sepulchers. A few weeks after the publication of Father Musiał's article, Father Chrostowski published a rebuttal, "A Rainbow Painted in Black" ("Tęcza na czarno," *Tygodnik Powszechny*, January 11, 1998). Musiał's response to Chrostowski's rebuttal, "The Sin of Anti-Semitism," was published on the same page as Chrostowski's piece, along with a short endorsement of Musiał's position by Stanisław Krajewski, the cochairperson—together with Chrostowski—of the Committee on Christian-Jewish Dialogue. The tenor of Father Chrostowski's article prompted a public conflict with the Jewish community, and Chrostowski shortly thereafter resigned from the committee (he was later replaced by Father Michał Czajkowski, an "open" Roman Catholic). Since then, Chrostowski, a traditional-conservative Catholic close to Cardinal Glemp, has been active in denouncing "Jewish excesses" and "Jewish anti-Polonism," from the "Judaization of Auschwitz" to the (American) Jewish attempt to prevent Mel Gibson's *The Passion of the Christ* from being adequately promoted in Poland. A translation of Musiał's "Czarne jest czarne" appears in *Polin: Studies in Polish Jewry* 13 (2000), pp. 303–9, and an account and discussion of the debate can be found in Oppenheim (1999). After contacting him repeatedly for an interview, Father Chrostowski told me at a public lecture that he refused to meet with me because he "did not trust 'American milieus'" (April 21, 2001).

23. In 1939, there were approximately 3,350,000 Jews in Poland. Only 50,000 remained in 1945 (the statistics for 1939 refer to prewar frontiers, and those of 1945 to postwar borders) (Hilberg 2003, 3:1128).

place Poles and Jews on an equal plane of losses and suffering—adding to the competitiveness of Poles with Jews over who holds the "monopoly" on suffering, a competitiveness heightened by the significant place of martyrdom as a root paradigm in the histories and identities of both Poles and Jews.

The distinction between "Poles" and "Jews" may seem arbitrary to sociologists, and may even appear to participate in the overall reification of groups as coherent, bounded wholes, a sacrilege in the discipline. Moreover, how can one classify and separate Polish Jews from ethnic Poles other than by using the criteria used by the Nazis? These numbers can only reflect that racist system, but avoiding it has posed even worse consequences, as I discussed earlier. Iwona Irwin-Zarecka points out that this conflation of ethnic Poles and Polish Jews does even more than simply boosting the numbers of Polish victims and legitimating the Polish narrative of martyrdom. It creates a distorted vision of the past:

> The figure of "six million Poles" . . . grants the dead Jew the status of a Pole, in a post-mortem acceptance of the Jews' membership in the Polish family. And this represents a reading of the past which renders that past unrecognizable. The Jew not only appears to be mourned on a par with others—which he was not—he also appears to have always belonged, which he did not. The destruction of the Jewish community, when reclaimed as the loss of Polish lives, acquires a sense of trauma which it did not have, at least for the majority. And the sharing in suffering, together with assigning all the blame to the Nazis, helps eliminate questions about the Poles' action and inaction towards the Jews. (1989b, 147)

The question of numbers is therefore much more salient than as mere historical record; it is meaningful in the creation of narratives and ultimately of identities.

In addition to revising the number of victims, the Auschwitz-Birkenau State Museum also revised its narrative. Although Auschwitz I remains the focus of guided tours and hosts the great majority of exhibits (because of its infrastructure), the museum and its guides now place more emphasis than before on Birkenau (Auschwitz II), where most of the killing was conducted, and where most victims were Jewish (as opposed to Auschwitz I, where most were ethnic Poles).[24] Guides were retrained to emphasize the Jewish

24. Despite these improvements, Auschwitz I undeniably remains the locus of the Auschwitz-Birkenau State Museum. Birkenau is presented as an "option" rather than as an integral part of the

identity of the majority of Auschwitz-Birkenau's victims and the uniqueness of the Holocaust, and various explanatory inscriptions were added throughout the museum to underscore the role of the camp in carrying out the Final Solution.[25] Perhaps not surprisingly, however, I noticed in the several tours I took with different guides that the younger generation of guides, trained in the 1990s, has integrated this improved narrative line more easily than their older counterparts, who often fall back into the Socialist narrative of the "martyrdom of Poles and other nations." This is significant, because Polish and foreign groups may be exposed to slightly different narratives during their guided visits, as newly trained guides are more likely than their older colleagues to emphasize the Jewish fact of Auschwitz, and as most foreign-language tours are conducted by younger cohorts of guides. This is so because guides who give tours in a foreign language are paid twice as much per visit as those who give their tours in Polish; the youngest generation of guides has therefore specialized in Western languages to accommodate the needs of a new flow of visitors since 1989. Older cohorts, however, who had specialized in the languages of the former Eastern Bloc countries, now find these linguistic skills largely unused, and presently give the majority of the Polish-language tours. Although this is anecdotal evidence, it has potential consequences for Polish visitors, especially schoolchildren, who may continue to be socialized into the older narrative until the older generation of guides retires and the entire corps is constituted by individuals trained after the fall of Communism.

When confronted by the new narrative line of the museum, Poles are often stunned, as was related to me by members of various cohorts brought up under Communism. One member of the museum's administration related the following to me:

> When I started working here in 1991 I started as a guide, and often when we stand by the urn, you know, the exhibit, and I give the number of victims there, often people were indignant: "How's that, 90 percent

visit. After a three-hour-long and difficult visit of Auschwitz I, the guide typically gives visitors a "break" and then asks them whether they wish to continue to Birkenau. In the high season (May–October), a free shuttle transports visitors to the other camp every thirty minutes; in the winter months, visitors must either walk or hire a cab for themselves and their guide to get to Birkenau.

25. From an assortment of unpublished seminar syllabi for the continuing education of the Auschwitz-Birkenau State Museum guides, and from an unpublished document prepared by Mirosław Obstarczyk in 1999 that gives specific instructions to guides on how to conduct visits. I'm grateful to Mr. Obstarczyk for making this document available to me.

> of victims were Jews! What about Poles? What? 70,000? What are you talking about?! What 70,000?!" And I had to explain to that person. . . . I had to explain, "Well, Sir, please imagine what it means, 70,000 people. It's a town, and not so small at that!" Poles felt we were taking away their holiness. (Interview, April 12, 2001)

The revision of numbers in the 1990s accomplished two things: it rectified the total number of victims away from the inflated four million (most of whom, as we have seen earlier, were implied to have been ethnic Poles) to a more accurate 1.1 million to 1.5 million; and it established the identity of the victims (most of whom, it is now clearly stated, were Jewish). The number of Polish deaths, now estimated at 70,000–75,000, is therefore shockingly low for Poles who were socialized into a narrative of millions.

This revision was symbolically enacted in the erasure of the commemorative plaques (in several languages) at the Birkenau Memorial, which until 1990 indicated that "four million people suffered and died here at the hands of the Nazi murderers between the years 1940 and 1945." The plaques were reinscribed three years later to reflect the revised numbers and the predominant identity of the victims: "For ever let this place be a cry of despair and a warning to humanity where the Nazis murdered about one and a half million men, women, and children, mainly Jews from various countries of Europe." It took that long for all members of the Auschwitz Council, composed of Jews from Israel, Poland, and other Western countries, as well of Polish intellectuals and government officials, to agree on the text of the new plaques, attesting to the weight given them. One problem, aside from the text itself, was to ensure the uniformity in the translation of the Polish original into more than twenty languages (interview with Krystyna Oleksy, March 19, 2001).[26]

Although the narrative of the museum was changed, the exhibit itself remains largely the same thus far, for lack of financial resources and ample disagreements over what, precisely, should replace it. The museum intends to design a new general exhibit, but to this date there is neither a definitive new plan nor concrete arrangements or schedules in place to realize it.[27]

26. The Auschwitz Council is since 2000 the "International Auschwitz Council." For a description of its activities, documents, and a list of its current members, visit: http://www.auschwitz.gov.pl/. See Webber (1993) and Young (1993, 141–43, 152–54) for a description and analysis of the process of erasure and reinscription of the memorial plaques.

27. Interviews with Teresa Zbrzeska, head of the Exhibitions Section (April 18, 2001, and May 17, 2004). In addition to the general exhibit, some blocks host "national exhibits" that are not included on the regular tour circuit and that were designed long ago by committees from specific

Most improvements involve the addition of informational panels along the former camp's alleys. While these may seem to be purely cosmetic or practical, they reflect the narrative shift described above, and should therefore be seen as improvement not only in the form of the message's dissemination, but also in its content.

Fighting the Conflation of Auschwitz and Oświęcim

In another symbolic indication of a shifting ideological climate, the museum changed its official name in 1998 from State Museum Oświęcim-Brzezinka to State Museum Auschwitz-Birkenau in Oświęcim. The rationale behind this modification, I was told by members of the museum administration, was twofold: first, the appellation should reflect the historical record, that is, the original German designation of the two camps. Second, reestablishing their "Germanness"—via the museum's renaming—would dissociate the towns of Oświęcim and Brzezinka, in which the camps were established and where the museum now lies, from the former camps themselves. In addition to this official name change, guides were formally instructed to refer to the camps in their original, German-language designations.[28] The change was made in a conscious effort toward "setting the record straight" and shaping world opinion: by incorporating the German-language place-names

nation-states: Poland, France, Hungary, etc. (There is also a "Jewish Block," whose presence amidst other national blocks implies—in a way analogous to the above-cited enumeration of all the groups victimized at Auschwitz—that Jews were just *one* of many national groups who were imprisoned and killed at Auschwitz.) Until very recently, all national exhibits from the Eastern Bloc as well as some from western Europe (such as France) presented strong Socialist narratives of resistance to Fascism or even straightforward histories of nation-states' respective Communist parties. After the fall of Communism and before their recent narrative revision and redesign, these exhibits were completely obsolete. "Auschwitz" is such a potent symbol that individual countries had refused to give them up despite the expressed desire of the Auschwitz-Birkenau State Museum to close the exhibits down (interviews with Krystyna Oleksy, March 19, 2001, and with Teresa Zbrzeska, April 18, 2001). Some of them have now been completely redesigned (e.g., Czech Republic, Slovakia, Hungary), and in order to better represent the extermination of the Roma, a national exhibit has been created specifically for this group. Poland has kept its national exhibit in Block 15, "The Fight and Martyrdom of the Polish Nation 1939–1945," but has since the fall of Communism added inscriptions to what was mostly a visual exhibit to better present the Polish narrative of "Oświęcim." I return to this case later in this chapter.

28. It was also stressed, in the visit synopsis distributed to the guides in 1999, that they must explain to visitors (especially to Polish ones, who tend to use the Polish names) why this semantic distinction is important: "The goal is to avoid the identification of the town, with its 800-year-old history and as part of Polish culture and tradition . . . with the camp created on its territory by the SS" (p. 3). Ironically, the title of this document used the very terms it instructed its guides not to use: "Synopsis of Tours on the Terrain and Permanent Exhibit of the State Museum *Oświęcim-Brzezinka*" (Obstarczyk 1999; my emphasis).

into the museum name, the curators wanted to counteract the common tendency, especially in the United States, to use the misnomer of *Polish camps* when referring to Nazi camps in today's Poland. This issue returned to the public front on the occasion of the sixtieth anniversary of Auschwitz's liberation on January 27, 2005. The international attention the commemoration received highlighted the need for unambiguous clarifications. David A. Harris, executive director of the American Jewish Committee, issued a statement three days after the event in which he condemned the frequent use of the expression "Polish camps":

> The American Jewish Committee . . . would . . . like to remind those who are either unaware of the facts or careless in their choice of words, as has been the case with some media outlets, that Auschwitz-Birkenau and the other death camps, including Belzec, Chelmno, Majdanek, Sobibor and Treblinka, were conceived, built and operated by Nazi Germany and its allies. The camps were located in German-occupied Poland, the European country with by far the largest Jewish population, but they were most emphatically not "Polish camps." This is not a mere semantic matter. Historical integrity and accuracy hang in the balance. . . . It should also never be forgotten that, in addition to Polish Jews, who were targeted for total annihilation by the Nazi Final Solution, other Poles . . . were also seized by the Nazis and incarcerated in concentration camps. Any misrepresentation of Poland's role in the Second World War, whether intentional or accidental, would be most regrettable and therefore should not be left unchallenged. (January 30, 2005)[29]

"These were not *Polish* camps," a member of the museum administration told me before this latest wave of confusion, "but *Nazi* camps where thousands of Poles were killed. This *must* be made clear" (interview with Andrzej Kacorzyk, March 30, 2001). While the use of the term *Polish camps* suggests Poles' central role in the Holocaust, for Poles the fact that "the

29. Press release available on the American Jewish Committee's Web site, http://www.ajc.org/InTheMedia/PressReleases.asp?did=1499. The daily *Rzeczpospolita* also initiated a campaign against the term *Polish camps*, which was supported by David Peleg, the Israeli ambassador to Poland. It has collected several thousand signatures. Peleg insisted in an open letter published in the daily that Jews and Israelis would never accept the concept of "Polish concentration camps" (*Rzeczpospolita*, February 3, 2005). The Polish Ministry of Foreign Affairs keeps careful track of all references to "Polish camps" in the international news media on a special page of its Web site, where it posts letters condemning the use of the formulation and includes links to the *Rzeczpospolita* action, "Against Polish Camps." See http://www.msz.gov.pl.

death camps were located on Polish soil suggests... not their national complicity, but their ultimate violation" (Young 1993, 123). The implication of *Polish camps* is thus doubly offensive to them: not only does it diminish the suffering resulting from their country's having served as the primary site of the war, it accuses them of something that was conducted by their occupant and tormentor.

Many Poles also oppose the designation "Nazi camps in *Poland*," because in the case of Auschwitz, the camp was in a territory directly annexed to the Reich, whereas the other ones were in *occupied* Poland. Since Poland was not a sovereign state and had no say as to where Germans established the death camps, it is, according to many, unfair even to say that these were Nazi camps "in Poland," especially since it could imply that Poles were accomplices in the crimes. The Polish delegation to the EU therefore strongly protested when the European Parliament decided to issue a special resolution about the Holocaust on the sixtieth anniversary of Auschwitz's liberation. The first version of the text referred to Auschwitz as a "death camp in Poland," a formulation that was harshly criticized by Poles and immediately stricken from the text.

The museum's administration is also very keen on distinguishing Auschwitz, the former camp and current museum, from Oświęcim, the town in which it is located and which has much deeper roots than the Second World War:

> Oświęcim, it is 800 years of history; it is the year 1177, the first reference to it in documents. Already in 1312, the town had its German equivalent, "Auschwitzen," no? It attests to the rank of that town. There is no reason to link the Oświęcim principality's history, 800 years of age, its land, culture, and tradition, with what Germans created here. (Interview with Mirosław Obstarczyk, April 12, 2001)

As another museum employee emphasized to me in an interview, it is indeed crucial for the museum to distinguish Auschwitz the death camp from Oświęcim the town, where ordinary people go about their everyday lives:

> This is very important. After the war, a substantial town grew here; almost fifty thousand people, and these people don't live in Auschwitz, but in Oświęcim. We should not associate them with this place; they have their own life, this is their world, their workplaces, their stores, their industries, their recreational sites; this is where their children go to school. We have to separate, radically separate. The camp is Auschwitz-Birkenau,

> the town is Oświęcim. In order not to erase [Oświęcim's] entire history, let's keep all of this somewhere on the side. Here is the camp. (Interview with Andrzej Kacorzyk, March 30, 2001)

The need to distinguish the town from Auschwitz has been ardently felt in the last decade or so, after locals were engulfed in loud international controversies such as those of the Carmelite convent and the War of the Crosses, along with scandals that were often misrepresented in the foreign news media—such as the planned opening of a supermarket and the existence of a discotheque "in Auschwitz."[30]

The town of Oświęcim and its inhabitants must endure the legacy left to them by the Nazis. The Auschwitz-Birkenau State Museum, far from being a source of revenue for the town, is perhaps better described as a liability. Although the museum attracts tourists, the town enjoys very little of what significant tourist sites and pilgrimage centers usually bring with them. Virtually no cottage industry is worth developing (or allowed to develop) around the museum. Aside from books, videotapes, maps, and grim postcards, there are no "appropriate" souvenirs to sell at Auschwitz. And even if the town or some entrepreneur decided to build a hotel and restaurants for tourists-pilgrims, few would elect to spend the night in the shadow of a death camp.[31]

30. The opening of the supermarket was planned in a lot across the street from the Auschwitz-Birkenau State Museum's parking lot in Oświęcim. Commercial buildings already existed in that area, and the supermarket was to be opened in a building that was to be renovated and expanded. The discotheque was opened in August 2000 a few kilometers from the former camp, close to the International Youth Meeting Center in Oświęcim. It was housed in what was during the war a tannery that used forced labor. After 1942, the basement of that building was used to search victims' suitcases and shoes for valuables. Victims' hair was also sorted there (http://www.auschwitz.org.pl/html/pl/aktualnosci/dyskoteka_historia.html#6). For short analyses of several controversies associated with Auschwitz from the perspective of a Polish Jew, see Krajewski (1997, 228–36). In a later section, I come back to the implications such a conflation between Oświęcim the town and Auschwitz the camp entails for the inhabitants of the small town.

31. There are, of course, exceptions to this tendency to avoid longer stays in Oświęcim. There are now three important institutions in Oświęcim that cater to pilgrims and educational groups by offering various workshops and promoting Polish-Jewish-German dialogue: The International Youth Meeting Center in Oświęcim (http://www.mdsm.pl), the Centre for Dialogue and Prayer in Auschwitz (http://www.centrum-dialogu.oswiecim.pl), and the Auschwitz Jewish Center (http://208.184.21.217/welcome.asp?page=1). (Despite the names of the last two, the centers are all located off-museum, in the town of Oświęcim.) These institutions play an important part in the movement to revise the history of Auschwitz away from its Socialist and nationalist narratives by emphasizing the Holocaust and offering venues to discuss its religious and ethical implications. They are also important in fostering dialogue among the main groups involved—Jews, Poles, and Germans—by giving youth from these different nations the opportunity to meet, discuss, and sometimes work together on communal projects. Finally, the Auschwitz Jewish Center offers a space for individual Jewish visitors to connect and recollect, and learn more about Oświęcim. It

Visitors typically rush back to Cracow, where they can wash away what often turns out to be a difficult visit, and spend money in the royal city's numerous cafes, pubs, and restaurants. Cracow hotels and tourist agencies have rapidly realized the extent of Auschwitz's potential and therefore developed that market, offering—and loudly advertising—packages that include visits at Auschwitz ("You will meet a former prisoner!") and *Schindler's List* tours with "optional lunch" in the old Jewish (and currently hip bohemian) neighborhood of Kazimierz, amidst the tours' usual itinerary of the Wawel royal castle, Wieliczka salt mines, and evenings of folk dances.[32]

Auschwitz, as historical monument, memorial site, and prime symbol of the Holocaust, presents a series of challenges for the town of Oświęcim. Although the museum does employ the local population, various proscriptions severely curtail the development of business in the proximity of the former camp. This was not problematic under Communism, when there was little private industry and commerce, and when Oświęcim was a relatively well-off town, with two large industries employing most of the population. With the fall of Communism and concurrent restructuring, however, unemployment has risen significantly, and the need for the development of alternative sources of employment is deeply felt. Large numbers have left Oświęcim in search of work, most of them youth who see no future in their hometown. Restrictions regarding what kinds of business can be conducted and where, in relation to the former camp, are thus seen as a serious impediment for economic development, especially since the former camp is at the heart of the industrial district. As Jacek Urbiński, a town councilman, pointed out to me:

> There is a lot of incertitude, and people are afraid; they don't know what to do. For example, there was talk, at one point, of a buffer zone between Auschwitz and Birkenau. Can you imagine? *Three* kilometers separate both camps! Even if these are only gossips or rumors, or ideas suggested by people who have no influence, it frightens the local population. People here feel like they have no say in what is going on in their own town. Warsaw can always step in and change the rules for whatever reason. Take

---

also provides the local population and other Polish visitors with important educational resources about the history and culture of Polish Jews before World War II.

32. This market is primarily aimed at non-Jewish individual tourists and groups. The vast majority of Jews who visit Poland do so within the framework of tour groups organized in their home countries and do not require the services described above. Survivors and their children, however, rarely join groups. For them, the visit is personal rather than communal (Kugelmass 1993, 402). On the cultural production of Kazimierz in Cracow, see Lehrer (2005).

> the supermarket. Its establishment was totally within the city codes. Then there was a scandal, the media blew this out of proportion, and the laws were changed. So there is no supermarket there. (Interview, April 4, 2001)

A clear tension exists between Warsaw and Oświęcim over local affairs, a tension palpable between the Auschwitz-Birkenau State Museum, under the jurisdiction of the Ministry of Culture, and the town.[33] The residents of Oświęcim live in what for many in the world is the symbol of the Holocaust, and see their daily activities restricted, not so much by the legacy of history, but by the *weight given to that history*. As the town councilman told me with a deep sigh, "Everything here is under a microscope. The world is constantly watching us." A prime example of the sort of news media coverage lamented by many locals is the scandal over a new discotheque that the international news media proclaimed to be "in Auschwitz."[34] The news of the disco's opening created a controversy worldwide. How could such an establishment be opened in one of the most notorious sites of the Holocaust? Mr. Urbiński, the town councilman, tried to clarify and explain the situation:

> Well, yes. People worked there [the disco building] during the war. But people worked everywhere [in Oświęcim]. For example, this road on which we were just driving . . . that straight road, well, it was built by the Germans [that is, by prisoners]. The road to the industry was built by prisoners, the industries were built by prisoners. . . . And these places were not even places of genocide, they were places of labor! In the tannery, two people perished. Now, if two people died in the tannery, and other people died while building this road, and still others died working in other industries . . . then what next? It was the war, and people inevitably died in several places. People died all over this town. This is Poland, after all. The war was fought here, so death is everywhere. But people now also live in this town, in this land. So the situation is tense.

These "scandals" partly result from the common misuse of the name Auschwitz to designate the town of Oświęcim, and from the indiscriminate use of the name Auschwitz in referring to the complex of camps and

33. On this tension and its impact on local politics, see the investigative report by Michał Olszewski in the Cracow supplement to *Gazeta Wyborcza*, May 21, 2004.

34. See note 30 above.

subcamps throughout the region. This leads to disturbing conclusions, such as reports of the opening of a supermarket and the existence of a discotheque "in Auschwitz." But such conclusions also stem from a different notion of "Auschwitz" the symbol and its spatial location. As we will see in greater depth in chapter 5, Poles clearly demarcate the physical site of Auschwitz I from its surroundings, Oświęcim, whereas for many Jews the containment of "Auschwitz," the symbolic site of the Shoah, within the physical space occupied by the former camp Auschwitz I and Auschwitz II-Birkenau is not appropriate. Since the entire area is filled with Jewish ashes, "Auschwitz" extends well beyond the physical walls of Auschwitz I; it spreads its sacredness into every corner of Oświęcim, which Poles in turn regard as an unfair imposition.

But if it is so important now for Poles to distinguish Oświęcim the Polish town from Auschwitz the Nazi camp, why was the name Oświęcim-Brzezinka used in the museum's official documents until recently? As noted at the beginning of the chapter, Poles from the beginning of the camp's existence referred to it by its Polish name. The original Polish designations Oświęcim and Brzezinka were also used in the museum's initial name as an attempt to combat the Germanization of a multitude of Polish sites that had occurred during the war, a practice that emphasized German domination and Polish subordination. Using the Polish names therefore underlined the sovereignty of the Socialist nation-state after the war. This "return" to the Polish place-names was effected at the same time as the Polonization of German cities that were annexed to Poland following its borders' shift to the west: Breslau and Stettin ceased to exist; Wrocław and Szczecin were the cities of the past, present, and future.

In view of the attempts to distinguish the town from the former camp, the museum's recent name change seems reasonable enough, and yet it is still quite rare to hear Poles refer to the site as Auschwitz. As a museum administrator pointed out to me, "When we are speaking of the camp, we should be using the name Auschwitz. But in the consciousness of Poles, Oświęcim is Oświęcim [and not Auschwitz], as you will find when you go even to the other end of Poland" (interview with Mirosław Obstarczyk, April 12, 2001). In the summer of 2004, members of the town council emphasized in a letter to the mayor the need to distinguish Oświęcim from Auschwitz in designations of streets and in names of organizations that refer to the Holocaust and its history rather than to the town per se:

> Given such a difficult past, the precise designation of historical facts... ha[s] fundamental significance. The adjective "Oświęcimski" has no

> relation to the camp. What did Oświęcim, that is, its inhabitants, do to the victims of KL Auschwitz? That is why it is difficult to still use the terms *Oświęcim victims* . . . or the *Oświęcim Council* to describe the international organ related to the Museum of the former KL Auschwitz-Birkenau. These changes must be made in the consciousness of the town's inhabitants, political activists, and in the shapers of public opinion [in Poland] and abroad, so that Auschwitz means something different from Oświęcim. So that outside the borders of [Poland] the town would be referred to as Oświęcim, and Auschwitz be used only to refer to the Museum. . . . If we do not do that, there will be more and more references like "Polish extermination camps," which work on the same principle as the "Oświęcim camp." (*Gazeta Wyborcza*, June 24, 2004)

There is, to be sure, the force of habit behind this insistence on referring to the site by its Polish name, especially in older cohorts of Poles. Only 9 percent of Poles use the German term, according to the results of an extensive survey conducted by Marek Kucia, a sociologist at Jagiellonian University in Cracow, while the name Oświęcim was used in reference to KL Auschwitz in almost all the spontaneous answers given by respondents (2005, 103–4). But there is also strong *ideological* resistance to shifting from one term to the other in certain right-wing milieus. This linguistic change is seen as the recognition and acceptance of the symbol's semantic shift from Polish martyrdom to Jewish Holocaust and universal evil. These right-wing groups therefore insist on calling the camp and the museum by its Polish designation. This reaction is especially surprising coming from the very organizations that incessantly insist on the victimization of Poles by Germans, yet it attests to the potency and value of "Oświęcim" as a symbol.

Shifting Clienteles and the "East-West" Inversion

Another significant element in the so-called de-Polonization of the site concerns tourism and visitors at the Auschwitz-Birkenau State Museum. Before 1989, most visitors to the museum were from the Eastern Bloc (see table 1), with Poles constituting the overwhelming majority (see table 2).

Auschwitz was an important Socialist pilgrimage site, and Eastern Bloc visitors conjoined duty with pleasure by procuring goods that may not have been available in their own countries. With the fall of Communism, however, the flow of tourists has been dramatically altered. Most foreign visitors are now from "the West"—the United States, Israel, and western and northern Europe, as the data in table 1 show.

Table 1. Foreign visitors to the Auschwitz-Birkenau State Museum, by country (selection), 1959–2003

Citizens	1959–90	(avg./year)	1991–2003	(avg./year)
Eastern Europe				
USSR	937,436	(30,240)	—	—
Russia	—	—	8,236	(634)
Ukraine	—	—	15,378	(1,183)
Belarus	—	—	2,007	(154)
Hungary	196,509	(6,339)	44,826	(3,448)
Bulgaria	117,963	(3,805)	1,375	(106)
Czechoslovakia	830,063	(26,776)	—	—
Czech Republic	—	—	40,627	(3,125)
Slovakia	—	—	29,997	(2,307)
East Germany	214,705	(6,926)	—	—
Western Europe/USA/Israel				
West Germany	249,911	(8,062)	—	—
Germany	—	—	471,902	(36,300)
France	197,595	(6,374)	243,335	(18,718)
Netherlands	44,046	(1,421)	116,983	(8,999)
Great Britain	52,254	(1,686)	242,118	(18,624)
Denmark	50,032	(1,614)	129,046	(9,927)
Norway	13,136	(424)	121,918	(9,378)
Sweden	33,472	(1,080)	96,011	(7,385)
Israel	23,496	(758)	198,438	(15,264)
USA	225,089	(7,271)	471,195	(36,246)

Source: Unpublished data, Auschwitz-Birkenau State Museum, Visitors' Service Section.
Note: Dashes indicate that a country did not exist in those given years.

Table 2. Visitors to the Auschwitz-Birkenau State Museum, 1946–2003

	Total no. visitors	Polish citizens	Foreigners	% Polish visitors
1946–50	923,045	881,533	41,512	95.5
1951–55	1,075,218	1,037,525	37,693	96.4
1956–60	1,132,132	1,010,195	121,937	89.2
1961–65	2,022,207	1,659,552	362,655	82.1
1966–70	2,839,092	2,273,027	566,065	80.1
1971–75	3,556,594	2,789,596	766,998	78.4
1976–80	3,373,462	2,429,350	944,112	72.0
1981–85	2,468,748	2,134,548	334,200	86.5
1986–90	2,935,200	1,882,050	1,053,150	64.1
1991–95	2,407,800	1,310,983	1,096,817	54.4
1996–00	2,448,032	1,415,100	1,032,932	57.8
2001–3[a]	1,322,455	513,053	809,402	38.8

Source: Unpublished data, Auschwitz-Birkenau State Museum, Visitors' Service Section.
[a]See note 37 in the text.

The East/West inversion is striking: for example, thirty-five times fewer Bulgarians have visited the museum on average per year since the fall of Communism; five times fewer Czechs and Slovaks have come to Auschwitz than Czechoslovaks; and half as many Hungarians. There are, however, three times more French visitors to the museum, five times more Americans, eleven times more citizens from Great Britain, and twenty times more Israeli visitors now than there had been on average for every year during the 1959–90 period.

This dramatic shift can be explained by two sets of factors. First, it has become much easier for Westerners to visit Poland since the fall of Communism. Most of these tourists no longer need visas to enter the country, a formerly complicated procedure involving receiving formal "invitations" and other formalities. In addition, the tourism infrastructure is much more developed now than it was before the end of Communism, with several flights a day to Warsaw and Cracow from all over Europe and North America, and comfortable hotels and restaurants for all tastes (a rare few now offering kosher meals)—all still relatively affordable to Western wallets compared with other destinations. For former Eastern Bloc groups, however, recent political and economic transformations decrease the likelihood of travel to Poland. For one, the cost of transportation has dramatically increased, and tours to Socialist shrines such as Auschwitz are no longer organized or subsidized by the government. Moreover, incentives for visiting other former Comecon countries have dwindled: why go to Poland for a vacation when one can go to Greece or even to Germany or England, with the possibility of earning some hard currency?

Most new, "Western" visitors come to Auschwitz to learn and teach about the Holocaust, not about martyrs of the resistance to Fascism or the Soviet heroes who liberated them. Many are even surprised to hear that the camp was initially established for Poles. Jews in particular now constitute an important group of visitors. Most come in organized groups, their presence often made visible by the identical white-and-blue jackets individual group members wear. They come to Auschwitz on pilgrimages and educational tours, the most important being the much-publicized March of the Living. This event is important for me to address next, not only because it is a striking example of the new kinds of visitors who come to Auschwitz since the fall of Communism. Just as important, the place Auschwitz occupies in the march's narrative and the vision of Poland that the event is built around clash with special intensity with the Polish understandings of "Oświęcim" and of World War II more broadly.

Jewish Tourism and Visions of Poland

Since 1988, on Yom HaShoah (Holocaust Remembrance Day) Jews from all over the world—mostly youth from the United States and Canada—gather at Auschwitz I and march the three kilometers to Birkenau (Auschwitz II). The two-week-long educational tour ends in Israel in time to observe Yom HaZikaron, Israel Memorial Day, and Yom Ha'Atzmaut, Israel Independence Day. Here is how the event is presented on the March of the Living official Web site (http://www.motl.org; all emphases are in the original text):

> You are about to embark upon an exciting experience, one that may just change your life. . . . You will be transported, along with 6,000 other teens from all over the world, back in time to one of the darkest chapters in human existence, to one of the most terrifying times in Jewish history. Then, before you can take a deep breath, you will travel to Israel, the Jewish Homeland, to celebrate with the people of Israel, Independence Day. *It will be a journey of darkness to light. It will be an experience of a lifetime.* You will be one of the chosen few who will walk in the footsteps of the 6,000,000. The march from Auschwitz to Birkenau will be along the same path which once two million of our people marched to their death in the gas chambers and crematoria of hell. You will visit the death camps of Treblinka and Majdanek. You will be witness to the remnants of the once vibrant Jewish population centers of Warsaw, Cracow and Lublin. You will see Israel as you have never seen it before, through the prism of your Polish experience. . . . We look forward to meeting all of you soon. Mark the date. Afterwards, you may never be the same! And you may like what you will become.

The event is told following the narrative script of the book of Exodus: from Poland to Israel, Egypt to the Promised Land, darkness to light, bondage to freedom. Poland is represented as the site where Jewish culture once flourished but was extinguished. In another section of the Web site, teens are exhorted to keep a diary of their feelings during the experience. In model examples presented there, "proper" perceptions of Poland are subtly prescribed to the pilgrimage candidates:

> Day 1. The departure date has finally arrived, after months of mental and physical preparation. We leave the comfort and security of our parents' arms, boarding the plane with excitement and anticipation. Although we realize these next two weeks will be no vacation, we really have no true

> concept as to the powerful, emotional experiences that await us. Day 2. We arrive at the Warsaw airport on a brisk, clear morning after a long, tiring flight. As we disembark, we are greeted by our first harsh, alien sight—a young, grim-faced, Polish soldier in uniform with rifle in hand—an eerie experience for many of us, particularly the Holocaust survivors traveling with us. . . . We receive long stares from construction men who stop their work on a modern glass building next door. It will be the first of many stares we receive during our week in Poland. We experience our first Polish meal—a dull lunch of a hard roll, raw radishes with the roots still attached and, yes—an Israeli chocolate wafer! Like the unwelcome stares, it will be one of many such unappetizing meals to follow, with the exception of the wafer, of course.

Poland here stands for the death camps, guarded by armed soldiers, with dry bread as the only food for its temporary prisoners. The Israeli wafer is the only comfort and promise of better days to come, when the students finally reach Israel: "Then Israel! Your emotions will skyrocket as you step foot in the Land of Israel. Some of you may kiss the ground as our ancestors have done for hundreds of generations. Some will laugh and others will cry."[35]

The March of the Living is not the only event that starts in Poland and ends in Israel. Jack Kugelmass points out that the symbolism of most organized visits of Jews to Poland is the same: the tours are structured around the themes of destruction and redemption, and almost all of them conclude their travel in Eastern Europe, with time allotted for a longer tour of Israel (1993, 404). According to him, what is unique about Jewish tourism in Poland is its "antiquarian" rather than "ethnographic" nature: Jewish "tourists" are interested in the dead rather than the living, and the experiences they remember tend to be "those that enhance an already negative opinion. Indeed, they are the experiences they expect to have in Poland, and because they confirm deeply held convictions, they are almost a desired part of the trip" (ibid., 411). Visiting Poland has now become what Kugelmass calls a "secular ritual" that confirms the identity of the participants as Jews (ibid., 419).

Such a narrative is problematic for some Polish Jews (that is, Jews living in Poland), since it rests on the idea that not only Poland but also the Jewish

35. For several other similar examples, see Kugelmass (1993); for a discussion of the Zionist narrative in the event, see Novick (2000, 16); and for an excellent analysis of the Israeli memory of the Shoah and the historical and symbolic creation of Yom HaShoah, Yom HaZikaron, and Yom Ha'Atzmaut, see Friedlander and Seligman (1994).

Diaspora living in Poland signifies death, or at least represents a serious anomaly that should remain hidden. Until recently, Polish Jews were not invited to participate in the March of the Living, according to Konstanty Gebert,

> because we are the living proof of that basic thesis's falseness. For me, what was unacceptable was that a thousand years of the Polish Jewry's wonderful history is reduced to five years of murder. I mean, the premise is that we've been here for all that time only for Hitler to come exterminate us, so that we could be remembered like that? Polish Jews from Venezuela were invited, no problem, but Polish Jews from Poland were not invited because we did not fit in the picture and spoiled the image. (Interview, May 25, 2004)[36]

Polish Jews have often assumed the role of mediators between Roman Catholic Poles and non-Polish, mostly American Jews. They have been instrumental, for example, in making the organizers of the March of the Living remove what was widely regarded by gentile and Jewish Poles alike as "shameful expressions of hatred toward Poles for their participation in the horrors of the war" from the brochures distributed to the march's participants (*Gazeta Wyborcza*, March 21, 1998). The contentious line was "You shall see the local habitants. You will hate them for the part they played, but you will pity them for their miserable living conditions" (Gebert, interview, May 25, 2004).

Polish Jews are also engaged in important "translation work": explaining to Christian Poles the Jewish prerogatives, and elucidating to non-Polish Jews what "Oświęcim" means for Poles. The Union of Jewish Communities, for example, stresses the significance of "Auschwitz" for Jews and the world while acknowledging "Oświęcim" as a Polish symbol—a position meant to appease agitated actors from both sides during the War of the Crosses:

> With pain and sorrow we observe the rising atmosphere of conflict around the cross at Auschwitz. The tumultuous conflicts are completely inappropriate in the proximity of this place. Only dignity and respect for all the victims of the camp are appropriate. We want to honor the memory of over one million Jews, whose ashes cover the said terrain. It became

36. For a full exposé of Gebert's view of the meaning and the implications of the March of the Living, as well as changes in its organization, see his article "Living in the Land of Ashes," published in *Gazeta Wyborcza* on April 4, 1998, under his pen name, Dawid Warszawski.

> for the world the symbol of the Shoah—the war genocide of Jews. We pay homage to Poles, Roma, and all the other victims of the camp. We are deeply conscious of the fact that Oświęcim is also the symbol of suffering of the entire occupied Poland. (*Gazeta Wyborcza*, March 28–29, 1998)

Like Gebert, Baruch Levi laments that Polish Jews are largely ignored by Jews living outside Poland:

> Too bad that the voices of Jews living here and now have not been sufficiently listened to and taken into account. . . . Not because Polish Jews have some kind of magical way to reach agreements, but knowing the situation in situ and the changes under way in the Catholic Church under the pontificate of John Paul II with regards to the relationship to Jews and Judaism, they could be used to bring closer the views of both sides. (*Słowo Żydowskie*, August 7, 1998)

While the symbolic March of the Living is incorporated into a Zionist narrative replicating the biblical story of the Exodus from Egypt, for Poles it marks the takeover of Auschwitz (the camp) and Oświęcim (the town). This "takeover" is reflected in the physical appropriation of the site and town by marchers proudly displaying their Jewish identity with Israeli flags and banners, and windbreakers in the colors of the flag (some with yellow stars on their sleeves), a white-and-blue human sea occupying the very space where more than one million Jews were sent to their death (see figs. 22, 23).

For the march's participants, this presence is not only a commemoration of the death of six million Jews, but also a powerful corrective to a (Polish) narrative that had downplayed the role played by Auschwitz in carrying out the Nazi Final Solution. Traffic between Auschwitz and Birkenau is blocked for the event, and stalled residents wait at intersections, watching the procession in silence, while marchers observe the observers, sometimes taking photographs of them. It is correct to say that the event creates a certain discomfort within the local population and between it and the marchers.

Resocializing Poles, Educating Non-Poles

The recent influx of Western visitors and visible events such as the March of the Living and the fiftieth and sixtieth anniversaries of Auschwitz's liberation (1995 and 2005) have brought Poles in greater contact with the Jewish narrative of "Auschwitz," and appear to many Poles of nationalist bent as the desecration of "Oświęcim," the Polish symbol. Significantly, however,

Figure 22 March of the Living, April 19, 2001. Groups assemble before the march at Auschwitz I. The march also is the occasion for social encounters. Here a group poses on the steps of Block 15 for a souvenir photo of the event. Photo: Geneviève Zubrzycki.

Poles remain the largest group of visitors at the Auschwitz-Birkenau State Museum, although their numbers, too, are in sharp decline since the fall of Communism (see table 2).[37] As many as half of adult Poles, according to national surveys conducted since 1995, have visited the museum in their lifetime (CBOS 1995, OBOP 2000, CBOS 2005).[38] Many of the Polish visitors are schoolchildren from the eighth grade and above, touring the museum as part of their Polish history class.[39] Since 1960, over six million Polish

37. The decline in visit frequency at the Auschwitz-Birkenau State Museum in the 2001–3 period is due to two main factors: aside from the fact that the data include only two years instead of the five used in table 2, the museum noticed a significant reduction in the number of visitors, especially in 2001. For foreign visitors, this is explained by the reduction in travel following the terrorist attacks of September 11, 2001, and for domestic visitors by the education reform in Poland, which impacted the number of Polish schoolchildren visiting the museum.

38. CBOS 1995 ($N = 1{,}011$); OBOP 2000 ($N = 1{,}111$); CBOS 2005 ($N = 1{,}133$).

39. Visits to the Auschwitz-Birkenau State Museum are not part of the official school curriculum, but they have traditionally been included on the "day-trip" circuit, especially in southern Poland. Students from farther regions also visit the museum when they visit Cracow and Zakopane, a small resort town in the Tatra Mountains. Guides reported to me that the pedagogical benefit for these latter groups was not all that clear, since they visit the museum on their way

Figure 23 Some two thousand March of the Living youth and organizers leave Auschwitz I through the infamous *Arbeit Macht Frei* gate. They symbolically replicate the March of Death by walking the three kilometers to Birkenau. Photo: Geneviève Zubrzycki.

youth have visited the former camp (unpublished data from the Auschwitz-Birkenau State Museum Visitors' Service Section). The museum is clearly a crucial socializing institution on the history of World War II and the Holocaust, and it takes its educational mission very seriously. Its current pedagogical section has put in place special programs for the continuing education of teachers, in order for them to better prepare pupils and students for their visit at Auschwitz-Birkenau, and to sensitize them to the Holocaust.[40]

to more "attractive" destinations. Unlike groups that come specifically to the museum as part of their history or Polish class, these school/tourist groups are not prepared intellectually or "culturally" to visit the site: "For them, it's just another attraction, and it's not a very attractive one. . . . They want to get back on the bus and go to the mountains to have fun. So it's hard on us, especially because their teachers have to deal with them nonstop for three to four days in a row, so when they come to the museum they take a break and relax on our backs. We end up having to do some disciplining, remind the brats of where they are, not to chew gum, to let other visitors go through, and the like" (informal interview with guide).

40. The first consists of two 4- to 6-day-long seminars on Auschwitz, its history and symbolism. The second, "Totalitarianism, Nazism, Holocaust," is more involved and detailed. Directed toward teachers of history, Polish, religion, and ethics, it consists of 206 hours of lectures on various topics by professors from Polish universities, experts, public intellectuals, and survivors.

While the museum has made a great effort to revise its narrative and meet the needs of Western visitors (by hiring and training guides fluent in English, French, German, Italian, Japanese, and several other "western" languages), it is also conscious of the fact that most of these visitors know very little about the Polish history of the site. On the occasion of the 2002 March of the Living, the Polish minister of education therefore arranged with her Israeli counterpart for Polish and Israeli teachers to be trained so that the information about the Holocaust would not be "one-sided" (that is, strictly Jewish): "In the future," she declared, "Jewish groups coming to our country will have a Polish guide to speak about the Holocaust in its entirety by showing that Poles also perished in Auschwitz" (Polish Press Agency, April 9, 2002).

In order to inform the visitors of the Polish war experience while maintaining its revised narrative line, a typical visit at the museum now starts with the history of the camp divided into two periods: 1940–42, the "Polish" period, and 1942–45, the "Jewish" one. One museum employee, a former guide now in charge of training new guides and supervising certified ones, declared to me that, in his view, the narrative "Judaization" was sometimes going a little too far:

> This year we organized training for guides, because every year we have those training sessions, and we did stress the need for the guides to inform people or remind them about the Polish memory. Because we came to the conclusion, by observing our guides, that they are giving way to this wave, that there is talk about "Jews, Jews, and the Holocaust," and there's missing some place for Poles, especially from those [guides] offering tours to foreigners. "People," we told them, "don't forget that you have to present the history of Auschwitz with a measure of objectivity!" (Interview, April 12, 2001)

The third program is organized jointly with Yad Vashem, and consists of courses in Poland and Israel on Judaism, the history and culture of Polish Jews, and the Holocaust (Andrzej Kacorzyk and Alicja Białecka, "Jesteście po to by dać świadectwo. Program edukacji nauczycieli w Muzeum i Miejscu Pamięci Auschwitz," proposal submitted to the Ministry of Culture, 1999). Aside from the pedagogical initiatives of the Auschwitz-Birkenau State Museum, the first high school textbooks about the Holocaust have recently been published, accompanied with a teacher's program containing lesson plans, descriptions of specific issues that the Holocaust raises, topics for group discussion, exercises, etc. (see for example Szuchta and Trojańksi 2000, 2003). See also the volume edited by Ambrosewicz-Jacobs and Hońdo, *Dlaczego należy uczyć o Holokauście?* (2003), or its English translation, *Why Should We Teach about the Holocaust?* (2004). For a study of ethnic prejudices and anti-Semitism in Poland and educational pilot programs, see Ambrosewicz-Jacobs (2003).

With the same preoccupation in mind, "to keep a measure of objectivity," the Polish Block has also been slightly revamped in order to represent the Polishness of "Oświęcim." Several information panels were installed to add a written narrative to what had been almost exclusively a visual exhibit. As the curator in charge of these changes told me,

> I wanted to add a little bit of information, factual, substantial information that would allow someone who is entering this exhibit to get acquainted a little bit with the history of occupation in Poland. . . . What inclined me to present this exhibit? Well, it seemed to me that, I mean I *know* that, our history from the Second World War is completely unknown in the world. It's not surprising. We've been closed off into a defined system, we didn't have the possibility to get out there with our information, and anyway there wasn't any special interest. . . . After all, few know that Poland lost about 50 percent of her intelligentsia during the Second World War, people come here with the conviction, especially here to Auschwitz, that Auschwitz was created only and exclusively for the Jews. Many people come, especially from Jewish circles, and declare that the camp began in 1942. But in fact it was created in 1940, and the basis for its establishment—or let's say, to put it differently—the camp was created for Poles. It was to be an instrument in the extermination of the Polish nation. . . . So I wanted to transmit some information in this exhibit. Especially since it so happens that Block 15 is well located. In the summer, when there is an intensive flux of individual visitors, tons of people come in. A lot of people enter that block first. Mostly foreigners, and that's an opportunity to show, to "sell" our martyrdom a little bit. For sure it's not a reason to be proud, but I think that it's easier later on to understand certain things, certain positions of Poles. . . . You are from the United States, from America, so you must have seen several of those Holocaust museums and you must admit that there is no information there about Poles, not even rudimentary information. There's nothing—not just about Poles; there's nothing about Soviet prisoners of war, nothing about other victims. (Interview with Mirosław Obstarczyk, April 12, 2001)

In representing the Polish experience of the war, there is a genuine concern to inform the museum visitor of the extent of its ravages, the suffering inflicted, and the resistance to the occupant. That is the context in which "certain positions of Poles," to use the terms of my interlocutor—regarding the camp, Polish-Jewish relations, and a variety of other themes—should be

Table 3. Poles' Connotations of "Oświęcim"
("With what, above all else, do you associate the word 'Oświęcim'? What is 'Oświęcim' for you?")

	1995 (CBOS)	2000[a] (OBOP)	2005 (CBOS)
	%	%	%
Martyrdom of the Polish nation	47	36	37
Extermination of Jews	8	32	17
Martyrdom of both Poles and Jews	9	5	7
Martyrdom of several nationalities	26	10	16
Exterm./martyr. of Poles, Jews, other nationalities	b	b	6
Genocide irrespective of nationality	5	13	7
Other responses	3	2	8
Don't know anything about Oświęcim	1	0	0
Difficult to say	1	2	2

Sources: CBOS, *Oświęcim w zbiorowej pamięci Polaków,* 1995; OBOP, *Oświęcim: przeszlość a teraźniejszość w opiniach Polaków,* 2000; CBOS, *Po obchodach 60tej rocznicy wyzwolenia Auschwitz-Birkenau—Obóz w Oświęcimiu w świadomości Polaków*, 2005.
Note: For survey methods, see note 42 in the text.
[a]Designed by and conducted for Dr. Marek Kucia, Department of Sociology, Jagiellonian University.
[b] Response option not given in that survey.

placed; Poles' historical (and personal) experience of the war is the prism through which they understand the current situation at Auschwitz.[41] Making this known to foreigners is a way to explain and possibly even to justify Poles' reactions to the "Judaization" of the site and to the world's ignorance about Polish martyrdom. Ironically, the declared need to "sell" martyrdom in a marketplace of ideas is a key marker of the post-Communist transition at Auschwitz.

Translating the Symbols into Numbers

Before concluding this chapter on the symbolism of "Oświęcim"/"Auschwitz," it may be helpful to offer some survey data on Poles' understanding of it as it relates to the site and its history. Three surveys are especially useful to describe the extent of the Polishness of "Oświęcim," but also to indicate changes in that perception following a multitude of commemorative events,

41. The memory of the camps is a very personal one for many Poles: every ninth adult Pole currently living in Poland (11 percent) has or had loved ones who were prisoners at Auschwitz, and one in twenty (5 percent) actually lost a family member or someone close in the camp. About a fifth of respondents (22 percent) declare that members of their family or people close to them were prisoners in other Nazi concentration camps (CBOS 2005).

the museum's own revised narrative, and the wave of Western visitors that now place Poles in contact with the Jewishness of "Auschwitz" that Jews and the world espouse (see table 3).

The first survey, conducted in 1995 on the eve of the commemorative celebrations of the fiftieth anniversary of the liberation of Auschwitz, reveals, in accordance with Socialist propaganda, that Auschwitz was above all else, for almost three-quarters of adult Poles, the place of martyrdom "of the Polish nation" or "of several nationalities" (47 percent and 26 percent respectively).[42] Only 8 percent of Poles associated the site above all else with the Holocaust.

The same questions were asked again five years and ten years after the date of the first survey. Most striking in these data is the respondents' increased consciousness of Auschwitz as the site of the Holocaust: the proportion of those who identified the site with the extermination of Jews was four times greater in 2000 than in 1995 (from 8 percent to 32 percent), although in 2005 the association of "Oświęcim" with the extermination of Jews had dropped to 17 percent. While that number still had doubled from ten years earlier, it is less than half that of those who understand "Oświęcim" as the place of martyrdom of the Polish nation. The significant boost in the association of the former camp with Jews in 2000 could be a result of the War of the Crosses and the intense campaign in the news media on this history of the former camp.

Another significant change is the growing perception of the former camp as the symbolic site of universal evil, of genocide regardless of national/ethnic identity or citizenship. Almost three times more respondents identified the site as such in 2000 than in the previous survey.[43] Finally, the

42. The first CBOS survey was conducted on January 13–16, 1995, on the basis of a representative random sample of adults living in Poland ($N = 1{,}011$). OBOP conducted two surveys, one on January 15–17 ($N = 1{,}008$) and the other on January 28–30, 2000—that is, before and after the commemorative events of the fifty-fifth anniversary of Auschwitz's liberation. The same questions were administered in both surveys to measure the impact of the event on the population's knowledge and perceptions of Auschwitz. The results cited in table 3 are those of the *second*, postcommemorative survey. The 2005 CBOS survey was conducted on January 28–February 1 of that year ($N = 1{,}333$), after the sixtieth anniversary of Auschwitz's liberation. The questions for all three surveys were identical. I am grateful to CBOS and OBOP for making the 1995 and 2000 surveys available to me at no charge. For analyses and discussions of these (and other) surveys, see Sułek (1998) and especially Kucia (2001).

43. The 2005 survey has "other responses" that could be added to the view that Oświęcim is the site of genocide regardless of nationality: for example, 2 percent of respondents declared that they understood Oświęcim as the place of torture, cruelty, and death without reference to the victims' origins, and another 6 percent identified Oświęcim with the martyrdom and genocide of Poles, Jews, and other nationalities.

acceptance of the Socialist narrative of "Oświęcim" as the site of martyrdom of the Polish nation and other nations had decreased from 26 percent to 10 percent between 1995 and 2000, gaining back a few points in 2005.

We learn from surveys conducted throughout the last decade that overall, Poles still predominantly associate "Oświęcim" with the martyrdom of the Polish nation. Most interesting is that only a small fraction of them understand "Oświęcim" as the symbol of martyrdom for both Poles *and* Jews, as if the sharing of the symbol were not imaginable. It is important to note, moreover, that the Polishness of the former camp was most often selected by people over forty years of age and least often by teenagers, who in turn most frequently indicated the Jewishness of the site (Kucia 2001, 13). In other words, those socialized in the People's Republic were least likely to associate "Oświęcim" with the Holocaust.

A key caveat here: the question was formulated to capture Poles' association with the symbol of "Oświęcim," not "Auschwitz." Other questions were intended to measure not the associations with the name "Oświęcim," but the actual historical knowledge about Auschwitz. In another question posed in the 2000 OBOP survey (not in table 3), 67 percent of respondents correctly identified Jews as the group with the largest number of victims. This suggests that most Poles *know* that Jews constitute the majority of the former camp's victims. That knowledge, however, does not seem to alter radically the meaning of "Oświęcim" as a symbol, which suggests the dissociation of the symbol "Oświęcim" from Auschwitz the historical site and event. "Oświęcim" belongs to the symbolic sphere of collective memory.

Nevertheless, despite its popularity, surveys show that the Polish meaning of "Oświęcim" is in slow decline. This could be attributed to the growing knowledge and awareness of Auschwitz's Jewishness. Since it seems difficult to "share" the symbol (only between 5 percent and 9 percent of respondents in 1995, 2000, and 2005 associated "Oświęcim" with the martyrdom of both Poles and Jews), "Oświęcim" has forfeited some of its sanctity for Poles.

A second factor for this decline may be the introduction of a "new" and rival symbol in public and official memory, which prior to the fall of Communism was taboo: "Katyń." Unlike "Oświęcim," which was appropriated by the state and given a strong nationalist and Socialist emphasis, "Katyń" was an important symbol in the underground, and was commemorated outside the state—not surprisingly, given that the Soviets were the perpetrator. With the end of Communism and the official recognition of the crime by the USSR in 1990, "Katyń" was brought into the foreground of Polish discussions of the war, leaving the private and underground spheres of memory to enter its public and official one, and now competing with "Oświęcim" for the status of the nation's holy site of martyrdom.

Conclusion

A significant source of the current memory war between Poles and Jews, and among Poles, is related to the attempt by the Communist regime to redefine Polish national identity along civic lines. Polish authorities designed the museum at Auschwitz according to a Marxist interpretation, which defined the Polish nation in civic terms. Jewish victims from Poland thus became "Polish citizens," and their number was conflated with that of "ethnic Poles." Since the nation in Poland is primarily understood in ethnic terms, receptors of this discourse "read" it in the sense that a great number of Auschwitz's victims were "Polish," that is, ethnic Poles, creating yet another example of semantic confusion. For half a century, Polish visitors—a majority of them schoolchildren who had no direct experience of the war and very few, if any, contacts with Jews—and Poles in general regarded "Oświęcim" as their own site of collective memory and suffering. The extent to which collective memories of Auschwitz are contested today is therefore, in part, a perverse effect of the Communist regime's attempt to restructure Polishness along civic lines.

Post-Communist nationalism is thus closely related to the legacy of Communism. First, the meaning of the transition derives from the interpretation of the Communist period as one during which Poland was not fully sovereign and independent. Second, despite open resistance to it, the Socialist state was successful in the socialization of its citizens: Poles' current narrative shock regarding not only their status as prime victims of World War II, but also their role in some of the horrors of the war, demonstrates as much. The old, convenient "truths" are hard to displace.[44] Even the most fervent right-wing anti-Communists have integrated the official discourse of the state regarding the postwar meaning of "Oświęcim."

But the disputed memory of Auschwitz is also the result of different understandings of the event and the creation of separate symbolic universes around it: "Oświęcim" for Poles, "Auschwitz" for Jews. The symbols' integration into long-standing ethno-national and ethno-religious narratives of

44. I have in mind here the official discourse of the Communist state on Auschwitz as the main site of Poles' martyrdom and on the murder of Jews on July 10, 1941, in Jedwabne, until recently attributed to Germans.

suffering, that of Christ of nations for Poles and the chosen people for Jews, makes them even more potent. Although Poles know that Jews constitute the largest group of Auschwitz's victims, they have appropriated the memory of Auschwitz and woven it into the grand narrative of Polish martyrdom. The prominence of "Oświęcim" in the Polish national narrative and collective memory serves to justify nationalist Poles' claims to the "ownership" of Auschwitz.

Given the meaning of "Oświęcim" for Poles and "Auschwitz" for Jews, the planting of crosses at that specific site carried powerful reverberations for both groups, as I analyze and discuss in the next chapters. The action was a doubly symbolic gesture: it marked one symbol—"Oświęcim"—as Polish and Roman Catholic through the use of another symbol—the cross. The action was also undertaken at a specific historical juncture, and at a specific moment in the site's history. The War of the Crosses was initiated when the camp's history was being revised and the symbol reworked by the legitimate authorities (the Auschwitz-Birkenau State Museum and the state) and the news media, as well as through the increased flow of visitors-tourists-pilgrims carrying a different understanding of what "Auschwitz" means and represents. It is at this liminal moment that Polish ultranationalists embarked on this project to firmly ground Auschwitz within Polish national history and memory by marking the physical site with a symbol associated with the Polish nation that could not be shared with Jews.

What makes the War of the Crosses doubly significant, on the symbolic front, is that the other symbol involved in the controversy, the cross, was itself undergoing a process of redefinition and contestation. As we have seen, Poles have been intensely debating, through the 1990s, the appropriateness of the fusion of religious and national identities as symbolized in the cross, and a significant part of the Roman Catholic Church has been trying to retheologize the cross away from its national(ist) interpretation, as we shall see in chapter 5. The planting of crosses just outside Auschwitz was therefore—and we shall see this in detail—about something even bigger than a fight over "Oświęcim" and Auschwitz. It was, ultimately, also about yet another symbol: "Poland."

Understanding and interpreting the cultural dimension of the post-Communist transition demands that we pay attention to key sites of national identity, such as Auschwitz and its attending (Polish) symbol, "Oświęcim," and the ways in which they not only contain the ashes of the dead, but also carry key structuring narratives into the present and future.

Plate 1 Rosary, with Auschwitz's "Block of Death" in the background, at the beginning of the summer of 1998. A few crosses have been erected in the gravel pit, indicating the beginning of the War of the Crosses, which lasted until May 1999. Photo: PAP/CAF Roman Koszowski.

Plate 2 Papal cross surrounded by other smaller crosses at the height of the War of the Crosses in late summer 1998. Photo: from the personal archives of Kazimierz Świtoń.

Plate 3 Processional flag used on the ritual occasion of the erection of a cross dedicated by members of the Polish-American diaspora. "The cross is our salvation" is embroidered in gold letters above the medallion of Pope John Paul II; below it, the affirmation "Father, we defend the cross." Mr. Świtoń gave weekly reports from the gravel pit to Polish-language newspapers in Chicago. Photo: from the personal archives of Kazimierz Świtoń.

Plate 4 Foot of the papal cross, transformed into an improvised altar. Photo: PAP/Roman Koszowski.

Plate 5 A Roman Catholic priest blesses crosses planted at the gravel pit during the summer of 1998 despite the official condemnation of the action by the Episcopate of Poland in late August. Photo: from the personal archives of Kazimierz Świtoń.

Plate 6 Mass celebrated just outside the gravel pit in September 1998. Photo: PAP/Roman Koszowski.

Plate 7 Mountaineers in their traditional regional garb, worn on special occasions, attaching an inscription to the cross they erected in the winter of 1999, well after the Episcopate of Poland officially condemned the War of the Crosses. Photo: PAP/Roman Koszowski.

Plate 8 Papal cross in the spring of 2004. The small altar by the fence is where a few men and women meet every day to pray "for the safe return of the Carmelite nuns and the defense of the papal cross." Photo: Geneviève Zubrzycki.

CHAPTER FOUR

The Aesthetics of the War of the Crosses: Mobilizing "the Nation"

Ah, it was beautiful...
—Kazimierz Świtoń, *instigator of the War of the Crosses*

Introduction

The Polish army removed the crosses from the gravel pit adjacent to the former Auschwitz concentration camp in May 1999, and re-erected them on the grounds of a Franciscan sanctuary in a small village nearby. Because of the inflammatory nature of the crosses' removal by soldiers, which took place in the middle of the night (echoing the stealth of the papal cross's planting a decade earlier), the Franciscans have devoted careful attention to the display of the crosses, the chapel, and various crucifixes and rosaries that had adorned the gravel pit's fence, with the objective of restoring the order of their original deployments. All are fastidiously maintained in the sanctuary's manicured backyard, a large grassy area surrounded by bucolic woods and pasture. Order and calm prevail. The grounds are empty and unperturbed by journalists, cameras, speeches, or crowds. The only action at the new location of the religious items is the occasional mowing of the grass and the occasional presence of the sanctuary's housekeeper during the warm seasons, hanging linens to dry in the wind a few yards away.

The atmosphere at the gravel pit during the War of the Crosses was quite different. People came and went, and at the height of the controversy in the summer of 1998, television stations had crews at the site twenty-four hours a day, reporting live the events of the day: a pilgrimage, a new cross, an inflammatory speech, or perhaps nothing more than the familiar Mr. Świtoń outside his trailer reading the papers, napping, or talking on his cell phone. On many days, there were more reporters and photographers at the gravel pit than actual supporters of the cross-planting action. The War of the Crosses soon became a media event, and "the gravel pit" a household word and topic of discussion. In the press, public intellectuals, politicians, clergymen, and the episcopate used the event as a catalyst for earnest editorial debate about Polish-Jewish relations, Polish national identity, collective memory, and the nature of Polish Catholicism while newspaper readers hurled fiery rejoinders to editors, brimming either with righteous indignation at the demands to remove the papal cross and with support and justification of the cross-planting action, or with its equally vehement condemnation.

In this chapter, I focus specifically on the aesthetics of the War of the Crosses. I analyze the form and content of symbols used in that conflict, primarily crosses and their inscriptions, as they offer a rich collection of iconographic and discursive representations. I show that the specific iconographic collage and the specific ritualizations used by Świtoń's advocacy group, the Defenders of the Cross, and by those bringing crosses to the site were borrowed from a cultural repertoire of nationalist protest that carries high emotional resonances. The aesthetics of the War of the Crosses evoked another moment of nationalist collective action, that of Solidarity in 1980. Actors attempted to recreate that historically transformative emotional effervescence at the gravel pit, and thereby to legitimize the cross-planting action. I argue that the aesthetics of the event were central to the successful mobilization of nationalist groups and the symbolic hijacking of Auschwitz.

The focus on symbols and collective action draws on a theoretical genealogy most notoriously descended from Émile Durkheim to Victor Turner. Durkheim argued, in *The Elementary Forms of Religious Life* ([1912] 1995), that the collective effervescence brought about by collective rituals reinforced the participants' identity as members of a given group, and reinforced moral and emotional attachment to the social order. Less developed in Durkheim's theory of ritual was the role symbols played in the process. Turner picked up the issue and has developed the most extensive theory of ritual in relation to symbols. Symbols, for Turner, are objects, activities, events, gestures, or spatial units in a ritual situation. Because a symbol's meaning is not absolutely fixed, it may become the object of fights over its definition, with the meaning eventually being determined by those with sufficient power, authority, or prestige. Turner went on to distinguish types or levels of meaning: a symbol's "exegetic" meaning is the one articulated by the actors themselves, while "operational" and "relational" meanings emerge through the observation and analysis of the ritual process. Operational meaning is derived from the actual use made of the symbol, the social composition of the groups performing the ritual, and the affective quality generated, while relational meaning is revealed through the analysis of a given symbol's relationship to other symbols in the total ritual system.

According to Turner, the power of dominant symbols derives from their unification of two poles of meaning: the ideological and the "orectic." While the ideological pole is a cluster of significations referring to the moral and social orders as well as to norms and values that structure relationships, the orectic pole primarily refers to sensory, emotional processes. What is not sufficiently addressed in Turner's theory is why certain symbols have especially strong emotional resonance. He viewed the orectic pole as one usually associated with the body and physiological functions (mostly reproduction). In this work, by contrast, I show the historical process of symbolic meaning-making and so drag Turner "into history." While Turner viewed the emotional pole of symbols as primarily "biological," I see it as historically built through past events and narratives about those events. Dominant symbols harness values and norms to emotions. Sentiments of nationness, then, are aroused through individual and collective mnemonic associations with key historical narratives, such as those analyzed in chapter 1.

The processual symbolic analysis I therefore propose here is inspired by the work of Turner but goes beyond it by exploring the meaning of symbols as they are transformed over time and in specific relation to historical narratives. Between "sender" and "receiver," a series of complex operations must be performed: the evocation of key historical narratives condensed into a given aesthetic "set" that a symbol draws upon for its depth; the structural refinement of what a symbol "is" by determining what it is not; and the constant looping back of a symbol's immediate political effect on a given arena into its present and future performance. It is in specific macropolitical contexts that symbols take on meaning and are disseminated in mass media, becoming part of the available, familiar shared repertoire of the "public sphere." Our attention to this set of issues offers a refinement and advancement of Turner's model.

In this chapter, then, I closely examine the cross as a dominant symbol in its exegetical, relational, and operational processes of signification, and work within the "gaps" of the signifying process. I interpret the cross's exegetical meaning by analyzing inscriptions left on those erected at the gravel pit, and its relational meaning by situating it in relation to other symbols, most significantly "Oświęcim" but also the flag; the Black Madonna, Our Lady of Częstochowa; and John Paul II. I ground these firmly in the history and historical narratives that constitute their layers of meaning. But the full meaning of the cross (and the significance of the War of the Crosses) will not emerge until we analyze its operational meaning through the various discourses and debates about it and the event in the public sphere, a task engaged in the next chapter. For now, we approach the cross not as romantically backlit from a distance, but viewed close enough that the wood screws and glue trails of its assembly begin to appear, and then even the knots and grain, where a riddle is hidden: of how two planks of wood became, and are still becoming, a platform and frame of a nation. It is the nation not of councils and constitutions, but of the humble materials that summon, mobilize, and sustain sentiments of affinity for some, and estrangement for others.

The Auschwitz Crosses: Martyrdom, Memory, and Identity

All crosses brought to the gravel pit were planted under the supervision and with the assistance of Kazimierz Świtoń, who arranged them in a semicircle around the papal cross. The great majority of them bore a small commemorative plaque indicating the name and prisoner number of the victim in whose memory the cross was being erected, or a specific slogan, message, poem, biblical inscription, or testimony: Defend the Cross, For God and Fatherland, Only Poland (fig. 24). Most of them were signed by their sponsors, whether private individuals or organizations: A. Biedak and F. Binkiewicz; Zbydniów Parish, Sandomierz; Patriotic Association "Wola-Bemowo" in Warsaw; Falanga (a Fascist group); Society of Saint Pius X; Polish-American Committee in the Defense of the Cross. Some preferred to remain anonymous: Academic teacher from Warsaw; Son; Attorneys of the Capital.

While some crosses were delivered individually in a relatively anonymous, subdued manner without agitation or ceremony, others were transported with maximal flourish and fanfare in processions accompanied by songs and prayers. Typically, a small ceremony under the supervision and with the help of Świtoń would accompany the planting, complete with speeches, personal testimonies, flowers, banners, and flags. The subsequent blessing of crosses was accompanied by more developed ritual performances such as prayers, religious chants, and the sprinkling of holy water as photographers and crowds of the curious observed the congregants from the distance of the street, standing behind the gravel pit's chain-link fence that bounded and distinguished "sacred space" from everyday space. Crosses were brought from Poland's four corners: Warsaw, Cracow, Łódź, Łomża, Katowice, Sandomierz, and Wrocław, to name only a few. More precisely, crosses were *offered* by people from every part of the country, for one could order and purchase one in Oświęcim itself, where a small cottage industry of cross-building bloomed. At least three crosses were dedicated

Figure 24 Typical plaque left on the crosses to commemorate the documented death of the 152 Poles executed at the gravel pit in 1941. This one reads: "R.I.P. Janusz Chrzanowski from Warsaw, prisoner no. 80071. Lost at the gravel pit on March 13, 1941. [Signed:] Grateful people of the sea." Photo: Geneviève Zubrzycki.

by members of the Polish diaspora in the United States (Chicago), Canada (Toronto), and Australia, testifying to the transnational dissemination of the controversy.

The most common theme expressed on the crosses' inscriptions is the martyrdom of Poles and the implicit claim to Poles' right to the site. By commemorating Polish victims, the Jewishness of Auschwitz is contested. A great many inscriptions emphasize the Polish identity of the victims and their suffering, in an attempt to counteract the recent revision of the camp's history. Recall that the cross-planting action was initiated by Świtoń, who invited Poles to commemorate the execution of ethnic Poles at the gravel pit in 1941, thereby sufficiently Polonizing the site such that the papal cross would remain. In this vein, one woman intended her cross as a testimony of the crimes against Poles, her cross's inscription reading: "As an inhabitant of Harmęże [nearby village], I was a witness of those brutal murders of Hitlerites on Poles in the camp and at the Gravel pit. Let this birch Cross attest that I remember you. Anna Chrapczyńska." Another inscription was left by a former prisoner of Auschwitz, whose survival he attributed to the grace of God. His cross was dedicated to the memory of Saint Maksymilian Kolbe, in whose hunger cell he himself had spent forty days. Another cross, offered by Świtoń's son, is dedicated to the memory of five priests "tortured to death on August 26 1941 . . . martyrs for [their] Faith and for Poland," marking the site as a holy Roman Catholic and national one. The Social Committee for the Defense of the Crosses[1] dramatically rejected the revised historical narrative concerning the number of Poles killed at Auschwitz (now estimated at 70,000–75,000), and opposed the "Judaization" of the site by emphasizing on its cross the Polish and Christian identity of victims:

> To the memory of Poles shot by Germans and to the *hundreds of thousands of [Poles]* murdered in the years 1940–45 in the former Konzentrationslager Auschwitz-Birkenau. This Cross at the Gravel pit in Oświęcim, the *site of Christians' slaughter*, was erected in August 1998 by members of the Social Committee in the Defense of the Oświęcim Crosses from Kędzierzyno-K, Gliwice, Bielsko, Oświęcim, and Katowice. (My emphases)

This latter offers clues for how the following cross might be interpreted. Quite simple in design and inscription, the message is nevertheless bewilderingly complex. It is dedicated to the memory of "Blessed Edyta Stein, Jew. Teresa Benedykta of the Cross found death in the gas chamber on August 9, 1942." The victim here is commemorated as a saint, yet her Jewishness is noted. The last line nevertheless implies that the victim found death as a Catholic. The presence of this cross at the gravel pit hence suggests an attempt not only to emphasize the existence of numerous Polish and Christian victims, but also to appropriate some Jewish ones. This is certainly how the beatification of Edith Stein is understood by many Jews.[2] As is often noted by Polish Jewish intellectuals, what is especially offensive to them is the exclusion of pre–World War II Jews from the nation when they were alive, compared with their postmortem discursive inclusion, a problem I discussed in the last chapter. This reproach is usually made in the

1. Note here the plural form of *cross*. The committee's mission was initially to defend the papal cross, but as mobilization grew and more crosses appeared at the gravel pit, the group's goal was redefined to defend *all* the crosses at the site, hence the change in their name from "Defenders of the Cross" to "Defenders of the Crosses."

2. Baruch Levi, a Polish Jew, argued that the "appropriation" of Edith Stein, far from being negative, was an indicator of Roman Catholics' full acceptance of Jews. Jews are good enough to be not only Catholics, but also Catholic *saints* (*Słowo Żydowskie*, October 30, 1998). This position is, however, an exception; it is the only such opinion I have found thus expressed.

context of the "numbers war" concerning Auschwitz victims and the conflation of Polish Jews and gentile Poles within the single category of "Polish Citizens" or simply Poles. The argument put forward is that before the war, Jews were second-class citizens and, following an ethnic understanding of national identity, were not considered Polish at all. With the Marxist interpretation of the war and its civic discourse, these same Jews, killed in Nazi camps, suddenly became members of the nation as Polish citizens. The victims' Jewishness, however, was concealed. Their appropriation in state propaganda was thus doubly offensive.

In the few examples given here, we notice Poles' implicit competition with Jews for the "ownership" of the site. Some use a discourse reminiscent of the Jewish discourse on the Holocaust: "At this place Fascists murdered 152 people *only for that they were Poles.* Lord Jesus, forgive..." (my emphasis). One could read in this an attempt to place Poles on an equal plane of suffering with Jews. Another author went one step further by dedicating his cross to the memory of Poles killed for hiding Jews. Many Poles, it is implied, were killed *because* of Jews.[3] Some even went so far as to claim that Poles had been killed *by* Jews: Mr. Świtoń "revealed" to me that, for example, the Kapos at the gravel pit were Jewish. Their hatred of Poles, he explained, was used by the Germans to do the dirty work of torturing the victims before their execution. On other occasions, such as the March of the Living in April 1998, the Holocaust was borrowed and freely reinterpreted. On a political banner displayed on the gravel pit's fence, one could read (in English): "Polish Holocaust by Jews 1945–56," a reference to the repression suffered under Stalinism and the widely held belief that the Secret Police of that period was overwhelmingly constituted by Jews (see fig. 4).

Other crosses emphasized the Roman Catholic identity of Poles by fusing, sometimes in creative ways, Catholicism and Polishness. In addition to a multitude of crosses bearing inscriptions such as "To the Poles-Catholics murdered at the Gravel pit" and "Here died Polish patriots-Catholics," many featured verses inspired by poetry commonly attributed to Adam Mickiewicz, Poland's national bard: "Only under this cross / Only under this sign / Poland is Poland / and a Pole is a Pole." The author of one inscription, in a significant inversion, replaced the poem's last verse with the line "and a

3. This came up in my informal conversations with members of the Oświęcim Covenant in the Defense of the Papal Cross at the Gravel Pit. According to them, about two hundred thousand Poles lost their lives for saving Jews, and they were quick to emphasize that Poles have been awarded the largest numbers of Yad Vashem medals and trees for having saved Jews: "And they don't appreciate this at all. They just want to eliminate us through the structures of the European Union. Please show me *one* Jew who saved a Pole. There aren't any. None" (April 4, 2001).

Catholic is a Pole" (my emphasis), illustrating the complete conflation of national and religious categories.[4]

The cross, moreover, is often described as Poland's protector and main attribute, its totem. Without it, Poland would no longer be Poland, as the short poem suggests, or exist at all, as Świtoń argued: "This cross, it is for Poland to be or not to be" (*Rzeczpospolita*, July 20, 1998). Poland, moreover, is on other inscriptions personified and addressed in the vocative form: "Poland! Since centuries the Cross is your Defense. We, attorneys of the capital, are your servants" or "Poland! We are defending the Cross." Opposing the cross is equal to treason: "He who fights the Cross, who sells Polish land and the Nation's property, is the enemy of and traitor to the Fatherland." A true Pole, according to this inscription's author, is a traditional Catholic opposing the presence of foreign capital in Poland. Jews are the obvious enemy, and liberal secular elites their accomplices if not actually Jews disguised as Poles, like wolves under sheepskins. This is a position widely expressed in the pages of the right-wing Catholic daily *Nasz Dziennik*, associated with Radio Maryja. Its editors encourage the boycott of foreign products, oppose the selling of Polish land and industries, and specifically promote a traditional Catholicism in a section of the paper called "The Faith of Our Ancestors." In it, ethnic, religious, and economic nationalism are fused into a conservative, traditional vision of Poland closing itself off to the West and the European Union because the designs of both are supranational, therefore antinational. Jews are represented as linked to both Communism and capitalism; either way, they deal with money, whereas "good Poles" cultivate the land, their national traditions, and their Catholic faith.

Other crosses contain general references to the Christian salvation narrative now applied to the nation, such as "With faith in the victory over evil" or "The cross is the salvation for *everyone*" (my emphasis). It is precisely this all-inclusiveness that is read by Jews as an unwelcome invitation or even an imposition. Still other crosses, a tiny minority, contain strictly personal inscriptions: "To my father, prisoner of Oświęcim—Son," or "Jesus, I trust You. Protect all my family." Although these inscriptions are not in themselves political, when viewed in the context of their appearance on crosses planted at this specific site during that particular summer—viewed, that is, in their material totality as a symbol rather than as decontextualized discourse—they are emphatically political.

4. I was unable to trace the origins of these verses, but it is certain that they are part of a well-known hymn that in the 1980s was frequently sung not only in pilgrimages and Masses for the homeland, but also during vigils, political demonstrations, and strikes (Rogozińska 2002, 28).

Figure 25 Example of a cross plaque containing biblical references (Matt. 23:1–3, 34–36). Photo: Geneviève Zubrzycki.

Several crosses bear biblical quotations and conjoin religious anti-Semitism with Polish nationalism. Two especially merit our attention. The first is four meters high, ornately decorated by metal panels attached to its sides, painted in green, and inscribed by hand in white. Beneath the main inscription is a coat of arms in red metal featuring an embossed white eagle that has a crown nailed onto its head, symbolizing Polish independence (fig. 25). The main inscription contains a passage from the Gospel according to Matthew that is frequently invoked to explain (and justify) the tragic fate of Jews:[5]

> Then said Jesus to the crowds and to his disciples, "The scribes and the Pharisees sit on Moses' seat; so practice and observe whatever I tell you, but not what they do; for they preach, but do not practice. Therefore I

5. This biblical passage was also, among other verses from the Gospel according to Matthew, at the center of a controversy surrounding Mel Gibson's film *The Passion of the Christ* (2004).

> send you prophets and wise men and scribes, some of whom you will kill and crucify, and some of whom you will scourge in your synagogues and persecute from town to town, that upon you may come all the righteous blood shed on earth. . . . Truly, I say to you, all this will come upon this generation." (Matt. 23:1–3, 34–36 [RSV])

Jews are therefore being punished for the killing of Christ, and the Holocaust is interpreted as one of many deserved punishments for that sacrilege. A second biblical quotation, inscribed on a metal panel on the side of the same cross, reads: "But he who denies me before men will be denied before the angels of God (Luke 11:9 [RSV])." In this case, the warning is addressed to those denying Jesus. In the context of the War of the Crosses and more broadly of post-Communism, the reference appears to be addressed not only to Jews who never recognized Christ, but also to those Christians who "deny Jesus before men": "bad Catholics," liberal Roman Catholic elites, and secularists, all of whom argued for the removal of the crosses.

While Jews are depicted as Christ-killers whose death at Auschwitz is therefore justified, Poles, in contrast, are rendered as truly sacrificial victims and heroes. In a messianic interpretation of their fate, Poles were not killed at Auschwitz as a punishment for any sin, but rather *to redeem sin*, to save the world, as we can see from the inscription on another cross. More somber than the previously described one, the sign is professionally engraved, and like the aforementioned one, its authorship remains anonymous, although the author's gender, profession, and place of residence are revealed:

> "And the whole earth followed the beast with wonder. Men worshiped the dragon, for he had given his authority to the beast, and they worshiped the beast, saying, 'Who is like the beast, and who can fight against it?'" (Revelation 13.3–13.4 [RSV]).
>
> In the name of the Lord Jesus Christ, the Holy Spirit and God the Father, let no human dare to raise his unworthy hands on this Cross—symbol of the Catholic faith and of a free Poland, but also of the bloodiest Golgotha of Poland and of the heroism of Poles murdered at this gravel pit and in Oświęcim—since It stands on Polish Land, soaked with Polish blood.
>
> —Offered by an Academic Teacher from Warsaw [Capital letters in original text]

The inscription mixes a biblical passage with a personal interpretation of the events and issues at stake in the War of the Crosses. Since the first century, this passage from the book of Revelation has often been read as an end-times prophecy of an Antichrist/world power that represents the ultimate manifestation of evil. In the Polish context, the passage could be used to describe a multitude of enemies: colonizers and occupiers as well as traitors. It is not clear who "the beast" is, in the eyes of the academic teacher from Warsaw: Nazism? A Jewish world conspiracy against Poland? The personal inscription proffers other indications. First, the cross is here again the symbolic fusion, within one material sign, of Catholicism and Polishness. The cross is the symbol of Catholic faith *and* of Poland—not any Poland, however, but more specifically a *free* Poland. Removing the cross, by implication, would signify the loss of independence. The cross also stands for another symbol, "Oświęcim," invoked here as Poland's "bloodiest Golgotha," a religious metaphor borrowed from John Paul II's homily during his Mass at Birkenau in 1979. Just like Jesus, Poland was crucified to save the world from evil, a powerful contemporary extension of the Romantic messianic myth of Poland as the Christ of nations. Thus, the cross also represents the sacrificial, redemptive heroism of Poles. The last part of the inscription justifies the presence of the cross at the site and warns against its removal: the cross cannot be removed because it stands on "Polish Land" ("Land" spelled with a capital *L*, emphasizing its sacredness and sovereignty), and because that land is soaked with Polish blood (as opposed to Jewish ashes), which sanctifies its grounds. The injunction against the cross's removal, made in the name of the Holy Trinity, could be addressed either to Jews or to Poles who supported the relocation of the papal cross.

Still another cross, carried to the gravel pit by the Patriotic Youth of Wrocław and Lower Silesia, bears an inscription to the memory of Poles murdered at the site, with the Latin invocation "Exoriare aliquis nostris ex ossibus ultra!" (Someone will arise from our bones!) Polish bones not only sanctify the gravel pit's grounds; these sacred remains guarantee the resurrection of Poles and Poland.

Finally, let's examine the cross brought to the gravel pit by the Priesthood of the Working People in Łódź, the iconography of which is especially rich. The three-meter-high cross is proudly signed by the organization in brass letters nailed onto the two wooden beams. It stands out from the forest of other crosses by virtue of its boldly colored laminated inscription, which was added on later in the summer (fig. 26). Unlike most crosses, its message is expressed in an iconographic collage and in the text of a song.

A cameo at the top center of the cross is divided in three, each portion presenting important Polish symbols: the Black Madonna of Częstochowa,

Figure 26 Cross planted by The Łódź Priesthood of the Working People. The memorial board is especially rich, mixing religious and secular symbols and imagery. Photo: Geneviève Zubrzycki.

Queen of Poland; the First Partition of Poland (1772), between Prussia, Russia, and Austria; and the Constitution of May Third (1791). These two historic moments are captured and represented by Poland's most famous painter, Jan Matejko (1838–93). The first one, on the left, is a detail of his *Rejtan, The Downfall of Poland* (1866) (fig. 27), depicting the official recognition of the First Partition by the Polish Sejm on April 21, 1773. Three magnates stand under a portrait of Catherine the Great; gold lies at their feet. One of them holds the signed document while a feeble nobleman turns away, holding a clock in his hand: it is only a matter of time before Poland's complete annihilation. At their feet lies the noble Rejtan, deputy at the Sejm, who attempts to prevent the act by blocking the door, since leaving the conference room meant that the deputies agreed with the decision to ratify the document and recognize the Partition. He heroically bares his chest, threatening to kill himself: "Over my dead body" can be read in his despairing eyes. The painting narrates the story of national betrayal: a few Poles selling out Poland to her neighbors, placing

Figure 27 Jan Matejko, *Rejtan, The Downfall of Poland.* Collection of Zamek Królewski, Warsaw. Photo: Maciej Bronarski.

their own selfish interests before that of the republic. But it also recognizes the existence of true patriots, those for whom Poland was worth their own sacrifice.

The second painting, on the right side of the cameo, is *The Constitution of May Third* (1891), which depicts the euphoria immediately following the ratification of this historic document (fig. 28). Ecstatic crowds celebrate in the streets while a victorious speaker of the house, carried by fellow members of the Sejm, proudly holds the document. It is a scene of joy, honor, and pride. The painting is not only the sequel to *Rejtan, The Downfall of Poland*; in addition to telling the second part of the Partitions' story, *The Constitution of May Third* is offered as a contrast to the vile betrayal of the Polish magnates twenty years earlier. It is also a reminder of Poland's enemies and traitors: if some nobles were ready to relinquish their privileges for the sake of a stronger Poland, others refused to agree to the constitution's profound restructuring, placing their own class interest over the state's. This was already clearly depicted in *Rejtan, The Downfall of Poland* through the portrayal of the magnates' selfishness juxtaposed with Rejtan's selflessness. In *Constitution*, Matejko picks up this theme again: in the lower portion of the painting, a father tries to kill his child in order to divert attention and prevent the constitution from taking effect. It is an abject gesture that

Figure 28 Jan Matejko, *The Constitution of May Third.* Collection of Zamek Królewski, Warsaw. Photo: Maciej Bronarski.

stands in sharp contrast with Rejtan's noble one. Both paintings, although created a quarter of a century apart (and representing events separated by two decades), are episodes within a single narrative. It is common to place them together (in history or art books), as they tell the story of the decline of the Polish-Lithuanian Republic and its attempt at reform and revival before its complete disappearance from the map of Europe in 1795. Both warn against the egoism and megalomania of Sarmatians.[6] They are hung side by side at the Royal Castle in Warsaw.

At the top of the cameo, Our Lady of Częstochowa on her throne presides over the other two representations with the inscription "Long live May Third." A white-and-red banner displaying the inscription "Queen of Poland, bring us back our Constitution" rims the religious icon. As we saw in chapter 1, May 3 is both the anniversary of the 1791 Constitution and

6. Sarmatism denotes Polish noble culture from the beginning of the sixteenth century to the mid-eighteenth century. The term itself comes from the nobility's myth of origins: the Polish *szlachta* was said to descend from the Sarmatians, a people of Iranian descent who settled in Europe in the third century. Sarmatism denotes, more broadly, an ideology justifying the nobility's exclusive control of the government, the guarantee of nobles' unlimited personal freedoms, and intolerance toward other political, religious, and cultural systems (*Mała encyklopedia powszechna* 1997). As a class and cultural formation, sarmatism is directly opposed to the ideology of the Enlightenment and is characterized by love of liberty and chivalry, excessive disregard for trade and craft, and austerity of morals (Waśko 1995).

the Feast of Our Lady. In the Roman Catholic narrative of the nation, both represent Polish sovereignty. Thus the Virgin, guarding the constitution, is protecting Polish national identity and independence. Remember that the summer of 1998, when the War of the Crosses was in full deployment, was only one short year after the ratification of the new constitution, to which the Right had been fiercely opposed. The Right even characterized it as a "non-Polish" constitution that "threatened Polish independence." It is in this postconstitutional context that this juxtaposition of events should be understood.

The banner curving beneath the Madonna is carried by white eagles. Underneath the cameo is an official crest of the Republic of Poland, a crowned white eagle on a red background with the words "Constitution of the Polish Republic" inscribed in bold black letters. Finally, on each side of the cameo, one can read the lyrics of a song accusing Jews of complicity with Germans in the "selling out" of Poland at the end of the 1990s, and predicting Polish revenge, eternal Jewish defeat, and German humiliation:

End of the nineteenth century
From the Vistula to the Varta
The bells are warning, Silesia is unprotected[7]
End of the twentieth century
From the Neisse to the Oder
There are Germanic hordes once again
They are buying out Polish land
Yewreye are in business with them[8]

7. The author most probably refers to the acceleration of German colonization and expropriation activity that took place in the Prussian partition from the 1890s onward. Most German expropriation and purchasing, however, did not occur in Silesia per se, but rather in the Poznań/Posen region (i.e., between the Vistula and the Varta rivers). I am grateful to Jim Bjork for clarifications on this point. The Oder-Neisse is Poland's western border with Germany. As a result of the agreement among the Allied powers at Potsdam in August 1945, Poland's borders were moved westward. Eastern Silesia, which is referred to in the song, was annexed to Poland and commonly referred to in state propaganda (and later on in everyday discourse) as the "Recovered Lands."

8. The Russian word for "Jews," *Jewreje*, is used in the original Polish version. *Jewreje* does not have a negative connotation in Russian—as opposed to the word *Zhid*, for example, which in Polish is the official, neutral name for "Jew" (although it can be an insult as well, as in "you Jew"). *Żydek*, the diminutive for "Jew" (literally "little Jew") is the condescending, offensive term for "Jew" in Polish. In the specific context of the song, the use of *Jewreje* is clearly pejorative: it refers to the myth of an all-powerful *Żydokomuna*, the belief that Communism was installed in Poland by Russian Communist Jews. Hence the use of the Russian term to describe Jews. My thanks to Konstanty Gebert for clarifying this point.

They are tearing Polish land apart
Let them buy, let them do business
Let them buy, let them trade
The Eagles are flying up over Poland
And they will carry out the revenge
Until the eternal calamity of the Jews
And the humiliation of the Teutons
All their lands they will plough
Once for all they will be done with them
They will kill every single one of them
And the entire Polish land
Will then recover the splendor of *Sarmacja*
—*Sarmata*[9]

These lyrics describe the buying back by Germans of land formerly owned by them in Silesia. Since the fall of Communism, this has been a hot-button issue in Poland. One of the first mandates of Tadeusz Mazowiecki, first prime minister of post-Communist Poland (1989–90), was to have the present Polish-German border officially recognized by a united Germany. The influx of German tourists and prospective buyers in western Poland after the fall of Communism has caused anguish among the inhabitants of these lands. Would their houses, land, small businesses, and factories be returned to their previous owners? Would Silesians, impoverished by the closing down of mines, factories, and heavy industries, be forced to sell to Germans in order to survive? Similar anxieties were felt in Lithuania and western Ukraine with the increased travels of Poles to their "hometowns," Wilno (Vilnius), Kowno (Kaunas), and Lwów (L'viv), to visit in pilgrimage-like tours their birthplaces, their schools, their old family estates, and cemeteries where their parents and grandparents were buried. Such travels also occur with Jews revisiting the places where they were born and had lived before the Second World War. Informal networks of private guides take

9. The song is signed by its author as "Sarmata." The references to sarmatism in the song and in its signature are puzzling, for sarmatism commonly connotes a megalomania that is dangerous for the nation. The Partitions of Poland are often attributed to the Sarmatians' egoism and shortsightedness, which is precisely what Matejko's *Rejtan* illustrates. We can only assume that the cross's *bricoleur* is confused or embracing another, less popular interpretation of Sarmatians, for surely he would not present himself as one of those whom his own collage denounces as the nation's traitors, as one of those who "sold" Poland to her neighbors and then opposed the Constitution of May Third? The plate's author could thus either be less educated, thus seeing sarmatism as denoting the golden age of the First Republic before its fall, or have a narrow understanding of sarmatism as an ideology opposed to the Enlightenment and its values.

Holocaust survivors and their families to their hometown, or shtetl. In a period of great economic incertitude and undefined privatization laws, fears of previous owners coming back to claim their own were, and still are, common.[10]

The song also describes Germans as being in cahoots with Jews in the fleecing of Poland. Both groups are rebuked for their putative capitalist talents, talents supposedly "sharpened on Poles' backs." This is a common theme in Polish discourse, widely exploited in literature as well as in films based on classical novels.[11] *The Promised Land* (1899), a novel written by Nobel Prize–winner Władysław Reymont (1867–1925), and its cinematographic adaptation by Andrzej Wajda (1975) explore this theme through the complex relationship between a Pole, a German, and a Jew in nineteenth-century Łódź. The "three brothers from Łódź" have plans for starting a business in the then-booming textile industry, but the story ends with the betrayal of the Pole, pushed aside by his two friends. In Oświęcim, Poles' lives are once again intertwined with those of Germans and Jews, occasioning the reprise of a familiar national theme. This stereotype, as we have seen in the previous chapter (note 31), is vigorously combated by centers promoting Polish-Jewish-German dialogue.

This cross mixes religious and secular imagery, official state symbols, high-cultural artifacts, and vulgar, popular anti-Semitic and anti-German discourse. It tells stories of betrayal (by Polish magnates, Germans, and Jews) and hearkens nostalgically back to Poland's grandeur before its fall through the embrace of the Black Madonna of Częstochowa and the Constitution of May Third, two powerful symbols of Polish resilience (in the first case *miraculous* resistance to the invader). The Black Madonna is invoked to protect the nation by restoring the constitution, while the Polish eagles exact violent revenge from the nation's enemies. If Matejko's paintings represent the inevitable fall of Poland, the presence of the Black Madonna and the cross itself, together with the prophetic song, emphasize its resurrection and its ultimate victory over evil Others.

10. An article in the Polish edition of *Newsweek* played on exactly these fears, adding a solid dose of anti-Semitic stereotypes (no. 14, April 4, 2004, pp. 14–21). The story made the weekly's first page, which depicted hands holding an old set of keys, with the title "Jews Are Coming Back for Their Property." The eight-page-long article was amply illustrated with photographs of small-town misery: dilapidated pre–World War II apartment buildings and local inhabitants, many of them elderly, in difficult economic situations. The article opened with the statement "A young generation of pragmatic functionaries has made a move for former Jewish property. For them, money is money and a house is a house. It is inconsequential whether it is located in Łomża or in Jedwabne." *Newsweek* was harshly criticized for the publication of such an offensive article.

11. For a study of the image of the Jew in Polish literature, see Inglot (1999).

Aesthetics and Mobilization

What is difficult to render, in my description of the crosses and the analysis of their inscriptions, is the overall aesthetic appeal of the gravel pit site and the War of the Crosses event, the impression both made on participants and observers, and the emotions both expressed *and* created, then encouraged and sustained. In the remainder of this chapter, I show the narrative connection between the War of the Crosses and the aesthetics of Solidarity almost two decades earlier. This narrative bridge was constructed through the specific symbolism of the site and the emotions it sought to evoke in Poles. Before going any further, however, let us examine the gravel pit's aesthetics and its visual impact.

Beauty and the Beast

The crosses' new location thoroughly removed them from the public sphere. Świtoń reflected on the difference between their current site and their former heyday: "But when they were standing in their place, *that* made an impression! Ah, it was beautiful . . . " Beauty, of course, is in the eye of the beholder. Those opposed to the presence of crosses in the proximity of Auschwitz, especially Jews, often described them as "disgusting," "shameful," and "offensive." But of interest here is what Świtoń suggests in his effusive response: that the crosses at the gravel pit made a greater impression than they do in their current location, and that there is a link between the site's "beauty" and the mobilizing impact it catalyzed.[12] This raises difficult qualitative problems: where was the "beauty" that seems to have eroded or even disappeared with the crosses' relocation? For Świtoń and his allies, it resided in the site itself and the context of public action, the heat of conflict and its emotional intensity, and the eruption of religious ritual and news media activity around the War of the Crosses. Let us examine how the crosses were spatially organized in the context of their original deployment.

The crosses formed an ensemble behind the tallest and most sacred one of all, the papal cross, wrapped in a white-and-red banner, its base transformed into an improvised altar where people laid flowers and lit candles. The papal cross was strategically placed at the epicenter of the gravel pit,

12. On the aesthetics of nationalism, see Mosse (1975), especially chapter 2, "The Aesthetics of Politics"; and Falasca-Zamponi (1997). On religious and/or secular rituals and the use of symbols in politics, see Hobsbawm and Ranger (1983); Gusfield and Michalowicz (1984); Kertzer (1988); Berezin (1997); Wedeen (1999); Etzioni (2000); and Pfaff and Yang (2001).

right in front of the Block of Death. From the street, the cross is thrown into relief against the camp's building (fig. 5; plates 6, 8). The tall cross structured the gravel pit's space by serving as the organizational axis for all other crosses, which were placed in a semicircle behind it, filling the space to the maximal degree possible. They served as the papal cross's "acolytes," and gained sanctity by contagion, by virtue of their proximity to it. Removing them from the shadow of the papal cross rendered them trivial, an exhibition rather than a social action. They were no longer an army of soldiers defending their sovereign in the battlefield, but crippled veterans forgotten in an infirmary after the battle was over, mere pieces of decorated wood in a lonely backyard.

The gravel pit itself, as the site of murders, was defined during the summer of 1998 as sacred space and as an arena of ritual action, thereby heightening the significance of the crosses sunk in its dirt. Prior to the dispute over the Carmelite convent, the terrain was a profane no-man's-land. It was abandoned, overrun by tall weeds and litter. The gravel pit was discursively sacralized during the initial Carmelite convent conflict in the late eighties *as convent ground*, and then ritually sacralized by the planting of the papal cross. It was further distinguished during the War of the Crosses a decade later through discourses of the site as one "soaked with Polish blood" and "filled with Polish bones," and by the ritual erection of hundreds of crosses by "pilgrims." The site was therefore made sacred by specific performative discourses and actions and the sufficiently reverential audience they attracted, while the crosses themselves, as objects, gained sanctity by their contact with that specific site. The gravel pit and the crosses, sacred space and sacred objects, were thus mutually constituted by a shared arena of ritual performance.

Serving as the background for the crosses, moreover, was not merely a pasture or a wooded area, but Auschwitz's "Block of Death," where prisoners were starved and tortured before being shot at the nearby execution wall. Juxtaposing two symbols of martyrdom, the cross(es) and Auschwitz's Block of Death, created a visual narrative suggesting individual and collective pain and suffering. The cross, however, gives specific meaning to that suffering by promising redemption. Further, the gravel pit is bordered by the former Carmelite convent at one end and a guard tower at the other. While separated from the camp per se by a brick wall and two barbed-wire fences, it is nevertheless very much part of Auschwitz's aesthetics and history. Finally, because it is visible from a busy street, the gravel pit was like a stage for the play performed there, the chain-link fence acting as the opened curtain for watching the ongoing drama created by the display of crosses and the ritual bows of the actors, who posed for photographers like movie stars. Sometimes they even signed autographs.

It is therefore not surprising that the crosses at the gravel pit were more "beautiful" and made a greater "impression," that is, generated a greater emotional response (whether positive or negative), in their performative context than in the relatively arbitrary site to which their careers as symbols have been retired. The crosses at the Franciscan sanctuary, one might presume, also are less "ugly" and offensive to Jews than they were at the gravel pit. Although they still retain their nationalist and anti-Semitic inscriptions, away from Auschwitz they are no longer "shoved" in Jews' faces to spite them, nor are they any longer the "tight fist of opposition," as they were called by Father Stanisław Musiał (*Tygodnik Powszechny*, August 8, 1998). In fact, they remain invisible. As symbols, the crosses cannot be detached from the site; their meaning is constituted by it. Their relocation not only deprives them of their capacity to generate emotional reactions, since they no longer have a viewing public, but also strips them of their "authenticity." Despite the Franciscans' efforts at displaying the crosses with a sense of order reminiscent of that of the gravel pit, the site of re-creation is a poor pastiche. They fail to engage the passerby; they look out of place, insignificant, and almost risible. Symbols are inseparable from their operational and relational context; what the crosses *are* was therefore transformed by their relocation.

Legitimacy by Association and Mimesis

The gravel pit was strewn not only with crosses, but with additional iconographic artifacts that adorned it as well. Polish flags were attached to the crosses, Polish coats of arms were nailed to them, and promises of the nation's faithfulness to Roman Catholicism were made through the waving of *Polonia semper fidelis* processional flags. Political slogans on white banners were frequently stretched across the fence, and inscriptions in the shape of Poland's map, Solidarity pins and logos, and stations of the cross were added to the arena to create a powerful juxtaposition of religious and secular national iconography. Also added to this scene were altars with offerings of flowers, candles, rosaries, and pictures of John Paul II; the Vatican's yellow-and-white banners fluttered in the wind as pictures of the Black Madonna were lifted in processions by pilgrims and left to "protect and defend Poland." Public prayers, vigils, and religious and patriotic songs provided the soundtrack of the action as photographers and television crews simultaneously consumed and created "the story."

Kazimierz Świtoń, in his narrative of the event, described his "mission" in terms of "Divine Providence" watching over him as he "sacrificed" himself and his family for the defense of the cross and for God, honor, and country. Also, the Defenders of the Cross commonly cited Pope John Paul II to justify and legitimize the War of the Crosses. One quotation in particular, spoken by the pope in Zakopane during his 1997 visit to Poland, became the crusade's motto: "Defend the cross. Do not be afraid—Be strong in your faith." Two inscribed crosses and several banners refer to that homily, and respond to the Holy Father with the written exclamation, "Yes, Father, every cross!"

Though references to the pope are commonplace in Poland, they were especially abundant during the War of the Crosses. The Defenders of the Cross designed, produced, and distributed postcards that iconographically linked Świtoń and the War of the Crosses to the Pope's Mass at Birkenau, conducted during the pontiff's first official visit to his homeland in 1979. Each card presents a collage of images: the papal Mass at Birkenau; the papal cross at the gravel pit surrounded by dozens of smaller crosses, flowers, and flags; the papal invocation "Defend the Cross"; the contours of the map of Poland in white and red; and a dignified Świtoń wearing a sober dark suit and tie.

One of the postcards (fig. 29) shows two pictures of the gravel pit—on the left, a placard containing the "pope's quote" placed between two cypresses; on the right, the papal cross adorned by a white-and-red banderole with Auschwitz's Block of Death in the background. Between those two images, bold white-and-red letters against a black background exhort, "By Defending the Cross, We Are Defending Poland," and a picture of Świtoń appears between both lines of the exhortation. Świtoń is (self)represented here as Poland's knight, the nation's defender in a crusade for the maintenance of a free and Catholic Poland, justifying his action-mission with the papal imperative.

Another postcard suggestively juxtaposes events and individuals, thereby creating a visual narrative about Poland and the cross (fig. 30). The card is divided in two: on the left, Pope John Paul II kneels and prays at the Birkenau memorial during his 1979 visit, with a small inset photo depicting the "Defend the Cross" placard. On the right-hand side is the gravel pit at the height of the War of the Crosses, with a red-and-white map of Poland at the lower right corner and a picture of Świtoń at the top right corner. The papal cross occupies the center of the postcard, linking the two events in a visual narrative: the papal Mass at Birkenau in 1979, the War of the Crosses at Auschwitz in 1998. Once again, the cross-planting is legitimized by the

Figure 29 Postcard produced and distributed by the Defenders of the Cross at the gravel pit in the summer of 1998.

Figure 30 Postcard produced and distributed by the Defenders of the Cross at the gravel pit in the summer of 1998.

pope's exhortation to defend the cross. The pontiff and Świtoń are juxtaposed, each occupying his respective section of the postcard—the former is the nation's father and savior, the latter its defender. The pope saved Poland from Communism; Świtoń defends it from Communists, atheists, and Jews, preserving the nation's sovereignty. Both images claim, and proclaim, the sacredness of "Oświęcim" for Poles and legitimize the War of the Crosses by presenting it as the dutiful response to papal orders. The crusade is a divine mission for the nation.

The aesthetics of the War of the Crosses—the symbols, rituals, and strategies of resistance—are strikingly reminiscent of those of the historic sit-down strike at the Gdańsk shipyard in 1980, which marked the birth of Solidarity and the beginning of the end of Communism in Poland and in Eastern Europe. The Defenders of the Cross created an event that borrowed from a repertoire of actions and symbols that could easily be recognized by participants and observers alike. Hunger strikes, political speeches, prayers and Masses, flags, pictures of Our Lady of Częstochowa and of the pope, flowers and candles, posters, and banners along with leaflets distributed at the gate repeat a well-known script in an effort (conscious or not) to recreate—or at least give the impression of recreating—the power of August 1980, a rare moment of collective effervescence and unprecedented social solidarity (itself replicating a Romantic script developed during the nineteenth-century insurrectionary period) (figs. 11–12, 16).

By borrowing well-established aesthetics, the Defenders of the Cross placed themselves in a long lineage of "Poles-Patriots" that includes Rejtan, Adam Mickiewicz, Pope John Paul II, and Solidarity's heroes, thereby attempting to generate a strategic narrative link with other significant historical events such as national insurrections, the pope's first visit to Poland, and the Solidarity strikes. The latter two events mobilized unprecedented national consensus. The Solidarity lineage was often explicitly and squarely exploited: Świtoń and his friends signed their cross as members of Solidarity, and several other crosses bore the labor union's famous logo (fig. 31).

Hunger strikes recapitulated a privileged and well-established nonviolent gesture of protest under Communism. In fact, Świtoń had become a master in this particular art of protest over the last two decades. He emphasized, in his own self-representations during our first meeting, his links to Solidarity and to the pope by showing me several pictures of himself and union leader Lech Wałęsa, one of them during a special audience at the Vatican with John Paul II.

Figure 31 Cross dedicated by the initial members of the Social Committee for the Defense of the Cross. Three of them explicitly claim affiliation with Solidarity. Photo: PAP/Marian Koszowski.

Świtoń and the Defenders of the Cross(es) thus actively called upon the symbolic and moral capital they had acquired during their previous struggle against Communism during the Solidarity movement (Bourdieu 1991b; Lamont 1992; Verdery 1996). Through the manipulation of key symbols and through ritual performances, they generated emotional responses that mobilized a certain group of Poles to social action. In its discourse, the Defenders of the Cross attempted to recreate the "us/them" master frame that had proved effective for mobilizing citizens under Communism and transfer it to a new conflict. The "us/them" frame employed during the War of the Crosses was not only used to differentiate "us/Poles" from "them/Jews," but also to distinguish "we, the Catholic nation, real Poles" from "them, atheist Communists, fake Poles" and even "us, true Catholics" versus "them, washed-out Catholics or crypto-Jews," as I analyze in the next chapter.

Posters on the gravel pit's fence offered promises to the pope to defend the cross from the "hierarchists," the insinuated word being *Communists*. A list of highly ranked government officials, deputies, the prime minister, and the president (from both the Left and the Right) was posted, with the warning to them that "he who fights the cross, dies under the cross." A marginal and extreme group, the Defenders of the Cross attempted to portray itself as "the nation" in a way similar to what Solidarity had done two decades earlier—with the important difference that the union did indeed represent ten million members, a quarter of Poland's total population. "*We* are the nation," the group proclaimed at the gravel pit, attempting to create the illusion of unity against "external Others" (American and Israeli Jews) and "internal Others" (Communists, atheists, Masons, and "Jews")[13] at a moment of intense social, economic, and political division in the country.

The Periphery at the Center

The Defenders of the Cross(es) were successful in mobilizing a small segment of the population—and even some members of the international Polonia—but it, like others who participated in the event, remained a marginal group. There is no doubt that Kazimierz Świtoń and his followers were not mainstream personae. Although they were the main characters in the War of the Crosses drama, they remained marginal in the sociopolitical landscape. Świtoń was demonized in the mainstream Center-Left news media, presented as a madman who symbolized fundamentalist Roman Catholic nationalists and their crusade. The church, meanwhile, depicted him and his group as quasi heretics, especially after the schismatic Society of Saint Pius X became a vocal actor in the controversy. Despite their sympathy for his cause and ideological affinities, the right-wing news media largely ignored Świtoń as the event degenerated, because he was perceived as too dangerous a liability.

Granted, Świtoń had once been an active member of the opposition (which gave him some access to Solidarity's "greats," such as Lech Wałęsa, as well as some privileges, such as an audience with the pope), and he had been a deputy in the Sejm representing the right-wing party Konfederacja Polski Niepodległej (KPN—Confederation for an Independent Poland). But it was all downhill from there: he was laid off from his job with the advent of post-Communist restructuring, had failed at several small-business initiatives, and soon became known as a loose cannon. This label was attached to him after he was sued for distributing home-printed tracts accusing several politicians of being former KGB agents or members of a Jewish conspiracy planning the takeover of Poland.

13. I address the notion of symbolic Jews ("Jews") in a subsequent chapter. See also note 27, chapter 2.

Świtoń and his acolytes are for the most part unemployed older men with little hope of improving their circumstances in the new context of post-Communism. They are the uncontested economic losers of the transition, unable to adapt and/or too old already to develop the skills needed to make it in the new market economy and its employment exigencies. Under these circumstances, many have turned to the Right (and the Far Right) to make sense of their plight. Despair and anger over their situation is channeled against the "invisible hands" of "Communists," "atheists," and "Jews" suspected of controlling the future of Poland, in what David Ost calls the "politics of anger" (2005). In fact, Ost argues that right-wing nationalist discourse in post-Communist Poland stems from the Left's inability to call a spade a spade, and address the issue of the working class's disenfranchisement following the fall of Communism.

After years of Communist rhetoric, the discourse of class conflict was avoided by the post-Communist liberal Left. The Right quickly capitalized on this void by directing the working classes' economic discontent during the destabilizing transition away from class-cleavages explanations toward identity ones instead. Ost sees nationalist discourse in post-Communist Poland as the "political mobilization of anger." In places without Poland's civic legacy and cultural homogeneity, he points out, "movements of rage" found other targets or other outlets, sometimes violent ones (Ost 2005, 7). In more homogenous settings like Poland's, the result was the discursive scapegoating of "Communists" and "atheists" (and I would add "Jews," often conflated with the other two groups). The turning of a large segment of Polish labor to the Right, the main puzzle Ost seeks to solve, therefore "results from [working class] economic anger being captured by parties proposing non-economic solutions. And these parties were able to do so because the political liberals who led the country after 1989 consistently refused to organize workers" (ibid., 36).

I find Ost's thesis convincing, but what it lacks is an explanation of why precisely the nationalist discourse of the Right resonated below. So far, I have argued that it has for two main reasons: first, the post-Communist transition was largely understood as a "national" one, as the "recovery of national independence" and the reconstruction of a "genuinely" Polish state. That project, in turn, opened the discursive field on what Polishness is and should be, making room for the redefinition of symbolic boundaries of what constitutes a "real" Pole. So, as old enemies disappeared with the fall of Communism, new ones had to be invented. But the Right has also succeeded in capturing the imagination of disenfranchised groups because of the symbols it had at its disposal. Soon after the fall of Communism, the Right quickly appropriated the symbols of Solidarity as its own, so that Solidarity's left wing no longer had usable emblems and rituals in its arsenal.

Świtoń and the Defenders of the Cross made ample use of these symbols and the aesthetics of protest to channel discontent and mobilize nationalist feelings against Jews (actual and symbolic) and "Communists." They found sympathetic ears in the listeners of Radio Maryja, which promotes a culture of fear and despair even though it claims to offer hope and peace; and in the readers of newspapers such as the national-Catholic daily *Nasz Dziennik*, related to Radio Maryja, and *Nasza Polska*, a Far-Right weekly.[14]

But Świtoń and the other members of his ad hoc group are much more marginal even than these right-wing media outlets. For example, *Nasz Dziennik* kept its distance from the Defenders of the Cross once the War of the Crosses was unequivocally condemned by the episcopate in late August. In addition, most publications of these extreme groups, such as political tracts, pamphlets, postcards, and short books, are self-published, often through the use of home computers and storefront photocopying services. Groups like the Defenders of the Cross are part of a subculture feeding on elaborate conspiracy theories exposing how the international Jewry and Freemasonry are out to destroy Poland from within and from without. According to members of the Oświęcim Covenant in the Defense of the Papal Cross, for example, Jews know that Israel is seriously threatened by the conflicts in the Middle East, and are therefore planning their return to Poland, the Promised Land, through the European Union's structural elimination of Poland (interviews, April 4, 2001).

These extreme groups are also often in conflict with each other: the Oświęcim Covenant in the Defense of the Papal Cross closed ranks with the church after the ecclesial institution officially condemned the cross-planting action several weeks after it had begun, whereas Świtoń and the Defenders of the Cross continued the action in association with the Society of Saint Pius X, a sectarian group whose founder was excommunicated by John Paul II. Both the Oświęcim Covenant in the Defense of the Papal Cross and the Defenders of the Cross have conspiracy theories about the other: the covenant's leader told me that Świtoń and his acolytes were in fact Communist Jews whose goal was to create such a controversy that the papal cross would be removed (interviews, March and April 4, 2001). Świtoń, on

14. See appendix A for circulation numbers.

the other hand, told me that the members of the covenant were crypto-Jews, since they sided with the church's ecclesial hierarchy (interviews, April 25 and May 23, 2001). In both theories, the adversary is represented as "against the cross," and therefore "Jewish"—yet another example of "magical anti-Semitism" (Michnik 1999).

It should therefore be clear that Świtoń and the others involved in the War of the Crosses are peripheral actors in Poland. Nevertheless, the cross-planting action did mobilize grassroots support; and the issues it raised were not themselves marginal but, rather, became a lightning rod for mainstream commentary and debate on Polishness, the state of the Roman Catholic Church, and the history and memory of World War II. What has enabled characters like Świtoń and the Defenders of the Cross to become so influential despite their obvious marginality? First, they were master manipulators of powerful symbols, creating, through the event itself, an aesthetic that could be recognized by Poles of all ages and classes even though it mobilized only a small subpopulation to action. It was not Świtoń's charisma that motivated ordinary Poles to come to Oświęcim to erect their crosses just outside Auschwitz, but the symbols themselves that held charismatic authority through the powerful collective memories and emotions they transmitted.[15] The discourse and aesthetics of the event, moreover, evoked issues that had been at the center stage of public debates throughout the 1990s: not only was the War of the Crosses the third act in a vocal social drama involving the meaning of "Oświęcim,"[16] but it was also an event that directly challenged the ongoing dissociation of Polish national identity from Catholicism. It touched on the issues of Polish collective memory and anti-Semitism, the relation between Polishness and Catholicism, and the place of religious symbols in the public sphere. The event generated a new wave

15. I noticed that right-wing newspapers generally remained mute on Świtoń himself, focusing instead on the events at the gravel pit, demands from Jews, and the meaning of the cross and of "Oświęcim" for Poles. Interesting viewpoints can be found in numerous letters to the editor in *Nasz Dziennik*. These letters indicate widespread support of the action by readers of the Right's newspapers. Świtoń privately reports that he received congratulatory phone calls from right-wing newspaper editors—all off the record, of course. Moreover, when Świtoń was briefly imprisoned for threatening to blow up the gravel pit (and himself) if the crosses were removed, prison guards commonly asked to have their photos taken with him. He showed me several such photographs, but declined to make me copies, since it "could get these good folks in trouble." We might surmise, therefore, that he was something of a folk hero for those on the Right despite his official marginalization in the news media.

16. The first one, the reader may recall from the book's introduction, was the establishment of the Carmelite convent in 1984 and the controversy surrounding its relocation (1987–93), while the second was the erection of the papal cross at the gravel pit in 1988.

of intense public debate about the nature of the nation and Catholicism, as we shall see in the next chapter.

Conclusion

In addition to the anger and indignation initially aroused by rumored plans by the Polish government to remove the papal cross, the symbols and iconography of the War of the Crosses evoked key historical events that resonate strongly with Poles: the Partitions, World War II, the totalitarian Communist regime, and the "salvation" of Poland thanks to Pope John Paul II and Solidarity. The cross was given a specifically "national" dimension, representing at once oppression from, and resistance to, foreigners. It symbolizes Polish national independence and arouses feelings of pride in Polish national identity. Our Lady of Częstochowa, with her scarred face, likewise was used to remind Poles of their historical suffering and their miraculous survival as a nation. The specific aesthetics of the War of the Crosses—crosses, flags, flowers, posters, pictures of the pope, paintings of the Black Madonna—and the specific ritualizations at the gravel pit—prayer vigils, Masses, patriotic chants, hunger strikes—were borrowed from a familiar cultural repertoire of nationalist protest. It was in part the evocation of emotions created through the aesthetics of the event that mobilized support for the cross-planting action. But it was also the case that these aesthetics mobilized many Poles *against* the War of the Crosses. The specific use of the symbols was perceived as their instrumentalization for goals that were not recognized as legitimate, an issue I turn to in the next chapter.

In what became the most influential theoretical intervention on the emotional force of symbols, Victor Turner argued (most clearly in his 1967 *Forest of Symbols*) that symbols occupy a middle position between an emotional, or "orectic," pole and an ideological pole, acting as something like conductors between the two. What was not made adequately clear in Turner's theory is precisely how symbols focus, acquire, and maintain the ability to evoke emotion. It is precisely on this score that we can critique and revise his seminal formulation. Whereas for Turner symbols' force and capacity to link emotion to ideology were explained by physical characteristics—their mimesis of the body and its universal parts and functions—in this work I drag his ahistorical theory into history. The power of symbols such as the cross cannot be wholly detached from the fact of its human form, and its design as an instrument of bodily torture grants it visceral immediacy even to nonadherents. But its force in mobilizing *nationalist* emotions in Poland, I showed, derives from the historical narratives that have accrued around it: Poland as the Christ of nations or the cross in Solidarity's resistance to Communism. Symbols' ability to evoke and channel emotions depends on their location in historically compelling narratives as these are more or less successfully reactivated by political activists in the present.

CHAPTER FIVE

Debating Poland by Debating the Cross

If a Pole allows the removal of crosses, he stops being a Pole.
—Kazimierz Świtoń, *instigator of the War of the Crosses*

May Christ not cry over us as He cried over Jerusalem, where conflicting elites of the Pharisees and Sadducees were colliding. May He not cry over us, when we quarrel about [who has] the monopoly over patriotism.
—Archbishop Józef Życiński, *on November 11, 1998 (Independence Day)*

Introduction

So far I have analyzed representations made by a very specific group of Poles who expressed anger and indignation at the possibility of the papal cross's removal. These activists condensed and materialized their sentiments into symbolic representations that they then actually brought to the gravel pit, even in open disobedience of the Episcopate of Poland's late-August request to stop erecting crosses at the site. The actors' obdurate persistence in the ritualizations gave evidence of their conviction and dedication to "the cause." But this dedication was far from universal, and interpretations of the event and of the symbol itself were far less unanimous than the Defenders of the Cross attempted to portray. As this chapter shows, the cross is not only a multivocal or polysemic symbol; it contains various sets of associations, various layers of meaning for various social groups. The War of the Crosses, as event, polarized and mobilized different segments of Polish society and, ultimately, is linked to central cleavages in Polish society. It is related to a crisis in Polish-Jewish relations, but also, if not primarily, as one within Polish society and even within the Roman Catholic Church. As Ronald

Jacobs points out in his study of the Rodney King beating in Los Angeles, "The cultural construction of social problems in civil society occurs in multiple media that are connected to different communities of discourse" (1996, 1265). A single event, he shows, can be constructed as several different problems in several different public spheres. He therefore argues for an approach to the study of civil society that takes into account its multiple public spheres and communities, the consequences of particular events, and the different forms of their narration. A similar point obtains here: the study of a single symbol reveals the fault lines of its layered construction—not only of the material object, but of the narrative construction, discursive representation, and normative evaluation of the cross as a symbol, and of the War of the Crosses as it was rendered an "event" by different social groups.

The same symbol that evoked sentiments of pride in those involved in the event created feelings of shame in those opposing it. By analyzing the multiple and often contradictory meanings of the cross in various communities of discourse as the event evolved, this chapter uncovers the "operational" layer of its meaning. My focal point for the analysis of discourses of these multiple "publics" is the arguments made for or against the removal of the cross(es) from the proximity of Auschwitz.[1]

Theology, Space, and Religious Symbols

Arguments favoring or opposing the removal of the papal cross and the other crosses placed in the gravel pit in 1998–99 were made from a myriad of perspectives: theological, legal, spatial, symbolic, and political. At the basis of the conflict between Poles and Jews lies the contested meaning of "Oświęcim"/"Auschwitz," symbolically and politically constructed and reconstructed since World War II. To this is added a theological layer, the level at which differences between the Christian and Jewish faiths are consciously experienced and articulated.

1. I restrict my analysis to the discourses about the cross and the event as they were expressed in *Poland*. To be sure, the War of the Crosses attracted international attention and was discussed and debated in several other communities of discourse, most prominently in Israel and the United States within the Jewish and Polish diasporas. While those are no doubt important, since the subject of this book is Polish nationalism, I included views expressed outside Poland only insofar as they were addressed, engaged with, and debated in the Polish public sphere. My analysis of the War of the Crosses therefore in no way aspires or pretends to be "total"; it is analyzed from the broader perspective of Polish nationalism and religion in the post-Communist period. For an analysis of the event's representation in the German, English, French, American, and Israeli press, see Ryzner (2000).

There are two primary theological positions concerning the meaning of "Auschwitz" for Jews: one is that Auschwitz should remain empty and absolutely silent, that it should present the territorial equivalent of God's absence and silence during the Shoah. Religious symbols should not be present, nor prayers said at Auschwitz.[2] This is the theological argument of René-Samuel Sirat, chief rabbi of the Central Consistory of France, based on this Bible passage:

> And they have built the high place of Topheth, which is the valley of the son of Hinnom, to burn their sons and their daughters in the fire; which I did not command, nor did it come to my mind. Therefore, behold, the days are coming says the Lord, when it will no more be called Topheth, or the valley of the son of Hinnom, but the valley of Slaughter: for they will bury in Topheth, because there is no room elsewhere. And the dead bodies of this people will be food for the birds of the air, and for the beasts of the earth; and none will frighten them away. And I will make to cease from the cities of Judah and from the streets of Jerusalem the voice of mirth and the voice of gladness, the voice of the bridegroom and the voice of the bride; for the land should become a waste. (Jer. 7:31–34 [RSV])

The valley of Slaughter is now Auschwitz; the reciting of prayers at Auschwitz is therefore "the worst idolatry," according to Sirat (in Krajewski 1997, 253).

The other theological position, more popular, is that Jews should recite the Kaddish, a mourning prayer, at Auschwitz. But as Poland's chief rabbi, Pinchas Menachem Joskowicz, explained several times in the Polish news media,

> Our old religion forbids us to pray where other gods stand. The cross is holy for Catholics, but it should not stand in the holiest site for Jews, and for all the others who perished there. What sin have I committed so that I cannot pray at that holy site, the largest Jewish cemetery in the world? (*Wprost*, August 23, 1998)

The cross disturbs and even prevents Kaddish at Auschwitz, "the holiest place in the world. Holier than the Wailing Wall in Jerusalem" (Joskowicz, ibid.).

2. There exists an extensive post-Holocaust theology and philosophical treatises on God, history, and humanism after Auschwitz. It is beyond the scope of my analysis to discuss that literature here.

Auschwitz is therefore sacrilege for some, requiring total silence, and sacred for others, demanding the Kaddish.[3] If Jews differ as to whether or not they should pray at Auschwitz, according to either theological interpretation the Carmelite nuns' prayers and the presence of the cross in sacred Jewish sites violate Hebraic prohibitions. Christians, on the other hand, are prescribed to place crosses to mark the graves of their coreligionists, to signify eternal life after corporeal death.

This theological divergence between Christians/Poles and Jews is further developed at the level of space. As we have seen in chapter 3, what is commonly referred to as "Auschwitz" is in fact an elaborate system of camps and subcamps: Auschwitz (or Auschwitz I), the mother camp; Birkenau (or Auschwitz II); and Monowitz (or Auschwitz III, which is not part of the Auschwitz-Birkenau State Museum [fig. 19]). Auschwitz I was initially created in 1940 primarily for Polish political prisoners; in 1942, Birkenau was established and became the epicenter of the Final Solution. Monowitz was a network of labor camps, and as such did not enter Holocaust symbology and Polish martyrology. Given those spatial distinctions, it was suggested by Poles that the museum and memorial site be clearly divided between Auschwitz I, where most of the prisoners were ethnic Poles and where, therefore, Poles could commemorate "their" dead as they wish; and Birkenau (Auschwitz II), built three kilometers away in the village of Brzezinka, where the overwhelming majority of the victims were Jewish and where, following Jewish request, no religious symbols would be present. In this Polish "solution" to the impasse, the spatial argument rests upon the (allegedly clear-cut) identity of the victims at each camp and the theological differences between Judaism and Christianity.

Poles rebut the Jewish argument against the presence of the symbol of the cross at the gravel pit with the assertion that the papal cross is located outside the former camp per se, and that in any case, Auschwitz I is the "Polish" camp, whereas Auschwitz II-Birkenau is the "Jewish" one (fig. 32). Jews, on the other hand, refuse this distinction, arguing that "Auschwitz" as

3. The (philosophical) position of Elie Wiesel regarding Auschwitz is different from either of these two theological ones. For Wiesel, himself a survivor of Auschwitz, the former camp should remain silent. It should remain silent because the Holocaust is impossible to communicate, since it is itself about silence. The Holocaust, for Wiesel, is a cursed universe and Auschwitz a blasphemy. That said, Wiesel recounts his spontaneous recitation of the Jewish martyrs' prayer during a visit to Birkenau (1999, 193) as well as his insistence on the recitation of the Kaddish at the commemoration of the fiftieth anniversary of Auschwitz's liberation in 1995 (ibid., 194–98). Wiesel sees his storyteller role as one that paradoxically communicates the impossibility of communication.

Figure 32 Aerial photograph of Auschwitz I. On the upper right corner, the gravel pit and the former Carmelite convent are visible; on the lower right is the parking lot and the visitors' center, once a reception center for prisoners of the camp. Photo: Auschwitz-Birkenau State Museum, 1996.

a whole is the symbol of the Shoah. For them, the division between "inside" and "outside" Auschwitz I is not pertinent either, since the entire area, filled with Jewish ashes, is sacred. Moreover, even if the inside/outside distinction were to be accepted as legitimate by Jews, the cross, while being outside, is still visible from *inside* its wall. In Jewish discourse reported in the Polish news media, the cross is variously referred to as "overlooking," "towering," or "dominating" the camp (*krzyż "góruje" nad obozem*). Poles supporting the presence of the papal cross at the site respond to that assertion by insisting that it is barely visible, merely "peeking" over Auschwitz's wall. Both contentions are exaggerated: the cross is in a sunken area—from the street outside the camp, it is fully visible; from one alley inside the camp, one can see its top over the wall and barbed-wire fences separating the gravel pit from the camp. It is, however, clearly visible from a window in the staircase leading to Block 11's second floor (figs. 33, 34). Many Jews, like Poland's then chief rabbi Joskowicz, thus insist that it be removed because it disturbs and ultimately prevents Jewish prayers at the largest Jewish cemetery (*Wprost*, August 23, 1998).

Figure 33 View of the papal cross from inside Auschwitz I in 2001. Photo: Geneviève Zubrzycki.

Several proposals have been made to remedy the situation and appease the inflamed passions on both sides. It was suggested, for example, that a wall of special one-way glass be erected between the papal cross and the former camp so that the cross would be visible from the street outside the former camp and current museum, but not from inside it. Other, less creative proposals have included reducing the height of the cross such that it would be invisible from within the camp, or removing the cross and replacing it with a commemorative monument dedicated to Polish victims, with a small cross inscribed on it. In the end, a row of evergreen trees was planted to create a natural screen between the cross and the former camp (interviews with Stefan Wilkanowicz, April 23, 2001, and Stanisław Krajewski, May 24, 2004).

Another problem derives from the historical and symbolic status of the gravel pit.[4] That site, where the papal cross stands, is a liminal space: it is outside the fenced area of the former camp, but it is bordered by a guard tower. Poles argue that the gravel pit thus is not part of the former camp,

4. The legal status of the gravel pit during the War of the Crosses was also unclear, as discussed in the book's introduction (note 20).

Figure 34 View of the papal cross from the staircase leading to the second floor of Block 11, the "Block of Death," in 2001. Photo: Geneviève Zubrzycki.

using the wall and barbed-wire fences as the dividing line between inside and outside, between Auschwitz the camp and Oświęcim the town. This spatial interpretation is contested by a historical one, however: prisoners used to work at the gravel pit, where many were executed, and it is immediately adjacent to a building that was used to store Zyklon B during the war (the so-called Old Theater, which served as a convent for the Carmelite nuns from 1984 to 1993). It is also contradicted by the spatial claims of the Auschwitz-Birkenau State Museum in a quasi-legal document: although the museum did not have formal jurisdiction over the gravel pit, it included it in its maps when it sought formal recognition by UNESCO and succeeded in gaining Auschwitz's and Birkenau's inclusion on the World Heritage List in 1979. This supranational connection, in turn, was used to justify arguments for the extraterritoriality of Auschwitz-Birkenau made by prominent Jewish spokespersons such as Kalman Sultanik, then vice-president of the World Jewish Congress, and Menachem Pinchas Joskowicz, then chief rabbi of Poland.

The gravel pit is therefore at the center of a border dispute between Poles and Jews about where Auschwitz begins and ends. In the battle over the location of some critical line in space, Poles reject the all-encompassing symbolic field of "Auschwitz" and rely on physical demarcations to contain the site. For Jews, "Auschwitz" stands outside any physical construction and exists within its own universe: for some it is not even part of Poland, hence the possibility of requesting its extranational territoriality.

The Cross in the Crossfire: Debating a Polysemic Symbol

Beyond the arguments as to the meaning of "Oświęcim" and "Auschwitz" and the legitimacy or illegitimacy of the presence of religious symbols at the site or in its proximity, many of the discourses emerging from the War of the Crosses were focused on the symbol of the cross itself and on the meaning of the cross-planting action. Analysis of the discourse of various factions involved in the debate highlights the various (and conflicting) meanings of the cross in Polish history and in contemporary post-Communist Poland, and suggests that the debate about the cross in Poland was not merely a fight over a Christian symbol at the Holocaust's prime symbolic site and a conflict between Christians and Jews, but a debate among Poles over what constitutes a legitimate *national* symbol. Let's consider the main positions.

Bracketing the theological arguments against the presence of the cross and other religious symbols at Auschwitz, for Jews the cross has traditionally been seen as a sign of menace, standing as a symbol of indifference or even aggression and persecution during the Holocaust (Krajewski 1997). In the words of Dawid Warszawski, a Polish Jew,[5]

> This cross in Auschwitz is in our eyes the sign of the persecutors, not of the victims. Its erection at the cemetery of Jewish victims by Christian Europe insults us.... In Auschwitz, the place of death not of one Jew, but of one million, there should be no crosses. (*Gazeta Wyborcza*, April 21, 1998)

A similar argument was made by a reader of the Jewish monthly *Midrasz* in a letter to its editors:

> In Jerusalem, one Jew died on the cross—Christ. At Auschwitz, more than one million Jews perished, and this with much greater suffering. In

5. Dawid Warszawski is the pen-name of Konstanty Gebert, the editor-in-chief of *Midrasz*, a Jewish monthly, and a frequent contributor to *Gazeta Wyborcza*.

> Oświęcim, Jews constituted almost 99 percent of victims. . . . This cross is the disgrace of Polish Catholicism. (Narmi Michejda, *Midrasz*, April 1998)

Here the argument against the presence of the cross is cast in religious categories (Jews versus Christians), and suffering is measured quantitatively and qualitatively. The cross, however, is not only a universal Christian symbol: its presence at that site is more specifically associated with Polish Catholicism. The cross at the gravel pit thus signifies an attempt to "Christianize" Auschwitz and to "Polonize" its memory. According to Stanisław Krajewski, Jewish activist, public intellectual, and cochair of the Committee on the Christian-Jewish Dialogue, "The planting of crosses is the expression of Christian triumphalism" (1997, 247). For many ethnic Poles, on the other hand, efforts to remove the cross are understood as attempts at "de-Polonizing" "Oświęcim" and further "Judaizing" Auschwitz: it is interpreted as the exclusive appropriation of the symbol by Jews and their refusal to allow Poles to commemorate their own victims.

Under Communism, the presence of the cross in the public sphere was seen as something desirable by many opposed to the Communist regime, including atheists and Jews. As we have seen in chapter 1, this was especially true in the 1980s, when the secular Left took pride in the Polish pope and his human rights message, supported workers demonstrating with religious symbols in Gdańsk, and more generally embraced the church following the declaration of martial law in 1981. The cross was understood as a sign of diversity against an imposed monolithic worldview, and its physical presence served as a reminder of the regime's fragility. In 1983, for example, during the fortieth anniversary of the Warsaw Ghetto Uprising, Marek Edelman, the uprising's last living leader, decided that Solidarity's independent commemoration of the event should be marked by the laying of a cross with flowers at the Ghetto's Heroes monument.

In post-Communist Poland, however, the cross in the public sphere—and especially at Auschwitz and its proximity—now signifies for liberal intellectuals from the Left (and for some liberal Roman Catholic circles) the imposition of a set of values and an intolerance toward Others. It stands as the rejection of the principles of the *Rechtsstaat*, where particular allegiances are relegated to the private sphere—an opinion that was similarly expressed in debates about the constitution's preamble. The symbol of the cross at Auschwitz for them stands for an ethno-Catholic vision of Poland which excludes not only Jews from its present and past, but also all of those who do not think of themselves or of Poland in those terms. It is a sign of opposition to, instead of reconciliation with, Jews; a sign of Poles' refusal to engage in an open dialogue with the Other. For liberal Catholics associated with the Catholic publications *Tygodnik Powszechny*, *Znak*, and *Więź*, such as Stefan Wilkanowicz, the large papal cross is a political instrument, a provocation contrary to the Christian meaning of the symbol (*Gazeta Wyborcza*, August 7, 1998), while for others it is the shameful expression of Polish nationalism.

For editors of Far-Left, anticlerical publications such as the satirical weekly *Nie*, the cross stands for fundamentalist tendencies in Poland since the fall of Communism and represents the "narrow-minded clericalism and bigotry" of the so-called Catho-Right. In the words of Jerzy Urban, *Nie*'s owner and editor-in-chief, the "crossomania" is a comedy in which the crusaders, like madmen escaped from mental institutions, play "Cathonationalist gardeners . . . planting crosses on gravel, like dogs and cats feeling the need to mark their territory" (*Nie*, no. 35, 1998).

In the discourse of conservative Catholic groups, attempts at removing the cross are still associated with the Communist past of forced atheization and religious repression. The presence of the cross in the public sphere here signifies, in an interesting twist, the religious freedom and religious *pluralism* associated with Western culture and values, as expressed in this Catholic organization's declaration against the removal of the papal cross from the gravel pit:

> Signs and symbols are the testimony of [the living's] faith and national identity, their dignity and freedom, their endurance and hope. For Christians, for the majority of Poles, the cross is such a sign. In our forefathers' history, the partitioning powers or the occupants more than once have fought against the presence of the sign of the holy cross on Polish land. Today, in a free and independent European country, in a state based on the rule of law and democracy, the battle with the symbols of religious faith is contrary to the spirit of Europe and the expression of lack of respect for people of other faith or nationality. (Civitas Christiana, printed in Katolicka Agencja Informacyjna, *Biuletyn*, no. 12, March 24, 1998)[6]

6. Civitas Christiana's declaration was also read by Father Adolf Chojnacki during a Mass at the gravel pit on July 5, 1998. After the homily, speeches were made by activists and Radio Maryja personalities. The Mass ended with the singing of "Boże coś Polskę" (*Nasz Dziennik*, July 15, 1998). Civitas Christiana is the direct heir of Pax, a lay Roman Catholic organization that until 1989 recognized the Socialist system and the leading role of the Communist Party. In 1994, the organization changed its name and in 1997 was officially recognized by the Catholic Church as a

If the second part of the argument made sense under Communism, it is clearly anachronistic in post-Communist Poland. Nevertheless, the message finds a ready audience.

Generally speaking, the cross for Christians symbolizes suffering, love, and victory over evil. But it is also said to refer more specifically to Poland's Christian heritage, to resistance against occupation under the Partitions, during World War II, and under Communism. Consider, to wit, Józef Cardinal Glemp's words about the cross at the beginning of the summer of 1998, when people were mobilizing for its defense but were not yet erecting additional crosses at the gravel pit:

> The Polish people [*lud*] have been put up on the cross. That is why they love this cross, a sign of love in suffering wherever it is: in the shipyards, in Warsaw, or in Oświęcim. In Oświęcim the cross has been standing and will stand.... The Eiffel Tower did not and does not please everyone, but it is not a reason to remove it and take it down. (*Tygodnik Powszechny*, June 6, 1998)

The sites enumerated by Cardinal Glemp are closely associated with the nation, with Polish martyrdom and resilience. All three are symbols of the moral victory of Poles under occupation: Oświęcim and Warsaw during the Second World War, and the Gdańsk shipyards under Communism. The Polish nation is identified here with Christ, in continuation with Polish Romantic thought: its history and destiny are intimately linked to the cross. Most striking, however, is the analogy drawn by Glemp between the cross at Auschwitz and the Eiffel Tower in Paris, which shows the extent to which he misunderstood, downplayed, and belittled the Jewish position.

For traditionalists and the Roman Catholic Right, the cross represents the endurance of the Polish nation through the centuries, the resurrection of the Polish state, and now the reaffirmation of Poland's mission in the new Europe as well. In a more narrow connection to Auschwitz, it represents years of national domination and religious repression during the German occupation, but also under the Communist rule. The cross stands as a sign of resistance to occupants and oppressors and as a sign of victory over them. For many Poles, then, the cross at Auschwitz is above all a symbol of Polish

"Catholic organization." The shadow of Pax, however, remains. The director of the Małopolska division indicated to me in an interview that the organization was quite isolated in the public sphere for two main reasons: its anti-Semitic legacy through Bolesław Piasecki, for milieus of the Center-Left; and its collaboration with the regime under Communism, for traditionalist and right-wing groups and newspapers (interview with Marian Ćwik, June 11, 2001).

sovereignty. This is especially so after pressure from various international Jewish organizations and groups to remove it and in the face of proposals for the extraterritoriality of the camp. In the words of Kazimierz Świtoń, "The time has come to make a choice: the Cross or servitude. . . . If we do not defend this Cross—the time has come for the Fifth Partition of Poland" (in Marszałek 1999, unnumbered pages).[7] One hundred and thirty parliamentarians, mostly from the right-wing coalition AWS,[8] signed a letter to the prime minister, Jerzy Buzek, asking him to ensure the presence of the cross at the gravel pit because the defense of the cross is the state's "legal and moral duty." The parliamentarians justified their position by, among other arguments, defining the cross as part of the "national heritage" and the site where it stands as the site of "Polish martyrdom":

> The cross standing in the site sanctified by the mass martyrdom of Poles and of representatives of other nations should last as a sign of suffering and sacrifice and at the same time as the sign of faith and hope for those who in great numbers gave their lives in this inhuman place. . . . The sovereign Polish Republic guards all those signs [of faith, and of religious and national identity] against all attacks. (Katolicka Agencja Informacyjna, *Biuletyn*, no. 12, March 24, 1998)

One recognizes in the letter the Socialist discourse of "Oświęcim" as the site of martyrdom of "the Polish Nation and other Nations," which de facto sacralizes the gravel pit.[9] Here again the cross is associated with national identity in addition to Christian faith. It is implied that the republic has the duty, now that it is sovereign, to defend the symbol against all attacks, whether from secular post-Communists, Jews, or foreign powers.

The Christian symbol thus evokes historical and contemporary associations far removed from its religious semantics. In the Right's discourse, it is clearly related to what a free and "truly Polish" Poland should be. For the Defenders of the Cross especially, the cross symbolizes the Catholic "essence" of Polishness. Here is what Mr. Świtoń told me:

7. The Molotov-Ribentropp pact, which divided Poland between Nazi Germany and the Soviet Union, and the conferences of Postdam and Yalta are commonly referred to as the Fourth Partition of Poland.

8. 109 were from AWS; the rest were from PSL and ROP.

9. Note here the tension between interpretations of the status of the gravel pit in Polish discourses: it is sometimes argued that the gravel pit is outside the sacred grounds of Auschwitz the former camp and belongs instead to the profane sphere of Oświęcim the town; and sometimes argued that it is sacred ground, given the murders of Poles at the site.

> The cross is the foundation of our identity—that's the cross. Poles have won under the cross, they went to death with the cross. If a Pole is not defending the cross, I think he's not a Pole; he's just an ordinary person. If a Pole allows the removal of crosses, he also stops being a Pole. (Interview, April 25, 2001)

Polishness here is equated with Catholicism, and the cross, for Świtoń, is the symbol of that fusion. Therefore, the removal of the cross signifies not only the stripping of one's Catholic identity, but also of one's national identity. Without the cross one is condemned to her presocial state with no "self," an "ordinary person," in the words of Świtoń. Polishness, we may also deduce from this view, is "extra-ordinary."

Divided We Stand: The Roman Catholic Church and the Cross

Even among Catholics the cross has various significations, linked with a variety of positions that could be heard during the War of the Crosses. In fact, that event brought to light serious differences and divisions within the institutional church itself. The hierarchy's position on the papal and the other crosses was far from unified, and clearly unfolded and shifted in accord with developing events. Bishops expressed different opinions, and Cardinal Glemp's declarations were inconsistent, ranging from open approval to condemnation of the action. I now turn to the analysis of the different understandings of the cross as a symbol and of the War of the Crosses as an event *within* the Roman Catholic Church and the Catholic community at large, and document the shifts in the evaluation of the event as it unfolded in the summer of 1998.

The Cross as Ecclesiastic Bone of Contention

Once the War of the Crosses was fully engaged, the harshest critique of the church's position—or lack thereof—came from Father Stanisław Musiał, known for his trenchant opinions, direct style, and vehement denunciations of anti-Semitism.[10] In an article published in the liberal Catholic weekly

10. This was not the first time that Father Musiał publicly expressed a critical stance toward the church. Recall his intervention concerning the church's soft stance vis-à-vis anti-Semitism within its ranks in his article "Black Is Black" (chapter 2). Father Musiał was reprimanded by his superiors for publicly criticizing the church, and was threatened with exile from Cracow, where he had a high public profile in liberal Catholic circles and was actively involved in

Tygodnik Powszechny, Father Musiał expressed not only his indignation at the cross action, but additionally, if not primarily, his disapproval of the church's passivity in response to the controversy:

> The shameful cross game at Auschwitz continues. What is going on here does not have anything to do with God or with the commemoration of the victims. For almost forty-five years after the war this place did not interest either Catholics or patriots.... There is in this country an Authority that, from the raison d'être of its mission, should put an end to this battle of the crosses at Auschwitz. Everything, however, points to the fact that this Authority has buried its head in the sand, and what is worse, wants national and world public opinion to interpret this gesture of silence as a sign of virtue, discernment, and civic consideration.... It is high time for the church in Poland to awaken and raise its voice against the abuse of religious symbols for extrareligious goals. In truth, those against Christ's Cross are not the ones demanding that the crosses be removed from the gravel pit... but rather those who planted the crosses, and those who want them to remain. Christ's cross is not a tight fist. And that is what the crosses at the gravel pit at Auschwitz are. (*Tygodnik Powszechny*, August 9, 1998)

A few days later, in a message perceived by many, including Świtoń, as supporting the retention of the papal cross (interview, April 25, 2001), Glemp replied that the church had no monopoly on the symbol of the cross, and therefore could not authoritatively intervene:

> The cross is not the property of the Catholic Church, but is linked with Christianity, and as a symbol it is understood and recognized in Western civilization as a sign of love and suffering. Conceived in that way, not only the episcopate but all those who accept this cross with faith have the right to its use and its defense. (August 6, 1998; published in Katolicka Agencja Informacyjna, *Biuletyn*, no. 32, August 11, 1998)[11]

Christian-Judaic and Polish-Jewish dialogue. He became a persona non grata in the official corridors of the Catholic Church (interviews with Stanisław Musiał, April 9, 2001; and Stanisław Obirek, May 22, 2004).

11. Father Musiał's article was submitted to *Tygodnik Powszechny* on August 5, but appeared in the weekly three days later, on the eighth. Meanwhile, Cardinal Glemp was given a copy, and reacted to it in public immediately, on the sixth. This is why Cardinal Glemp's response to Father Musiał's editorial appeared before that editorial was even on the newsstands.

By emphasizing that the cross is not the church's exclusive property, Cardinal Glemp indirectly justified the passivity of the church in the affair. And although Glemp stressed the right to defend the cross as a *Christian* symbol, he also indirectly justified its political instrumentalization by attributing responsibility for the crisis to the "Jewish side":

> This is Polish land, and any imposition by others is taken as interference with sovereignty.... Mr. Świtoń and his group... are often singled out as the cause for the escalation of tensions. We have to say, in the name of truth, that this group did not come out of nowhere, but rather in reaction to the constant and increasingly strident pestering by the Jewish side for the rapid removal of the cross. (Ibid.)

In the same declaration, Cardinal Glemp also directly and contemptuously denounced Father Musiał's position:

> Some are decidedly for the defense of the cross, others are supporters of the Jewish option... such as Father Musiał, editor of *Tygodnik Powszechny*. The one-sided condemnation of the episcopate for its not satisfying the Jewish side cannot bear fruit, mostly because it is unfounded.... We have to ponder how the planting of new crosses can be used in the process of agreement and unification. The affair must find a positive resolution on the condition that people at the service of a one-sided solution, like Father Musiał for example, will not inflame [popular feelings] with their apodictic judgments. (Ibid.)

In this expressly personal rebuttal, Cardinal Glemp accused Musiał of supporting the "Jewish option" instead of defending the cross, as a Roman Catholic priest should. More significant, however, was Cardinal Glemp's intimation that the planting of new crosses was a positive and potentially productive action, demonstrating once more how oblivious he was to the gravity of the situation. The same week, however, Archbishops Henryk Muszyński and Damian Zimoń characterized the cross-planting action as both a provocation and the hurtful manipulation of the religious symbol for political purposes.[12] In an appeal to stop planting crosses in which he

12. Archbishops Muszyński and Zimoń are "purist" Roman Catholics. Contrary to Cardinal Glemp's traditional model of Polish Catholicism, which accentuates the public dimension of faith and politicizes religion, "purists" focus on the deepening of faith, on its active internalization.

publicly contradicted his superior, Archbishop Muszyński declared, "Those who are using the cross as an instrument in the fight against anyone are actually acting as *enemies of Christ's cross*" (Katolicka Agencja Informacyjna, *Biuletyn*, no. 32, August 11, 1998; emphasis in the text).[13] In response to this new twist, only four days after rebutting the argument put forth by Father Musiał, Cardinal Glemp issued a new statement, in which he charged that the cross-planting had been orchestrated by "irresponsible groups." Their action, he said, diminished the symbol of the cross: "The gravel pit, this way, loses its gravity" (*Rzeczpospolita*, August 11, 1998). The Primate thus appealed to those concerned to stop planting crosses at the gravel pit, and asked bishops to "try to control the rise of this unchurch-like action" (ibid.). Bishop Tadeusz Pieronek similarly characterized the groups involved in the action as an "anti-Church" (*Wprost*, August 23, 1998).

Finally, at the end of August—nearly two months after the War of the Crosses was declared by Świtoń—the Episcopate of Poland issued a much-awaited official declaration in which it condemned the action, echoing the position of Archbishop Muszyński, vice-chair of the episcopate's commission, instead of the earlier ones of its chair, Cardinal Glemp:

> As shepherds of the church we address our words to the faithful, expressing our gratitude to those who have suffered for the cross during the unlawful Communist period. . . . At the same time, we categorically

According to them, traditional Catholicism is overly associated with secular emotions; it has become a political religion. They warn against the conflation of nation and religion. Instead of emphasizing Polish Catholic exceptionalism, like the traditionalists and integrists do, "purists" stress the universality of Catholicism. They also consistently promote the principles of Vatican II: dialogue, ecumenism, and attempts to modernize the Polish church. "Purists" should therefore not be characterized as resistant to change; rather, the changes they endorse are those devoted to a universalist construction of faith-based Catholic renewal. Despite their multiple critiques of traditional Catholicism, they do not reject it altogether, but rather aim at modifying it so that it can better adapt to the new exigencies of the contemporary moment. The "purist" model has a strong base in the church hierarchy and is particularly popular among younger priests (Gowin 2000). For a typology of Catholics and an analysis of cleavages within the church following the fall of Communism, see Zubrzycki (2005).

13. Archbishop Muszyński very early on, even before the actual declaration of the War of the Crosses, had condemned the agitation taking place around the papal cross in a homily that he concluded with the following prayer: "Save us, Holy Spirit, from stupidity masquerading as wisdom, from lie masquerading as truth, from blindness masquerading as foresight, from fanaticism masquerading as faith, from filth masquerading as purity, from hatred masquerading as love; Save us from slavery masquerading as freedom, from hypocrisy masquerading as honesty, from pride masquerading as humility; Save us from the rule of Satan" (printed in *Gazeta Wyborcza*, May 10, 1998).

> underline that it is forbidden for anyone to overuse the holy sign of the cross and turn it *against the church in Poland*, by creating agitation and conflict. We declare that the action of planting crosses at the gravel pit has been undertaken *without the permission of the concerned diocesan Bishop, and even against his will.*... Planting crosses *on one's own initiative* at the gravel pit is provocative and is contrary to the dignity that such a place requires.... *Organized in such a fashion*, the action equally hurts the memory of the murdered victims, the well-being of the church and the nation, in addition to inflicting pain on the different sensibility of our Jewish brothers. The cross, which for us Christians is the highest sign of love and sacrifice, can never serve as an instrument in the fight against anyone. ("Oświadczenie Rady Stałej Konferencji Episkopatu Polski w sprawie krzyży w Oświęcimiu," August 26, 1998, published in *Tygodnik Poszechny* on September 6, 1998; my emphases)

Note here that the primary reasons for condemning the cross-planting were that it had negative repercussions on the church and had been undertaken without the hierarchy's permission, even against its expressed will. It is revealing that in this statement the Jewish perspective occupies the last position in the list of concerns. The action was said to hurt the memory of the victims, the church, and the nation, and only then was it observed to offend the "different sensibility of our Jewish brothers." In the wake of this declaration, it was decided that the papal cross would remain but that the other crosses should be removed. It was suggested that any person or group who had brought a cross to the gravel pit could reclaim it. As I noted in the book's introduction, the crosses were finally removed only much later, in May 1999.

For Father Musiał, the episcopate's declaration, while welcome, came too late and did not go far enough, especially with regards to Polish-Jewish relations (interview, April 9, 2001). Other prominent "open" Roman Catholics, however, were satisfied by the episcopate's resolution. Stefan Wilkanowicz, liberal Catholic intellectual editor-in-chief of the monthly *Znak* and cochair of the Auschwitz International Council, reiterated that for Christians, the site cannot be deprived of the cross. The absolute proscription of religious symbols demanded by the Jewish side, according to him, is untenable for Christians. That said, Mr. Wilkanowicz stressed that the presence of a Christian symbol at the gravel pit need not be the papal cross, eight meters high and visible from inside the former camp. A modest monument commemorating the death of Christians with a small cross on it should be satisfactory to Christians without giving offense to Jews (interview, April 23, 2001).

For Archbishop Muszyński, the meaning of the cross for Christians at large, and for Poles especially, is in tension with Jewish demands for the removal of the symbol, ultimately leading to a seemingly unsolvable impasse:

> For us Christians, the cross will always be the greatest holiness, the sign of salvation and the symbol of the highest love freely accepted for saving the world. From the beginning of Polish history, the cross also became deeply inscribed in our forefathers' land so that there is no way to understand Poles and the Polish nation without the cross and resurrection, of which the cross is the symbol, the condition, and the sign. Conceived in this way, the cross deserves to be defended always and everywhere, because it is the most complete symbol and sign of the entire Christendom. One cannot forget, however, that our non-Christian Jewish Brothers associate with the cross a completely different content. They expect the same respect of their convictions as we Christians do. The content of those cannot be reduced to a common denominator. (Katolicka Agencja Informacyjna, *Biuletyn*, no. 32, August 11, 1998)

Although the Christian and Jewish views cannot be reconciled, Archbishop Muszyński, unlike Cardinal Glemp in his early declarations, pointed out that the outcome of the War of the Crosses was the instrumental exploitation of the cross and its Christian meaning, resulting in the negation of the Christian spirit (ibid.). The archbishop also tried to rescue the words of John Paul II from their illegitimate use:

> The reference to the words spoken in Zakopane by the pope, "Defend the Cross," to justify the action of the crosses at the gravel pit constitutes an abuse, and is the evident deformation of the actual intentions of the pope, just as it is the instrumentalization of the cross, which is made into a tool for one's own, unclear interests that affect the good of the Church, our Homeland, and Christian-Jewish dialogue. . . . One must really be completely deprived of any common sense to think that the Holy Father desires that the defense of the cross be used in the fight against whomever. (Ibid.)

In a way reminiscent of the episcopate's official condemnation of the War of the Crosses, Muszyński's statement, while very critical of the Defenders of the Cross, shows the extent to which the controversy was primarily understood as one detrimental to the church and the nation, and only secondarily relevant to the "Christian-Jewish dialogue" (Jews themselves are not mentioned at all).

If at the beginning of the War of the Crosses Cardinal Glemp attributed the event to the "constant . . . pestering by the Jewish side," as the event unfolded and clearly escaped the control of the church, it was essentially placed in the framework of an *internal affair*: a conflict between the Roman Catholic Church and disobedient Catholics, which was harmful to both the church and the fatherland. It is only then that the church finally took an official stand and decided that the papal cross would remain while the other crosses would be removed. Indeed, the attitude of the church's hierarchy toward the War of the Crosses evolved throughout the summer from implicit approval to indifference, to apprehension, and, finally, to condemnation. These changes in perception and response went hand in hand with the drama's unfolding.

From the moment the church issued its official position on the papal cross and "Świtoń's crosses," its hierarchy attempted to restrict the semantic orbit of the cross and regain discursive and ritual control of the symbol. The bishops convened to emphatically promote a "correct theology of the cross," since it had become apparent that "a deeper reflection about the meaning of the cross [was] lacking" (August 25–26, 1998, in Katolicka Agencja Informacyjna, *Biuletyn*, no. 35). Archbishop Muszyński characterized the incorrect theology as "a great problem internal to the church" (ibid.). According to him, "the cross is a sign of love, forgiveness, and unity, and not exclusively the symbol of a rather narrow conception of identity that can then be freely exploited in the fight with others" (ibid.). As he saw it, it had been easy to mobilize Poles around the symbol "because of their emotional attachment to the cross, attacked and destroyed by two totalitarian regimes," which had therefore become "a beautiful patriotic-religious symbol, worshiped as such" (ibid.).

Interviews with priests, scholars, and other public figures on the meaning of the cross appeared in the press. While Świtoń claimed in right-wing Roman Catholic publications that the cross was the symbol of Polishness, Father Wacław Oszajca asserted that

> when one says that the cross is a sign of national identity, the meaning of the cross is denied—national identity is put above the cross. For Christians, it should be the opposite: national identity, the identity of every human being . . . is understandable only through the cross and Christ. (*Wprost*, August 23, 1998)

Priest and philosopher Józef Tischner similarly insisted that the cross must be above national conflicts—which is how he understood the War of the Crosses—otherwise it is merely two intersecting pieces of wood (*Gazeta Wyborcza*, October 17, 1998). Father Andrzej Zuberbier, a respected theologian, diagnosed the War of the Crosses as revealing the problem of different understandings of the cross *within the church itself* more than the problem of the different understandings of the cross held by Christians and Jews (*Tygodnik Powszechny*, August 2, 1998).

Toward Sectarianism?

The church's rather late efforts at disseminating a "more orthodox" theology of the cross were in vain. The episcopate's condemnation of the action and its active promotion of a "correct" theology of the cross had no real effect on those who continued to bring crosses to the gravel pit throughout the fall of 1998. In fact, two priests even consecrated the crosses as well as a small chapel built by Świtoń—an act that supplied the Defenders of the Cross with fresh ammunition (plate 5). The group could now argue that not only the papal cross but all the other crosses must not be removed. According to Kazimierz Świtoń and the Defenders of the Cross, the church had no monopoly on the symbol—a position Cardinal Glemp himself had articulated in an early declaration. What was more, they argued, "*We* are the church." Mr. Świtoń explained this statement to me:

> Our church did not defend [the cross]. Because the church is divided: there's the administration and there's the People of God. . . . But the church, in fact, it is the People of God, just like Christ founded it, and not the administration, bureaucrats who are priests, bishops, or cardinals. (Interview, April 25, 2001)

In this explanation, Świtoń distinguishes between the institutional church—the administration and its bureaucrats who did not come to the defense of the cross and Polishness—and the People of God, a "truer" church, faithful to its mission of guarding the nation. Alhough the statement "*We* are the church" is reminiscent of the democratic, post–Vatican II definition of the church as a "community of believers," Świtoń's comment smacks of something closer to the Weberian distinction between church and sect, between a routinized and institutionalized movement and a charismatic one whose objectives have not been bent by the needs of the institution (M. Weber 1978, 456). What defines Świtoń's "People of God," however, is their "true" Polishness. According to him, "a Pole who does not defend the cross stops being a Pole." Moreover, for him the hierarchy of the Catholic Church in Poland was no longer Catholic at all, since at one point the bishops stopped defending the cross *as the symbol of Polishness*.[14] Just as only those who defend the cross are Poles, only those who defend the cross qua Polishness are Catholic. The statement "*We* are the church," therefore, opposes the "no longer Catholic" Catholic Church (because not nationalist enough) to promote a truer church, the People of God, defined here as "true Poles," that is, those who defend the cross as a symbol of Polishness. "By defending the cross," Mr. Świtoń told me, "I was defending Polish identity. *Polish identity*. Because Poland without the cross would not be Poland. Mickiewicz already said it a hundred-something years ago: 'Only under this cross / Only under this sign / Poland is Poland / and a Pole is a Pole'" (interview, April 25, 2001). Indeed, many crosses at the gravel pit bore on their inscriptions these verses, commonly attributed to the Romantic national bard. As we have seen earlier, one cross, in either a creative inversion or a Freudian slip, replaced the poem's last verse with "and a *Catholic is a Pole*" (my emphasis). These reflections might be the best contemporary articulations of the fusion of Roman Catholicism and Polishness within a single category, that of Polak-katolik.[15]

As these few quotations illustrate, for Świtoń, the Defenders of the Cross, and many other national-Catholic groups, Catholicism is so closely associated with the Polish nation that there is no perceived tension between the universalism of the religion and its nationalist interpretation, a phenomenon typical of religious nationalism when the religion in question is universalist in scope. The supranational dimension of Catholicism is simply absent from the logic of this discourse, and although the Defenders of the Cross borrow freely from the rhetoric of Vatican II, the group's interpretation is far removed from the postcouncil teachings. In fact, the National Council of Lay Catholics came to the defense of the church and

14. Mr. Świtoń also explained to me why the hierarchy was neither truly Polish nor truly Roman Catholic. According to him, the church's hierarchy is controlled by crypto-Jews: children who had been saved from the Holocaust by nuns and priests and converted to Catholicism, and who were now out to destroy the church from within (interview, April 25, 2001). This view is commonly reported in newspapers and publications of the Far Right, like *Nasz Dziennik* and *Nasza Polska*.

15. See Czarnowski ([1934] 1988) for a classical ethnography of the Polak-katolik stereotype; Zawadzki (1996) for an analysis of the Catholicization of the national tie, a process which was accentuated and generalized only under Socialism; Nowicka (1991) for an analysis of the contemporary significance of the Polak-katolik stereotype in processes of inclusion and exclusion; and Koseła (2003) for the most recent reappraisal of the stereotype, mostly through survey data.

denounced the usurpation of the language of Vatican II for what it perceived to be political ends:

> The fanatic agitators from the Oświęcim gravel pit declared that "*they* are the church." We categorically protest against such a caricatured vision of Catholicism. The teachings of the Second Vatican Council about the church as the People of God are very dear to us. That is why we do not agree with its perversion, when, in the name of a private conception of Christianity, the slogan "*We* are the church" is used in the fight against the ecclesial hierarchy. The National Council of Lay Catholics expresses solidarity with the pastors of our church, and deplores the actions of those persons who insult the bishops, disrespecting their mission in the church. We appeal to all Catholics—lay and religious—for whom the words "We are the church" are not the call for fighting anyone but the expression of the deepest identity: Let us give . . . the testimony of our position and affirm that "to be in the church" means to live according to the commandment of love. (Katolicka Agencja Informacyjna, *Biuletyn*, no. 34, August 25, 1998)

It was the illegitimate use and claim to ownership of Catholic rhetoric that prompted the reaction of this lay Catholic group, not the nationalist and anti-Semitic sentiments and actions such rhetoric suggests. Once again, the Defenders of the Cross's discourse was perceived and interpreted as a direct attack on the church, and was as such denounced.

Since the Catholic Church's hierarchy had "deserted the nation," the Defenders of the Cross saw no reason to abandon its mission—quite the contrary. Then the Society of Saint Pius X donned its cape and came to the rescue. The brotherhood was founded in 1970 by Archbishop Marcel Lefebvre, who refused to submit to the teachings of Vatican II and was subsequently excommunicated for schism by John Paul II in 1988. It was present for ritualizations at the gravel pit at least three times over the summer, celebrating Tridentine Masses, erecting its own cross (second highest after the papal cross), and blessing all the newly delivered crosses.[16] Before the official declaration of the episcopate, Lefebvre's society had celebrated two Masses at the site, which may have provided an additional incentive for the church

16. The schismatic group was present at the gravel pit on July 21, August 15 (the Feast of the Assumption), and August 30, 1998. A Tridentine Mass is a Mass celebrated in Latin, with a strict ritualistic code. The Second Vatican Council replaced the Tridentine Mass with the New Mass, celebrated in vernacular languages. Although the public celebration of Tridentine Masses is not banned, it is restricted by most bishops.

to finally react to the War of the Crosses. The society's involvement in the War of the Crosses clearly had an impact on the framing of the events as an internal crisis.

At one such ritual in mid-August, a priest from the Society of Saint Pius X insisted in his homily that

> by defending the Cross... we are not only defending a piece of wood... and the place where it is standing. The issue at stake here is the defense of our Faith and of our national identity. [National identity] is the guarantor of our Faith's maintenance. (Oświęcim, August 15, 1998)

Officiants moreover insisted in their homilies that the Society of Saint Pius X not only *was* Catholic, but that it was actually representing the "true" Catholic faith, untarnished by the corrupt teachings of Vatican II:

> The Society of Saint Pius X is here today to help the faithful. Canonical law demands from the chaplain that he serve the faithful... [who] feel abandoned by their shepherds and cannot find another way to take the sacraments. We are acting in complete accord with canonical law of the Roman Catholic Church. I repeat and confirm: a Roman Catholic Priest is standing before you.... It is not the Defenders of the Cross who accelerated the war: it was a spontaneous defensive reaction of the entire nation, which however surpassed all expectations. Those who should defend the cross are on the opposite side of the barricades. How is that possible? Where does this tragic situation come from? Allow me to explain something to you, why we are here now and where this great crisis in the church is coming from. Because in effect, everything that we are experiencing now has its cause. This cause is the crisis, the terrible crisis in the church... : ecumenism. (Homily, Oświęcim, printed in *Zawsze Wierni*, no. 24, September–October 1998)

Like Cardinal Glemp in his first declaration, the Society of Saint Pius X exonerated the Defenders of the Cross, which had merely initiated a nationwide defensive reaction to Jewish demands. But while Glemp attributed blame to the "Jewish side," the Society of Saint Pius X accused the *church* of not defending the cross firmly enough.

The religious disobedience of Catholics and the infiltration of the schismatic group were a catalyst and cause for alarm within the Roman Catholic Church. Catholic and secular media initiated an information campaign about the Society of Saint Pius X, and it became the occasion to discuss not only problems within the church and the conflicts between the church and self-proclaimed Poles-Catholics, but also the state of Polish Catholicism more generally. By the end of the summer, it became increasingly clear to many observers (and shapers of public opinion) that the cross action was directed less against Jews than against "secular society" and a church modernizing in the spirit of Vatican II. According to Jacek Żakowski, a journalist associated with *Gazeta Wyborcza* and invested in a dialogue with "open" Catholics, "at the horizon of the debate we can see with increasing clarity the attempt at creating a folk, populist, integrist church acting independently from canonical structures" (*Gazeta Wyborcza*, August 31, 1998).[17]

In an editorial in a Center-Left weekly magazine, *Wprost*, Father Wacław Oszajca summarized the challenges before the church: "The church stands here before the very difficult issue of internal dialogue. What is happening now may be for us an opportunity—on the condition that we start talking to each other and not excommunicate" (August 23, 1998). Allusions to potential excommunications were indeed eventually made. The episcopate devoted a special communiqué to explain to Catholics what the Society of Saint Pius X was, and what the implications were for orthodox Catholics associating with it:

> The Society of Saint Pius X created structures outside the Catholic Church. A group of priests and those faithful to the Society of Saint Pius X rejected the resolutions of the Vatican II Council, which John Paul II is implementing with such intensity. This group rejected as well post–Vatican II legislation and does not recognize the power of the pope in the Catholic Church. Despite the efforts of the Holy See, the members of the Society of Saint Pius X . . . broke in 1988 its unity link with the Holy Father, Bishop of Rome and the Successor of Saint Peter. In this way, they became a schismatic group separate from the one Catholic Church, and accordingly do not have the right to use the designation Catholic in their activities. It is necessary here to remember that the affiliation of a Catholic with this schismatic group entails the punishment of excommunication. (*Konferencja Episkopatu Polski*, November 27, 1998 [http://www.episcopat.pl])

Note in the above communiqué the repeated references to John Paul II, who was and still is an uncontested authority and a national hero in Poland,

17. Żakowski published a book-length interview with Jerzy Turowicz (1990), and coauthored a book of conversations with Adam Michnik and Father Józef Tischner (1995).

as an attempt to further delegitimate the schismatic group. The Society of Saint Pius X also made multiple references to the pope in its homilies, publications, and Web site in an attempt to counter the claim that the group is not Roman Catholic and to gain legitimacy. As we have seen in the previous chapter, the Defenders of the Cross also purportedly acted to defend the "papal" cross and obey the pope's summons "to defend the cross." John Paul II, then, served as a legitimating currency, a symbol competed over to legitimize competing views, positions, and actions. That the pontiff was Polish, moreover, further blurred the universality of the Catholic Church: the pope was seen, in Poland, as the national spiritual leader, an uncontested and uncontestable authority.[18]

In an interesting turn of events, the Lefevrists, as the followers of Marcel Lefebvre's Society of Saint Pius X are commonly called in Poland, became a chief scapegoat of the church's fiasco. By the fall of 1998, voices such as that of Father Musiał had been muted: the culprits in the War of the Crosses and the crisis in the church—Jews and the schismatic group—were forces *external* to the church yet creating *internal* damage to the Polish Catholic body. The War of the Crosses was compared to the attempts by the Communist regime to divide and conquer:

> Do you realize, dear brothers and sisters, what a terrible and absurd paradox, that someone wants to turn the cross against the church in Poland and awaken the distrust of the faithful toward the bishops . . . ? We know those methods well. We are keeping them fresh in our memory and in the live tissue of our hearts. The serpent entwined its slippery belly around the tree of paradise, but it cannot entwine this tree's life, which is the cross at Golgotha. No one has the right to turn the cross against a free and democratic fatherland and its current struggle to define its present and future shape. (Bishop Tadeusz Rakoczy's homily, August 14, 1998, printed in Katolicka Agencja Informacyjna, *Biuletyn*, no. 34)

Indeed, as the last line suggests, the War of the Crosses was also about what the new Poland should be and become. But if Bishop Rakoczy saw in that event an attack on the church reminiscent of Communists' old battles, Archbishop Józef Życiński abandoned that simplistic explanation and understood it instead as a "pathology of the past," as the swinging back

18. This has led Stanisław Obirek, a Jesuit priest, to describe the adoration of John Paul II in Poland as a sort of uncritical "papofilia" that functions at a very superficial level, ultimately preventing the faithful from fully engaging the papal teachings. Father Obirek was severely reprimanded by his superiors for expressing this view (interview, May 22, 2004).

of the pendulum from imposed internationalism to an immature patriotism. On November 11, on the occasion of Independence Day, he preached:

> Until now we did not have the conditions to learn a deep and mature patriotism. In the official propaganda of the Polish People's Republic we were prescribed proletarian internationalism, and talk about the Fatherland was treated as a nationalist deviation. The pathologies of the past can still take revenge. Today, some milieus direct their entire energies toward a fight with slogans contending who is the greater patriot. This is the kind of patriotism that leaves injuries, [marked by] intrigues and [used by] shrewd people with phraseology in their mouths. May Christ not cry over us as He cried over Jerusalem, where conflicting elites of the Pharisees and Sadducees were colliding. May He not cry over us, when we quarrel about [who has] the monopoly over patriotism. (Printed in Katolicka Agencja Informacyjna, *Biuletyn*, no. 46, November 17, 1998)

Father Tischner argued, in a similar vein, that the War of the Crosses is symptomatic of a part of Polish Catholicism: "The gravel pits are within ourselves," he argued, "growing from pain, loss, and fear. Could anyone have predicted twenty years ago that this is the 'gift' we would offer the Polish pope for the anniversary of his papacy?" (*Gazeta Wyborcza*, October 17, 1998)

Keeping a Measure of Authority

Our analysis would not be complete without asking how wide the support of the cross action was—that is, how representative the views of the Defenders of the Cross were, and how authoritative the declarations of Cardinal Glemp (August 10) and of the episcopate (August 25) proved in that matter.

If the Defenders of the Cross and even some Roman Catholic priests ignored the episcopate's condemnation of the cross action and persevered in their performance, public opinion polls suggest that the majority of Poles closed ranks with the hierarchy of the Catholic Church and followed its official line. Two polls highlight the significance of the official position of the church: one was taken after the personal request of Cardinal Glemp to halt the planting of crosses but *before* the official declaration of the episcopate; the other, after the said declaration (table 4).

According to the nationwide survey conducted before the official declaration of the episcopate concerning potential solutions to the conflict, 35 percent of respondents were of the opinion that the papal cross should remain at the gravel pit but that the other crosses should be removed;

Table 4. Support for the presence of the papal cross and other crosses at the gravel pit *before* and *after* the episcopate's official declaration on August 25, 1998

	***Before* the declaration: CBOS, Aug. 14–19, 1998** %	***After* the declaration: OBOP, Sept. 5–8, 1998** %
Keep only the papal cross	35	49
Keep all crosses	34	15

Source: CBOS (1998, $N = 1{,}085$) and OBOP (1998, $N = 1{,}011$).
Note: The questions for both surveys were slightly different. CBOS asked respondents, "How, according to you, should the conflict about the crosses erected at the gravel pit in Oświęcim be resolved?" whereas OBOP asked, "How should Poles murdered in Oświęcim be commemorated?"

27 percent thought that the other crosses should remain, but that no other crosses should be erected; and 7 percent thought that all the crosses should stay and that additional ones should continue to be brought to the site (for a total of 34 percent in favor of the presence of crosses in addition to the papal cross).

After the episcopate's declaration on August 25, however, the number of respondents who agreed that only the papal cross should remain at the site jumped by twelve percentage points (to 49 percent), while the proportion of those who did not agree with the official position of the church (and instead thought that Poles murdered at Auschwitz should be remembered by leaving *all* the crosses erected at the gravel pit) dropped by more than half, from 34 percent to 15 percent. This suggests that for the ordinary, "statistical" Pole, the church retains a significant measure of authority. This data led some observers to suppose that if the church had reacted earlier and had firmly and officially opposed the cross mobilization, the conflict at Auschwitz might not have assumed the proportions it ultimately did (Sułek 1998). But in fact, even before the official declaration, 74 percent of Poles felt that those participating in the War of the Crosses should submit to the personal appeals of Cardinal Glemp and other bishops and stop erecting crosses, while only 16 percent thought the right course of action was to "defend the papal cross" and erect new crosses in spite of the various appeals from prominent ecclesiastical figures (CBOS 1998).[19] It is likely for

19. Ten percent of the population was still unclear on the topic. Unlike the question posed by CBOS in table 4 ("How should the conflict be resolved?"), the question asked here was intended to *directly* address the relation of the respondent to requests of church authorities, such as Cardinal Glemp and Archbishop Muszyński, to stop planting crosses. The question was "According to you, the participants in the action for the defense of the cross should . . . " with the following options: (1) Submit to the request of the Primate and bishops and stop erecting new crosses; (2) Defend the cross and erect new ones regardless of the appeals from the church hierarchy; (3) Difficult to say.

Table 5. Preferred modes of commemorating Poles murdered at Auschwitz

	%
Papal cross/papal cross + other crosses	64
Replace papal cross with a smaller cross	1
Monument with a small cross on it	20
No reason for separate commemoration of Poles	10
Difficult to say	5

Source: OBOP (1998, $N = 1{,}011$).

this last group's opinion that the official declaration of the episcopate had the greatest effect.

These data do not contradict or invalidate my earlier claim articulated in chapter 2 concerning the significant decline of the church's authority in Polish public life since the fall of Communism. In fact, they confirm it by highlighting that it is the *political* involvement of the church that Poles reject, not its authority over matters of religion. The findings suggest that the church retains a measure of authority in what is perceived as its legitimate field and appropriate sphere of influence. The semantic and ritual manipulation of religious symbols was identified as the church's business; within this arena, a majority of Poles deferred to the ecclesial institution's decision, especially once its position was clearly articulated. The data also confirm the marginality of the Defenders of the Cross within the broader Polish landscape of public opinion.[20] Survey data, however, indicate that Poles decidedly favor the presence of the symbol of the cross (and more specifically the continued presence of the papal cross) at the gravel pit: as we can see in table 5, 65 percent of the population wish to commemorate Poles with crosses, as opposed to 30 percent who either would prefer a monument or do not see the need for a separate form of commemoration for Poles at Auschwitz.

Other data, concerning who has the right to decide how to commemorate the dead at Auschwitz and dictate the rules of management of the site, show that the stakes of the War of the Crosses were not only or merely religious, but depended on the understanding of "Auschwitz"/"Oświęcim" as symbols, and of Poland as a sovereign nation-state. Only 5 percent of the respondents recognized the right of the Israeli government and international Jewish organizations to demand the removal of religious symbols from the

20. Even *Nasz Dziennik*, while clearly supporting the presence of the papal cross at the gravel pit, did not endorse the War of the Crosses after the official declaration of the Episcopate of Poland. According to Świtoń, the newspaper refused to print a paid appeal by the Defenders of the Cross to continue planting crosses at the gravel pit (interview, April 25, 2001).

proximity of the camp, with the logic that Auschwitz is the site of collective memory of all nations and religions, and most of all the place of the extermination of Jews. For 34 percent of the adult population of Poland, Jews have no right to demand the removal of crosses from the grounds of the former camp and its proximity, because Auschwitz is located in a sovereign nation-state; therefore Poles alone are entitled to decide how to manage the site. Fifty-two percent nevertheless recognized that Poles should exercise that right with respect for the religious feelings of other groups. According to the overwhelming majority of the respondents (86 percent), then, Poles have the sovereign right to decide how to manage the grounds of the former camp and its surroundings, because Auschwitz is on the ground of the sovereign Republic of Poland (CBOS 1998).[21]

Conclusion

The specific crosses' inscriptions, their spatial arrangement at the gravel pit, and the diverse discourses about the symbol in general in post-Communist Poland and at Auschwitz in particular suggest important leads for our consideration.

The War of the Crosses highlights the divisions within Polish society and the different ways in which social groups actually articulate, "on the ground" and in the public sphere, the relationship between national identity and religion. The controversy came to be interpreted as a largely internal affair: as a debate among Poles about Poland, and a discussion among Roman Catholics about Catholicism in post-Communist Poland. The symbol of the cross, in this context, does not represent monolithic unity, but rather contains and brings to light religious and national conflict and fragmentation. The analysis of the discourses surrounding its presence at the gravel pit and its ritual use by Catholic nationalists allows us to deconstruct the homogeneity of Polish society: the overwhelming majority of Polish citizens are ethnically Polish and (at least nominally) Catholic, but what Polishness and Catholic identity "are," and the way they intersect, are polysemic and contested. This is not to say that the War of the Crosses was not about something other than tensions concerning visions of the nation and discord within the Catholic Church, for it obviously was. There is no question that anti-Semitism was a catalyst of the event; but it was interpreted as a national debate, and reframed as a crisis of Catholicism.

21. In the original Polish-language options for replying to the question "With which following opinion do you agree?" the term *Oświęcim* was used to refer to Auschwitz.

The meaning of the War of the Crosses changed as the crisis persisted and deepened. It was at first interpreted by diverse communities of discourse as a conflict over the meaning of "Auschwitz"/"Oświęcim," and narrated as a "war" waged by Poles to keep the memory of "Oświęcim" alive. The normative evaluations of the event, we have seen, diverged greatly: while some denounced the takeover of the gravel pit as a despicable anti-Semitic gesture, others saw in the event the just and legitimate fight of Poles for their nation and its symbols. However, after the episcopate's declaration, the continuous disobedient action of the Defenders of the Cross, and the persistent involvement of the Society of Saint Pius X, the War of the Crosses was progressively reframed as a problem originating not from within the church, as Father Musiał decried in his forceful editorial intervention, but outside it, and developing without, in spite of, and even against it. The culprits in the War of the Crosses were forces *external* to the church—Jews and disobedient Catholics—who caused *internal* damage to the Polish Catholic body. Although the framing of the War of the Crosses as an "un-church-like action" could be interpreted as a tactical device (Poles were certainly more likely to rally on behalf of the church rather than in support of the Jews), it also reflected the episcopate's real concern regarding Catholic disobedience, especially as the conflict continued to escalate and as the Society of Saint Pius X became involved in the action. Once the event was reconfigured as primarily a crisis of Catholicism and more specifically an attack on the church and on the good name of the nation, different communities of discourse, previously split in their normative evaluation of the event, converged to condemn the action. The Jewish objections were not enough for unanimous condemnation of the War of the Crosses; what prompted an unequivocal reaction to the event was the threat posed to Catholicism.

The analysis suggests that the controversy had two interlaced layers: the first one, the most apparent, concerned the presence of a Christian symbol at the symbolic site of the Holocaust, and brought out tensions between Christians/Poles and Jews. The second layer concerned the meaning of the cross in post-Communist Poland, or more precisely, of the cross in *independent* Poland. This debate, as we have seen, was more broadly about the association of Roman Catholicism and Polishness, and about the role of the church in the new Poland. Contrary to the myth of Poland's intrinsic Catholicism and of the monolithic authority of the church in that country, tension, fissures, and lines of division run deep. The Pole-Catholic association of identifications is reproduced only by determined cultural work on specific symbols and events and their meanings. This cultural "work," moreover, is carried by specific social groups and their media staging grounds to create communities of discourse, the formulations of which are disseminated—yet not necessarily assimilated—more or less successfully throughout the population at large. In this way, though the actors and groups involved may themselves be marginal figures, the event of the War of the Crosses became a crucible for mainstream articulations of religion and the nation in addition to their relation.

We have now considered the War of the Crosses from manifold analytical perspectives: key historical narratives (chapters 1 and 2) that informed performance; key symbols as situated in liminal space (chapter 3); aesthetics and the evocation of nationalized emotions (chapter 4); and the discursive flows in and through which relatively marginal actions became "an event" (chapter 5). In the conclusion that follows, I explore the significance of these manifold analytical points of purchase for broader reflections on religion and nationalism.

CONCLUSION

Nationalism and Religion Reexamined

During the summer and fall of 1998, while the War of the Crosses was being fought in Oświęcim, debated in Poland, and discussed throughout the world, the Łódź court rendered judgment on a civil case filed the year before by a self-proclaimed atheist. The plaintiff had sued the City of Łódź for displaying a cross in its city hall since 1990. He claimed that his personal well-being was threatened by the presence of the religious symbol, which was visible in the city-hall chambers during televised local proceedings that he had watched from home. The suit was grounded on article 25, law 2 of the 1997 Constitution of the Third Republic of Poland, which concerns the religious and philosophical neutrality of public organs. Though founded upon the constitutional guarantees of the state's neutral worldview, the regional court of Łódź rejected the lawsuit. It ruled that the plaintiff's well-being had not been infringed on by the presence of the cross, because, among other things, the cross as a traditional symbol in Polish culture had been objectified to the extent that its presence did not constitute a threat to anyone (*Rzeczpospolita*, June 30, 1998).

Upon the plaintiff's appeal, the Court of Appeals upheld the regional court's decision, adding that the display of crosses is not expressly forbidden by the constitution. Besides, it argued, the constitution even refers to God in its preamble (*Orzecznictwo sądów polskich*, 1999, 487). After demonstrating that the cross did not impinge on the plaintiff's freedom of conscience, the Court of Appeals grounded its judgment in an unusually long and detailed examination of the cross's symbolic meanings. It argued that in the Polish patriotic tradition, the cross has not only played a religious role, but also expressed a specific set of moral and historical values:

> Personal well-being cannot be understood abstractly, without reference to the tradition, culture, and history of the collectivity in which persons live and function. The symbol of the cross in the experiences of the Polish nation, in addition to its religious meaning . . . has also been inscribed in social consciousness as a symbol of death, pain, and sacrifice, and as a way of honoring all those who fought for and cared about freedom and independence in the struggle for national liberation during the Partitions and during the war with invaders. For centuries, the symbol of the cross has designated the graves of ancestors and the place of national memory. In nonreligious collective behavior, this last signification of the cross as an expression of respect for and unity with the liberators of the fatherland even has precedence, since other universal means to express respect have not been developed. . . . Understood and felt in that way, the symbolism of the cross, independently of its reference to an Absolute, is inscribed in the history of the country from its early dawn. (Ibid., 488)

Moreover, according to the court, the cross is expressly related to secular state institutions:

> The symbol of the cross in Polish society, in addition to its religious meaning, expresses moral order on which the idea of the state and society is based. . . . From the First Republic through the period of the Partitions and then after the recovery of national independence, the cross has been, in Polish tradition, linked with the legislative and judiciary powers. This fact itself does not prevent dialogue among people representing different worldviews. (Ibid.)

The symbol's religious semantics were overshadowed, in both courts' decisions, by its secular, merely "cultural" connotations. In this instance at least, the meaning of the cross in Poland's historic struggles and national values predominated over the symbol's putative Christian "essence." The cross is described as a sacred, yet thoroughly secular symbol, a phenomenon to which I return below.

Granted, the courts' decisions could be read in the context of the ongoing conflict in Oświęcim, but this case, like the other ones I analyzed in greater depth in this study, is telling. Behind an apparently straightforward, "commonsensical" legal verdict lies a complex, multilayered relationship between national identity and religion. Does the Polish case suggest a diminution of the public centrality of religion, with the cross deemed tolerable because sufficiently secularized, and thus not evocative of religious sentiments whatsoever? Or, conversely, does it present a hypertrophy of religion, with the cross now grown so omnivorous and all-encompassing as to devour the *Rechtsstaat* entirely, such that its religious meaning, however occluded as merely "cultural," is the champion left standing not only at Auschwitz but over the nation as a whole? Or perhaps we need a new alternative for evaluating the nation-religion relation? Before suggesting new theoretical avenues, it may be useful to pause and briefly retrace the path this study has traveled thus far.

Recapitulation of the Arguments and Empirical Findings

Deconstructing Polish National Identity

In chapter 1, I analyzed the historical formation and transformation of Polish nationalism and deconstructed the myth of an eternally and primordially Catholic Polish nation. The ethno-Catholic vision of Polish national identity is historically specific; the nation was (re)defined along ethnic lines with the disappearance of the Polish state. In the absence of "national" territorial boundaries and political sovereignty, Polishness lost its civic signification and was slowly reimagined as a primarily cultural affinity rooted not in political institutions but rather in a shared language and a repertoire of Roman Catholic symbols and rituals. The free borrowing of religious symbols and metaphors by messianic poets as well as the simultaneous targeting of religion and ethnicity in the discriminatory policies of the Russian and Prussian partitioning powers contributed to link Polishness and Roman Catholicism in the social sphere. Most important, this association was codified and politicized at the turn of the century, especially by the nationalist Endecja, at the crucial moment of the democratization of national consciousness and the canonization—the bounding and stabilization—of "national culture." The ethno-Catholic vision of Polishness is therefore a relatively recent construction that was solidified, expanded in scope, and invested with a mantle of legitimacy only in the twentieth century, especially under Communism.

The Second World War and the subsequent Soviet takeover of Poland reified the Polak = katolik equation through two main processes: the reconfiguration of the ethnic and religious landscape of postwar Poland, and the Roman Catholic Church's resistance to the Communist party-state. The structure of domination in Communist Poland presented a privileged niche for the church as the sole institution that retained relative autonomy, which in turn facilitated the creation of a coherent myth surrounding the ecclesial institution. Although the Catholic Church was neither the creator nor the protector of the nation during the Partitions, it appropriated as its own the very messianic narrative it had opposed in the nineteenth century, and represented itself as both victim of the Communist system and timeless heroic defender of the nation, the foot-soldier entrenched against an illegitimate, foreign, and colonialist party-state. A narrative equivalence between the postwar era and the Partitions was created, pressed as a claim, and secured, remaining virtually unassailable until 1989.

This means that the Polak-katolik is a specific construction of Polish national identity, closely related to the structural contexts in which it was first formulated, took root, and became naturalized as doxa. Representations of the nation and narratives of history are intimately linked to the institutional and structural contexts in which they are articulated and propagated, and in which they may, or may not, become memorable or mobilizing. The historical analysis of Polish nationalism's formation in chapter 1 demonstrated as much.

Historical Narratives and the Cultural Dimension of the Post-Communist Transition

It is against the modern historical experience of statelessness, or, to be more precise, the lack of *national* statehood (and the paradigmatic national narrative it created) that the post-1989 period must be read. Perhaps ironically, given that Fascism, Communism, and the cold war were the defining political themes of the twentieth century, they were in the *longue durée* "banal" for Poles. This does not mean that they did not have enormous consequences, but rather that, as events, they looked less like landmark oaks than like hedge-shrubs in a row, planted in a familiar historical narrative of foreign oppression and religious repression. Their significance in the Polish social imagination resided in their perpetuating a familiar script. For Poles, the Communist "occupation" was merely one more in a long string of unwelcome foreign squatters. The year 1989 and the post-Communist period therefore do not simply mark the transition from a centrally planned economic system to a free-market economy, and from a totalitarian regime to a democracy. Rather, they signify the recovery of national independence, territorial sovereignty, and the reconstruction of a "truly national" nation-state.[1]

1. It is interesting to note that the Communist state, which de facto created the Polish nation-state—that is, which succeeded in matching its political borders with the ethnic nation, as per Gellner's definition (1983)—was not deemed "truly national" or "truly Polish." Polishness, then, is perhaps less ethnically based than usually assumed. The "truly Polish" nature of the state, or

Without historicizing the transition and examining its meaning, many of the political fights and public debates that have shaped and divided post-Communist Polish society remain simply unintelligible. The post-1989 transition is essentially a nationalist one, that is, the attempt at building a national state, a state of and for Poles, hence the need to define Polishness and its relation to both Roman Catholicism and the Roman Catholic Church. Given the mechanisms behind the fusion of Polishness and Catholicism, the doxic model of the Polak-katolik was bound to be questioned once Poland "recovered her independence." The last decade has thus been characterized by increasing tensions between rival visions of the state and of national identity, of religion's role in defining national identity, and of the church's role in the post-Communist state.

This study thus pointed to the necessity of attending to the *meaning* of the transition, an aspect too often overlooked in so-called transitology studies, which focus primarily on structural and institutional transformations in the political and economic spheres and neglect the transition's cultural dimension[2] (Linz and Stepan 1996; Stark and Bruszt 1998; Elster, Offe, and Preuss 1998; Eyal, Szelényi, and Townsley 1998; Eyal 2003).[3] While these studies are no doubt important and have yielded significant findings about the transition, in order to understand the decade that followed the fall of Communism in Poland and explain the debates that have punctuated it, we must pay attention to how the transition is understood and framed by the people living in Polish post-Communist society. This understanding in turn depends on the narratives constructed out of historically sedimented tropes on the one hand, and contemporary needs and resources on the other. It is perhaps obvious, but worth recalling, that nationalism is the partially

lack thereof, is evaluated in ideological terms, not in ethnic or geopolitical ones. I return to this important point below.

2. I do not assume here a sharp division between these dimensions, and do not see culture as a separate domain from social structure, economics, politics, and so on. Culture should not be conceptualized apart from social structure, a common fallacy in sociological works. Rather, culture is constitutive of the social structure. It is the domain of symbols, discourse, and meaning that mediates broader social structures and individual action, social reproduction, and creation. When I say that I focus on the "cultural dimension" of the transition, therefore, I mean that I examine the symbols and narratives through which the economic and political structures are given coherence and "make history," and on which social actors depend for models of action. See the introductory chapter for a clarification of the theoretical underpinnings of my use of the concept of "culture."

3. This is especially true in political science and sociology. Noted exceptions in sociology include the works of Kennedy and Harsanyi (1994); Bonnell (1996); Ekiert and Kubik (1999); Burawoy and Verdery (1999); Glaeser (2000); Kennedy (2002); and Kumar (2001).

shared sentiments of affinity created, condensed, and mobilized around specific symbols and material sites. Understanding and interpreting the cultural dimension of the post-Communist transition demands that we pay attention to key symbols of national identity, such as the constitution's preamble, "Oświęcim," and the cross, and analyze the ways in which they create and transmit key structuring narratives. What did these symbols and events, as well as the discourses surrounding them, tell us about nationalism in post-Communist Poland, and about the relationship between nationalism and religion more broadly?

The Revenge of the Polak-Katolik

The War of the Crosses contained within it multiple sites of conflict. The most obvious of these is the ongoing Polish-Jewish dispute about the meaning of Auschwitz, and the Christian-Judaic dispute about the presence of the cross at this site of the Shoah. But as we have seen, the War of the Crosses was not only an interfaith or an interethnic conflict. I argued that its *intra*national and *intra*religious axes were equally important. The War of the Crosses divided ethno-religious from secular nationalists; members of the clergy and of the episcopate from others; and the Roman Catholic Church's hierarchy from self-defined Poles-Catholics planting crosses at the gravel pit—the latter perhaps the most surprising cleavage brought to light by the controversial event.

In Poland, the event was primarily understood as an internal affair; it was a debate among Poles over the meaning of the nation, the nature and future of Polish Catholicism, and what constitutes a legitimate *national* symbol. The debate over the War of the Crosses, moreover, rarely involved Poles and Jews in direct dialogue, although Jews remained the implicit (and often explicit) external and internal Other in exchanges between Poles. Jews and Jewishness served as a trope to discuss Polishness and the role of Catholicism in defining and shaping the latter. Thus, while at the core of the conflict between Catholic Poles and Jews was the cross used as a religious symbol, it was the cross used as a national symbol that was at the core of tension among Poles, and within the Catholic Church itself.

As the court judgment cited at the beginning of this chapter clearly articulated, the cross in Poland, like the icon of the Black Madonna, Our Lady of Częstochowa, is not merely a religious symbol. It is a secular symbol as well. Debates on the cross within Poland concerned not only whether religious symbols should or should not be present at Auschwitz or its immediate proximity—which is at the core of theological arguments between

Christians and Jews—but what the cross in Poland *means*. In other words, the debates about the cross(es) at Auschwitz, and about the *invocatio Dei* in the constitution's preamble, were for Poles debates about the association of the national and religious dimensions, the appropriateness and legitimacy of their association in the post-Communist context, and the perceptions and possible consequences of such a fusion.

The latter debates were prompted by a change in the structural relation between state, nation, and church. In the traditional model that was operative, *grosso modo*, during the Communist period, the nation and the church were united against a "foreign" state. National identity was consciously constructed through religion and supported by the church in opposition to the state.[4] The religion-nation fusion therefore gained force and was largely taken for granted. When the state acquired legitimacy and became "truly Polish," however, it was no longer the "third element" against which nation and church could be mobilized, but rather the prism through which identities could be viewed and consciously constructed. As a result, religion has declined in its ability to carry national identifications, and the provisional nature of what appeared to be a solid fusion begins to show its seams. The War of the Crosses should therefore be seen as an attempt to revitalize what is now an increasingly contested version of national identity that fuses ethnicity and religion into one category. It is precisely at the moment when the fusion of religious and ethno-national categories is being questioned in public discourse and civic life that strident counterefforts by minority voices—such as the members of the Defenders of the Cross—are deployed in an attempt to ossify a vision of the nation that is slowly disintegrating.

The change in the form of the state (and its symbolic status) therefore entails the redefinition of relations between the state and the nation, the state and the church, and the church and the nation. The structural redefinition of the triangle is, essentially, what characterizes post-Communist Poland.

Defining Symbolic Boundaries: Roman Catholicism and "Jews"

Roman Catholicism and the cross under Communism served to mark the nation's symbolic boundaries: "us," the nation, against "them," the alien atheistic Communist regime. It managed to coalesce different social groups

4. This does not mean that the state was not shaping subjects; it obviously was, as I explain above. But subjects did not *identify* with the state, and instead built their national identity through the church.

against the party-state, including atheists and Jews. In post-Communist Poland, however, the cross is used *within* civil society to define the boundaries between "true" Poles and "non-Poles": in addition to Jews, "bad Catholics," "cosmopolitan secularists," and Freemasons have also become categories of symbolic exclusion from the nation. The latter two categories are also code words for "Jews." Religion is therefore used by the Right and the Far Right to define the symbolic boundaries of the "Polish nation," where the determination of who truly belongs depends to a great extent on one's commitment to a very specific—and narrow—vision of Polishness: that of the Polak-katolik.

Jewishness, in this context, itself becomes a symbol, standing for a civic-secular Poland. Through a complex chain of associations, a "Jew," in the discursive universe of the Right, is anyone who does not adhere to a strictly exclusive ethno-Catholic vision of Poland. Even certain bishops, as we have seen in the last chapter, are accused of being "crypto-Jews," and the civic nation, according to the editor of Far-Right weekly *Nasza Polska*, is an invention of Jews. Among "closed" Catholics and Polish ultranationalists, the European Union is similarly held to be the product of Jewish machinations aimed at the institutional and structural annihilation of nation-states. From this perspective, Poland is ruled by "Jews," that is, by *symbolic* Jews. Kowalski and Tulli (2003, 486–89) observed that the invention of Jews in right-wing milieus is a response to the ideological creation of "imaginary Poles." Imaginary Poles are, in the eyes of the Right, the ideal representatives of the national soul, embodying the "true" qualities and values of Polishness: Catholicism, patriotism, traditionalism, and economic conservatism. This ideal Pole is rarely matched by actual persons, which creates in Right-leaning social actors a disturbing cognitive dissonance between what they see as "real Poles" and real existing ones. That uncomfortable gap between the ideal Pole and his less-than-perfect empirical twin is explained through conspiracy theories of infiltration by Others. Those Poles who don't really fit the Polak-katolik mold are not really Poles after all; they are "Jews."

This points to an interesting paradox. The category of Polishness is generally understood in ethnic terms, following the German Romantic model of nationhood. But it is simultaneously articulated by the Right in ideological-political terms, even while insisting on its primordial, blood-based character.[5] As we have seen in several chapters, certain Poles, because of their

5. Of course, even though its ideologues insist on its primordial character, the ethnic nation, like any other form of nation, is a social construction. Whereas the civic nation is conceived as a construct, the ethnic nation is conceived of as a given. This is not, however, what I am underlining

political allegiances and ideological positions (mostly with the liberal Left), are deemed "un-Polish" or "anti-Polish," or else dismissed as "fake Poles" or "Jews" by the Far Right. Recall Mr. Świtoń's statement that a Pole who does not defend or stops defending the cross is no longer a Pole. Whereas such symbolic exclusion is typical of places where the nation is understood in civic terms, and where, therefore, one's national identity—at least ideally—is determined by his or her adhesion to the principles of the social contract,[6] it seems unlikely in and ill-befitting a place where the nation is primarily understood in *ethnic* terms. In Poland, national identity is largely perceived as being transmitted through birth, flowing through one's veins. In line with this conception, national identity can be neither chosen nor escaped; it is constitutive of the self. How is it possible, given this understanding of national identity, to encounter *ideological forms of exclusion* from the ethnic nation? How is the tension between these two modes of social closure, one based on blood and culture, the other based on ideological orientations and political bonds, reconciled?

In the Polish case, the answer is that ideological difference is "ethnicized" such that an "un-Polish" or "Polish-speaking" (that is, "non-Polish") liberal intellectual advocating a civic-secular Poland becomes a "Jew."[7] Magical anti-Semitism is activated against a specific set of values, whether capitalism or Communism, since either of these threatens a traditional way of life and its religious values. Both Communism and Western-style capitalism are associated with cosmopolitanism, and both are associated with Jewishness. But why Jews instead of Ukrainians or Germans, for example? Jews are the paradigmatic Other because Jewishness is an ethno-religious category that is perceived as the opposite of the Polak-katolik. While Polishness is defined in opposition to Jewishness, Poles nevertheless share with Jews important characteristics: both groups see themselves as a chosen people and

---

here. Rather, I am pointing out the ideological criteria used by the Right in determining one's Polishness (or lack thereof) and the tension such criteria entail for the (ideally) ethnically defined nation. For discussions of the principles behind ethnic and civic nationalism, see Brubaker (1992); Schnapper (1994); Yack (1996); Nielsen (1999); and Zubrzycki (2001, 2002).

6. The American case is the paradigmatic example of ideologically defined national identity, where "being" American means the support of a specific set of values and practices, and therefore where it is possible to be "un-American," say, for supporting Communism during McCarthyism or, more recently, by criticizing the Bush administration in the post-9/11 United States. See Lipset's *Continental Divide* (1990) for an analysis of this mechanism.

7. In my informal meetings with members of the Oświęcim Covenant in the Defense of the Papal Cross throughout the spring of 2001, for example, *Nasz Dziennik* was referred to as the "Gospel," the "only Polish daily on the market." *Gazeta Wyborcza*, on the other hand, was nicknamed *Gazeta Koszerna*, the "kosher newspaper." The implication here is clear: the right-wing *Nasz Dziennik* is "Polish," the Center-Left liberal *Gazeta Wyborcza* is "Jewish."

understand their historical suffering within a messianic narrative. These similarities, instead of creating a rapprochement, actually encourage Poles' rivalry with Jews over the question of which nation is morally superior. In fact, Ireneusz Krzemiński and his colleagues found that Polish messianism is at the basis of Polish anti-Semitism (1996, 20–21, 102–4).

"Jewishness" serves to exclude "unwanted ideological elements" that do not fit with the Right's ideally defined model of Polishness. Hence we witness the strange phenomenon of anti-Semitism in a country virtually without Jews.[8] Under Communism, the notions of a *Żydokomuna* and later of a Zionist plot were used to purge Polish society of "undesirable social elements." The state's anti-Zionist campaign of 1968 purged the old Communist guard, but also rid the country of a significant contingent of young students, a reservoir of proto-opposition. Whereas most of those targeted in 1968 were actually Jewish, the purges and repression also included several symbolic "Jews." This logic of exclusion was not used by the Communist party-state alone, however; it also pervaded the opposition. It is indeed following this familiar logic that Communist elites could not be "Poles." Thus, in spite of the party-state's success in establishing a homogeneous nation-state for the first time in Polish history, the Polish People's Republic was not considered "Poland." Hence Solidarity's mission, which followed the motto taken from a popular song, "So that Poland be Poland . . . "

By using the cross at Auschwitz, the Defenders of the Cross were therefore actively engaged in the production of symbolic categories. Here we arrive at what Pierre Bourdieu (2000), David Kertzer (1988), and others have described under the rubric of Symbolic Violence. Neither direct coercion nor direct persuasion, symbolic violence instead entails the establishment of categories and divisions that inform social reproduction. Even those who reject the cross at Auschwitz or on television, or the *invocatio Dei* in the constitution's preamble, articulate their mutiny using those very symbols. Everyone speaks in those terms, whether their lips are poised to reverently praise or pursed to spit with disgust.

Yet even within these structuring categories, there is the radical malleability both of the symbol of the cross and of its moral valuation. Under Communism, it was regarded by a great number of Polish citizens as "good" because it marked the line dividing atheist colonizers from "authentic Poles" and marked an area of (relative) freedom from the state. Engaging in religious practices or articulating religious discourse in the public sphere were activities that, de facto, created a "plural" society in place of the

8. See note 26 in chapter 2 for a discussion of the current number of Jews in Poland.

totalizing one that the Communist party-state endeavored to construct and impose. In the post-1989 context, that argument is not persuasive. Though the most reactionary groups attempt to sustain the symbolic potency of the cross by planting it before a new Other, the civic-secular-internationalist West (a.k.a. "Jews"), the majority of Poles, we have seen, reject this effort. Indeed, for many Poles the cross has come to stand not for a free and independent Poland but for right-wing oppression within the nation. Far from creating or expressing social cohesion, the cross serves both to sharpen existing divisions within Polish society and to exacerbate social conflicts.

Historicizing Symbols

As I pointed out several times throughout the book, the extreme views the Defenders of the Cross presented were marginal, but its discourse and action nevertheless mobilized significant support; moreover, the issues the group raised were not themselves peripheral, but central in focusing mainstream commentary on national identity and its link to religion. Świtoń touched a sensitive nerve in Polish society, and was a successful manipulator of core symbols. But those symbols are core symbols because of their historical weight and because of the specific social context in which they were evoked and used. To demonstrate this, we examined the process of the cross's and "Oświęcim's"/"Auschwitz's" social construction through time. Also, the symbols' respective meanings were relationally constituted within the narrow context of post-Communism itself: the juxtaposition of the cross and "Oświęcim" at the very moment of "Oświęcim's" narrative reconfiguration as "Auschwitz" certainly gave special potency to both symbols and to the War of the Crosses, the event that brought them together. Remember, moreover, that the event's meaning and significance were shaped by the debates over national identity and the role of religion in the new polity that have punctuated the post-Communist period.

The War of the Crosses thus tells us something about the mobilizing power of key symbols. It is here that Victor Turner's approach to symbols must be left behind. Whereas the dominant symbol of the Ndembu milk tree highlighted in Turner's classic *Forest of Symbols* (1967) was relatively stable and, at least in Turner's summation, less historically than "biologically" built, the cross only signifies within the context of specific historical narratives and political-structural situations. It is a "dominant symbol," but the form of its semantic domination is radically contingent precisely because it is semantic, not somatic. My conception of symbolic process is therefore much more fully historical than Turner's approach. Turner's functionalism implied a concept of temporality that assumes the existence of a sociocultural equilibrium that is constantly being reestablished, rather than an open-ended process of eventful historical change. Turner, moreover, did not expand on how the orectic (or emotional) pole meets the ideological one; I showed that this was accomplished through historical narratives that are carried not only through discourse but also through aesthetics.

Aesthetics and Emotions

Every Pole recognized the familiar and distinct aesthetics of Polish protest in the War of the Crosses, the event's peculiar mix of religious and secular imagery and its nonviolent practices of dissent. But while for some this generated a flow of emotions that mobilized their support of the action, for others it aroused feelings of shame, disgust, and anger at the small group of marginal men who claimed to represent "Poland." The aesthetics of the War of the Crosses and the emotional reactions aroused by the protest were key in the mobilization process for and against the crosses at the gravel pit. They played a fundamental role in the War of the Crosses and the national, international, and supranational controversy surrounding it. The site itself, in the shadow of the former concentration camp, is already loaded with painful memories, and the War of the Crosses prompted and was initiated by intense feelings of anger, indignation, and fear on both the Jewish and the Polish sides. Jews were offended, repulsed, hurt, and angered by the presence of the papal cross at Auschwitz, while many Poles were offended, hurt, and angered by demands to remove the symbol.

Emotions, their expression, and their reproductions in the media were important in every step of the protest. Recall that the War of the Crosses, as the third act of a wider drama, began with rumors regarding the papal cross's imminent removal from the proximity of Auschwitz. As described in the book's introduction and again in chapter 5, reactions were immediate: surprise, disbelief, and anger were expressed by many politicians and even from the head of the Polish Catholic Church, Józef Cardinal Glemp. These reactive emotions, however, were soon transformed into moral shock and indignation, as discourse against "Jews and secularists" was articulated. Jews, it was argued, infringed on the nation-state's sovereignty and offended Polish memory, whereas secularists, by not defending the cross, were yielding to foreigners and relinquishing the Polish nation's defining character. The demonization of both groups and the constant depictions of imminent threats fueled and amplified further emotions of disgust and even hatred toward Jews and "bad Poles."

Once discursively articulated, such sentiments legitimized the action, now framed as righteous revenge and a noble defense of national property, memory, and tradition. Sentiments of pride, love of the nation, and self-righteousness were central to the event, which the participants clearly perceived to be of crucial importance. Świtoń fasted for forty-two days in protest, and camped at the gravel pit for nearly a year, seriously jeopardizing his health. Many Roman Catholics took part in gatherings in the summer and fall, assemblies that by late-August had been officially condemned by the episcopate; and the few priests blessing crosses risked severe reprimands from their ecclesiastical superiors, all for the righteousness of their "mission," as Świtoń called the War of the Crosses.

The role of aesthetics in nationalist expression and mobilization should not be taken lightly; it was partly through them and the historical narratives they conjured up—of victimhood, suffering, and resistance in the case at hand—that emotions were awakened and stimulated in the War of the Crosses.

Narrative Shock and Identity

So how could such a marginal group as Świtoń's ad-hoc organization, the Defenders of the Cross, mobilize support and generate a societywide debate? So far, I have argued that it was successful because (1) it manipulated dominant symbols using an aesthetics of protest that evoked key historical narratives, which together generated a flow of emotions; and (2) the War of the Crosses touched upon issues that had been debated sporadically but intensely since the fall of Communism, namely what Polishness "is" and what its relationship with Roman Catholicism should be.

Closer to the event itself, I also argued that (3) the civic mobilization organized by the Defenders of the Cross and the ability of such a marginal group to initiate a public debate are related to the widespread shock to the social and historical consciousnesses of Poles caused by the narrative reconfiguration of "Oświęcim" as "Auschwitz." The War of the Crosses can be interpreted as the resistance, by many Poles, to the so-called Judaization of Auschwitz and as the attempt to re-Polonize the physical site by marking it with symbols traditionally associated with the nation. What I call Poles' *narrative shock*, the shock to their historical and social identities as victims, is related to the threat posed by the Jewish and universal symbol of "Auschwitz" to the core Polish narrative of victimhood, which took shape in the nineteenth century, was developed in the twentieth through Poles' direct experience of the war, and was reinforced by the socialization efforts of the Communist party-state. The People's Republic capitalized on the Polish core narrative of martyrdom by presenting "Polish citizens" as the main victims of the war, distorting reality in a way that is difficult to repudiate now. The War of the Crosses was thus partially caused by the perverse effects of civic-Socialist nationalism; by the discursive reconceptualization of the nation as a "nation of citizens" in official representations that were addressed to what became, after World War II, an ethnically and confessionally homogeneous nation. The party-state on the one hand factually built an ethnic nation-state, while on the other hand it used in its discourse the language of civic nationalism. Both strengthened, de facto, the popularity of the ethno-Catholic vision of the nation.

With this analytical summary in mind, let us consider the contributions of the approach developed to the study of nationalism.

Contributions to the Study of Nationalism

A Multilevel Approach

The book developed an approach that shows how identities, cultural practices, and memory-making are related to broad institutional-structural processes, and how that relationship is mediated by symbols, material sites, and ritual performances. It linked political and social change with cultural representations by looking at the triadic relationship between state (re)formation, the (re)construction of national identity, and the (re)definition of religion's role in society.

By looking at specific symbols and events, I related microsociological processes to macropolitical transformations, showing how social actors' interpretations of history and representations of the nation are interrelated with systemic change. In so doing, the study challenges the ways in which the transition from Communism to post-Communism has been defined primarily as structural change in the political and economic spheres. That perspective can only very partially appreciate the transition. Cultural and historical understandings of the past and of the present affect the current shape of the polity, and define Poland's international relations and role in suprastatal organizations such as NATO and the EU. I have shown how cultural representations impact institution-building, and vice versa. The central lesson is that even for the study of macropolitical formations, *culture matters.*

The study also underlined how nations and nationalism are discursively created. The nation is constituted by a multitude of interrelated voices, regardless of their relative strength or weakness. Political outsiders and marginal groups can sometimes "symbolically hijack" (Bourdieu 2000, 185) the nation and usurp the power of definition usually restricted to the state by using sacred speech or sacred symbols (religious or not). While Świtoń failed to impose his vision of Polishness, he did manage to orient and shape public debates, and ultimately determined the outcome of the War of the Crosses, with the papal cross firmly anchored in Auschwitz's gravel pit.

The broader point is that there is no single understanding of the nation at any time in the history of modern nations. The nation only exists in and through discursive networks and the ability of these to mobilize significant constituencies and provisionally affix the terms of the nation's definition. This ability is ultimately dependent on political contexts and institutional arrangements, so that a given discourse of the nation does not have the same symbolic weight, political salience, and mobilizing potential in all contexts. Yet while the nation is constituted by various discursive representations—and its meaning, ipso facto, is contested—the nation itself, as a category of practice, is nevertheless taken for granted. That there does indeed "exist" a Polish nation is a given for all social actors involved in the contest for the control of its definition. The book was thus concerned with the examination of the internal social dynamics of nationalism—the sphere of contestation *within* the nation, *about* the nation. The nation ultimately is a discursive space constituted by a web of representations articulated by various communities of discourse around specific events, and constituted also through the practical uses of symbols commonly understood as "national." The nation is relatively malleable, but its malleability is contained within the boundaries of more or less durable narrative structures and sets of symbols. For example, martyrdom and messianism are dominant narratives; the cross and the Black Madonna, dominant symbols. The specific social implications of "Poland under the cross" are contested, contextually determined, and only provisionally fixed, but no group could legitimately bid to disconnect Poland from the cross *tout court*.

The focus on a text, a memorial site, and a religious/national symbol, as well as the focus on the public debates and conflicts these generated, warrant an expansion of the idea that the nation is constructed through discourse. Discourse here is not restricted to enunciated speech, but also includes symbolic artifacts and their ritual articulation in a series of positions within a field of debate. It is in that expanded notion of a shifting discursive field that the nation takes form. The move from constitutional debates—an elite, official, and officialized symbol—to the social drama of the War of the Crosses—a popular, spontaneous movement—provided different vantage points from which to observe the nation in its cultural production. My focus gradually narrowed from examining nationalism as expressed in debates between Poles and Jews (the nation defined vis-à-vis Others) to those among Poles (the nation defined in competing visions of Polishness), and finally to debates within a key institution of the "authentic nation," the Roman Catholic Church. The use of these lenses allowed for the scrutiny of the nation from within, as it is contested and reconstructed in and by key institutions, such as the church; through pivotal events, such as the War of the Crosses; and in the productive tension between discourses by government and church officials, intellectuals, and politicians, as well as by the practical experiences of "ordinary Poles."

An Eventful Sociology of the Nation

In order to avoid the reification of the nation, a problem that plagues studies on nations and nationalism, Rogers Brubaker suggests that we reconceptualize "nation" from a bounded notion of the group to "nationhood" and "nationness," concepts that suggest the nation's mutability and processual quality. He incites us to think of nationness itself as a contingent "event," as something that "suddenly crystallizes rather than gradually develops, as a contingent, conjuncturally fluctuating, and precarious frame of vision and basis for individual and collective action, rather than as a relatively stable product of deep developmental trends in economy, polity, or culture" (1996, 19). Such a perspective, according to him, would shed light on how nationness "happens."[9]

Brubaker's framework relies on a double contrast: the first is between nation as entity and nationness as the variable property of groups, relationships, and relational settings; the second is between nationhood and nationness as something that "happens" as opposed to nation as the result of a slow development. But the evidence of this study suggests that the nation (or nationness) "happens" somewhere in between. It is slowly constructed, but crystallizes in specific events such as the War of the Crosses. Rather than seeing the nation as occurring in either a kind of slow, incremental crawl or a "big bang" explosion, I offer a volcanic analogy: the nation is like an active volcano, made of the sporadic eruptions of competing discourses

9. This is a key theoretical agenda for the future of nationalism studies, but what makes it tricky is Brubaker's double-use of *events*: the nation, or nationness, is itself an "event," which happens *through* contingent events with transformative consequences. While adding complexity, this makes the concept difficult to operationalize.

and practices about what a given nation purportedly is and should be. The nation happens through these bursts of creativity, contestation, and redefinition that do not appear ex nihilo but are, rather, embedded in and caused by their social, historical, cultural, and economic environments. Events bring to light the underlying forces that otherwise remain hidden. It is in *this* sense, then, that the nation "happens."

Not only did nationness "happen" in and through the War of the Crosses, its symbols were melted down and transformed. The specific symbols of the nation and religion are closely layered in narrative strata and sediments gathered over centuries, then sporadically erupted into space at moments of their violent "heating" at key junctures of political compression. The eruption of the War of the Crosses, for example, revealed that Polish nationness is not ethno-religious in any strong sense. The cross, likewise, was revealed to be not a monument of robust union but of disunion. With the eruption by now mostly subsided to smoke, the symbol of the cross was left fragile and precarious, a cross of volcanic dust, just as most of the crosses planted at Auschwitz were emptied from the battlefield of public contestation to a quiet retirement in the Franciscan monastery's yard. All but one, the papal cross. It remains at Auschwitz to remind us how eruptions of nationness unearth and re-embed symbols in new contexts, shifting their meaning—and also remind us that this volcano is far from dormant.

Theories of Nationalism and Religion Revisited

The empirical analysis suggests that contrary to the neat, overly simplified evolutionist-functionalist models I discussed in the book's introduction, nation and religion are variously interrelated in different historical and political contexts—in Communist versus post-Communist Poland, for example—and are evoked and mobilized differently by various social groups. This study demonstrates that the relationship between nationalism and religion is a dynamic one that cannot be reduced to linear, evolutionist, or simplistic functionalist terms, but is instead contingent on the form of the state. Instead of thinking of the relationship between religion and nation as a dyad, I have shown that we need to look at it as part of a triad in which the state plays a key role. Reading the relationship between nation and religion in Poland requires the analysis of the triadic relationship between state (re)formation, the (re)construction of national identity, and the (re)definition of religion's role in society.

Whereas dominant paradigms in the field maintain that nationalism replaced traditional religion and even is a modern religion itself through the sacralization of politics, this case suggests a much more complex and subtle relationship between nationalism and religion. Historically, the formation of Polish nationalism cannot be related to religious decline, as the evolutionists claim. Religious symbols and stories instead provided a vocabulary and grammar to speak of the nation and its mission after the Partitions. Romantic messianism found a congenial niche for the expression of this emerging form of nationalism in Roman Catholic rituals and everyday practices. Through a slow and complex process in the nineteenth and twentieth centuries, Polish national identity and Catholicism became fused.

This is far from conforming to the functionalist model, however, according to which nationalism, after having superseded religion, replaces it, or even becomes a religion itself. The paradigmatic term for this model is *civil religion*, sometimes defined as an empirical object, sometimes as an analytical dimension of all social groups. Civil religion, following the Durkheimian trajectory, attempts to describe or interpret the social sacralization of a given group's symbols.[10] In the modern era, according to this view, civic or state symbols such as the flag are worshiped by citizens as religious icons or totems, and state martyrs are revered as "saints." Nationalism becomes a religion, as treason and heresy become one and the same. But this will not do either.

Sacred-Secular Religious Nationalism

Liah Greenfeld (1996) suggested that the confusion between religion and nationalism stems from the fact that nationalism is a form of consciousness that sacralizes the secular, hence the temptation to treat it as a religion, albeit a "civil religion." Although this is useful, it does not go far enough. The Polish case points to a different and overlooked process. Because of Poland's peculiar political history, it was not political institutions and symbols that were sacralized and became the object of religious devotion (following the French revolutionary model), but religious symbols that were first secularized and then *resacralized as national*. Biblical allegories, religious symbols, hymns, and iconography as well as religious practices such as processions, pilgrimages, or simple participation in Sunday Mass were largely politicized

10. The term *civil religion* was first coined by Jean-Jacques Rousseau in the *Social Contract*. Mostly associated with Durkheim and Durkheimian perspectives, it was popularized in the United States in the late 1960s with Robert Bellah's article "Civil Religion in America" (1967), on the heels of which a veritable sociological industry grew up before again receding by the 1990s. For an interesting resurrection of the concept after the events of September 11, 2001, see Johnson (2005).

as carriers of national identity during the period when the Polish state disappeared from the European map. As such, religion, during the Partitions and under Communism, served as an alternative space providing civil society with an area of relative freedom of action in defiance of an oppressive or totalitarian state. A pilgrimage to Częstochowa, in this context, was a way to publicly "vote with one's feet" (Michel 1986, 85). Catholic identity, symbols, and acts were secularized through their politicization and ultimate fusion with national identity. Their significance was heightened or loaded; they became neon hypermarkers, but of Polishness.

The Polish case therefore suggests a peculiar form of the secularization of religion and religious symbols through their political instrumentalization and then their *resacralization* as *national* symbols. The cross in Poland is therefore a *sacred secular* symbol. It is sacred not only because of its Christian semantics (or even in spite of them), but because it traditionally represents, since the nineteenth century, Poland. In the place of religion yielding to nationalism or nationalism becoming a religion, here *religion becomes nationalism*.[11] The national sacralization of religious symbols, however, is meaningful and garners consensual support only in specific politico-structural contexts. The study therefore points to the necessity of looking at the relationship between religion and nationalism as it is embedded within broad systemic processes related to state formation on the one hand, and as it is reflected in specific social dramas and cultural practices on the other.

Beyond Secularization

It is in their secular form that Roman Catholicism and its symbols were resacralized. They became the sacred symbols of national identity, only to be contested and potentially "secularized" again in the post-Communist period. *Secularization* in the sense I am using the term here would mean, however, returning to a more distinctly (or theologically orthodox) religious interpretation of "Catholicism" (or of the cross). That is precisely the

11. This is far from the perennialist model of the relationship between nationalism and religion, which claims that the modern nation grew out of already existing religious communities. I showed throughout this study, in contradistinction to that view, that the association between Roman Catholicism and Polishness was not natural but historically specific. It is the result of a hard process of construction that is never totally completed and that requires extensive maintenance and upkeep in institutions of social reproduction—pedagogy, law, the state, the church—and by public leaders through speeches, publication, political mobilization, and ritual performance.

agenda of "open Catholics" and "purists": to shift the Catholic Church's role in Poland away from identity politics back to faith. "The challenge now," in the words of the late priest-philosopher Józef Tischner, "is to return to the essence of the Church's mission—to religion," even at the cost of lower church attendance.[12] The goal for those Catholic groups is the depoliticization of religion and a deepening of faith. After Catholicism's long public career, they invite its privatization. Privatization, usually understood as one aspect of secularization, would, paradoxically, be salutary for Catholicism now that there is no reason for its political role in the public sphere, and now that the "practicing nonbeliever" lost her reasons to practice.

The Polish case thus turns secularization theory on its head: what is commonly seen as religion's revenge—the undeniable strength and pervasiveness of Catholicism in Communist Poland's public life (Casanova 1994)—could instead be regarded as its ultimate defeat—its instrumentalization and its reduction to the role of symbolic vehicle of national identity and institutional support to civil society. Indeed, I would argue, contra José Casanova (1994), that it was the public role of Catholicism and of the church in Poland that presented its secularization, and that the attempt to de-publicize and privatize it now would not signify its decline but rather present the possibility of its revitalization.

What secularization means is thus much more complex than the usual "decline of religion" one-size-fits-all proposition (Casanova 1994; Gorski 2000a). For Mark Chaves, for example, secularization is, more specifically, the declining *scope* of religious authority. It is a process, moreover, rooted in concrete social struggles: "Secularization occurs, or not, as the result of social and political conflicts between those social actors who would enhance or maintain religion's social significance and those who would reduce it" (1994, 752). In the Polish case, this struggle is taking place not only between liberal, civic, and secular actors and conservative ethno-nationalist religious elites, but also between two great camps within the church: that of post–Vatican II "open Catholics" and "purists," who argue for a de-politicization of religion and a deepening of faith, and that of "traditionalists" and "integrists," who maintain that Roman Catholicism is primordially linked with Polishness and that the church's mission is necessarily political. Bruce Lincoln (2003), for example, calls these "minimalist" versus "maximalist" articulations of religion. The tension is between privatizing and publicizing

12. Father Tischner spoke these words during a public discussion at the Dominican church in Cracow on November 22, 1993. This is also the opinion expressed by Father Stanisław Obirek in an interview on May 22, 2004.

forces, between opposed views of the role of religion and of the church in the public sphere. In the religious field, the post-1989 period is best described by the polarization, within the church, between these two orientations.

But this relative decline in the scope of religious authority and the ensuing privatization of religion do not necessarily imply the decline of religion, merely its decline as a carrier of sentiments of national affinity and solidarity. The point to be made here is that secularization turns on multiple axes: one is the level of public engagement in a given national environment; another is the level of authority over the public sphere in a given national context; and still a third reflects the level of privately held and enacted religious sentiments. Secularization, it turns out, does not mean very much as a theoretical tool until it is operationalized within a given articulation of nationness. The comparative study of nationalism and religion, I suggest, would be more productively advanced by devoting less energy to secularization and more to the specific configurations of religious authority and religious cultures, on one hand, and national institutional contexts and national cultures, on the other. Religion and nationalism each have both institutional and symbolic or discursive forms, such that what began as an apparently straightforward problem of examining religion and nationalism, and their fission or fusion, has now become a more complex one that "secularization" does not usefully address.

For Poland, as for other cases where national identity in certain political contexts is experienced and expressed through religious channels, the estimation of religious decline or ascent in relation to nationalism is a quixotic mission. Where the sacred is secularized and then resacralized in national form, and this transmutation repeated over and over again, the quest for neat models of the substitution of one for the other is a charging of windmills. Far from being fixed, as if on a predetermined course, the relationship between nationalism and religion is in constant motion. It is this movement that I attempted to capture and analyze in this study.

APPENDIX A

Periodicals Consulted

Newspapers consulted, from Left to Right: *Nie, Polityka, Gazeta Wyborcza, Wprost, Tygodnik Powszechny, Nasz Dziennik, Gazeta Polska*, and *Nasza Polska*. Each is loosely associated with a party:[1] *Nie* with SLD, *Polityka* with SLD and UW, *Gazeta Wyborcza* with UW, *Tygodnik Powszechny* with the conservative wing of UW, *Gazeta Polska* with AWS and ROP, and *Nasz Dziennik* and *Nasza Polska* with AWS, ROP, LPR, and various small National-Catholic parties.

Gazeta Wyborcza, a daily of the Center-Left edited by Adam Michnik, is by far the most popular newspaper in Poland. With a circulation of 570,000 (720,000 on Saturdays) and an average issue readership (AIR) of 2 million, it is read by 7.2 percent of Poles above the age of fifteen. It has consistently been the most popular and influential nationwide daily since the fall of Communism, and its circulation is actually higher than any other paper in Eastern Europe (Ekiert and Kubik 1999, 15). The daily *Nasz Dziennik*, for comparative purposes, has a circulation of 300,000 and an AIR of 170,000 (0.6 percent), according to research conducted by OBOP in February 1999 ($N = 2{,}931$; $+/-1.2$ percent). (See Ośrodek Badań Prasoznawczych [2000], *Katalog mediów polskich 1999/2000* (Cracow: Jagiellonian University); Ośrodek Badań Opinii Publicznej [1999], *Index Polska: Badania czytelnictwa prasy*, http://www.obop.com.pl/index_polska9902.htm).

Gazeta Polska and *Nasza Polska* are Far-Right weeklies with much smaller readerships. Very graphic in their language and strident in the tone of their interventions, they should not be considered "mainstream." They remain relatively marginal in Polish society, although they do not go unnoticed, especially when church authorities or politicians give them

1. The names of the political formations given here are those in use in 1996–2004.

interviews. For a useful characterization of the radical Right in Poland and its relative weakness, see Ost (1999).

In the words of its editor, Jerzy Urban, the weekly *Nie* is "a satirico-critical newspaper, attacking nationalism, clericalism, parties from the Right, parties issued from Solidarity, and Wałęsa." *Nie* is on the extreme Left, not so much in terms of the content of its interventions, but in its form. Famous for its satire, its hostility toward the church, and its vulgar caricatures, the weekly is comparable to the *National Lampoon*. (Urban was General Jaruzelski's spokesman in the 1980s.)

I also reviewed the Catholic Church's weekly press bulletin, the Katolicka Agencja Informacyjna's *Biuletyn*, in which official statements by the Primate and the episcopate, pastoral letters, sermons, and interviews with the church's hierarchy are published, as well as two Jewish publications, *Midrasz* and *Słowo Żydowskie*. I have consulted *Rzeczpospolita* as a source of information in order to reconstruct the events that took place.

APPENDIX B

Official Translation of the Preamble, Constitution of the Third Republic of Poland

Having regard for the existence and future of our Homeland,

Which recovered, in 1989, the possibility of a sovereign and democratic determination of its fate,

We, the Polish Nation—all citizens of the Republic,

Both those who believe in God as the source of truth, justice, good and beauty,

As well as those not sharing such faith but respecting those universal values as arising from other sources,

Equal in rights and obligations towards the common good of Poland,

Beholden to our ancestors for their labours, their struggle for independence achieved at great sacrifice,

For our culture rooted in the Christian heritage of the Nation and in universal human values,

Recalling the best traditions of the First and the Second Republic,

Obliged to bequeath to future generations all that is valuable from our over one thousand years' heritage,

Bound in community with our compatriots dispersed throughout the world,

Aware of the need for cooperation with all countries for the good of the Human Family,

Mindful of the bitter experiences of the times when fundamental freedoms and human rights were violated in our Homeland,

Desiring to guarantee the rights of the citizens for all time, and to ensure diligence and efficiency in the work of public bodies,

Recognizing our responsibility before God or our own consciences,

Hereby establish this Constitution of the Republic of Poland as the basic law for the State,

Based on respect for freedom and justice, cooperation between the public powers, social dialogue as well as on the principle of aiding in the strengthening the powers of citizens and their communities.

❧

We call upon all those who will apply this Constitution for the good of the Third Republic to do so paying respect to the inherent dignity of the person, his or her right to freedom, the obligation of solidarity with others, and respect for these principles as the unshakable foundation of the Republic of Poland.

APPENDIX C

Historical Cues

966: Baptism of Mieszko I. Poland is introduced to Latin Christianity. This year also is associated with the founding of the Polish state.

1079: Execution of Stanisław Szczepanowski, bishop of Cracow, by King Bolesław the Brave. Beatified, he will be proclaimed the patron saint of Poland in 1253.

1569–1795: Polish-Lithuanian Republic (elective monarchy).

1772: First Partition of Poland, between Russia, Prussia, and Austria.

1791: Proclamation of the Constitution of May Third.

1793: Second Partition of Poland, between Russia and Prussia.

1794: The Kościuszko Uprising.

1795: Third Partition of Poland, between Russia, Prussia, and Austria. The Polish state disappears from the map of Europe.

1830–31: November Uprising against Russia.

1831: Capitulation of Warsaw, defeat of the Uprising on September 7.

1831–32: Brutal repression of insurrectionists. "Great Emigration," notably to France. Paris becomes the center of Polish cultural and political life: Adam Mickiewicz, Juliusz Słowacki, and Frederyk Chopin are among those who make that city their adopted home.

1848: Abolition of serfdom in the Austrian Partition on April 22.

1848–49: Participation of Poles in the "Spring of Peoples" revolutions.

1863–64: January Uprising lasts from January 1863 to fall of 1864.

1864–65: Repression of insurrectionists. Approximately 30,000 Poles are deported to Russia. Massive emigration to western Europe.

1905: Revolution in Russian Poland.

1914–18: First World War. Poles from the different partitions find themselves fighting each other in enemy armies.

1918: The Treaty of Versailles officially proclaims the independence of Poland. Reconstitution of the Polish state.

1918–39: Second Republic.

1939: On August 23, the Molotov-Ribbentrop pact between Nazi Germany and the Soviet Union divides Poland into occupation zones, commonly called the "Fourth Partition." The German army invades Poland on September 1. Two weeks later, on the seventeenth, Soviet troops cross the Polish border. Poland disappears from the European map for the second time.

1939–45: Second World War.

1944: Yalta Conference, in February, during which Allies agree on dividing Europe into "zones of influence."

1945: Capitulation of the Third Reich on May 8–9, marking the end of the Second World War. Later that summer, at Potsdam, the Soviet Union pledges the holding of free elections in its zone of influence.

1953: Death of Joseph Stalin on March 5.

1953–56: "Thaw," a wave of relative liberalization in the Eastern Bloc.

1956: Poznań Workers' Uprising in June. In October, Władysław Gomułka becomes the Communist Party's First Secretary and promises reforms ("Polish October").

1957: Inauguration of the Great Novena in Częstochowa, in preparation for the millennial celebration of Poland's baptism in 1966.

1968: Violent repression of student protests, and anti-Zionist campaign and purges.

1970: Workers' protests in December, precipitated by rises in food prices, end in bloodshed on the Baltic coast (Gdańsk, Gdynia, Szczecin). In February 1971, Edward Gierek replaces Gomułka as Party leader.

1976: Workers' protests precipitated by food prices escalate in June. Violence in Radom and Ursus near Warsaw. In September, the KOR is formed.

1978: Election of Karol Cardinal Wojtyła, Archbishop of Cracow, to the Holy See on October 16.

1979: First visit of the "Polish pope" to Poland in June, on the occasion of the nine-hundredth anniversary of the death of Saint Stanisław, patron saint of Poland.

1980: Nationwide strikes, marking the birth of the Solidarity movement, in August. The martyrs' memorial is inaugurated on December 16, to commemorate the tenth anniversary of the death of workers during the December Events on the Baltic coast.

1981: Martial law is declared on December 13. It will be lifted in July 1983.

1984: Father Jerzy Popiełuszko, an outspoken supporter of Solidarity, is assassinated. Half a million people attend his funeral on November 3.

1989: Roundtable discussions, during which an agreement between the government and the opposition is reached. The government guarantees that 35 percent of the seats in the Sejm and all of those in the Senate will be open to free elections.

1990: Lech Wałęsa elected President of the Third Republic.

1997: Ratification of the Third Republic's Constitution.

REFERENCES

PRIMARY SOURCES

*Formal Interviews**

Ćwik, Marian (president of the Cracow section of the Catholic Association "Civitas Christiana"), Cracow, June 11, 2001.

Czajkowski, Michał (priest, cochair of the Committee on Christian-Jewish Dialogue), audio recording, Warsaw, May 25, 2004.

Folwarczny, Andrzej (president, Forum for the Dialogue among Nations), audio recording, Warsaw, May 28, 2004.

Gebert, Konstanty (public intellectual, frequent contributor to *Gazeta Wyborcza*, editor of the Jewish monthly *Midrasz*), audio recording, Warsaw, May 25, 2004.

Hutny, Wanda (coordinator of museum guides and their continuing education, Auschwitz-Birkenau State Museum), audio recording, Oświęcim, March 22, 2001.

Kacorzyk, Andrzej (member of the Pedagogical Section and coordinator of the postgraduate program for teachers, "Totalitarianism-Fascism-Holocaust," Auschwitz-Birkenau State Museum), audio recording, Oświęcim, March 30, 2001.

Kadlčik, Piotr (president of the Jewish Community in Warsaw), Warsaw, May 12, 2004.

Krajewski, Stanisław (cochair of the Committee on Christian-Jewish Dialogue, member of the International Council of the Auschwitz-Birkenau State Museum, and consultant for the American Jewish Committee), audio recordings, Warsaw, May 2001, and May 24, 2004.

Musiał, Stanisław (Jesuit priest actively involved in Polish-Jewish dialogue), audio recordings, Cracow, April 9, 2001, and May 10, 2001.

* See note 39 of the introduction for a methodological discussion of the distinction between formal interviews and informal, ethnographic ones.

Obirek, Stanisław (Jesuit priest actively involved in ecumenical dialogue), audio recordings, Cracow, May 20, 2004, and May 22, 2004.

Obstarczyk, Mirosław (curator, Exhibitions Section, Auschwitz-Birkenau State Museum), audio recordings, Oświęcim, April 14, 2001, and May 17, 2004.

Oleksy, Krystyna (vice-director of the Auschwitz-Birkenau State Museum and director of the Pedagogical Section, Auschwitz-Birkenau State Museum), Oświęcim, audio recording, March 19, 2001.

Oświęcim Covenant in the Defense of the Papal Cross at the Gravel Pit, Oświęcim, audio recordings, March 7, 2001, and April 4, 2001.

Smoleń, Kazimierz (Auschwitz survivor and director of the State Museum at Auschwitz, 1955–90), audio recording, Oświęcim, May 9, 2001.

Świtoń, Kazimierz (instigator of the War of the Crosses, ex-Solidarity activist, and former KPN deputy), audio recordings, Katowice, April 25, 2001, and May 23, 2001.

Urbiński, Jacek (councilman in Oświęcim), audio recording, Oświęcim, April 4, 2001.

Wilkanowicz, Stefan (editor-in-chief of Znak publishing house and cochair of the International Council of the Auschwitz-Birkenau State Museum), audio recording, Cracow, April 23, 2001.

Zbrzeska, Teresa (head of the Exhibitions Section, Auschwitz-Birkenau State Museum), audio recordings, Oświęcim, April 18, 2001, and May 17, 2004.

Newspapers and Magazines

Gazeta Polska

Gazeta Wyborcza

Katolicka Agencja Informacyjna—*Biuletyn*

Midrasz

Nasz Dziennik

Nasza Polska

Nie

Polityka

Polska Agencja Prasowa

Rzeczpospolita

Słowo Żydowskie

Tygodnik Powszechny

Więź

Wprost

Zawsze Wierni

Znak

Statistical Data and Reports

Centrum Badania Opinii Społecznej. 1992a. *Obawy Polaków i postulaty dotyczące kształtu państwa.* Warsaw: Centrum Badania Opinii Społecznej.

———. 1992b. *Opinia publiczna o prawie do przerywania ciąży*. Warsaw: Centrum Badania Opinii Społecznej.

———. 1992c. *Opinia społeczna o przerywaniu ciąży*. Warsaw: Centrum Badania Opinii Społecznej.

———. 1992d. "Polski katolicyzm Anno Domini 1992." *Polityka*, no. 50–51.

———. 1994. *Religijność Polaków: 1984–1994*. Warsaw: Centrum Badania Opinii Społecznej.

———. 1995. *Oświęcim w zbiorowej pamięci Polaków*. Warsaw: Centrum Badania Opinii Społecznej.

———. 1998. *Polacy o krzyżach w Oświęcimiu*. Warsaw: Centrum Badania Opinii Społecznej.

———. 1999. *Kościół w III Rzeczypospolitej*. Warsaw: Centrum Badania Opinii Społecznej.

———. 2001. *Religijność Polaków na przełomie wieków*. Warsaw: Centrum Badania Opinii Społecznej.

———. 2004a. *Stabilizacja opinii o wpływie Kościoła na życie w kraju*. Warsaw: Centrum Badania Opinii Społecznej.

———. 2004b. *Opinie o integracji w przeddzień rozszerzenia Unii Europejskiej*. Warsaw: Centrum Badania Opinii Społecznej.

———. 2005. *Po obchodach 60 rocznicy wyzwolenia Auschwitz-Birkenau—Obóz w Oświęcimiu w świadomości Polaków*. Warsaw: Centrum Badania Opinii Społecznej.

Główny Urząd Statystyczny. 1991. *Kościół katolicki w Polsce, 1918–1990: Rocznik statystyczny*. Warsaw: Główny Urząd Statystyczny.

Ośrodek Badania Opinii Publicznej. 1997. *Treść przyszłej konstytucji w opinii Polaków*. Warsaw: OBOP.

———. 1998. *Wokół Oświęcimia*. Warsaw: OBOP.

———. 1999. *Index Polska-Badania czytelnictwa prasy*, http://www.obop.com.pl/index_polska9902.html.

———. 2000. *Oświęcim: Przeszłość a teraźniejszość w opiniach Polaków*. Warsaw: OBOP.

Ośrodek Badań Prasoznawczych. 2000. *Katalog Mediów polskich 1999/2000*. Cracow: Jagiellonian Univ. Press.

Additional Published Sources

Białecka, Alicja, ed. 1999. *Los Polaków i los Żydów w KL Auschwitz: Materiały historyczne dla nauczycieli*. Oświęcim: Państwowe Muzeum Auschwitz-Birkenau.

Brand, William, ed. 2001. *Thou Shalt Not Kill: Poles on Jedwabne*. Warsaw: Więź.

Dmowski, Roman. [1927] 1964. *Kościół, naród i państwo*. London: Nakładem "Myśli Polskiej."

———. 1990. *Wybór pism*. Ed. Roman Wapiński. Warsaw: Państwowy Instytut Wydawniczy.

Glemp, Józef Cardinal. 1999. *Listy pasterskie Prymasa Polski 1981–1996*. Poznań: Pallotinum.

Gross, Jan Tomasz. 2003. *Wokół "Sąsiadów": Polemiki i wyjaśnienia*. Sejny: Pogranicze.

Jackowski, Jan Maria. 1993. *Bitwa o Polskę*. Warsaw: Ad astra.

———. 1997. *Bitwa o prawdę*. Warsaw: Ad astra.

Jan Paweł II w Polsce, 31 maja 1997–10 czerwca 1997: Przemówienia, homilie. Cracow: Znak.

Jedwabne: Spór historyków wokół książki Jana T. Grossa "Sąsiedzi." 2002. Warsaw: Biblioteka Frondy.

John Paul II. 1993. *Veritatis Splendor*. Boston, MA: St. Paul Books & Media.

———. 1995. *Spiritual Pilgrimage: Texts on Jews and Judaism 1979–1995*. Ed. Eugene J. Fischer and Leon Klenicki. New York: Crossroad.

Klein, Théo. 1991. *L'affaire du Carmel d'Auschwitz*. Paris: Éditions Jacques Bertoin.

Machcewicz, Paweł, and Krzysztof Persak. 2002a. *Wokół Jedwabnego*. Vol. 1, *Studia*. Warsaw: Instytut Pamięci Narodowej.

———. 2002b. *Wokół Jedwabnego*. Vol. 2, *Dokumenty*. Warsaw: Instytut Pamięci Narodowej.

Marszałek, Jan. 1998. *Broniąc Krzyża Polski bronimy*. Vol. 1, *Obrona konieczna Godności Polki i Polaka*. Warsaw: Polska Oficyna Wydawnicza.

———. 1999. *Broniąc Krzyża Polski bronimy*. Vol. 2, *Opis wielkiej żydowskiej krucjaty wojennej przeciwko katolicyzmowi na przykładzie Papieskiego Krzyża w hitlerowskim obozie zagłady Birkenau-Auschwitz w Oświęcimiu*. Warsaw: Polska Oficyna Wydawnicza.

Mickiewicz, Adam. 1944. *Poems by Adam Mickiewicz*. Ed. George Rapall Noyes. New York: The Polish Institute of Arts and Sciences in America.

Muszyński, Henryk Archbishop. 2002. *Europa ducha: Chrześcijańska wizja fundamentów jedności europejskiej*. Gniezno: Prymasowskie Wydawnictwo Gaudentinum.

———. 2003. *Na samym chlebie: Kościół w rodzinnej Europie*. Interview conducted by Dorota Maciejewska. Gniezno: Prymasowskie Wydawnictwo Gaudentinum.

"Obozy koncentracyjne hitlerowskie." 1966. In *Wielka Encyklopedia Powszechna PWN* 8:87–89. Warsaw: Państwowe Wydawnictwo Naukowe.

"Od Wydawnictwa" and "Obozy hitlerowskie." 1968. In *Wielka Encyklopedia Powszechna PWN*, erratum added to vol. 11. Warsaw: Państwowe Wydawnictwo Naukowe.

Orzecznictwo sądów polskich. 1999. Position 177. Pp. 486–88. Warsaw: Wydawnictwa Prawnicze PWN.

Polonsky, Antony, and Joanna B. Michlic, eds. 2004. *The Neighbors Respond: The Controversy over the Jedwabne Massacre in Poland*. Princeton, NJ: Princeton Univ. Press.

Smoleń, Kazimierz. 1960. *Oświęcim 1940–1945.* Oświęcim: Państwowe Muzeum w Oświęcimiu.

———. 1979. *Auschwitz 1940–1945: Guide du Musée.* Katowice: Krajowa Agencja Wydawnicza.

———. 1999. *Auschwitz-Birkenau Guide-book.* Oświęcim: Państwowe Muzeum w Oświęcimiu.

Stępniak, Marek. 2004. *Kościołowi w Europie napisz.* Kielce: Jedność.

Szuchta, Robert, and Piotr Trojański. 2000. *Holokaust: Program nauczania o historii i zagładzie Żydow na lekcjach przedmiotów humanistycznych w szkołach ponadpodstawowych.* Warsaw: Wydawnictwo Szkolne PWN.

———. 2003. *Holokaust: Zrozumieć dlaczego.* Warsaw: Oficyna Wydawnicza "Mówią Wieki," Dom Wydawniczy Bellona.

Tajne dokumenty: Państwo-Kościół 1980–1989. 1993. Warsaw: Aneks.

Tajne dokumenty: Państwo-Kościół 1960–1980. 1996. Warsaw: Aneks.

Turowicz, Jerzy, and Jacek Żakowski. 1990. *Trzy ćwiartki wieku: Rozmowy z Jerzym Turowiczem.* Cracow: Znak.

Wiesel, Elie. 1990. *From the Kingdom of Memory: Reminiscences.* New York: Summit Books.

———. 1999. *And the Sea Is Never Full: Memoirs 1969–.* Trans. from the French by Marion Wiesel. New York: Alfred A. Knopf.

Wyszyński, Stefan Cardinal. 1995. *Zapiski więzienne.* Warsaw: Wydawnictwo im. Stefana Kardynała Wyszyńskiego "Soli Deo."

———. 1996a. *Na szlaku Tysiąclecia: Wybór kazań.* Warsaw: Wydawnictwo im. Stefana Kardynała Wyszyńskiego "Soli Deo."

———. 1996b. *Zapiski milenijne: Wybór z dziennika "Pro memoria" z lat 1965–1967.* Warsaw: Wydawnictwo im. Stefana Kardynała Wyszyńskiego "Soli Deo."

SECONDARY SOURCES

Abbott, Andrew. 1990. "Conceptions of Time and Events in Social Science Methods." *Historical Methods* 23 (4): 140–50.

Alexander, Jeffrey C. 2002. "On the Social Construction of Moral Universals: The 'Holocaust' from War Crime to Trauma Drama." *European Journal of Social Theory* 5 (1): 5–86.

Alexander, Jeffrey C., and Philip Smith. 1993. "The Discourse of American Civil Society: A New Proposal for Cultural Studies." *Theory and Society* 22:151–207.

Althoen, David M. 2000. "That Noble Quest: From True Nobility to Enlightened Society in the Polish-Lithuanian Commonwealth, 1550–1830." Ph.D. diss., Department of History, Univ. of Michigan.

Ambrosewicz-Jacobs, Jolanta. 2003. *Me Us Them: Ethnic Prejudices among Youth and Alternative Methods of Education; The Case of Poland.* Cracow: Universitas.

Ambrosewicz-Jacobs, Jolanta, and Leszek Hońdo, eds. 2003. *Dlaczego należy uczyć o Holokauście?* Cracow: Uniwersytet Jagielloński, Katedra Judaistyki.

———, eds. 2004. *Why Should We Teach about the Holocaust?* Cracow: Judaica Foundation, Center for Jewish Culture.

Aminzade, Ronald R., and Doug McAdam. 2001. "Emotions and Contentious Politics." In *Silences and Voice in the Study of Contentious Politics*, ed. R. R. Aminzade, J. A. Goldstone, D. McAdam, E. J. Perry, W. H. Sewell Jr., and C. Tilly. Cambridge: Cambridge Univ. Press.

Anderson, Benedict. [1983] 1991. *Imagined Communities: Reflections on the Origins and Spread of Nationalism*. London: Verso.

Anusz, Andrzej. 2004. *Kościół obywatelski: Formowanie społeczeństwa obywatelskiego w PRL.* Warsaw: Agencja Wydawnicza i Reklamowa Akces.

Appleby, R. Scott. 2000. *The Ambivalence of the Sacred: Religion, Violence, and Reconciliation.* New York: Rowman & Littlefield Publishers, Inc.

Arjomand, Said Amir, ed. 1993. *The Political Dimensions of Religion.* Albany: State Univ. of New York Press.

Armstrong, John. 1996. "Nations before Nationalism." In *Nationalism*, ed. John Hutchison and Anthony D. Smith, 140–47. New York: Oxford Univ. Press.

Ash, Timothy Garton. 1985. *The Polish Revolution: Solidarity.* New York: Vintage Books.

Babiński, Grzegorz. 1993. "Religia i nacjonalizm w środkowej i wschodniej Europie: Zarys problematyki." In *Religie i Kościoły w społeczeństwach postkomunistycznych*, ed. Irena Borowik and Andrzej Szyjewski, 193–98. Cracow: Nomos.

Balibar, Étienne. 1991. "The Nation Form: History and Ideology." In *Race, Nation, Class: Ambiguous Identities*, ed. E. Balibar and I. Wallerstein, 86–106. New York: Verso.

Barkun, Michael. 1997. *Religion and the Racist Right: The Origins of the Christian Identity Movement.* Rev. ed., Chapel Hill: Univ. of North Carolina Press.

Bartnik, Czesław. 1982. *Chrześcijańska nauka o narodzie według Prymasa Stefana Wyszyńskiego.* London: Odnowa.

———. 2001. *Idea polskości.* Radom: Polskie Wydawnictwo Encyklopedyczne.

Bartoszewski, Władysław T. 1991. *The Convent at Auschwitz.* New York: George Braziller Inc.

Bauer, Yehuda. 2002. *Rethinking the Holocaust.* New Haven, CT: Yale Univ. Press.

Beiner, Ronald, ed. 1999. *Theorizing Nationalism.* Albany: State Univ. of New York Press.

Bell, David E. 2003. *The Cult of the Nation in France: Inventing Nationalism, 1680–1800.* Cambridge, MA: Harvard Univ. Press.

Bellah, Robert N. 1967. "Civil Religion in America." *Daedalus* 96:1–120.

Bendelow, Gillian, and Simon J. Williams, eds. 1998. *Emotions in Social Life: Critical Themes and Contemporary Issues.* New York: Routledge.

Berezin, Mabel. 1997. *Making the Fascist Self: The Political Culture of Interwar Italy*. Berkeley and Los Angeles: Univ. of California Press.

———. 2001. "Emotion and Political Identity: Mobilizing Affection for the Polity." In *Passionate Politics: Emotions and Social Movements*, ed. Jeff Goodwin, James M. Jasper, and Francesca Polletta, 83–98. Chicago: Univ. of Chicago Press.

Berger, Alan L., Harry James Cargas, and Susan E. Nowak, eds. 2004. *The Continuing Agony: From the Carmelite Convent to the Crosses at Auschwitz*. Lanham, MD: Univ. Press of America.

Berger, Peter L. 1969. *The Sacred Canopy: Elements of a Sociological Theory of Religion*. New York: Doubleday.

Berger, Peter L., and Thomas Luckman. 1967. *The Social Construction of Reality: A Treatise in the Sociology of Knowledge*. New York: Doubleday.

Bergmann, Olaf. 1998. *Narodowa Demokracja wobec problematyki żydowskiej w latach 1918–1929*. Poznań: Wydawnictwo Poznańskie.

Bernhard, Michael H. 1993. *The Origins of Democratization in Poland: Workers, Intellectuals, and Oppositional Politics, 1976–1980*. New York: Columbia Univ. Press.

Bhabha, Homi K., ed. 1990. *Nation and Narration*. New York: Routledge.

Bibó, István. 1993. *Misère des petits États d'Europe de l'Est*. Paris: Albin Michel.

Bjork, James. 2004. "Nations in the Parish: Catholicism and Nationalist Conflict in the Silesian Borderland, 1890–1922." In *Religion und Nation, Nation und Religion: Beiträge zu einer unbewältigten Geschichte*, ed. M. Geyer and H. Lehmann, 207–24. Göttingen: Wallstein Verlag.

Blanke, Richard. 1981. *Prussian Poland in the German Empire (1871–1900)*. New York: Columbia Univ. Press.

Blobaum, Robert. 2001. "The Politics of Antisemitism in Fin-de-Siècle Warsaw." *Journal of Modern History* 73 (2): 291–305.

———. 2005. "Introduction." In *Antisemitism and Its Opponents in Modern Poland*, ed. R. Blobaum, 1–19. Ithaca, NY: Cornell Univ. Press.

———, ed. 2005. *Antisemitism and Its Opponents in Modern Poland*. Ithaca, NY: Cornell Univ. Press.

Bloch, Maurice. 1989. *Ritual, History, and Power: Selected Papers in Anthropology*. Atlantic Highlands, NJ: Athlone Press.

Boć, Jan, ed. 1998. *Konstytucje Rzeczypospolitej oraz komentarz do Konstytucji RP z 1997 roku*. Wrocław: Kolonia Ltd.

———, ed. 2001. *Konstytucje Rzeczypospolitej 1997, 1952, 1935, 1921, 1791*. Wrocław: Kolonia Ltd.

Bocheński, Józef M. 1999. *Szkice o nacjonalizmie i katolicyzmie polskim*. Warsaw: Wydawnictwo Antyk.

Bogucka, Teresa. 1997. *Polak po komunizmie*. Cracow: Znak.

Bonnell, Victoria E., ed. 1996. *Identities in Transition: Eastern Europe and Russia after the Collapse of Communism.* Berkeley: Center for Slavic and East European Studies, Univ. of California at Berkeley.

Bonnell, Victoria E., and Lynn Hunt, eds. 1999. *Beyond the Cultural Turn: New Directions in the Study of Society and Culture.* Berkeley and Los Angeles: Univ. of California Press.

Borowik, Irena. 1992. "Miejsce Kościoła i religii w nowej sytuacji społeczno-politycznej Polski." *Nomos, Kwartalnik religioznawczy* 1:156–72.

———. 1993. "Religijność społeczeństw postkomunistycznych-katalog pytań i paradoksów." In *Religie i Kościoły w społeczeństwach postkomunistycznych,* ed. Irena Borowik and Andrzej Szyjewski, 117–26. Cracow: Nomos.

———. 1997. *Procesy instytucjonalizacji i prywatyzacji religii w powojennej Polsce.* Cracow: Wydawnictwo Uniwersytetu Jagiellońskiego.

———. 2000. *Odbudowywanie pamięci: Przemiany religijne w Środkowo-Wschodniej Europie po upadku komunizmu.* Cracow: Nomos.

Borowik, Irena, and Tadeusz Doktór. 2001. *Pluralizm religijny i moralny w Polsce.* Cracow: Nomos.

Bourdieu, Pierre. 1977. *Outline of a Theory of Practice.* Cambridge: Cambridge Univ. Press.

———. 1980. "L'identité et la représentation: Élément pour une réflexion critique sur l'idée de région." *Actes de la Recherche en Sciences Sociales* 35.

———. 1991a. "Genesis and Structure of the Religious Field." *Comparative Social Research* 13:1–44.

———. 1991b. *Language and Symbolic Power.* Cambridge, MA: Harvard Univ. Press.

———. 2000. *Pascalian Meditations.* Stanford, CA: Stanford Univ. Press.

Breton, Raymond. 1988. "From Ethnic to Civic Nationalism: English Canada and Quebec." *Ethnic and Racial Studies* 11 (1): 85–102.

Breton, Raymond, and Władysław Kwaśniewicz. 1990. "Ethnic Groups, Regions and Nationalism in the Formation of Canadian and Polish Society." In *National Survival in Dependent Societies: Social Change in Canada and Poland,* ed. Raymond Breton, Gilles Houle, Gary Caldwell, Edmund Mokrzycki, and Edmund Wnuk-Lipiński, 101–35. Ottawa: Carleton Univ. Press.

Breuilly, John. 1993. *Nationalism and the State.* Chicago: Univ. of Chicago Press.

———. 1996. "Approaches to Nationalism." In *Mapping the Nation,* ed. G. Balakrishnan, 146–74. New York: Verso.

Brock, Peter. 1994. "Polish Nationalism." In *Nationalism in Eastern Europe,* by Peter F. Sugar and J. Lederer, 310–72. Seattle: Univ. of Washington Press.

Bromke, Adam. 1987. *The Meaning and Use of Polish History.* New York: Columbia Univ. Press.

Browning, Christopher R. 1993. *Ordinary Men: Reserve Police Battalion 101 and the Final Solution in Poland.* New York: HarperCollins.

Brubaker, Rogers. 1992. *Citizenship and Nationhood in France and Germany.* Cambridge, MA: Harvard Univ. Press.

———. 1996. *Nationalism Reframed: Nationhood and the National Question in the New Europe*. Cambridge: Cambridge Univ. Press.

———. 1999. "Myths and Misconceptions in the Study of Nationalism." In *The State of the Nation: Ernest Gellner and the Theory of Nationalism*, ed. John A. Hall, 272–306. Cambridge: Cambridge Univ. Press.

Brubaker, Rogers, and Frederick Cooper. 2000. "Beyond 'Identity.'" *Theory and Society* 29:1–47.

Brzezinski, Mark. 1998. *The Struggle for Constitutionalism in Poland.* New York: St. Martin's Press.

Brzozowski, Mieczysław. 1990. "The Problem of the Nation in the Preaching of Archbishop Jan Pawel Woronicz, 1757–1829." In *Faith and Identity: Christian Political Experience*, ed. David Loades and Katherine Walsh, 137–46. Oxford: Blackwell.

Buckley, Anthony. 1995. *Negotiating Identity: Rhetoric, Metaphor, and Social Drama in Northern Ireland*. Washington, DC: Smithsonian Institution Press.

Budziło, Krzysztof, and Jan Pruszyński, eds. 1996. *Dla dobra Rzeczypospolitej: Antologia myśli państwowej.* Warsaw: Wydawnictwo Sejmowe.

Burawoy, Michael, and Katherine Verdery, eds. 1999. *Uncertain Transition: Ethnographies of Change in the Postsocialist World.* Lanham, UK: Rowman & Littlefield.

Cała, Alina. 1995. *The Image of the Jew in Polish Folk Culture.* Jerusalem: Magnes Press, Hebrew University.

Calhoun, Craig. 1993. "Nationalism and Ethnicity." *Annual Review of Sociology* 19:211–39.

———. 1996. "The Rise and Domestication of Historical Sociology." In *The Historic Turn in the Social Sciences*, ed. Terrence J. McDonald, 305–38. Ann Arbor: Univ. of Michigan Press.

———. 1997. *Nationalism.* Minneapolis: Univ. of Minnesota Press.

Caplan, Richard, and John Feffer, eds. 1996. *Europe's New Nationalism: States and Minorities in Conflict.* New York: Oxford Univ. Press.

Casanova, José. 1994. *Public Religions in the Modern World.* Chicago: Univ. of Chicago Press.

Castellan, Georges. 1981. *"Dieu garde la Pologne!" Histoire du catholicisme polonais (1795–1980).* Paris: Robert Laffont.

Chałasiński, Józef. 1968. *Kultura i naród: Studia i szkice.* Warsaw: Książka i Wiedza.

Chaves, Mark. 1994. "Secularization as Declining Religious Authority." *Social Forces* 72:749–74.

Chevallier, Jacques. 1996. "Essai d'analyse structurale du préambule." In *Le Préambule de la Constitution de 1946: Antinomies juridiques et contradictions politiques*, ed. Geneviève Koubi. Paris: Presses universitaires de France.

Chlebowczyk, Józef. 1980. *On Small and Young Nations in Europe: Nation-Forming Processes in Ethnic Borderlands in East-Central Europe.* Warsaw: Ossolineum.

Chrostowski, Waldemar. 1996. *Rozmowy o dialogu.* Warsaw: Vocatio.

———. 1999. *Dialog w cieniu Auschwitz.* Warsaw: Vocatio.

———. 2001. "Drogi i bezdroża dialogu katolicko-żydowskiego." Lecture given at the Cardinal Stefan Wyszyński University in Warsaw, March 5.

Chrypinski, Vincent C. 1989. "Church and Nationality in Postwar Poland." In *Religion and Nationalism in Soviet and East European Politics,* ed. Pedro Ramet, 241–63. Durham, NC: Duke Univ. Press.

Chwalba, Andrzej. 2000. *Historia Polski, 1795–1918.* Cracow: Wydawnictwo Literackie.

Cole, Tim. 2000. *Selling the Holocaust: From Auschwitz to Schindler; How History Is Bought, Packaged and Sold.* New York: Routledge.

Comaroff, John. 1987. "Of Totemism and Ethnicity: Consciousness, Practice, and the Signs of Inequality." *Ethnos* 52:302–23.

Connor, Walker. 1994. *Ethnonationalism: The Quest for Understanding.* Princeton, NJ: Princeton Univ. Press.

Corrsin, Stephen D. 2005. "Works on Polish-Jewish Relations Published since 1990: A Selective Bibliography." In *Antisemitism and Its Opponents in Modern Poland,* ed. Robert Blobaum, 326–41. Ithaca, NY: Cornell Univ. Press.

Cywiński, Bohdan. 1993. *Ogniem próbowane.* Vol. 1, *Korzenie tożsamości.* Warsaw: WSP.

———. 1994. *Ogniem próbowane.* Vol. 2, *I was prześladować będą.* Warsaw: WSP.

Czarnowski, Stefan. [1934] 1988. "La culture religieuse des paysans polonais." *Archives des Sciences sociales des Religions* 65 (1): 7–23.

———. 1956. *Kult bohaterów i jego społeczne podłoże: Święty Patryk bohater narodowy Irlandii.* Warsaw: Państwowe Wydawnictwo Naukowe.

Davies, Norman. 1982. *God's Playground: A History of Poland.* Vol. 1, *The Origins to 1795;* vol. 2, *1795 to the Present.* New York: Columbia Univ. Press.

———. 1992. *Heart of Europe: A Short History of Poland.* Oxford: Oxford Univ. Press.

Delannoi, Gilles. 1991a. "Nations et Lumières, des philosophies de la nation avant le nationalisme: Voltaire et Herder." In *Théories du nationalisme,* ed. Gilles Dellanoi and Paul-André Taguieff. Paris: Kimé.

———. 1991b. "La théorie de la nation et ses ambivalences." In *Théories du nationalisme,* ed. Gilles Dellanoi and Paul-André Taguieff. Paris: Kimé.

Déloye, Yves. 1996. "Gouverner les citoyens: Normes civiques et mentalité en France." *L'année sociologique* 46 (1): 87–103.

Dieckhoff, Alain. 1996. "La déconstruction d'une illusion: L'introuvable opposition entre nationalisme politique et nationalisme culturel." *L'année sociologique* 46 (1).

Duara, Prasenjit. 1995. *Rescuing History from the Nation: Questioning Narratives of Modern China.* Chicago: Univ. of Chicago Press.

Dudek, Antoni, and Ryszard Gryz. 2003. *Komuniści i Kościół w Polsce (1945–1989).* Cracow: Znak.

Dumont, Louis. 1983. "Interaction between Cultures: Herder's *Volk* and Fichte's *Nation*." In *Ethnicity, Identity and History*, ed. J. B. Maier and C. Waxman, 13–24. New Brunswick, NJ: Transaction Publishers.

Dunn, Dennis J. 1987. "Nationalism and Religion in Eastern Europe." In *Religion and Nationalism in Eastern Europe and in the Soviet Union*, ed. D. Dunn, 1–14. London: Lynne Rienner Publishers.

Durkheim, Émile. [1912] 1995. *The Elementary Forms of Religious Life*. Trans. K. Fields. New York: Free Press.

Eglitis, Daina Stukuls. 2002. *Imagining the Nation: History, Modernity, and Revolution in Latvia*. University Park: Pennsylvania State Univ. Press.

Ekiert, Grzegorz, and Jan Kubik. 1999. *Rebellious Civil Society: Popular Protest and Democratic Consolidation in Poland, 1989–1993*. Ann Arbor: Univ. of Michigan Press.

Eley, Geoff, and Ronald G. Suny. 1996. "Introduction: From the Moment of Social History to the Work of Cultural Representation." In *Becoming National: A Reader*, ed. Geoff Eley and Ronald G. Suny. New York: Oxford Univ. Press.

Elias, Norbert. 1978. *The History of Manners*. New York: Pantheon Books.

Elster, Jon, Claus Offe, and Ulrich K. Preuss. 1998. *Institutional Design in Post-Communist Societies: Rebuilding the Ship at Sea*. Cambridge: Cambridge Univ. Press.

Enloe, Cynthia. 1996. "Religion and Ethnicity." In *Ethnicity*, ed. John Hutchison and Anthony D. Smith, 197–202. New York: Oxford Univ. Press.

Etzioni, Emitai. 2000. "Toward a Theory of Public Ritual." *Sociological Theory* 18 (1): 44–59.

Eyal, Gil. 2003. *The Origins of Postcommunist Elites: From Prague Spring to the Breakup of Czechoslovakia*. Minneapolis: Univ. of Minnesota Press.

Eyal, Gil, Iván Szelényi, and Eleanor Townsley. 1998. *Making Capitalism without Capitalists: Class Formation and Elite Struggles in Post-Communist Central Europe*. London: Verso.

Fedyszak-Radziejowska, Barbara. 2003. "Zmiany społeczne i przystąpienie Polski do Unii Europejskiej jako zadanie i wyzwanie dla Kościoła katolickiego: Opinie duchowieństwa parafialnego." In *Kościół katolicki w przededniu wejścia Polski do Unii Europejskiej*, ed. Piotr Mazurkiewicz, 61–89. Warsaw: Instytut Spraw Publicznych.

Fejtö, François. 1992. *La fin des démocraties populaires*. Paris: Éditions du Seuil.

Figa, Józef, and Hank Johnston. 1988. "The Church and Political Opposition: Comparative Perspectives on Mobilization against Authoritarian Regimes." *Journal for the Scientific Study of Religion* 27 (1): 32–47.

Filipowicz, Hanna. 2001. "Taboo Topics in Polish and Polish/Jewish Cultural Studies." *Journal of the International Institute* 9 (1).

Finkelstein, Norman G. 2000. *The Holocaust Industry: Reflections on the Exploitation of Jewish Suffering*. London: Verso.

Fischer-Galati, Stephen. 1993. "The Political Right in Eastern Europe in Historical Perspective." In *Democracy and Right-Wing Politics in Eastern Europe in the 1990's*, ed. Joseph Held, 1–12. Boulder, CO: East European Monographs.

Friedland, Roger, and Richard Hecht. 2000. *To Rule Jerusalem*. Berkeley and Los Angeles: Univ. of California Press.

Friedlander, Saul, and Adam B. Seligman. 1994. "The Israeli Memory of the Shoah: On Symbols, Rituals, and Ideological Polarization." In *NowHere: Space, Time, and Modernity*, ed. R. Friedland and D. Boden, 356–71. Berkeley and Los Angeles: Univ. of California Press.

Friedman, Jeffrey. 1996. "Nationalism in Theory and Reality." *Critical Review* 10 (2): 155–67.

Froese, Paul, and Steven Pfaff. 2001. "Replete and Desolate Markets: Poland, East Germany, and the New Religious Paradigm." *Social Forces* 80 (2): 481–507.

Fuszara, Małgorzata. 1993. "Abortion and the Formation of the Public Sphere in Poland." In *Gender Politics and Post-Communism: Reflections from Eastern Europe and the Former Soviet Union*, ed. Nanette Funk and Magda Mueller, 241–52. New York: Routledge.

Gach, Piotr Paweł, ed. 1995. *Otwórz Twój skarbiec ... Antologia modlitwy za Ojczyznę*. Cracow: Wydawnictwo WAM.

Gal, Susan. 1991. "Bartok's Funeral: Representations of Europe in Hungarian Political Rhetoric." *American Ethnologist* 18 (3): 440–58.

Gauchet, Marcel. 1985. *Le désenchantement du monde: Une histoire politique de la religion*. Paris: Gallimard.

Gebert, Konstanty. 1991. "Anti-Semitism in the 1990 Polish Presidential Election." *Social Research* 58 (4): 723–55.

Geertz, Clifford. 1973. *The Interpretation of Cultures: Selected Essays*. New York: Basic Books.

Gellner, Ernest. 1983. *Nations and Nationalism*. Ithaca, NY: Cornell Univ. Press.

———. 1997. *Nationalism*. New York: New York Univ. Press.

Gillis, John R. 1994. "Memory and Identity: The History of a Relationship." In *Commemorations: The Politics of National Identity*, ed. John R. Gillis, 3–24. Princeton, NJ: Princeton Univ. Press.

Gitelman, Zvi. 1993. "Soviet Reactions to the Holocaust, 1945–1991." In *The Holocaust in the Soviet Union: Studies and Sources on the Destruction of the Jews in the Nazi-Occupied Territories of the USSR, 1941–1945*, ed. Lucjan Dobroszycki and Jeffrey S. Gurock, 3–27. Armonk, NY: M. E. Sharpe.

Glaeser, Andreas. 2000. *Divided in Unity: Identity, Germany, and the Berlin Police*. Chicago: Univ. of Chicago Press.

Głownia, Marek, and Stefan Wilkanowicz, eds. 1998. *Auschwitz: Konflikty i dialog*. Cracow: Wydawnictwo Św. Stanisława.

Goban-Klas, Tomasz. 1995. "Pamięć podzielona, pamięć urażona: Oświęcim i Auschwitz w polskiej i żydowskiej pamięci zbiorowej." In *Europa po Auschwitz*, ed. Zdzisław Mach, 71–91. Cracow: Universitas.

Gomułka, Stanisław, and Antony Polonsky. 1990. "Introduction." In *Polish Paradoxes*, ed. Stanisław Gomułka and Antony Polonsky, 1–17. New York: Routledge.

Goodwin, Jeff, James M. Jasper, and Francesca Polletta, eds. 2001. *Passionate Politics: Emotions and Social Movements.* Chicago: Univ. of Chicago Press.

Gorski, Philip S. 2000a. "Historicizing the Secularization Debate: Church, State, and Society in Late Medieval and Early Modern Europe, ca. 1300 to 1700." *American Sociological Review* 65:138–67.

———. 2000b. "The Mosaic Moment: An Early Modernist Critique of Modernist Theories of Nationalism." *American Journal of Sociology* 105 (5): 1428–68.

———. 2003. *The Disciplinary Revolution: Calvinism and the Rise of the State in Early Modern Europe.* Chicago: Univ. of Chicago Press.

Górski, Piotr. 1994. *Socjalistyczno-niepodległościowa idea narodu polskiego 1908–1914.* Cracow: Apostrof.

Gowin, Jarosław. 1995. *Kościół po komunizmie.* Cracow: Znak.

———. 2000. *Kościół w czasach wolności 1989–1999.* Cracow: Znak.

Grabowska, Mirosława. 1992. "L'Église de Pologne à un tournant." In *Les religions à l'Est*, ed. Patrick Michel, 109–27. Paris: Ed. du Cerf.

Graczyk, Roman. 1997. *Konstytucja dla Polski: Tradycje, doświadczenia, spory.* Cracow: Znak.

———. 1999. *Polski Kościół-polska demokracja.* Cracow: Universitas.

Greenfeld, Liah. 1992. *Nationalism: Five Roads to Modernity.* Cambridge, MA: Harvard Univ. Press.

———. 1996. "Is Nationalism the Modern Religion?" *Critical Review* 10 (2): 169–91.

Grewe, Constance, and Henri Oberdoff, eds. 1999. *Les Constitutions des États de l'Union européenne.* Paris: Documentation française.

Grosfeld, Jan, ed. 1996. *Kościół wobec integracji europejskiej.* Warsaw: Societas.

Gross, Jan Tomasz. 1992. "Poland: From Civil Society to Political Nation." In *Eastern Europe in Revolution*, ed. I. Banac. Ithaca, NY: Cornell Univ. Press.

———. 2000. *Sąsiedzi: Historia zagłady żydowskiego miasteczka.* Sejny: Pogranicze.

Gross, Jan Tomasz, and Leszek Kołakowski. 1980. "Church and Democracy in Poland: Two Views." *Dissent* 3.

Grott, Bogumił. 1993. *Religia, Kościół, etyka w ideach i koncepcjach prawicy polskiej: Narodowa Demokracja. Wybór tekstów z komentarzem autora.* Cracow: Nomos.

———. 1999. *Nacjonalizm chrześcijański: Narodowo-katolicka formacja ideowa w II Rzeczypospolitej na tle porównawczym.* Krzeszowice: Ostoja.

Grudzińska-Gross, Irena. 1997. "Introduction: When Polish Constitutionalism Began." *East European Constitutional Review* 6 (2–3): 64–76.

———, ed. 1994. *Constitutionalism in East Central Europe: Discussions in Warsaw, Budapest, Prague, Bratislava*. Bratislava: Czecho-Slovak Committee of the European Cultural Foundation.

Gusfield, Joseph R., and Jerzy Michalowicz. 1984. "Secular Symbolism: Studies of Ritual, Ceremony, and the Symbolic Order in Modern Life." *Annual Review of Sociology* 10:417–35.

Gutman, Yisrael. 1986. "Polish and Jewish Historiography on the Question of Polish-Jewish Relations during World War II." In *The Jews in Poland*, ed. Chimen Abramsky, Maciej Jachimczyk, and Antony Polonsky, 177–89. Oxford: Basil Blackwell.

Gutman, Yisrael, and Shmuel Cracowski. 1986. *Unequal Victims: Poles and Jews during World War Two*. New York: Holocaust Library.

Halbwachs, Maurice. 1992. *On Collective Memory*. Ed., trans., and with an introduction by L. A. Coser. Chicago: Univ. of Chicago Press.

Hall, John A., ed. 1999. *The State of the Nation: Ernest Gellner and the Theory of Nationalism*. Cambridge: Cambridge Univ. Press.

Handler, Richard. 1988. *Nationalism and the Politics of Culture in Quebec*. Madison: Univ. of Wisconsin Press.

———. 1994. "Is 'Identity' a Useful Cross-Cultural Concept?" In *Commemorations: The Politics of National Identity*, ed. John R. Gillis, 27–40. Princeton, NJ: Princeton Univ. Press.

Harootunian, Harry. 1999. "Memory, Mourning, and National Morality: Yasukuni Shrine and the Reunion of State and Religion." In *Nation and Religion: Perspectives on Europe and Asia*, ed. Peter Van der Veer and Hartmut Lehmann, 144–60. Princeton, NJ: Princeton Univ. Press.

Hastings, Adrian. 1997. *The Construction of Nationhood: Ethnicity, Religion and Nationalism*. New York: Cambridge Univ. Press.

Hauser, Ewa, Barbara Haynes, and Jane Mansbridge. 1993. "Feminism in the Interstices of Politics and Culture: Poland in Transition." In *Gender Politics and Post-Communism: Reflections from Eastern Europe and the Former Soviet Union*, ed. Nanette Funk and Magda Mueller, 257–73. New York: Routledge.

Hayes, Carlton. 1926. *Essays on Nationalism*. New York: Macmillan Co.

———. 1960. *Nationalism: A Religion*. New York: Macmillan Co.

Hilberg, Raul. 2003. *The Destruction of the European Jews*. 3 vols. 3rd ed. New Haven, CT: Yale Univ. Press.

Hirszowicz, Łukasz. 1993. "The Holocaust in the Soviet Mirror." In *The Holocaust in the Soviet Union: Studies and Sources on the Destruction of the Jews in the Nazi-Occupied Territories of the USSR, 1941–1945*, ed. Lucjan Dobroszycki and Jeffrey S. Gurock, 29–59. Armonk, NY: M. E. Sharpe.

Hobsbawm, Eric J. 1983a. "Introduction: Inventing Traditions." In *The Invention of Tradition*, ed. Eric J. Hobsbawm and Terence Ranger, 1–14. Cambridge: Cambridge Univ. Press.

———. 1983b. "Mass-Producing Traditions: Europe, 1870–1914." In *The Invention of Tradition*, ed. Eric J. Hobsbawm and Terence Ranger, 263–307. Cambridge: Cambridge Univ. Press.

———. [1992] 1995. *Nations and Nationalism Since 1780*. New rev. ed. New York: Cambridge Univ. Press.

Holc, Janine P. 2005. "Memory Contested: Jewish and Catholic Views of Auschwitz in Present-Day Poland." In *Antisemitism and Its Opponents in Modern Poland*, ed. Robert Blobaum, 301–25. Ithaca: Cornell Univ. Press.

Houle, Gilles, Piotr Łukasiewicz, and Andrzej Siciński. 1990. "Social and National Consciousness Transformations in Dependent Societies." In *National Survival in Dependent Societies: Social Change in Canada and Poland*, ed. Raymond Breton, Gilles Houle, Gary Caldwell, Edmund Mokrzycki, and Edmund Wnuk-Lipiński, 137–76. Ottawa: Carleton Univ. Press.

Hroch, Miroslav. 1996. "From National Movement to the Fully-Formed Nation: The Nation-Building Process in Europe." In *Becoming National: A Reader*, ed. Geoff Eley and Ronald G. Suny, 60–77. New York: Oxford Univ. Press.

Huener, Jonathan. 2003. *Auschwitz, Poland, and the Politics of Commemoration, 1945–1979*. Athens: Ohio Univ. Press.

Hunter, James Davison. 1991. *Culture Wars: The Struggle to Define America*. New York: Basic Books.

Igniatieff, Michael. 1993. *Blood and Belonging: Journeys into the New Nationalism*. New York: Farrar, Strauss and Giroux.

Inglot, Mieczysław. 1999. *Postać Żyda w literaturze polskiej lat 1822–1864*. Wrocław: Wydawnictwo Uniwersytetu Wrocławskiego.

International Institute for Democracy, ed. 1996. *The Rebirth of Democracy: 12 Constitutions of Central and Eastern Europe*. Strasbourg: Council of Europe Publishing.

Irwin-Zarecka, Iwona. 1989a. *Neutralizing Memory: The Jew in Contemporary Poland*. New Brunswick, NJ: Transaction Publishers.

———. 1989b. "Poland after the Holocaust." In *Remembering for the Future: Working Papers and Addenda*, vol. 1, ed. Y. Bauer, Alice L. Eckardt, F. H. Littell, E. Maxwell, R. Maxwell, and D. Patterson, 143–55. New York: Pergamon Press.

Iwaszko, Tadeusz. 1985. "The Prisoners." In *Auschwitz: Nazi Extermination Camp*, 47–85. Warsaw: Interpress.

Jachymek, Jan, ed. 1995. *Religia i Kościół rzymskokatolicki w polskiej myśli politycznej*. Lublin: Wydawnictwo Uniwersytetu Marii Curie-Skłodowskiej.

Jacobs, Ronald N. 1996. "Civil Society and Crisis: Culture, Discourse, and the Rodney King Beating." *American Journal of Sociology* 101 (5): 1238–75.

Jaffrelot, Christophe. 1991. "Les modèles explicatifs de l'origine des nations et du nationalisme." In *Théories du nationalisme*, ed. Gilles Dellanoi and Paul-André Taguieff, 139–77. Paris: Kimé.

Jakubowska, Longina. 1990. "Political Drama in Poland: The Use of National Symbols." *Anthropology Today* 6 (4): 10–13.

Janion, Maria, and Maria Żmigrodzka. 1978. *Romantyzm i historia*. Warsaw: Państwowy Instytut Wydawniczy.

Janowitz, Morris. 1980. "Observations on the Sociology of Citizenship." *Social Forces* 59:1–24.

Jasiewicz, Krzysztof. 1999. "Democratic Transition and Social Movements in Poland: From Solidarność to Rodzina Radia Maryja." Presented at the annual meeting of the American Association for the Advancement of Slavic Studies, November 18, St. Louis, MO.

———. 2000. "Dead Ends and New Beginnings: The Quest for a Procedural Republic in Poland." *Communist and Post-Communist Studies* 33:101–22.

Jedlicki, Jerzy. 1990. "Holy Ideals and Prosaic Life, or the Devil's Alternatives." In *Polish Paradoxes*, ed. Stanisław Gomułka and Antony Polonsky, 40–62. New York: Routledge.

———. 1999. *A Suburb of Europe: Nineteenth-Century Polish Approaches to Western Civilization*. Budapest: Central Univ. Press.

Jerschina, Jan. 1990. "The Catholic Church, the Communist State and the Polish People." In *Polish Paradoxes*, ed. Stanisław Gomułka and Antony Polonsky, 76–96. New York: Routledge.

Jewsiewicki, Bogumił. 1995. "The Identity of Memory and the Memory of Identity in the Age of Commodification and Democratization." *Social Identities* 1 (2): 227–62.

Johnson, Paul Christopher. 2005. "Savage Civil Religion." *Numen* 52 (3): 289–324.

Johnston, Hank. 1992. "Religious Nationalism: Six Propositions from Eastern Europe and the Former Soviet Union." In *Religion and Politics in Comparative Perspective: Revival of Religious Fundamentalism in East and West*, ed. Bronisław Misztal and Anson Shupe, 67–79. Westport, CT: Praeger.

Juergensmeyer, Mark. 1993. *The New Cold War? Religious Nationalism Confronts the Secular State.* Berkeley and Los Angeles: Univ. of California Press.

Kaldor, Mary. 1996. "Cosmopolitanism versus Nationalism: The New Divide?" In *Europe's New Nationalism: States and Minorities in Conflict*, ed. Richard Caplan and John Feffer, 42–58. New York: Oxford Univ. Press.

Kamiński, Andrzej Sulima. 2000. *Historia Rzeczypospolitej wielu narodów 1505–1795: Obywatele, ich państwa, społeczeństwo, kultura*. Lublin: Instytut Europy Środkowo-Wschodniej.

Kapralski, Sławomir. 1998. "Oświęcim: Miejsce wielu pamięci." *Pro Memoria* 8 (January): 17–24.

———. 2001. "Battlefields of Memory: Landscape and Identity in Polish-Jewish Relations." *History and Memory* 13 (2): 35–58.

Kaufman, Stuart. 2001. *Modern Hatreds: The Symbolic Politics of Ethnic War.* Ithaca, NY: Cornell Univ. Press.

Kedourie, Elie. 1960. *Nationalism.* New York: Blackwell.

Kempny, Marian. 1997. "Patriotyzm wspólnoty narodowej i obywatelstwo a treści demokracji w świadomości zbiorowej Polaków." In *Elementy nowego ładu,* ed. Henryk Domański and Andrzej Rychard, 446–58. Warsaw: IFiS PAN.

Kennedy, Michael D. 1991. *Professionals, Power, and Solidarity in Poland: A Critical Sociology of Soviet-Type Society.* New York: Cambridge Univ. Press.

———. 1999. "Poland's Critical Sociological Significance: A Comparative and Historical Approach to a Nation and Difference." In *Power and Social Structure: Essays in Honor of Włodzimierz Wesołowski,* ed. A. Jasińska-Kania, M. L. Kohn, and K. M. Słomczyński, 239–63. Warsaw: Wydawnictwo Uniwersytetu Warszawskiego.

———. 2002. *Cultural Formations of Postcommunism: Emancipation, Transition, Nation, and War.* Minneapolis: Univ. of Minnesota Press.

Kennedy, Michael D., and Nicolae Harsanyi. 1994. "Between Utopia and Dystopia: The Liabilities of Nationalism in Eastern Europe." In *Envisioning Eastern Europe: Postcommunist Cultural Studies,* ed. Michael D. Kennedy. Ann Arbor: Univ. of Michigan Press.

Kennedy, Michael D., and Maurice D. Simon. 1983. "Church and Nation in Socialist Poland." In *Religion and Politics in the Modern World,* ed. P. H. Merkl and N. Smart, 121–54. New York: New York Univ. Press.

Kersten, Krystyna. 1992. *Polacy, Żydzi, komunizm: anatomia półprawd 1939–68.* Warsaw: Niezależna Oficyna Wydawnicza.

Kertzer, David I. 1988. *Ritual, Politics, and Power.* New Haven, CT: Yale Univ. Press.

Kieniewicz, Stefan. 1986. "Polish Society and the Jewish Problem in the Nineteenth Century." In *The Jews in Poland,* ed. Chimen Abramsky, Maciej Jachimczyk, and Antony Polonsky, 70–77. Oxford: Basil Blackwell.

———. 1987. *Historia Polski 1795–1918.* Warsaw: Państwowe Wydawnictwo Naukowe.

———. 1990. "Polish Revolutionaries of the Nineteenth Century and the Catholic Church." In *Faith and Identity: Christian Political Experience,* ed. David Loades and Katherine Walsh, 147–60. Oxford: Blackwell.

Klein, Emma. 2001. *The Battle For Auschwitz: Catholic-Jewish Relations under Strain.* Portland, OR: Vallentine Mitchell.

Kłoczowski, Jerzy. 1979. "The Polish Church." In *Church and Society in Catholic Europe of the Eighteenth Century,* ed. W. J. Callahan and D. Higgs, 122–37. Cambridge: Cambridge Univ. Press.

———. 1991. *Dzieje chrześcijaństwa polskiego.* Paris: Editions du Dialogue.

———. 1992. *Chrześcijaństwo w Polsce: Zarys przemian 966–1979.* Lublin: Towarzystwo Naukowe Katolickiego Uniwersytetu Lubelskiego.

———. 2000. *A History of Polish Christianity.* Cambridge: Cambridge Univ. Press.

Kłoskowska, Antonina. 2001. *National Cultures at the Grass-Root Level.* Budapest: Central European Univ. Press.

Koćwin, Lesław. 1996. "'Narodowcy' i 'Europejczycy' wobec problemu jedności europejskiej." In *Współczesna polska myśl polityczna*, ed. Bronisław Pasierb and Krystyna A. Paszkiewicz, 39–64. Wrocław: Wydawnictwo Uniwersytetu Wrocławskiego.

Kohn, Hans. 1944. *The Idea of Nationalism: A Study in Its Origins and Background*. New York: Macmillan Publishing Co.

———. 1946. *Prophets and Peoples: Studies in Nineteenth Century Nationalism*. New York: Macmillan Publishing Co.

———. 1996. "Western and Eastern Nationalisms." In *Nationalism*, ed. John Hutchison and Anthony D. Smith, 162–65. New York: Oxford Univ. Press.

Kołakowski, Leszek, and Jan T. Gross. 1979. "Christian Poland and Human Rights." *Index on Censorship* 6:27–32.

Koopmans, Ruud, and Paul Statham. 1999. "Ethnic and Civic Conceptions of Nationhood and the Differential Success of the Extreme Right in Germany and Italy." In *How Social Movements Matter*, ed. M. Giugni, D. McAdam, and C. Tilly, 225–51. Minneapolis: Univ. of Minneapolis Press.

Korboński, Andrzej. 1993. "The Revival of the Political Right in Post-Communist Poland: Historical Roots." In *Democracy and Right-Wing Politics in Eastern Europe in the 1990's*, ed. Joseph Held, 13–31. Boulder, CO: East European Monographs.

Koseła, Krzysztof. 2003. *Polak i katolik: Splątana tożsamość*. Warsaw: Wydawnictwo Instytutu Filozofii i Socjologii PAN.

Koubi, Geneviève, ed. 1996. *Le Préambule de la Constitution de 1946: Antinomies juridiques et contradictions politiques*. Paris: Presses universitaires de France.

Kowalski, Sergiusz, and Magdalena Tulli. 2003. *Zamiast procesu: Raport o mowie nienawiści*. Warsaw: Instytut Studiów Politycznych PAN.

Krajewski, Stanisław. 1997. *Żydzi, judaizm, Polska*. Warsaw: Vocatio.

Królewska, Jadwiga. 1990. "Uroczystości religijne organizowane przez NSZZ Solidarność od sierpnia 1980 do grudnia 1981: Ich funkcje, charakter i wymowa." In *Religijność polska w świetle badań socjologicznych*, ed. W. Piwowarski and W. Zdaniewicz, 142–46. Warsaw: Pallotinum.

Krzemiński, Ireneusz. 2002. "Polish-Jewish Relations, Anti-Semitism and National Identity." *Polish Sociological Review* 137:25–51.

———, ed. 1996. *Czy Polacy są antysemitami? Wyniki badania sondażowego*. Warsaw: Oficyna Naukowa.

Kubik, Jan. 1994. *The Power of Symbols against the Symbols of Power: The Rise of Solidarity and the Fall of State Socialism in Poland*. University Park: Pennsylvania State Univ. Press.

Kucia, Marek. 2001. "KL Auschwitz in the Social Consciousness of Poles, A.D. 2000." In *Remembering for the Future: The Holocaust in an Age of Genocide*, ed. E. Maxwell and J. K. Roth, 632–51. New York: Palgrave.

———. 2005. *Auschwitz jako fakt społeczny: Historia, współczesność i świadomość społeczna KL Auschwitz w Polsce*. Cracow: Universitas.

Kugelmass, Jack. 1993. "The Rites of the Tribe: The Meaning of Poland for American Jewish Tourists." *YIVO Annual* 21:395–453.

Kulczycki, John J. 1981. *School Strikes in Prussian Poland, 1901–1907*. New York: Columbia Univ. Press.

———. 2001a. "The National Identity of the 'Natives' of Poland's 'Recovered Lands.'" *National Identities* 3 (3): 205–19.

———. 2001b. "Who is a Pole? Polish Nationality Criteria in the 'Recovered Lands,' 1945–1951." *Canadian Review of Studies in Nationalism* 28 (1–2): 107–18.

Kuleta, Magdalena. 2001. "Obraz Żydów i stosunków polsko-żydowskich w prasie (w artykułach dotyczących konfliktu o krzyże w Auschwitz)." M.A. thesis, Department of Sociology, Univ. of Warsaw.

Kumar, Krishan. 2001. *1989: Revolutionary Ideas and Ideals*. Minneapolis: Univ. of Minnesota Press.

———. 2003. *The Making of English National Identity*. Cambridge: Cambridge Univ. Press.

Kurczewska, Joanna. 1997. "Patriotyzm społeczeństwa polskiego lat 90: Między wspólnotą kultury a wspólnotą obywateli." In *Elementy nowego ładu*, ed. Henryk Domański and Andrzej Rychard, 419–45. Warsaw: IFiS PAN.

———. 2000. *Kultura narodowa i polityka*. Warsaw: Oficyna Naukowa.

———. 2002. *Patriotyzm(y) polskich polityków: Z badań nad świadomością liderów partyjnych lat dziewięćdziesiątych*. Warsaw: IFiS PAN.

Kurti, Laszlo. 1997. "Globalization and the Discourse of Otherness in the 'New' Eastern and Central Europe." In *The Politics of Multiculturalism in the New Europe: Racism, Identity and Community*, ed. P. Werbner and T. Modood. London: Zed Books.

———. 1998. "The Emergence of Postcommunist Youth Identities in Eastern Europe: From Communist Youth, to Skinheads, to National Socialist." In *Nation and Race: The Developing Euro-American Racist Subcultures*, ed. J. Kaplan and T. Bjorgo. Boston: Northeastern Univ. Press.

Lamont, Michèle. 1992. *Money, Morals, and Manners: The Culture of the French and American Upper-Middle Class*. Chicago: Univ. of Chicago Press.

Lecomte, Bernard. 1992. "Le Pape et l'après-communisme européen." In *Cet étrange post-communisme: Rupture et transitions en Europe centrale et orientale*, by Georges Mink and Jean-Charles Szurek. Paris: Presse du CNRS, La découverte.

Lehrer, Erica. 2005. "'Shoah-Business,' 'Holocaust Culture,' and the Repair of the World in 'Post-Jewish' Poland: A Quest for Ethnography, Empathy, and the Ethnic Self after Genocide." Ph.D. diss., Department of Anthropology, Univ. of Michigan.

Łepkowski, Tadeusz. 1989. *Uparte trwanie polskości: Nostalgie, trwanie, nadzieje, wartości*. London: Aneks.

Leszczyńska, Katarzyna. 2002. *Imprimatur dla Unii? Kościół rzymskokatolicki w Polsce i Czechach wobec Europy i procesów zjednoczeniowych*. Cracow: Nomos.

Łętowska, Ewa. 1995. "La Constitution, oeuvre de la société?" In *L'espace constitutionel européen*, ed. Roland Bieber and Pierre Widmer, 117–31. Zurich: Publications de l'Institut suisse de droit comparé.

———. 1997. "A Constitution of Possibilities." *East European Constitutional Review* 6 (2–3): 76–81.

Lewandowski, Jan. 1989. *Naród w nauczaniu Kardynała Stefana Wyszyńskiego*. Warsaw: Wydawnictwa Uniwersytetu Warszawskiego.

Libiszowska-Żółtkowska, Maria. 2000. *Wiara uczonych*. Cracow: Nomos.

Limanowski, Bolesław. 1906. *Naród i państwo: Studium socjologiczne*. Cracow: Drukarnia Narodowa.

Lincoln, Bruce, ed. 1985. *Religion, Rebellion, Revolution: An Interdisciplinary and Cross-Cultural Collection of Essays*. New York: St. Martin's Press.

———. 1989. *Discourse and the Construction of Society: Comparative Studies of Myth, Ritual, and Classification*. New York: Oxford Univ. Press.

———. 2003. *Holy Terrors: Thinking about Religion after September 11*. Chicago: Univ. of Chicago Press.

Linz, Juan J., and Alfred Stepan. 1996. *Problems of Democratic Transition and Consolidation: Southern Europe, South America, and Post-Communist Europe*. Baltimore, MD: Johns Hopkins Univ. Press.

Lipset, Seymour Martin. 1990. *Continental Divide: The Values and Institutions of the United States and Canada*. Washington, DC: Canadian-American Committee.

Lipski, Jan Józef. 1986. *KOR: A History of the Workers' Defense Committee in Poland, 1976–1981*. Berkeley and Los Angeles: Univ. of California Press.

Llobera, Josep. 1996. *The God of Modernity: The Development of Nationalism in Western Europe*. Oxford: Berg.

Łodziński, Sławomir. 2003. "Polish Citizenship and Ethnicity: Contribution to the Problem of Ethnic Boundaries and Issue of Citizenship in the Polish Society." Paper presented at the European Sociological Association Conference, Essex, England.

Lowenthal, David. 1985. *The Past Is a Foreign Country*. Cambridge: Cambridge Univ. Press.

Ludwikowski, Rett R. 1996. *Constitution-Making in the Region of Former Soviet Dominance*. Durham, NC: Duke Univ. Press.

Lukas, Richard C. 2001. *Forgotten Holocaust: The Poles under German Occupation 1939–1944*. Rev. ed. New York: Hippocrene Books.

Lukowski, Jerzy. 1991. *Liberty's Folly: The Polish-Lithuanian Commonwealth in the Eighteenth Century*. New York: Routledge.

Lukowski, Jerzy, and Hubert Zawadzki. 2001. *A Concise History of Poland.* Cambridge: Cambridge Univ. Press.

Mach, Zdzisław. 1992. "National Symbols in Politics: The Polish Case." *Etnologia europea* 22:89–107.

———. 1993. *Symbols, Conflict and Identity: Essays in Political Anthropology.* Albany: State Univ. of New York Press.

Mach, Zdzisław, Jacek Mucha, and Janusz Szmatka, eds. 1993. *Eastern European Societies on the Threshold of Change.* Lewiston, NY: Edwin Mellen Press.

Maier, Charles S. 1988. *The Unmasterable Past: History, Holocaust, and German National Identity.* Cambridge, MA: Harvard Univ. Press.

Mała Encyklopedia Powszechna. 1997. Warsaw: PWN.

Markandan, K. C. 1984. *The Preamble: Key to the Mind of the Makers of the Indian Constitution.* New Delhi: National.

Markiewicz, Mariusz. 2004. *Historia Polski: 1492–1795.* Cracow: Wydawnictwo Literackie.

Markowitz, Andrei S., and Frank E. Sysyn, eds. 1982. *Nationbuilding and the Politics of Nationalism: Essays on Austrian Galicia.* Cambridge, MA: Harvard Univ. Press.

Markowski, Radosław. 1997. "Political Parties and Ideological Spaces in East Central Europe." *Communist and Post-Communist Studies* 33.

Marvin, Carolyn, and David W. Ingle. 1999. *Blood Sacrifice and the Nation: Totem Rituals and the American Flag.* Cambridge: Cambridge Univ. Press.

Marx, Anthony W. 2003. *Faith in Nation: Exclusionary Origins of Nationalism.* New York: Oxford Univ. Press.

Mathernova, Katarina. 1993. "Czecho? Slovakia: Constitutional Disappointments." In *Constitution Making in Eastern Europe,* ed. A. E. Dick Howard, 57–92. Washington, DC: The Woodrow Wilson Center Press.

Mazurkiewicz, Piotr, ed. 2003. *Kościół katolicki w przededniu wejścia Polski do Unii Europejskiej.* Warsaw: Instytut Spraw Publicznych.

Meinecke, Friedrich. 1970. *Cosmopolitanism and the National State.* Princeton, NJ: Princeton Univ. Press.

Mendelsohn, Ezra. 1986. "Interwar Poland: Good for the Jews or Bad for the Jews?" In *The Jews in Poland,* ed. Chimen Abramsky, Maciej Jachimczyk, and Antony Polonsky, 130–39. Oxford: Basil Blackwell.

Michel, Patrick. 1986. "Y a-t-il un modèle ecclésial polonais?" *Archives des Sciences sociales des Religions* 62 (1): 81–92.

———. 1988. *La société retrouvée: Politique et religion dans l'Europe soviétisée.* Paris: Fayard.

———. 1990. "Légitimation et régulation étatique de la religion dans les systèmes de type soviétique: L'exemple du catholicisme en Pologne, Tchécoslovaquie et Hongrie." *Social Compass* 37 (1).

———. 1991. "L'Église entre Gdańsk: Rome et Varsovie." In *Le religieux dans le politique.* Paris: Editions du Seuil.

———. 1992a. "Églises et religion à la croisée des chemins." In *Cet étrange post-communisme: Rupture et transitions en Europe centrale et orientale*, ed. Georges Mink and Jean-Charles Szurek. Paris: Presse du CNRS, La découverte.

———. 1992b. "Religion, sortie du communisme et démocratie en Europe du Centre-Est." In *Les religions à l'Est*, ed. Patrick Michel. Paris: Ed. du Cerf.

Michnik, Adam. 1990. "Le prêtre et le bouffon: La polonité entre Wyszynski et Gombrowicz." In *La deuxième révolution*, ed. A. Grudzińska and G. Mink. Paris: Editions La découverte.

———. 1991. "Le nouvel évolutionnisme vingt ans après." In *Vers une mutation de société: La marche de l'Europe de l'Est vers la démocratie*, ed. Miklos Molnar, Georges Nivat, and André Reszler. Paris: Presses universitaires de France.

———. 1993. *The Church and the Left.* Ed., trans., and with an introduction by David Ost. Chicago: Univ. of Chicago Press.

———. 1998. *Letters from Freedom: Post-Cold War Realities and Perspectives.* Berkeley and Los Angeles: Univ. of California Press.

———. 1999. "Wystąpienie." In *Kościół polski wobec antysemityzmu, 1989–1999: Rachunek sumienia*, ed. Bohdan W. Oppenheim, 69–76. Cracow: Wydawnictwo WAM.

Michnik, Adam, Józef Tischner, and Jacek Żakowski. 1995. *Między Panem a Plebanem.* Cracow: Znak.

Michowicz, Waldemar. 1988. "Problemy mniejszości narodowych." In *Polska Odrodzona, 1918–1939*, ed. J. Tomicki, 285–321. Warsaw: Wiedza Powszechna.

Millard, Frances. 1995. "Nationalism in Poland." In *Contemporary Nationalism in East Central Europe*, ed. P. Latawski, 105–26. New York: St. Martin's Press.

———. 1996. "The Failure of Nationalism in Post-Communist Poland 1989–1995: A Historical Perspective." In *Nation and Identity in Contemporary Europe*, ed. B. Jenkins and S. A. Sofos, 201–22. New York: Routledge.

———. 1999. *Polish Politics and Society.* New York: Routledge.

Misztal, Bronisław, and Anson Shupe, eds. 1992. *Religion and Politics in Comparative Perspective: Revival of Religious Fundamentalism in East and West.* Westport, CT: Praeger.

Modras, Ronald. 1994. *The Catholic Church and Antisemitism: Poland, 1933–1939.* Jerusalem: Harwood Academic Publishers.

Molnar, Miklos, Georges Nivat, and André Reszler, eds. 1991. *Vers une mutation de société: La marche de l'Europe de l'Est vers la démocratie.* Paris: Presses universitaires de France.

Morawska, Ewa. 1984. "Civil Religion vs. State Power in Poland." *Society* 21 (4): 29–34.

———. 1995. "The Polish Roman Catholic Church Unbound: Change of Face or Change of Context?" In *Can Europe Work? Germany and the Reconstruction of Postcommunist Societies*, ed. S. E. Hanson and W. Spohn, 47–75. Seattle: Univ. of Washington Press.

Morgan, David. 1998. *Visual Piety: A History and Theory of Popular Religious Images*. Berkeley and Los Angeles: Univ. of California Press.

Mosse, George. 1975. *The Nationalization of the Masses: Political Symbolism and Mass Movements in Germany from the Napoleonic Wars through the Third Reich*. Ithaca, NY: Cornell Univ. Press.

Mucha, Janusz L., and Maciej K. Zaba. 1992. "Religious Revival or Political Substitution: Polish Roman Catholic Movements after World War II." In *Religion and Politics in Comparative Perspective: Revival of Religious Fundamentalism in East and West*, ed. Bronisław Misztal and Anson Shupe, 55–66. Westport, CT: Praeger.

Mushkat, Marian. 1992. *Philo-Semitic and Anti-Jewish Attitudes in Post-Holocaust Poland*. Lewiston, NY: Edwin Mellen Press.

Nairn, Tom. 1993. "Demonising Nationalism." *London Review of Books*, February 25.

———. 1997. *Faces of Nationalism: Janus Revisited*. New York: Verso.

Nielsen, Kai. 1999. "Cultural Nationalism, Neither Ethnic nor Civic." *Philosophical Forum: A Quarterly* 28 (1–2): 42–52.

Nora, Pierre, ed. 1997. *Les lieux de mémoire*. Vol. 1, *La République, La Nation*. Paris: Gallimard (Quarto).

Novick, Peter. 2000. *The Holocaust in American Life*. New York: Mariner Books.

Nowak, Stefan. 1981. "Values and Attitudes of Polish Society." *Scientific American*, January, 45–53.

Nowicka, Ewa. 1991. "Polak-katolik: O związkach polskości z katolicyzmem w społecznej świadomości Polaków." In *Religia a obcość*, ed. Ewa Nowicka, 117–38. Cracow: Nomos.

Nowicka, Ewa, and Sławomir Łodziński. 2001. *U progu otwartego świata: Poczucie polskości i nastawienia Polaków wobec cudzoziemców w latach 1988–1998*. Cracow: Nomos.

Obrebski, Joseph. 1976. *The Changing Peasantry of Eastern Europe*. Cambridge, MA: Schenkman Publishing Company, Inc.

Olszewski, Daniel. 1996. *Polska kultura religijna na przełomie XIX i XX wieku*. Warsaw: Instytut Wydawniczy Pax.

Opalski, Magdalena, and Israel Bartal. 1992. *Poles and Jews: A Failed Brotherhood*. Hannover: Brandeis Univ. Press.

Oppenheim, Bohdan W., ed. 1999. *Kościół polski wobec antysemityzmu, 1989–1999: Rachunek sumienia*. Cracow: Wydawnictwo WAM.

Osa, Maryjane. 1992. "Pastoral Mobilization and Symbolic Politics: The Catholic Church in Poland, 1918–1966." Ph.D. diss., Department of Sociology, Univ. of Chicago.

———. 1996. "Pastoral Mobilization and Contention: The Religious Foundations of the Solidarity Movement in Poland." In *Disruptive Religion: The Force of Faith in Social Movement Activism*, ed. Christian Smith, 67–85. New York: Routledge.

———. 2003. *Solidarity and Contention: Networks of Polish Opposition.* Minneapolis: Univ. of Minnesota Press.

Osiatyński, Wiktor. 1995. "The Referendum, Popular Initiative and the Issue of Legitimacy in Consitution-Making in Poland." In *L'espace constitutionel européen*, ed. Roland Bieber and Pierre Widmer, 345–58. Zurich: Publications de l'Institut suisse de droit comparé.

———. 1997. *Twoja konstytucja.* Warsaw: Wydawnictwa Szkolne i Pedagogiczne.

Ossowski, Stanisław. 1984. *O ojczyźnie i narodzie.* Warsaw: Państwowe Wydawnictwo Naukowe.

Ost, David. 1990. *Solidarity and the Politics of Anti-Politics: Opposition and Reform in Poland since 1968.* Philadelphia: Temple Univ. Press.

———. 1999. "The Radical Right in Poland: Rationality of the Irrational." In *The Radical Right in Central and Eastern Europe since 1989*, ed. Sabrina P. Ramet, 85–107. University Park: Pennsylvania State Univ. Press.

———. 2005. *The Defeat of Solidarity: Anger and Politics in Postcommunist Europe.* Ithaca, NY: Cornell Univ. Press.

Oxford Dictionary of Sociology. 1994. London: Oxford Univ. Press.

Paszkiewicz, Krystyna A. 1996. "Koncepcje 'Powrotu do Europy' we współczesnej polskiej myśli politycznej." In *Współczesna polska myśl polityczna*, ed. Bronisław Pasierb and Krystyna A. Paszkiewicz, 15–38. Wrocław: Wydawnictwo Uniwersytetu Wrocławskiego.

———, ed. 2000. *Partie i koalicje polityczne III Rzeczypospolitej.* Wrocław: Wydawnictwo Uniwersytetu Wrocławskiego.

Pawlicka, Katarzyna. 2004. *Polityka władz wobec Kościoła katolickiego (grudzień 1970–październik 1978).* Warsaw: Wydawnictwo Trio.

Pawlik, Wojciech. 1995. "The Church and Its Critics: The Spell of the Polish Ombudsman." *Polish Sociological Review*, 31–45.

Pawlina, Krzysztof. 2003. "Powołania kapłańskie i zakonne w Polsce na początku XXI wieku." In *Kościół katolicki w przededniu wejścia Polski do Unii Europejskiej*, ed. Piotr Mazurkiewicz, 42–60. Warsaw: Instytut Spraw Publicznych.

Petersen, Roger D. 2002. *Understanding Ethnic Violence: Fear, Hatred, and Resentment in Twentieth-Century Eastern Europe.* New York: Cambridge Univ. Press.

Pfaff, Steven, and Guobin Yang. 2001. "Double-Edged Rituals and the Symbolic Resources of Collective Action: Political Commemorations and the Mobilization of Protest in 1989." *Theory and Society* 30 (4): 539–89.

Piper, Franciszek. 1992. *Ilu ludzi zginęło w KL Auschwitz: Liczba ofiar w świetle źródeł i badań 1945–1990.* Oświęcim: Wydawnictwo Państwowego Muzeum w Oświęcimiu.

Piwowarski, Władysław. 1983. "Katolicyzm polski jako religijność narodu." In *Religia i życie społeczne*, ed. Witold Zdaniewicz, 66–82. Poznań: Pallotinum.

Plamenatz, John. 1973. "Two Types of Nationalism." In *Nationalism: The Nature and Evolution of an Idea*, ed. E. Kamenka, 22–37. Canberra: Australian National Univ. Press.

"Pod wspólnym niebem: Tematy polsko-żydowskie." 1998. *Więź* (special issue).

Polonsky, Antony, ed. 1990. *My Brother's Keeper: Recent Polish Debates on the Holocaust*. New York: Routledge.

Pomian, Krzysztof. 1982. *Pologne: Défi à l'impossible? De la révolte de Poznan à Solidarité*. Paris: Les éditions ouvrières.

Pomian-Srzednicki, Maciej. 1982. *Religious Change in Contemporary Poland: Secularization and Politics*. London: Routledge & Kegan Paul.

Porter, Brian. 2000. *When Nationalism Began to Hate: Imagining Modern Politics in Nineteenth-Century Poland*. New York: Oxford Univ. Press.

———. 2001. "The Catholic Nation: Religion, Identity, and the Narratives of Polish History." *The Slavic and East European Journal* 45 (2): 289–99.

———. 2002. "Marking the Boundaries of the Faith: Catholic Modernism and the Radical Right in Early Twentieth Century Poland." In *Studies in Language, Literature and Cultural Mythology in Poland: Investigating "the Other,"* ed. E. M. Grossman, 261–86. Lewiston, NY: Edwin Mellen Press.

———. 2005. "Antisemitism and the Search for a Catholic Identity." In *Antisemitism and Its Opponents in Modern Poland*, ed. Robert Blobaum, 103–23. Ithaca, NY: Cornell Univ. Press.

Postone, Moishe. 1986. "Anti-Semitism and National Socialism." In *Germans and Jews since the Holocaust*, ed. A. Rabinbach and J. Zipes, 301–14. New York: Holmes & Meier.

Prażmowska, Anita. 1995. "The New Right in Poland: Nationalism, Anti-Semitism and Parliamentarism." In *The Far Right in Western and Eastern Europe*, ed. L. Cheles, R. Ferguson, and M. Vaughan, 198–214. New York: Longman.

Preuss, Ulrich K. 1995. "Patterns of Constitutional Evolution and Change in Eastern Europe." In *Constitutional Policy and Change in Europe*, ed. Joachim Jens Hesse and Nevil Johnson, 95–112. New York: Oxford Univ. Press.

———. 1998. "Constitutionalism: Meaning, Endangerment, Sustainability." In *Rules, Laws, Consitutions*, ed. S. Saberwal and H. Sievers, 172–87. London: Sage Publications.

Prosono, Marvin. 1994. "Symbolic Territoriality and the Holocaust: The Controversy over the Carmelite Convent at Auschwitz." *Perspectives on Social Problems* 5:173–93.

———. 2004. "Cross Purposes: The Conflict over Symbolic Territory between Poles and Jews at Auschwitz." In *The Continuing Agony: From the Carmelite Convent to the Crosses at Auschwitz*, ed. Alan L. Berger, Harry James Cargas, and Susan E. Nowak, 55–75. Lanham, MD: Univ. Press of America.

Przybylski, Ryszard. 1995. "Romantyczne spory ze Stolicą Apostolską o istotę chrześcijaństwa." In *Nasze pojedynki o romantyzm*, ed. Dorota Siwicka and Marek Bieńczyk, 99–110. Warsaw: Instytut Badań Literackich PAN.

Radomski, Grzegorz. 2000. *Narodowa Demokracja wobec problematyki mniejszości narodowych w Drugiej Rzeczypospolitej w latach 1918–1926*. Toruń: Wydawnictwo Adam Marszałek.

Raina, Peter. 1985. *Kościół w Polsce*. London: Veritas.

———. 1991. *Spór o klasztor sióstr karmelitanek bosych w Oświęcimiu*. Olsztyn: Warmińskie Wydawnictwo Diecezjalne.

Ramet, Pedro, ed. 1989. *Religion and Nationalism in Soviet and East European Politics*. Durham, NC: Duke Univ. Press.

Ramet, Sabrina P. 1991. *Social Currents in Eastern Europe: The Source and Meaning of the Great Transformation*. Durham, NC: Duke Univ. Press.

———. 1997. *Whose Democracy? Nationalism, Religion and the Doctrine of Collective Rights in Post-1989 Eastern Europe*. New York: Rowman & Littlefield Publishers, Inc.

———. 1998. *Nihil Obstat: Religion, Politics, and Social Change in East-Central Europe and Russia*. Durham, NC: Duke Univ. Press.

———. 1999. "Defining the Radical Right: Values and Behaviors of Organized Intolerance in Post-Communist Central and Eastern Europe." In *The Radical Right in Central and Eastern Europe since 1989*, ed. Sabrina P. Ramet, 3–27. University Park: Pennsylvania State Univ. Press.

Rapaczyński, Andrzej. 1993. "Constitutional Politics in Poland: A Report on the Constitutional Committee of the Polish Parliament." In *Constitution Making in Eastern Europe*, ed. A. E. Dick Howard, 93–131. Washington, DC: The Woodrow Wilson Center Press.

Reddy, William M. 2001. *The Navigation of Feeling: A Framework for the History of Emotions*. New York: Cambridge Univ. Press.

Renan, Ernest. [1882] 1996. "Qu'est-ce qu'une nation." In *Becoming National: A Reader*, ed. Geoff Eley and Ronald G. Suny, 41–55. New York: Oxford Univ. Press.

Renaut, Alain. 1991. "Logiques de la nation." In *Théories du nationalisme*, ed. Gilles Dellanoi and Paul-André Taguieff. Paris: Kimé.

Riesebrodt, Martin. 1993. *Pious Passion: The Emergence of Modern Fundamentalism in the United States and Iran*. Berkeley and Los Angeles: Univ. of California Press.

Rittner, Carol, and John K. Roth, eds. 1991. *Memory Offended: The Auschwitz Convent Controversy*. New York: Praeger.

Rogozińska, Renata. 2002. *W stronę Golgoty: Inspiracje pasyjne w sztuce polskiej w latach 1970–1999*. Poznań: Księgarnia Św. Wojciecha.

Rothschild, Joseph. 1990. *East Central Europe between the Two World Wars*. Seattle: Univ. of Washington Press.

Rothschild, Joseph, and Nancy M. Wingfield. 2000. *Return to Diversity: A Political History of East Central Europe since World War II*. New York: Oxford Univ. Press.

Rudnicki, Szymon. 2005. "Anti-Jewish Legislation in Interwar Poland." In *Antisemitism and Its Opponents in Modern Poland*, ed. Robert Blobaum, 148–70. Ithaca, NY: Cornell Univ. Press.

Rudolph, Suzanne Hoeber, and James Piscatori. 1997. "Introduction: Religion, States and Transnational Civil Society." In *Transnational Religion and Fading States*, ed. Suzanne Hoeber Rudolph and James Piscatori, 1–24. Boulder, CO: Westview Press.

Rupnik, Jacques. 1992. "L'invention démocratique en Europe du Centre-Est." In *Cet étrange post-communisme: Rupture et transitions en Europe centrale et orientale*, ed. Georges Mink and Jean-Charles Szurek. Paris: Presse du CNRS, La découverte.

Rutkowski, Krzysztof. 1995. "Dlaczego Mickiewicz heretykiem był?" In *Nasze pojedynki o romantyzm*, ed. Dorota Siwicka and Marek Bieńczyk, 111–21. Warsaw: Instytut Badań Literackich PAN.

Ryzner, Janusz. 2000. "Konflikt na oświęcimskim żwirowisku w świetle prasy zagranicznej." *Biuletyn Żydowskiego Instytutu Historycznego* 4:575–85.

Sahlins, Marshall. 1981. *Historical Metaphors and Mythical Realities: Structure in the Early History of the Sandwich Islands Kingdom*. Ann Arbor: Univ. of Michigan Press.

———. 1985. *Islands of History*. Chicago: Univ. of Chicago Press.

Scarfe, Alan. 1984. "National Consciousness and Christianity in Eastern Europe." In *Religion and Nationalism in Soviet and East European Politics*, ed. Pedro Ramet, 31–38. Durham, NC: Duke Univ. Press.

Schnapper, Dominique. 1994. *La communauté des citoyens: Sur l'idée moderne de la nation*. Paris: Gallimard.

Schwartz, Herman. 2000. *The Struggle for Constitutional Justice in Post-Communist Europe*. Chicago: Univ. of Chicago Press.

Sells, Michael A. 1996. *The Bridge Betrayed: Religion and Genocide in Bosnia*. Berkeley and Los Angeles: Univ. of California Press.

Sewell, William H. Jr. 1992a. "A Theory of Structure: Duality, Agency and Transformation." *American Journal of Sociology* 98 (1): 1–29.

———. 1992b. "Introduction: Narratives and Social Identities." *Social Science History* 16 (3): 479–88.

———. 1996a. "Historical Events as Transformations of Structures: Inventing Revolution at the Bastille." *Theory and Society* 25:841–81.

———. 1996b. "Three Temporalities: Toward an Eventful Sociology." In *The Historic Turn in the Social Sciences*, ed. Terrence J. McDonald, 245–80. Ann Arbor: Univ. of Michigan Press.

———. 1999. "The Concept(s) of Culture." In *Beyond the Cultural Turn: New Directions in the Study of Society and Culture*, ed. Victoria E. Bonnell and Lynn Hunt, 35–61. Berkeley and Los Angeles: Univ. of California Press.

Shils, Edward A. 1975. "Primordial, Personal, Sacred, and Civil Ties." In *Center and Periphery: Essays in Macrosociology*, 111–12. Chicago: Univ. of Chicago Press.

Siwicka, Dorota, and Marek Bieńczyk, eds. 1995. *Nasze pojedynki o romantyzm.* Warsaw: Instytut Badań Literackich PAN.

Skotnicka-Illasiewicz, Elżbieta, and Włodzimierz Wesołowski. 1995. "The Significance of Preconceptions: Europe of Civil Societies and Europe of Nationalities." In *Notions of Nationalism*, ed. S. Periwal. Budapest: Central Univ. Press.

Smith, Anthony D. 1986. *The Ethnic Origins of Nations.* New York: Blackwell.

———. 2003. *Chosen Peoples: Sacred Sources of National Identity.* New York: Oxford Univ. Press.

Smith, Christian, ed. 1996. *Disruptive Religion: The Force of Faith in Social Movement Activism.* New York: Routledge.

Smith, David Norman. 1996. "The Social Construction of Enemies: Jews and the Representation of Evil." *Sociological Theory* 14 (3): 203–40.

Snow, David A., and Robert D. Benford. 1992. "Master Frames and Cycles of Protest." In *Frontiers in Social Movement Theory*, ed. A. D. Morris and C. McClurg Mueller, 133–55. New Haven, CT: Yale Univ. Press.

Snyder, Louis L. 1990. *Encyclopedia of Nationalism.* New York: Paragon.

Snyder, Timothy. 2003. *The Reconstruction of Nations: Poland, Ukraine, Lithuania, Belarus, 1569–1999.* New Haven, CT: Yale Univ. Press.

Sokolewicz, Wojciech. 1995. "The Relevance of Western Models for Constitution-Building in Poland." In *Constitutional Policy and Change in Europe*, ed. Joachim Jens Hesse and Nevil Johnson, 243–77. New York: Oxford Univ. Press.

Śpiewak, Paweł. 1997. "The Battle for a Constitution." *East European Constitutional Review* 6 (2–3): 89–96.

———. 2000. *Spór o Polskę 1989–99: Wybór tekstów prasowych.* Warsaw: Wydawnictwo Naukowe PWN.

Stark, David, and László Bruszt. 1998. *Postsocialist Pathways: Transforming Politics and Property in East Central Europe.* New York: Cambridge Univ. Press.

Staszyński, Edmund. 1968. *Polityka oświatowa caratu w Królestwie Polskim: Od powstania styczniowego do I wojny światowej.* Warsaw: Państwowe Zakłady Wydawnictw Szkolnych.

Stauter-Halsted, Keely. 2001. *The Nation in the Village: The Genesis of Peasant National Identity in Austrian Poland, 1848–1914.* Ithaca, N.Y.: Cornell Univ. Press.

Steinlauf, Michael C. 1997. *Bondage to the Dead: Poland and the Memory of the Holocaust.* Syracuse, NY: Syracuse Univ. Press.

Steinmetz, George, ed. 1999. *State/Culture: State-Formation after the Cultural Turn.* Ithaca, NY: Cornell Univ. Press.

Strassberg, Barbara. 1988. "Changes in Religious Culture in Post War II Poland." *Sociological Analysis* 48 (4): 342–54.

Sugar, Peter F. 1989. "The Historical Role of Religious Institutions in Eastern Europe and Their Place in the Communist Party-State." In *Religion and Nationalism in Soviet and East European Politics*, ed. Pedro Ramet, 43–58. Durham, NC: Duke Univ. Press.

———. 1994. "External and Domestic Roots of Eastern European Nationalism." In *Nationalism in Eastern Europe*, ed. Peter F. Sugar and J. Lederer, 3–54. Seattle: Univ. of Washington Press.

Sułek, Antoni. 1998. "Wokół Oświęcimia: Spór o krzyże na tle wyobrażeń Polaków o sobie i Żydach." *Więź* (November): 61–70.

Suny, Ronald Grigor. 1993. *The Revenge of the Past: Nationalism, Revolution, and the Collapse of the Soviet Union*. Stanford, CA: Stanford Univ. Press.

———. 2004. "Why We Hate You: The Passions of National Identity and Ethnic Violence." Paper presented at the American Historical Association, January 10, Washington, D.C.

Suny, Ronald Grigor, and Michael D. Kennedy, eds. 1999. *Intellectuals and the Articulation of the Nation.* Ann Arbor: Univ. of Michigan Press.

Swidler, Ann. 1986. "Culture in Action: Symbols and Strategies." *American Sociological Review* 51:273–86.

Symmons-Symonolewicz, Konstantin. 1983. *National Consciousness in Poland: Origin and Evolution.* Meadville, PA: Maplewood Press.

Szacki, Jerzy. 1990. "Polish Sociology and Problems of Nation-Building." In *National Survival in Dependent Societies: Social Change in Canada and Poland*, ed. Raymond Breton, Gilles Houle, Gary Caldwell, Edmund Mokrzycki, and Edmund Wnuk-Lipiński, 71–81. Ottawa: Carleton Univ. Press.

———. 1994. *Liberalizm po komunizmie.* Cracow: Znak (Fundacja im. Stefana Batorego).

———. 2004. "Is There Such a Thing as the Sociology of Nation?" *Polish Sociological Review* 1:3–14.

Szajkowski, Bogdan. 1983. *Next to God . . . Poland.* New York: St. Martin's Press.

Szawiel, Tadeusz. 2003. "Wiara religijna młodzieży polskiej (1992–2002)." In *Kościół katolicki w przededniu wejścia Polski do Unii Europejskiej*, ed. Piotr Mazurkiewicz, 119–49. Warsaw: Instytut Spraw Publicznych.

Szczur, Stanisław. 2002. *Historia Polski: Średniowiecze.* Cracow: Wydawnictwo Literackie.

Tambiah, Stanley. 1996. *Leveling Crowds: Ethnonationalist Conflicts and Collective Violence in South Asia*. Berkeley and Los Angeles: Univ. of California Press.

Tamir, Yael. 1995. "The Enigma of Nationalism." *World Politics* 47:418–40.

———. 1997. "Pro Patria Mori!: Death and the State." In *The Morality of Nationalism*, ed. R. McKim and J. McMahan, 227–41. New York: Oxford Univ. Press.

Tanay, Emanuel. 1991. "Auschwitz and Oświęcim: One Location, Two Symbols." In *Memory Offended: The Auschwitz Convent Controversy*, ed. Carol Rittner and John K. Roth, 99–112. New York: Praeger.

Tazbir, Janusz. 1978. *Kultura szlachecka w Polsce: Rozkwit, upadek, relikty.* Warsaw: Wiedza Powszechna.

———, ed. 1980. *Zarys historii Polski.* Warsaw: Państwowy Instytut Wydawniczy.

———. 1986. *La Republique nobiliaire et le monde: Études sur l'histoire de la culture polonaise à l'époque du baroque.* Wrocław: Wydawnictwo Polskiej Akademii Nauk.

———. 1990. "The Polonization of Christianity in the Sixteenth and Seventeenth Centuries." In *Faith and Identity: Christian Political Experience*, ed. David Loades and Katherine Walsh, 117–35. Oxford: Blackwell.

Teich, Mikulas, and Roy Porter, eds. 1993. *The National Question in Europe in Historical Context.* Cambridge: Cambridge Univ. Press.

Terry, Sarah M. 1993. "What's Right, What's Left, and What's Wrong in Polish Politics?" In *Democracy and Right-Wing Politics in Eastern Europe in the 1990's*, ed. Joseph Held, 33–60. Boulder, CO: East European Monographs.

Thomas, William Isaac, and Florian Znaniecki. 1927. *The Polish Peasant in Europe and America.* New York: A. A. Knopf.

Todorov, Tzvetan. 1989. *Nous et les autres: La réflexion française sur la diversité humaine.* Paris: Éditions du Seuil.

Tomaszewski, Jerzy. 1993. "The National Question in Poland in the Twentieth Century." In *The National Question in Europe in Historical Context*, ed. Mikulas Teich and Roy Porter, 293–316. Cambridge: Cambridge Univ. Press.

Touraine, Alain. 1982. *Solidarité.* Paris: Fayard.

———. 1996. "Le nationalisme contre la nation." *L'année sociologique* 46 (1): 15–41.

Turner, Victor. 1967. *The Forest of Symbols: Aspects of Ndembu Ritual.* Ithaca, NY: Cornell Univ. Press.

———. 1969. *The Ritual Process: Structure and Anti-Structure.* Ithaca, NY: Cornell Univ. Press.

———. 1974. *Dramas, Fields and Metaphors: Symbolic Action in Human Society.* Ithaca, NY: Cornell Univ. Press.

Turner, Victor, and Edith Turner. 1978. *Image and Pilgrimage in Christian Culture: Anthropolgical Perspectives.* New York: Columbia Univ. Press.

Van der Veer, Peter. 1994. *Religious Nationalism: Hindus and Muslims in India.* Berkeley and Los Angeles: Univ. of California Press.

Van der Veer, Peter, and Hartmut Lehmann, eds. 1999. *Nation and Religion: Perspectives on Europe and Asia.* Princeton, NJ: Princeton Univ. Press.

Van Gennep, Arnold. 1922. "Religion et nationalité." *Journal de Psychologie Normale et Pathologique* 19:24–46.

Van Pelt, Robert, and Debórah Dwork. 1996. *Auschwitz 1270 to the Present.* New Haven, CT: Yale Univ. Press.

Verdery, Katherine. 1991. "Theorizing Socialism." *American Ethnologist* 18:3.

———. 1993. "Whither 'Nation ' and ' Nationalism'?" *Daedalus* 122 (3).

———. 1994. "Beyond the Nation in Eastern Europe." *Social Text* 38.

———. 1996. *What Was Socialism and What Comes Next?* Princeton, NJ: Princeton Univ. Press.

———. 1999. *The Political Lives of Dead Bodies: Reburial and Postsocialist Change*. New York: Columbia Univ. Press.

Wagner-Pacifici, Robin, and Barry Schwartz. 1991. "The Vietnam Veterans Memorial: Commemorating a Difficult Past." *American Journal of Sociology* 97 (2): 376–420.

Walaszek, Zdzisława. 1986. "An Open Issue of Legitimacy: The State and the Church in Poland." *Annals of the American Academy of Political and Social Sciences* 48.

Walicki, Andrzej. 1982. *Philosophy and Romantic Nationalism: The Case of Poland.* Notre Dame, IN: Univ. of Notre Dame Press.

———. 1989. *The Enlightenment and the Birth of Modern Nationhood: Polish Political Thought from Noble Republicanism to Tadeusz Kościuszko.* Notre Dame, IN: Univ. of Notre Dame Press.

———. 1990. "The Three Traditions in Polish Patriotism." In *Polish Paradoxes*, ed. Stanisław Gomułka and Antony Polonsky, 21–39. New York: Routledge.

———. 1999. "Intellectual Elites and the Vicissitudes of 'Imagined Nation' in Poland." In *Intellectuals and the Articulation of the Nation*, ed. Ronald Grigor Suny and Michael D. Kennedy, 259–87. Ann Arbor: Univ. of Michigan Press.

———. 2000. "The Troubling Legacy of Roman Dmowski." *East European Politics and Societies* 14 (1): 12–46.

Wandycz, Piotr S. 1974. *The Lands of Partitioned Poland, 1795–1918.* Seattle: Univ. of Washington Press.

———. 1990. "Poland's Place in Europe in the Concepts of Piłsudski and Dmowski." *East European Politics and Societies* 4 (3): 451–68.

Waniek, Danuta, ed. 1991. *Problemy socjologii konstytucji.* Warsaw: Instytut Studiów Politycznych Polskiej Akademii Nauk.

Waśko, Andrzej. 1995. *Romantyczny sarmatyzm: Tradycja szlachecka w literaturze polskiej lat 1831–1863*. Cracow: Arcana.

Watson, Rubie S., ed. 1994. *Memory, History and Opposition under State Socialism.* Santa Fe, NM: School of American Research Press.

Webber, Jonathan. 1992. "The Future of Auschwitz: Some Personal Reflections." The First Frank Green Lecture, Oxford Centre for Postgraduate Hebrew Studies.

———. 1993. "Creating a New Inscription for the Memorial at Auschwitz-Birkenau: A Short Chapter in the Mythologization of the Holocaust." In *The Sociology of Sacred Texts*, ed. J. Davies and I. Wollaston, 45–58. Sheffield, UK: Sheffield Academic Press.

Weber, Eugen. 1976. *Peasants into Frenchmen: The Modernization of Rural France, 1870–1914.* Stanford, CA: Stanford Univ. Press.

Weber, Max. 1949. "'Objectivity' in Social Science." In *The Methodology of the Social Sciences*, ed. Edward Shils. New York: Free Press.

———. 1978. *Economy and Society.* Vols. 1 and 2. Berkeley and Los Angeles: Univ. of California Press.

Wedeen, Lisa. 1999. *Ambiguities of Domination: Politics, Rhetoric, and Symbols in Contemporary Syria.* Chicago: Univ. of Chicago Press.

Winter, Jay, and Emmanuel Sivan, eds. 1999. *War and Remembrance in the 20th Century.* Cambridge: Cambridge Univ. Press.

Wolff, Larry. 1994. *Inventing Eastern Europe: The Map of Civilization on the Mind of the Enlightenment.* Stanford, CA: Stanford Univ. Press

Wollaston, Isabel. 1996. *A War against Memory? The Future of Holocaust Remembrance.* London: SPCK.

Wronkowska, Sławomira. 1995. *Polskie dyskusje o państwie prawa.* Warsaw: Wydawnictwo Sejmowe.

Wuthnow, Robert. 1989. *Communities of Discourse: Ideology and Social Structure in the Reformation, the Enlightenment, and European Socialism.* Cambridge, MA: Harvard Univ. Press.

Wynot, Edward D. Jr. 1971. "'A Necessary Cruelty': The Emergencec of Official Anti-Semitism in Poland, 1936–39." *American Historical Review* 76 (4): 1035–58.

Xenos, Nicholas. 1996. "Civic Nationalism: Oxymoron?" *Critical Review* 10 (2): 213–31.

Yack, Bernard. 1996. "The Myth of the Civic Nation." *Critical Review* 10 (2): 193–211.

Yang, Guobin. 2000. "Achieving Emotions in Collective Action: Emotional Processes and Movement Mobilization in the 1989 Chinese Student Movement." *Sociological Quarterly* 41 (4): 593–614.

Young, James E. 1993. *The Texture of Memory: Holocaust Memorials and Meaning.* New Haven, CT: Yale Univ. Press.

———. 2000. *At Memory's Edge: After-Images of the Holocaust in Contemporary Art and Architecture.* New Haven, CT: Yale Univ. Press.

Zawadzki, Paul. 1996. "Le nationalisme contre la citoyenneté." *L'année sociologique* 46 (1): 169–85.

Zdaniewicz, Witold, and Tadeusz Zembrzuski, eds. 2000. *Kościół i religijność Polaków 1945–1999.* Warsaw: Instytut Statystyki Kościoła Katolickiego, Pallotinum.

Zerubavel, Eviatar. 1991. *The Fine Line: Making Distinctions in Everyday Life.* New York: Free Press.

Zerubavel, Yael. 1994. "The Historic, the Legendary, and the Incredible: Invented Tradition and Collective Memory in Israel." In *Commemorations: The Politics of National Identity*, ed. John R. Gillis, 105–23. Princeton, NJ: Princeton Univ. Press.

Ziołek, Jan. 1991. *Konstytucja 3 Maja: Kościelno-narodowe tradycje święta.* Lublin: Towarzystwo Naukowe Katolickiego Uniwersytetu Lubelskiego.

Znaniecki, Florian. 1952. *Modern Nationalities: A Sociological Study.* Urbana: Univ. of Illinois Press.

Zubrzycki, Geneviève. 1997a. "Changement social et construction identitaire: État, Église et identité nationale au Québec et en Pologne." In *La nation dans tous ses états: Le Québec en comparaison*, ed. G. Bouchard and Y. Lamonde, 221–50. Paris: L'Harmattan.

———. 1997b. "De la nation ethnique à la nation civique: Enjeux pour l'Église catholique polonaise." *Social Compass* 44 (1): 37–51.

———. 1998. "'Poland's Return to Europe': Reconstructing National Identity in a Global World." Paper presented at the Fourteenth World Congress of Sociology, July 26, Montreal.

———. 2001. "'We, the Polish Nation': Ethnic and Civic Visions of Nationhood in Post-Communist Constitutional Debates." *Theory and Society* 30 (5):629–669.

———. 2002. "The Classical Opposition between Civic and Ethnic Models of Nationhood: Ideology, Empirical Reality and Social Scientific Analysis." *Polish Sociological Review* 3:275–95.

———. 2005. "'Poles-Catholics' and 'Symbolic Jews': Jewishness as Social Closure in Poland." *Studies in Contemporary Jewry* 21:65–87.

Żywczyński, Mieczysław. [1935] 1995. *Watykan wobec powstania listopadowego.* Cracow: Universitas.

INDEX